Wilderness Areas
of
North America

Wilderness Areas of North America

BY ANN AND MYRON SUTTON

PHOTOGRAPHS BY THE AUTHORS

MAPS BY DON PITCHER

FUNK & WAGNALLS   New York

BY ANN AND MYRON SUTTON

The Wild Places
Yellowstone: A Century of the Wilderness Idea
The Wilderness World of the Grand Canyon
The Secret Places
New Worlds for Wildlife
The Appalachian Trail
The American West: A Natural History
The Life of the Desert

Animals on the Move
Guarding the Treasured Lands
Among the Maya Ruins
Exploring with The Bartrams
Journey Into Ice
Nature on the Rampage
Steller of the North
Wilderness Areas of North America

Title page photo: Quaking Aspen, Maroon Bells–Snowmass Wilderness, Colorado

Copyright © 1974 by Ann and Myron Sutton

Designed by Jill Schwartz and Marshall Henrichs

Manufactured in the United States of America

Library of Congress Cataloging in Publication Data

Sutton, Ann.
    Wilderness areas of North America.

    1. Wilderness areas--North America. I. Sutton,
Myron, joint author. II. Title.
QH76.S9 1974   333.9'5   74-8860
ISBN 0-308-10124-3
ISBN 0-308-10125-1 (pbk.)

1 2 3 4 5 6 7 8 9 10

To Jean and Fred Packard

Is there any front on which you two have not worked
in the cause of conservation? Scientific, international,
political . . . May there always be more like you,
so that there will always be wilderness.

Acknowledgments

We have personally visited nearly half of the areas listed in this book, but it would take several lifetimes to do them all justice, so we have relied on administering agencies and private organizations for advice—in the United States: the Bureau of Sport Fisheries and Wildlife, Bureau of Land Management, Forest Service, National Park Service, Appalachian Trail Conference, Sierra Club, Wilderness Society, and state park authorities in California, Florida, Michigan, Minnesota, Missouri, New Jersey, and New York; in Canada, México, Guatemala, Costa Rica and Panamá, the national and/or provincial governments and private groups.

Obviously the preparation of this book has involved the labors of hundreds of people. To make sure that the contents were as accurate as possible, each wilderness description went to the area manager for last-minute review, and to such persons we owe a lasting debt of gratitude. Space does not permit the listing of hundreds of names, but for special field assistance and extended help in making this book possible we should like to express our appreciation to the following: Panamá: Alfredo Castillero, Ricardo Gutierrez, Dario Tovar; Costa Rica: Mr. and Mrs. Mario Andrés Boza Loria, Alvaro Ugalde; Guatemala: Mr. and Mrs. Jorge Ibarra, Hugo Francisco Morales; México: José Arreola Tinoco, Jaime Carrillo Sanchez, Hector Fernandez de Castro, Horacio Gallegos Gamiochipí, Waldo Rodriguez, Luis Sangri; Canada: Rory Flanagan, Steve Kun, John I. Nicol, Shirley Popham, J. B. L. Walter; United States: Wallace Bailey, Percy Brown, Richard Burke, Rodney Churchwell, Otis Foiles, Edward Gaines, Robert Hayes, James Howe, James Husted, Harold Jones, Robert Kasparek, Don Kosin, Evelyn Kvernmo, William Lukens, Mr. and Mrs. James McLaughlin, Julio Marrero, Mr. and Mrs. James Metcalf, Carl Prince, Courtland Reid, Robert Sharp, Mr. and Mrs. Eldon Smith, Bert Speed, George H. Stankey, Mr. and Mrs. John Stratton, Larry Sutton, Michael Sutton, John Vogel, William Wallace, John Walther, and George Williams.

The authors and publishers are grateful for additional photographs provided by public and private agencies, as credited.

Ann and Myron Sutton

Massey Lake, Big Thicket, Texas.

Contents

Introduction

"The Street I Live On" was the title of a short essay written in longhand by an unknown schoolgirl on a single piece of loose-leaf notebook paper. It was found on a windy day, swirling in the dust of a midwestern street. It had been composed, apparently, as a school assignment, then discarded or lost. It was crumpled and soiled but the words could still be seen.

"The street I live on," it read, "is always filled with dogs, cars, and children running around trying to catch the bus. There is hardly no trees and no sweet things on our street just muddy little kids waiding in mud puddles with wet cloths on. There is always babys crying and squeaking bicycles and things like that and you can never get to sleep because there always trucks wizzing by and that is what the street I live on is like."

It is hardly necessary—and in fact rather painful—to suggest that this is more or less an accurate description of Main Street, North America, in these times of social progress and technological triumph. Although it comes about as a natural consequence of the overproduction of vehicles and people to drive them, the situation is rather alien to evolutionary human development. To have "trucks wizzing by" and "hardly no trees and no sweet things" appears to be contrary to normal life processes, if we are to judge from the record numbers of people trying to escape that kind of environment. Human beings are traveling to natural areas in such throngs, that some of the wild and wilderness places on this continent have become overfilled with refugees.

To get a touch of nature's tranquillity and energy in a clean and stable environment, humankind has inaugurated a sort of year-round migration to wilderness areas, national parks, and other havens from "wizzing trucks." On a lonely dune, or deep in mountain hemlock forests, present-day hikers are seeking a pristine world like that of early Indians, explorers, and naturalists, who knew how to appreciate wilderness. Alexander Humboldt penetrated the wildest parts of México and Central America and climbed into smoking craters. William Bartram found the Florida rivers so full of alligators he could almost walk across on their backs. Edgar Mearns rode out with the cavalry from Fort Verde, Arizona, in search of coyotes, quail, and flickers. Peter Kalm compared the plants of Canada with those of his native Sweden. To these eighteenth- and nineteenth-century naturalists, the North American wilderness seemed infinite. None knew how infinite, except that the wild horizon stretched as far as each could see. Their major, if not dominant, aim

1

was collecting scientific specimens; as Bartram phrased it: "discovering and introducing into my native country some original productions of nature which might become useful to society." They also got an immense enjoyment from just being there, as their journals show.

But in the early history of North America men also fought against wilderness as though it were an enemy and they managed to conquer it on very nearly a continental scale. So thorough were they that the words "untouched," "untrammeled," and even "wilderness" itself, took on archaic aspects. It is a wonder that any woods remain virgin or that the wolf and mountain lion live. In 1834 the first tourist came to the Yellowstone region, not to collect, trap, or hunt, but to see the wonders there. In 1872 Yellowstone's thermal features, wildlife, and scenery were set aside by Congress for national park purposes, though such a park concept was little known at the time and "wilderness" was even less familiar as a land-management term. The Adirondack clause "forever wild" in the New York State constitution of 1894 became a landmark phrase not only for New York but for North America.

As the wilderness diminished, what was left soon seemed to take on greater value. In the vigorous campaigns that followed, there were to become more than 60 million acres of national parks in North America, and more than 300 million acres in state and provincial parks, national forests, and national wildlife refuges.

The U.S.A. Wilderness Act of 1964 contained a concise definition of wilderness, but like other legal definitions it served the law and could scarcely embrace each nuance and contradiction of something so complex as open space. For example, it said that a wilderness was generally 5,000 acres or larger (except in the case of islands); but wilderness can be experienced in smaller areas. As the naturalist Darwin Lambert said not long ago in a widely publicized article, "We can have wilderness wherever we choose." And whenever, as well; some areas are wilder in spring and autumn, when the woods are filled with migratory birds, than in summer when so many human beings are present. In winter, the solitude is virtually complete in snowy regions. Much depends on what surrounds a given piece of open land, how remote it is from urban environments, and what the behavior is of other persons within it.

The Wilderness Act gave the term "wilderness" new technical meaning, implying the presence of uninterrupted and nonmanipulated natural environments, and land managers now use the term in this more restricted sense, often capitalizing it. But in this book we use the term in its more traditional or general sense, believing that wilderness can be experienced on disturbed and perhaps interrupted land, so long as naturalness and solitude prevail.

There is also a question of whether too restricted a terminology could delay or prevent the establishment of new wilderness areas.

The Wilderness Act provided clear guidelines for wilderness classification but much less for wilderness management. It permitted hunting, mining, and grazing in certain areas, though a valley filled with domestic cattle or sheep is hardly wilderness. Fundamental issues in caring for designated lands were not resolved, and conflicts have arisen, such as those over the ill-fated "enclaves" and "wilderness-threshold" concepts, which assumed that little spots of civilization within a wilderness, or buffer zones inside the borders, were acceptable. (They were rejected by citizens and the Congress.) A basic philosophical conflict developed over anthropocentric versus biocentric use. Both assume that wilderness is for man, but the biocentric philosophy argues that the presence of natural processes is an important source of human rewards, while the anthropocentric approach is to manipulate the environment for man's convenience. There are, of course, abundant examples of manipulated environments; it is often the degree of nonmanipulation that determines how "pure" a wilderness is. Some people feel that the anthropocentric approach would tend to eliminate many kinds of irreplaceable values that the biocentric approach would provide. In any case, national—or perhaps international—criteria are needed for uniform protection and use of wild places. The Wilderness Act was born of compromise and will likely be improved with age, but it was landmark legislation and the designation of wilderness under its provisions still goes on.

The problem now is caring for those areas. Many have grown so popular that their original values have become endangered. Wilderness-oriented recreation has been increasing at a rate of 10 percent a year, and visits to some sites have multiplied sevenfold in less than two decades. Visits to U.S.A. national parks alone exceed 200 million annually. In a single year recently the number of trips sponsored by the Wilderness Society rose 30 percent.

While the Wilderness Act has a dual objective of preservation and use, the unregulated admission of visitors could make a mockery of the act's preservation requirements. Evidence of diminishing values has been abundant. So many thousands of hikers, backpackers, riders, and canoeists have taken to the wilds that lonesome trails are losing their solitude. One forester in California's Sierra Nevada commented that a person could find more solitude in his backyard in Fresno than on the Pacific Crest Trail in August. Mount Whitney used to be a mecca for only a few hardy adventurers; but in 1973 some 15,700 people used the trail to its summit.

While not destroying the wilderness altogether, such use results in damaging concentrations of travelers. Canoe routes at certain localities in summer have begun to achieve the popularity of waterboat regattas on a

Sunday afternoon. Sites where cars assemble at jumping-off spots for trips into popular wilderness areas have the look of parking lots at a supermarket. Even where there is snow on the ground in early spring, it is hard to find a lean-to on The Appalachian Trail that is not overflowing with hiker-campers. Trails on high-country meadows have eroded into foot-deep trenches, and travelers choosing alternate routes have dug out half a dozen parallel trenches.

Wilderness rangers sometimes have trouble enforcing the rules against use of motorbikes or all-terrain vehicles on trails. In some cases hikers illegally take dogs into the wilderness and the shrieks of marmots echo up one valley and down another as the dogs excitedly probe into burrows. It doesn't take much disruption to force wildlife away from the trails and up into the high country, depriving visitors of opportunities to see these animals in their native habitats. Other violations with which the wilderness manager must contend include littering, illegal entry, cutting trees, camping too close to lakes and streams, failure to extinguish fires, use of chain saws and firearms, aircraft landings, vandalism, burning trash, noise, and boisterous conduct. Nevertheless, the typical wilderness user respects pristine territory because he knows how scarce it is. In fact, sociological studies and surveys conducted under the aegis of the U.S. Forest Service have altered the old public image of wilderness users.

It was long supposed that they were mostly elite and wealthy, but wilderness is actually used by all strata of society; income of visitors has little to do with use patterns. Education may be somewhat more of a factor—college students constitute a high percentage of users—but wilderness is also used by persons with much less formal education.

We might guess that the preponderance of wilderness visitors go into the backcountry for weeks, but not so. The average length of stay seems to be two or three days. Many wilderness areas, perhaps most, are popular chiefly for jaunts encompassing a single day, and it may turn out that most users do not even spend the night.

Thus if it is futile to seek social, economic, educational, or behavioral habits that most characterize wilderness visitors, perhaps we can say that people simply exercise their individual preferences—a rare privilege these days.

Still, the pressure of many visits, however altruistic, takes its toll. Moreover, the impact of man on wild places depends on factors other than number of visitor days; managers must consider size of party, length of stay, mode of travel, time of year, nature of the terrain, and general behavior of the user. No one knows what the carrying capacity of various kinds of wilderness is, but methodical studies through computer models are under way. Much data is already available, and solutions are being proposed and adopted. Some are questionable. A few wilderness managers are looking into the possibility of creating artificial lakes in order to spread the impact of public use. Others call for tramways to get people up on a mountain or down into a canyon. Still others suggest limited roads, primitive campgrounds and rest rooms, and horse corrals. These latter would ease maintenance and permit better protection of the environment, perhaps, but their very presence would render the wilderness less wild.

For the most part, however, new regulations reflect the assumption that users want their wilderness resources and solitude undisturbed, and hopefully someday a series of precise guidelines may be adopted.

As for new wilderness areas, most North American governments are actively setting aside as many as possible. In Canada, the United States of America, México, Guatemala, Honduras, El Salvador, Costa Rica, and Panamá, new areas are being investigated and inserted into the approval process. Alaska, under the 1971 Alaska Native Claims Settlement Act, will have vast roadless areas saved for public benefit, and special efforts are being made to establish wilderness areas in the eastern U.S.A. Some states have already set aside wilderness, including Ohio and Wisconsin, two that have been thoroughly settled, and Michigan has new legislation closely following the federal Wilderness Act.

Research programs are also under way on visitor use, trail and site deterioration, wildlife habitats, and fire ecology. Citizen cleanup teams have combined with administrative agencies to clean up trails, rehabilitate worn-out sites, and, in one case, even dismantle and pack out a wrecked aircraft.

The care and keeping of such areas depends, in the final analysis, on the capability and funding of the administering agency. One program coordinator wrote to his superiors, "Unless financing becomes available, the present high use we have experienced for the last two years will accelerate site deterioration on the heavily-used areas despite our best efforts to disperse use on a voluntary basis."

Some prime wilderness sites are disappearing altogether. Millions of acres were, of course, lost very early and very completely. Others survived for a while, but if they happened to be located on mineral deposits they were examined by exploration crews, opened to road and power easements, and endowed with a crazy-quilt pattern of roads that divested the land of its original charm. One almost lost in such a manner was the Uncompahgre Primitive Area in the highly scenic uplands around Ouray, Colorado.

At the other extreme, man has often been too protective of wild places, and his decades of forest-fire suppression have resulted in altered vegetational patterns that are unnatural.

Nowadays, uses and attitudes toward the wide-open spaces are rapidly changing. Regulations governing wilderness areas and the activities permitted in them now sometimes bear little resemblance to what applied a few years ago. One cherished principle to fall was that exhorting men to go into the wilderness as John Muir did—alone. Though this makes a person feel independent and self-reliant, a small mishap could mean disaster for lack of someone to summon help. Muir himself nearly came to an untimely end when he clambered about the brink of Yosemite Falls. To be sure, the hazards are part of what wilderness is all about. Many areas are at high elevations, where the sun can burn human skin severely, where high winds and lightning storms are likely to be more frequent, where sudden snowfall can catch a hiker unawares, and where wildlife such as grizzly bears may not be agreeable to human intrusion. Wilderness travel, requiring considerable preparation and "tuning in," is clearly not for everybody. Travelers who enter a wilderness should have some affinity for and familiarity with outdoor life already. Wilderness enjoyment is often thought of as a supreme personal experience and full enjoyment of it seems to follow some form of apprenticeship, such as visits to less remote or not quite so rugged county parks or forest recreation areas.

In the early days, few explorers went into the wilds; now, with many would-be Muirs and Thoreaus, families, and other groups exploring, the costs of public rescue have become excessive, not to mention the expense of tort claims. Since the public is invited to visit wilderness areas, accidents seldom seem to get classified as "acts of God." Government agencies accordingly try to persuade a person to protect himself, especially when economy moves make difficult the training and maintenance of protection crews.

Administrative agencies are coming to insist that wilderness travelers go forth in pairs at least. Actually, the wilderness experience is rather social; families or friends claim to have more personal relationships there than in busy everyday life. Whatever the case, few people do go in alone, some 2 percent according to one study.

Some agencies ask that an itinerary be filed in advance so that if a traveler becomes overdue, rangers will be able to narrow the search. This is a highly unpalatable measure that flouts the tradition of rambling at random, but with inexperienced people pouring into the backcountry, many getting lost or hurt, it is easy to understand the feelings of harried managers.

Since wilderness travelers as a whole have shown marked preferences for greater challenges in more rugged environments, entry must be rationed if wild places are to survive. New regulations—and the strengthening of old—have been enhancing wilderness values. For example, no longer are parties of ninety horses, ninety riders, and thirty head of pack stock permitted to sweep in a single party through fragile mountain wilderness. Strict limitations on number and size of groups are in effect, and wilderness managers have given notice that the restrictions will be made tighter if the impact on the resource does not lessen. No longer are people encouraged to bury or burn their refuse; everything packed in must be packed out. It is enough that thousands of visitors leave behind bodily wastes, for which trenches must be prepared far from sources of water; in a few wilderness campsites simple rest rooms have had to be constructed. Nor do campers go down to the creek with soap to take a bath, as in days of yore; the water for baths must be taken from the stream in a container and used and discarded away from the source.

That pristine waters must not be contaminated seems axiomatic, but administrators are dubious about complete voluntary compliance on the part of users. We have seen horse parties galloping across shallow lakes, and trails that seemed almost like the Washington Mall after a crisis march. Rangers attribute this not only to summertime users but also to hunters in autumn, who have been known to leave their camps completely unpoliced.

All this leads to sterner measures to protect the wilderness for those who care enough to leave it the way they found it. Rangers on foot patrols have been assigned to help visitors enjoy the wilderness and understand current regulations. A permit is required for entry and/or overnight trips into many, if not most, national park and national forest wilderness areas, and this system may well become universal. Studies indicate that mandatory registration is favored by most wilderness users, not only summer hikers but autumn hunters as well. The aim is to provide travelers with specific rules and regulations, and enable managers to match public use with the capability of fragile lands to take the impact. In some places, entry is during daylight hours only. Even swimming may be limited, especially where waterfowl congregate.

These curtailments of freedom in wild places are clearly and simply the result of man's population explosion. The more people fill their urban habitat with automobiles, housing developments, and roaring aircraft, the greater will be the number of human beings who try to escape into a dependable world of quiet trails and tranquil coves. But wilderness cannot accommodate so many people. The regulations are intended to prevent wild habitats from coming to resemble urban ones. Perhaps the best indicator of mature thought in this regard is the relatively new philosophy that if campers disturb bears, or vice versa, the campers and campgrounds will be removed rather than the bears.

Other practices once only frowned upon are now more strongly regulated. The cutting of living plants, especially where growing seasons are short, is becoming taboo. It is totally banned in many alpine and subalpine areas. No longer are campfires to be buried with dirt, which destroys the vicinity of the fire pit; they must be extinguished with water. Even the old familiar campfire itself is becoming a thing of the past because large numbers of wilderness users have picked the ground clean of dead and down wood, especially near popular high elevation meadows. Governing agencies are urging or requiring that hikers carry portable stoves that utilize alcohol, gas, or propane. And in the extreme, some wilderness areas are closed to public entry altogether during the months of highest fire danger—even if that is in the middle of summer.

Smoking while riding or hiking is prohibited at all times. Parties traveling with a string of pack animals are required to carry a water container of one gallon or more capacity, a thirty-six-inch shovel with an eight-inch blade, and an ax with at least a two-pound head and twenty-six-inch handle. Survival kits (whistle, mirror, waterproof matches, candle, bouillon, sugar, tea, knife, etc.) are becoming recommended equipment. Today's brightly colored packs, sleeping bags, and tents almost insure that a traveler can be easily seen from the air; however, there is a counterpoint to this splashing the landscape with artificial colors. Such bright trappings are now coming under critical scrutiny because they are indeed too visible, and at least one wilderness organization is returning to drab, natural-colored packs for its participants. The idea is to cross the land as quietly and unobtrusively as possible.

Restrictions are also being placed on that sacred wilderness companion, the horse, which is completely banned in some places because of its adverse effect on wild ecosystems. Pack or saddle animals are frequently prohibited from going within 200 feet of any wilderness lake or stream, except for purposes of watering, loading, unloading, or traveling on established trail routes. Carrying feed is advised in order to save natural forage but this feed may contain exotic species of plants whose introduction could be detrimental to native flora. As a result, some wilderness managers require that horse feed be pelletized or certified free of exotic plant species. The horses themselves are no longer to be picketed, which leads to scarred trees and trampled vegetation, but hobbled instead.

Motor vehicles of all kinds, from snowmobiles to aircraft, and motorized equipment such as power generators or chain saws, have been eliminated from nearly all wilderness areas. Pets are generally prohibited. Fishing is widely permitted, but firearms are illegal in all national parks and most state and provincial parks. Hunting is allowed only in certain provincial parks, wildlife refuges, and wilderness areas on national forest lands; both sports are usually controlled by local game laws and permitted only during specific seasons. (Surveys, however, have shown that many users do not condone hunting in established wilderness areas.) Fireworks and explosives are not allowed in any areas. Alcoholic beverages may be permitted (except in a few places, such as Florida state parks) but persons obviously intoxicated and guilty of disorderly conduct or disturbing the peace are subject to arrest. Regulations prohibit removal, destruction, defacement, or disturbance of plant and animal life—fish excepted. For prehistoric ruins, as well as fossils of any kind, the stringent provisions of antiquities laws usually apply. There is no hiking in the backcountry of Mesa Verde National Park except with a uniformed National Park Service employee. Some wilderness areas have special regulations that limit camping, overnight stays, fires, or even entry—as in the case of offshore islands containing delicate nesting colonies of seabirds.

If all this seems difficult to keep track of, especially since not all regulations apply to all areas, a prospective visitor can take heart in the fact that descriptive folders and printed regulations are available for nearly all wilderness areas, parks, forests, and wildlife refuges. Books and magazine articles on backpacking, camping, and specific sites are numerous. Nearly every governmental agency has public relations offices to meet the needs of prospective visitors. Under such circumstances there is no secrecy about the wilderness—and by law can be none.

Nevertheless, some people understandably fear that too much publicity attracts too many people who in turn destroy wilderness values, at least where controls are lacking. When an eastern state recently established a new park, the attendant publicity, combined with an absence of entry limits, brought about such an influx of visitors that the park was overwhelmed and had to be closed. Experience has shown that a surge of visitors comes to a new park or wilderness the first year, persons wanting to see something they had not known about before. But this is a natural evolution of human interest, and sometimes the visitation tapers off in subsequent years. Governing agencies should simply apply restrictions at the outset to assure that the new wilderness is not trampled.

Actually, evidence suggests that secrecy plays into the hands of wilderness opponents, who like to argue that a wilderness is "locked-up" land used only by "purists," which we have seen is untrue. Likewise, in a bizarre alteration of facts, they call it "single-use" land, as opposed to the familiar "multiple-use" principle whereby soils, woods, waters, and other resources are made available for commercial as well as recreational purposes. Of course, the U.S.A. Multiple-Use Act recognizes wilderness as a legitimate use of national forest land. But all public land activities, commercial as well as recreational, have legal restrictions.

Nothing could be more vital, therefore, for the continued preservation of wild lands than widespread publicity and a continuing clamor by wilderness lovers to get in. If that does not occur, lawmakers could commit the land to other purposes, especially in the face of "energy crises," "timber crises," and "land shortages." The more attractive these wild lands appear to the general public, and the more visits that are made to them, the more it will be seen that they are receiving "multiple use" of the highest order: hiking, camping, canoeing, inspiration, photography, fishing, and nature study. Limits on public entry could be construed as anomalous to the principles of freedom and free access, but the carrying capacity of wilderness, like the carrying capacity of schools, hospitals, or the earth itself, is finite. In numerous instances where government agencies closed off access to parts of the American heritage for protective reasons, the public went along with overwhelming approbation—sometimes to the surprise of the agencies. At present, most wilderness users seem to be in accord with closure of certain backcountry lakes and meadows so that they can recover from past overuse.

During production of this book, the U.S. Forest Service announced a program of wilderness investigations on an additional 237 study areas, and in time that number is likely to be expanded. So the work goes on. Public response to excessive industrial growth has become increasingly evident at the polls and at high government levels. Where growth conflicts with superlative natural environments, growth is being modified. Few better examples exist than California voter initiative in restricting coastal development, and the designation of Ontario's Quetico Provincial Park as a primitive park where commercial mining and lumbering are eliminated and previously logged areas must be rehabilitated. Such efforts are simply to keep man's habitat from becoming hopelessly urbanized.

Nevertheless, assaults against wilderness continue and grow stronger in the face of insufficient paper, petroleum, minerals, meat, and deep-water ports to supply an expanding population. So the efforts to keep a little stability in a hectic world will be hectic themselves. They call for expressions of opinion to government representatives, and the contribution of time, funds, and effort to organizations battling on behalf of the original heritage of North America.

Somewhere within us, perhaps as yet little understood, is the inevitable link to those evolutionary sources that show how limited man is after all, physically and environmentally. But with an appreciation of art and sculpture in the natural world, of wild music that fills the green vales, and of the ecological connections between organisms and environment, man's vision and enjoyment have no limit at all. The wilderness world becomes a living stage on which is enacted the most cosmic of dramas, the natural history of the universe itself. A visit to this universe is one of the most exciting human privileges. In the words of a Latin American park administrator, "when technology has nothing more for man, then nature will go on showing him her wonders."

Though the 500 areas listed in this book may seem at first like a great many, the shame is actually that there are so few. Scarcely 5 percent of the U.S.A. is devoted to parks, reserves, and wilderness areas, whereas New Zealand, Botswana, Dahomey, and other countries have up to 17 percent of their land surface reserved. The justification for doing likewise in North America could be drawn from the words of President Mobutu Sese Seko of the African Republic of Zaïre, who recently made the following remarks in opening his country's parliament:

The heritage of our ancestors is the natural beauty of our country: our rivers, forests, insects, animals, lakes, volcanoes, mountains, and plains. Nature is an integral and real part of our originality and personality.

Therefore, we refuse to follow blindly the trend of "developed" countries which want production at any price. We do not believe that peace and happiness are dependent on the number of cars in the garage, the television antennas on the roof, or on the amount of noise in your ears which, in the opinion of technicians, can be endured. Horror overcomes Zaïrans when we learn that in a city like New York, people slowly become more and more deaf beginning with the age of 25, whereas a farmer in our country might become so only toward the age of 70. What does it help to have innumerable factories if their chimneys spread poisonous products over us all day and night? We do not want these destructive industries which kill the fish in our rivers, depriving people of the pleasure of fishing or drinking clean water.

It should not surprise you when we declare that our ambition is to make our country, Zaïre, a paradise of nature. We have no intention of speculating upon public curiosity by selling the skins of crocodiles for handbags. We want first to study how these animals grow because we do not wish them to disappear in our national parks. When visiting the parks, tourists must be with guides and follow their instructions. We protect our waters, and mainly the river Zaïre, because to clean a river totally polluted never gives it back its original purity and virginity.

We believe that industrialized countries are running the risk every moment of becoming poorer. We desire only that when scientists will have transformed the world into an artificial one, in Zaïre an authentic nature will remain. Over the next few years, our national parks will be expanded to over 12 to 15 per cent of the country.

These words offer counsel for North American leaders, and for all heads of government. Of the trends now apparent to mankind, one seems to become more clear with the passing years: Wilderness is not a luxury. It is a necessity.

Our reasons for writing this book are many. One is to show that there are preserved wilderness areas in all parts of the continent, not just those famous places where visitors concentrate, and not just in remote places. There are

11

touches of wilderness near virtually all major cities—and should be a lot more.

We also want to make clear what the wilderness areas of North America are and, by extension, what they are not. From a reading of these descriptions of fragile sites it should be clear that human beings must behave differently in them than they do in areas devoted principally to other types of outdoor recreation. Every summer a number of visitors ill-prepared or ill-equipped don't enjoy the wilderness experience and leave in disgust, driven out by insects, boredom, discomfort, or other reasons; they sought a type of experience the wilderness was not meant to provide, and probably should not have come to it in the first place. Advance knowledge may, in fact, decide some persons against wilderness travel.

We should also like to suggest that the wilderness cause, having passed through an era of picture books and poetic appeals for protection of pristine areas, now needs more supporters to augment public understanding and appreciation of the problems involved in management and protection. This may not be as glamorous, but the agencies cannot do it alone. Fortunately, public participation is increasing, as in official citizen involvement in regional master planning.

This book will also serve, we hope, as a reminder that wilderness areas are made, not born. They can never be considered as securely established. The legislative bodies that so admirably make them can also unmake them. And it may be reasonably supposed that in all the North American republics there will continue to be, for many years, lawmakers who resolutely oppose the wilderness idea.

We describe in this book existing, proposed, and potential wilderness areas in North America, from Panamá to the Arctic. We have by no means covered every possible site; a comprehensive discussion of all wild or reasonably wild places on this continent would require encyclopedic treatment. But we have touched upon sites large and small, suburban and remote, where something of the original naturalness of the land remains, or is returning. Most of these sites are specifically designated as parks, refuges, or wilderness areas. A few areas were excluded either because we have not visited them or because we have not obtained convincing data that they possess at least a few touches of wilderness. On the other hand, some sites listed here for the U.S.A. have been rejected for inclusion in the national wilderness preservation system, or have not been considered at all; we simply concluded that the vestiges of wilderness in them were at least worth calling attention to. Researchers have discovered that there is a wide range of public opinion—even among users—as to what constitutes wilderness. And, of course, the quality of wilderness will be differently viewed by different people. In the final analysis, the designation of wilderness is done neither by congressmen nor by federal, state, or provincial officials. As one distinguished scientist said, "Despite an array of administrative and legislative edicts, wilderness remains largely a function of human perception."

The criteria we most consistently followed in judging a wild place were size (most areas in this book are larger than 5,000 acres) and some degree of public protection. But the rules for wilderness selection are often no more rigid than the rules for wilderness enjoyment. Some persons would reject a wild place that has aircraft constantly overhead; others would accept it. In most cases, where there are airports, power lines, resorts, or other "intrusions," we identify them so that the reader can be forewarned. Thus, these pages cover a spectrum from which readers may judge for themselves and make their own selections.

We describe more than 500 areas that have some degree of wildness. We could have included 500 more; many roadless parts of state and national forests are not specifically designated as wilderness. Also, more state parks doubtless deserve to be included. Thus, it is inevitable that this attempt to cover so many wilderness areas on so large a continent will miss some qualified sites. Moreover, new areas are being proposed or established so fast by so many legislative and administrative bodies that it is hard to keep track of them. Months must pass sometimes before complete and accurate data are prepared by governing agencies. Readers aware of significant omissions or errors herein are urged to notify the authors in care of the Funk & Wagnalls Company, 666 Fifth Avenue, New York, New York 10019. Wilderness areas missing from this book, or established and opened to the public after 1974, will be incorporated in future editions.

Descriptions include significant details of geology, flora and fauna, size, location, approach routes, what to see and do, where roads and/or trails reach, packers and outfitters available, campsites in the vicinity, accommodations nearby, who administers the area, unusual regulations, special features that should not be missed, and where to write for more information.

This book may serve as a general guide from which preliminary trip planning can be accomplished. For detailed planning and final arrangements, however, a traveler should consult the administrators of each area, whose addresses are given. In addition to folders, maps, trail guides, and other current data that a prospective visitor needs, these administrators can provide warnings of unusual or temporary hazards. Changes occur in roads, trails, boundaries, and access, and last-minute details about these cannot always be incorporated in a book such as this. Even under normal circumstances, entering the wilderness is an exercise that requires careful study and preparation.

PART I

The Far North

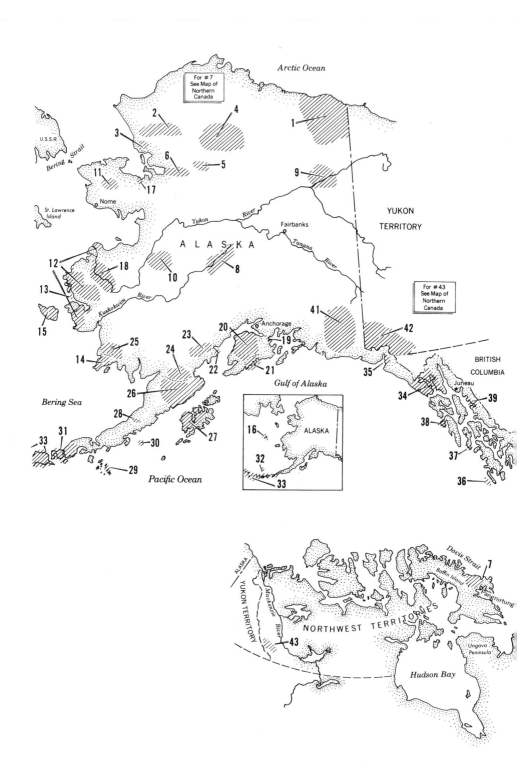

1. THE ARCTIC

1. Arctic National Wildlife Range, Alaska
2. Noatak National Arctic Range, Alaska
3. Cape Krusenstern National Monument, Alaska
4. Gates of the Arctic National Park, Alaska
5. Kobuk Valley National Monument, Alaska
6. Selawik National Wildlife Refuge, Alaska
7. Baffin Island National Park, Northwest Territories

2. INTERIOR AND WESTERN ALASKA

8. Mount McKinley National Park, Alaska
9. Yukon Flats National Wildlife Refuge, Alaska
10. Koyukuk National Wildlife Refuge, Alaska
11. Chukchi-Imuruk National Reserve, Alaska
12. Clarence Rhode National Wildlife Range, Alaska
13. Hazen Bay National Wildlife Refuge, Alaska
14. Cape Newenham National Wildlife Refuge, Alaska
15. Nunivak National Wildlife Refuge, Alaska
16. Bering Sea National Wildlife Refuge, Alaska
17. Chamisso National Wildlife Refuge, Alaska
18. Yukon Delta National Wildlife Refuge, Alaska

3. SOUTHWESTERN ALASKA

19. Nellie Juan Wilderness, Alaska
20. Kenai National Moose Range, Alaska
21. Harding Icefield–Kenai Fjords National Monument, Alaska
22. Tuxedni National Wildlife Refuge, Alaska
23. Lake Clark National Park, Alaska
24. Iliamna National Resource Range, Alaska
25. Togiak National Wildlife Refuge, Alaska
26. Katmai National Monument, Alaska
27. Kodiak National Wildlife Refuge, Alaska
28. Aniakchak Caldera National Monument, Alaska
29. Simeonof National Wildlife Refuge, Alaska
30. Semidi National Wildlife Refuge, Alaska

31. Izembek National Wildlife Range, Alaska
32. Bogoslof Island National Wildlife Refuge, Alaska
33. Aleutian Islands National Wildlife Refuge, Alaska

4. SOUTHEASTERN ALASKA AND ADJACENT CANADA

34. Glacier Bay National Monument, Alaska
35. Russell Fiord, Alaska
36. Forrester Island National Wildlife Refuge, Alaska
37. Hazy Islands National Wildlife Refuge, Alaska
38. St. Lazaria National Wildlife Refuge, Alaska
39. Tracy Arm, Alaska
40. Granite Fiords, Alaska
41. Wrangell–St. Elias National Park, Alaska
42. Kluane National Park, British Columbia
43. Nahanni National Park, Northwest Territories

17

1. THE ARCTIC

Much of Alaska is still wilderness, and not all of it, or in fact very much of it, is cold and perpetually frozen. John Muir referred to it as a garden. Thousands of square miles are carpeted with moss and flowers in summer; J. P. Anderson's *Flora of Alaska* contains 500 pages and is admittedly far from complete. The state is an ideal habitat for wildlife and, if saved from overexploitation, can remain an ideal habitat for men as well. Hiking there, one feels farther from industrial society than nearly anywhere else; one has the comfortable, challenging feeling that beyond the distant ridges are more forests, valleys, and gardens than could ever be explored. And for sheer spectacle there is little that surpasses such places as Glacier Bay, Cold Harbor, the Wrangell Mountains, the Brooks Range, Susitna River Valley. . . .

Few parts of North America are presently under as intensive land-use study. In accordance with the Alaska Native Claims Settlement Act of 1971, federal, state, and local governments are attempting to determine the future of the state's vast land areas. At issue are potential wilderness areas, parks, forests, wildlife refuges and wild rivers. The most outstanding are briefly described in these pages though their status may not be settled for years. With few exceptions, they are large and pristine, inaccessible by road, and virtually trailless.

These areas are so important in the progress of North American wilderness conservation that we list and describe them here even though sources of additional information are not given, as in most other entries in this book. Scientific and other details about the new areas are being assembled by government agencies, but there is no single office that provides a full range of public information. Some of the proposed areas are not yet administered as distinctive recreation or resource units.

Then, too, excessive public use prior to the installation of adequate access, facilities, and ranger protection could damage the superlative values that now make these areas so valuable. It does not take much uncontrolled use to destroy fragile features. This is not to deter serious examination of the sites for purposes of public debate, and a traveler may inquire locally about access

View from Sandy Cove, Glacier Bay National Monument, Alaska.

and places to stay; numerous guides and outfitters are available in Alaska. But it would be painful to see proposed wilderness areas damaged by concentrations of visitors before they had been approved—a real and present hazard that has been experienced in other places. Bills to establish the new areas have been introduced in Congress, so hopefully the legislation will be enacted and management commenced before too long.

Canada has also been active in preserving segments of its far-northern lands, as well as large portions of the rest of its domain. Indeed, at this writing, Canada has by far the world's largest system of national and provincial parks and related reserves, most of it managed as wilderness.

🌲 The most northerly national wildlife refuge in the United States covers nearly 9 million acres of northeastern Alaska and takes in parts of the Brooks Range, adjacent to Canada. Established in 1960 to preserve a biologically self-sufficient segment of the Arctic, the **Arctic National Wildlife Range** contains 9,000-foot glaciated mountains whose scenery alone merits protection. The southern slopes of the Brooks Range get warmed enough in summer to support a flourishing vegetation: buttercup, tundra rose, shooting star, fireweed, aster, monkshood, muskeg communities, and valleys of spruce and cottonwood. The rivers that give these systems life flow on south into the forests of the Yukon River plain.

North toward the Arctic Ocean, the landscape drops away in a series of rolling ridges and then goes on as a level, treeless tundra. Beset with bitter winter storms and temperatures far below zero, the land would seem forbidding to all but heavily furred or feathered life. Actually, many kinds of life exist, even smaller delicate forms protected in or under the tundra. Larger forms, which roam the surface, are indeed protected by fur: caribou (100,000 of them), moose, wolves, and grizzly bears.

In summer even the flattest tundra may be found appealing, for with continuous daylight it is green and warm, a botanical paradise as well as a feeding and breeding ground for animal life. The period of mildest weather is short, however; the land melts in June and freezes again in September. For hikers, the scenery and abundant wildlife are two major assets of this wilderness. The sight of Dall sheep on a mountain slope, or wolves hunting mice, or swans nesting, or mountain streams sifting in and out of gravel beds, suggests the primeval qualities of the range. Excellent walking routes can be followed, though hikers should check their plans with range officials and be sure to carry adequate equipment—including mosquito repellent. There are no campgrounds, food, lodging, or other facilities. Supplies should be

Kittiwakes nesting on southern Alaska coast.

(left) Cotton grass,
Mount McKinley National Park, Alaska.

(above) Mount St. Elias. Proposed Wrangell-St. Elias
National Park, Alaska. Courtesy National Park Service
(M. W. Williams)

Caribou, Mount McKinley National Park, Alaska.

obtained in Fairbanks but minimum facilities are available at Fort Yukon and Arctic Village. At this writing, the village of Fort Yukon, with a population of 500, has a grocery store, two restaurants, and a lodge.

Fishing is excellent, as are mountaineering, boating, canoeing, and even floating down the swift, wild rivers on a rubber raft. Millions of acres have been recommended for addition to the range for better protection of the ecosystems and in particular the Porcupine River caribou herd. If carried out, such an extension would abut the Yukon Flats area to the south, another outstanding wildlife area.

Access is chiefly by air. Commercial airlines serve Fort Yukon on the south and Barter Island on the north, and charter aircraft are available at Fort Yukon. Prospective visitors should obtain the latest details of access, weather, regulations, and routes.

Information: Manager, Arctic National Wildlife Range, 1412 Airport Way, Fairbanks, Alaska 99701.

🌲 The proposed **Noatak National Arctic Range** of 7,590,000 acres, examined under terms of the Alaska Native Claims Settlement Act, consists of glacier-sculptured valleys, deep canyons, lake-dotted plains, wild rivers, boreal forest, and tundra well above the Arctic Circle and deep within the Brooks Range. So far north is the area that the boreal forest reaches its northern and western limit here. Wildlife is abundant in the interior valleys and includes wolves, Dall sheep, grizzly bears, and two-thirds of the Arctic herd of 300,000 caribou. Ospreys, golden eagles, and peregrine falcons make their home in the area. Access is principally by air to Kotzebue and then by float plane to lakes within the area.

🌲 Extraordinarily rich archeological remains are a significant resource in the proposed 350,000-acre **Cape Krusenstern National Monument,** on the Chukchi Sea, forty miles north of Kotzebue. There are 114 beach ridges bearing evidence of nearly every major cultural period of Arctic prehistory, which suggests the possibility that this was where primitive hunters most often entered America from the now sunken Bering Land Bridge. Access is by air to Kotzebue, then by float plane to Krusenstern Lagoon or to an airstrip in the Kakagrak Hills. The intention is to build an interpretive center at Kotzebue, which would be a kind of staging center for travel to the area. This would keep facilities on the Monument at an absolute minimum and thus protect Monument features from construction damage.

🌲 The proposed **Gates of the Arctic National Park** takes in 8,360,000 acres of the central Brooks Range plus part of the Arctic slope in the Killik River region. The granitic Arrigetch Peaks, containing sharp spires, 7,000-foot ridges, and knife-blade crests have been spoken of as the most rugged and precipitous mountains in the United States. Caribou migrate through this region to calving grounds on the North Slope. For hikers it is a pristine wonderland fraught with Arctic challenges: rains, floods, unpredictable weather, uneven footing on tussocks and mosses of the tundra, tangles of willow to wade through, and hordes of mosquitoes. Anyone well-prepared will think of these only as minor matters; the remoteness, solitude, and scenic beauty should more than compensate.

A master plan prepared by the U.S. Department of the Interior states: "Most of the existing fine wilderness areas in national parks, forests, wildlife refuges, and other lands, public and private, are mere pockets of primitive America as compared with the immensity of the Gates of the Arctic National Wilderness Park. . . . The park proposal is based on the premise that the Nation can and should afford such a preserve and that little compromise should be made with its wilderness values. This latter premise stems not only from the area's environmental sensitivity but also from the conviction that it is neither necessary nor desirable to dilute its primitive primeval character in the name of either outdoor recreation or economic benefit."

Park headquarters will be at Bettles, just south of the park boundary. No roads are planned and access will be by canoe, on foot, by raft, or float plane. Trails will not be developed because of their erosional effect on tundra underlain by permafrost. Cross-country travel will be encouraged. The nearest transportation center at present is the Bettles airfield and the village of Evansville (both usually referred to as Bettles).

🌲 The proposed **Kobuk Valley National Monument,** 70 air miles east of Kotzebue, contains 1,850,000 acres of lake, river, tundra, and mountain country. In it is the best-known example of natural succession, soil development, and permafrost action on sand dunes in an Arctic climate. Some of the dunes are barren; others have been completely covered with vegetation and it is interesting to observe how this succession from scant to abundant plants occurs. In addition, scientists are probing the natural relationships between these dunes and surrounding bogs, tundra, and forests. It is no easy matter because natural fires alter the ecosystems and an abundant wildlife—caribou, moose, beaver, waterfowl—doubtless exerts a substantial influence. Nevertheless, this land is as it is because of interacting factors about which man has only begun to learn.

23

Access is by air and boat. Flights are scheduled three times a week from Kotzebue to Eskimo villages in the Kobuk Valley. Air taxi service is also available from Kotzebue into the proposed Monument area and boats may be chartered at Kiana, near the mouth of the Kobuk River, or at Ambler, eight miles east of the proposed Monument.

🌲 The proposed **Selawik National Wildlife Refuge** of 1.4 million acres, south of the Noatak region and 200 miles west-northwest of Fairbanks, consists of important waterfowl-producing areas averaging forty-four ducks per square mile, chiefly pintails, greater scaups, and widgeons. There are also large mammals such as caribou and grizzly bears on land areas, and whales, seals, and walruses in coastal waters. Musk-oxen, transplanted here a few years ago, are doing well. Access at present is by plane to Kotzebue and then by float plane into the proposed area. Plans call for a road across the southeast corner of the refuge.

🌲 Canada's vast empire of Arctic lands is commemorated by the setting aside of what is one of the world's most northern national parks. On Baffin Island, across the Davis Strait from Greenland, the Cumberland Peninsula juts southeastward for miles, at 66° north latitude. On that peninsula has been set aside **Baffin Island National Park,** 5.3 million acres of spectacular fjords, sharply eroded mountains, an immense ice cap, and numerous long glaciers. For most of the year the waters are locked in ice, the ground frozen, the silence broken by little more than the sweep of wind. In summer, however short, the bay ice melts, the glaciers retreat (perhaps almost imperceptibly), and the poppies and saxifrage brighten the tundra with their seemingly anomalous colors. From the edge of the sea some cliffs rise abruptly 3,000 feet. Inland rests the Penny Ice Cap, one of the largest ice caps in North America.

The waters of the fjords are home to whales, seals, and walruses. Other mammals of the park include polar bears, Arctic foxes, and barren-ground caribou. Approximately forty species of birds nest here, including Canada geese and snowy owls. Whistling swans may also be seen.

Baffin Island National Park, 1,500 miles north of Montreal, is still in the process of development. Commercial air service is available to Frobisher Bay and then to Pangnirtung, twenty miles from the southern boundary of the park. Prospective visitors should obtain the latest data and be prepared for the rigors of northern climate.

Information: Director General, Parks Canada, Department of Indian and Northern Affairs, 400 Laurier Avenue West, Ottawa, Ontario K1A 0H4.

2. INTERIOR AND WESTERN ALASKA

Central Alaska has much wider temperature ranges than the southern and western coasts, and temperatures can fall to more than 70° below zero. Yet in fleeting summers of nearly twenty-four hours' light and warmth, readings can rise to more than 70° above zero. Together with adequate rainfall, this produces an extraordinary richness of vegetation and one gets the impression that the tundra is several feet deep.

🌲 In **Mount McKinley National Park** a hiker sinks to his ankles in carpets of sphagnum moss. Flowers are copious, bright and varied, and it is possible to view the entire progression of spring, summer, and autumn plants at once because the melting snowbanks continually expose new patches to the sun. Predominant summer colors in central Alaska are green and magenta, the latter from slopes and flats of fireweed.

All this vegetation is the base upon which wild-animal populations are built, and at Mount McKinley may be seen a typical sample of Alaskan life. From the eighty-seven-mile road within the park, visitors look at grizzlies ambling awkwardly in search of Arctic ground squirrels or foraging for roots and insects, moose moving through the willows, caribou feeding on tundra, jaegers fluttering in the wind, and so on. Behind all, clouds permitting, we see the vast massif of McKinley itself, its summit, at 20,320 feet, the highest in North America. Though a challenge to mountaineers, its slopes are obviously for experienced climbers, and expedition leaders must submit applications to the park superintendent prior to attempting a climb.

The use of private automobiles in the park is restricted and the latest information should be secured. Free shuttle bus service is available daily in summer. Seven campgrounds are provided; space in four of them is by reservation only. There are visitor centers, nature trails, and publications. This park offers good chances to walk the taiga, an ice-heaved terrain of small-sized spruce and colorful, fragrant wild flowers. There are no trails but hiking routes lead through groves of aspen and willow, across meadows where grizzlies feed, and into copses of cranberry, blueberry, bearberry. The ubiquitous fireweed grows in magenta patches along with wild rose, and the cinquefoil adds a touch of yellow. The park offers a rare opportunity to understand the complex workings of both taiga and tundra.

The McKinley Park Hotel is open between May 15 and September 15. Food and camping supplies can be obtained at a small store. An all-weather paved highway and the railroad between Fairbanks and Anchorage pass through the east end of the park, and a landing field for light aircraft is located nearby. The Denali Highway, a rough, 163-mile gravel road between Paxson and the park, has sharp rocks that can play havoc with automobile tires, and loose gravel flung up between passing cars is a universal hazard on unsurfaced roads in Alaska and Canada. This road is not much used now since the Anchorage-Fairbanks highway was opened. The well-equipped, well-prepared traveler should have no difficulty, however, and the trip is worth the effort. Auto travelers are very much on their own because only limited repairs, food, and supplies are available at the park.

Under the Alaska Native Claims Settlement Act, nearly 3 million acres of new lands are being considered for possible addition to the park, which would nearly triple the original 1,939,493 acres. Only partial migration ranges of most major animal species are protected within the existing park, and, obviously, if men disturbed the remaining portions the migratory cycle might be seriously disrupted. "If wolf populations are to survive within Mount McKinley National Park," says the National Park Service, "it is urgent that consideration be given to protection not only of the entire range of park wolves but also to outranging animals which are their food supply, i.e., moose, caribou and sheep." For these reasons, the present boundaries of the park are being studied for possible more realistic ecological alignment.

More fully developed stands of spruce and larch grow north of the original park, and it is surprising to note that the southern slope of Mount McKinley, including major glacier systems, was never within the park. These two are being studied for inclusion.

Information: Superintendent, Mount McKinley National Park, Box 9, McKinley Park, Alaska 99755.

🌲 The proposed **Yukon Flats National Wildlife Refuge** of 3.6 million acres, where the Yukon River alters its course from northwest to southwest, is some of the richest waterfowl-producing area in North America, having at times an extraordinary density of ninety-nine birds per square mile. The terrain is ideally suited to bird life, since there are some 25,000 miles of streams and 40,000 small lakes and ponds. The summer residents in this environment include 120,000 pintails, 250,000 lesser scaups, 100,000 widgeons, and breeding populations of the much less abundant osprey, peregrine falcon, and bald eagle. Mammals also share the environment, some in great

Sitka spruce forest, Glacier Bay National Monument, Alaska.

numbers, such as 4 million muskrats, 15,000 beaver, and 10,000 mink. The Yukon River and its tributaries produce salmon and other species of fish. Aircraft to Fort Yukon or to native villages within the proposed refuge area affords the best means of access.

🌲 The proposed **Koyukuk National Wildlife Refuge** consists of two units totaling 4,430,000 acres, which host a half-million ducks and geese and serve as an important staging area for other bird species. Caribou winter in the area, and 40 percent of Alaska's beaver harvest is taken here. Millions of other furbearers inhabit the region. Fish include salmon, Arctic grayling, cisco, whitefish, and northern pike. Access is by dog sled, snow machine, aircraft, or boats capable of operation in undeveloped regions. Aircraft is the main method of transportation.

🌲 On the Seward Peninsula, ninety miles northeast of Nome, the proposed 2,690,000-acre **Chukchi-Imuruk National Reserve** embraces a delicate zone where the tundra meets the sea. It is a relatively warm sea, extremely rich with aquatic organisms, and the interaction between land and sea appears to be of unusual scientific interest. The evolution of coastal wild animals under natural Arctic conditions, as well as the progression of life on lava flows in the Imuruk Lake area and on volcanic ash deposits in the region of Devil Mountain and the Killeak Lakes, are not clearly understood. Prehistoric and recent Eskimo sites along the Chukchi shoreline have their origins very likely in unknown thousands of years of human transit over the Bering Land Bridge between Asia and North America. Village sites, caribou traps, cairns, and other evidence of past civilizations undoubtedly lie buried in these frozen soils. If the area is established as a public reserve, it may well become a major site for pondering the vast resources of the earth and the universe. Though not spectacular, the Chukchi-Imuruk area is nonetheless impressive. According to a preliminary report by the U.S. Department of the Interior: "Its scenic qualities lie in its vastness, its unbrokenness, its intimate, intricate complexities, in the opportunity to feel the vastness of the tundra, and in the contrasts of lava, tundra, lakes, bogs, rivers, and the sea."

In order to avoid disturbance to wildlife and the tundra environment, access is expected to be only by foot, boat and perhaps aircraft. At present, the area is reached through Nome or Kotzebue, which are served daily by commercial jet aircraft, and thence by scheduled airline flights to various localities on the peninsula. Air taxi service is also available. A gravel road, the Nome-Taylor Highway, runs north from Nome to points near the area.

🌲 In western Alaska, treeless deltas of the Yukon and Kuskokwim rivers are low, marshy, and covered with tundra vegetation, a major nesting ground of Canada geese, black brants, swans, eiders, pintails, mallards, teals, sandhill cranes, and other species. Such a vast congregation comes via North American flyways or from as far away as Australia, the Antarctic, and Hawaii to reproduce in the short summer and then return south. Several of the most significant parts of this vast and productive region have been set aside as wildlife refuges. The **Clarence Rhode National Wildlife Range,** 2,887,000 acres at the mouths of the Yukon and Kuskokwim rivers, lies nearly 500 miles west of Anchorage. The refuge headquarters is at Bethel, which can be reached by commercial aircraft, and is the last point of public accommodations. The wetlands, uplands, and volcanoes of the refuge itself lie more than 50 miles west of Bethel.

Plovers, sandpipers, curlews, godwits, loons, and other species take up residence on the 50,000 lakes and ponds that exist across mile after mile of watery tundra within the refuge. Lichens, mosses, shrubs, insects, and aquatic life provide abundant food to sustain this nursery. The number of bird species (ninety-six) is modest, but the population of individual birds is immense, as many as 10 million in good migration and nesting years. During winter, the flats are frozen and buried in snow, but each May the short renewal of life begins again.

The sites of most abundant waterfowl production lie along the Bering Sea. These areas can be reached only by chartered, float-equipped bush plane, which might cost over $600 at 1974 prices. Regular mail planes serving villages in the vicinity of the refuge could be utilized at a fraction of this cost, and Eskimo guides with boats could be hired for travel into the refuge. But these villages have no food, lodging, or supplies, so the traveler would have to be on his own. Persons who seriously wish to undertake an expedition into these remote localities should contact refuge personnel for a thorough review of plans, possibilities, and opportunities. Trips like this are so complex that travelers should have the latest specific advice from competent authorities.

Offshore is 6,800-acre Kigigak Island, administered jointly by range authorities as the **Hazen Bay National Wildlife Refuge.**

Information: Manager, Clarence Rhode National Wildlife Range, Box 346, Bethel, Alaska 99559.

🌲 Farther south, on Cape Newenham, a point that juts westward between Kuskokwim and Bristol bays, is **Cape Newenham National Wildlife Refuge,** where 265,000 acres were set aside to protect steep cliffs on which more than a million murres, kittiwakes, puffins, and other marine birds nest, one of the

Proposed Gates of the Arctic National Park, Alaska.
Courtesy National Park Service (M. W. Williams).

largest colonies in North America. Several hundred thousand migratory waterfowl also stop over here in spring and fall, lured by beds of eelgrass. There are also large runs of spawning fish, plus the usual contingent of bears, seals, sea lions, and walruses.

Information: Manager, Cape Newenham National Wildlife Refuge, Box 346, Bethel, Alaska 99559.

🌲 The natural history of **Nunivak National Wildlife Refuge**, in the Bering Sea, has been modified to some degree by men. Nunivak Island, 1,109,388 acres, lies at the same latitude as Anchorage, and usually its tundra vegetation and seaside cliffs glisten with cold rain, or are brushed by raging blizzards. During winter, pack ice locks the island in a frozen grip. Yet for all this seeming inhospitality, the climate is not only highly suitable for millions of gulls, puffins, and murres that come ashore to nest, but for ducks, geese, foxes, and other residents of marshes or meadows, and for walruses and seals, which inhabit the harbors.

Such biological productivity meant a great deal to early men, who for thousands of years caught and utilized wild animals here. By 1890 native caribou had been eliminated from the island. In 1920 reindeer were introduced; they thrived and multiplied to a population of thousands. Later a few caribou were reintroduced. The refuge itself was established in 1929. Rare musk-oxen were brought to Nunivak Island for propagation so that someday the species could be reestablished on its historic range in Alaska; the original herd of thirty-four, introduced from Greenland in 1936, grew to over 700, and for a time Nunivak Island was the home of the only musk-ox herd in the United States.

Visitors who go to Nunivak must be prepared for all kinds of weather. At the village of Mekoryuk, which is served by regularly scheduled air transportation, or by chartered bush plane, Eskimo guides may be available to conduct trips around the island. The route is across the Arctic prairie, which is very rough going, past willows and alders along stream courses, over sand dunes covered with beach rye grass, and near wave-cut cliffs with seething blankets of birds. The recommended method of sightseeing is to travel around the periphery of the island by boat or bush plane and then hike in to selected sites. Public accommodations are limited on the island. They may be secured in Mekoryuk by prior arrangement.

Information: Manager, Nunivak National Wildlife Refuge, Box 346, Bethel, Alaska 99559.

🌲 Nearly 200 miles to the west of Nunivak Island is a group composed of St. Matthew, Hall, and Pinnacle islands, which have been set aside as the **Bering Sea National Wildlife Refuge** of 41,113 acres. Once these rugged, tundra-covered islands had possibly the densest population of polar bears in the world, but hunters eliminated them within twenty years, and none remained after 1899. In addition to seabirds, which occupy a nesting area five miles long, the McKay's snow bunting visits here, and apparently nests nowhere else in the world. A herd of reindeer (introduced) fluctuates widely in population but is now declining because no males are left. Voles, foxes, and aquatic mammals have become adapted to the high winds, fog, humidity, and cold. The islands are so remote and difficult of access that public use is virtually nonexistent.

Information: Manager, Bering Sea National Wildlife Refuge, Box 346, Bethel, Alaska 99559.

🌲 Chamisso and Puffin islands and several islets in Kotzebue Sound, off the northwest coast of Alaska and near the Arctic Circle, have been established as the **Chamisso National Wildlife Refuge.** Although aggregating little more than 450 acres in area, these points of land are breeding grounds for large numbers of horned and tufted puffins, Pacific kittiwakes, and thick-billed and common murres. Harbor seals haul out on the wet, rocky shores and in winter, when the bay is frozen, there is an interchange of mammals with the mainland, three miles away. Foxes and Arctic hares live on Chamisso, at least part of the year, amid a tundra vegetation that includes crowberry, cranberry, Labrador tea, sedges, and lichens.

Human entry on the islands, or even a close approach, is not advisable when seabirds are nesting. The refuge is remote and subject to weather extremes. Nevertheless, bird observation is a significant recreational value. Access is by boat, or by light aircraft, which may land on sheltered waters in the lee of islands. The nearest accommodations are at Kotzebue or Nome.

Information: Manager, Chamisso National Wildlife Refuge, Box 346, Bethel, Alaska 99559.

🌲 The proposed **Yukon Delta National Wildlife Refuge** would add 5,160,000 acres of marshland and other types of terrain on the Yukon-Kuskokwim River delta to the protected waterfowl breeding areas of western Alaska. The region produces millions of waterfowl and the number of shorebirds nesting totals 50 million. "No other land area so small," says the U.S. Department of the Interior, "is so critical to so many species." Forty-three types of mammals have also been recorded, and the fish include salmon, pike, blackfish, whitefish, grayling, and rainbow trout. Access is by boat or barge on the Yukon and Kuskokwim rivers. Air transportation is available to village townships in and around the area. Winter travel is by dog team or snow machine.

🌲 For years much of the Alaska wilderness has been administered by the Bureau of Land Management, U.S. Department of the Interior. Recognizing the values of wild land recreation, especially by canoe, that bureau issued a folder entitled "Alaska Canoe Trails," a guide to water routes accessible by road. Included are guides to parts of the Fortymile, Delta, Gulkana, Kenai, Swanson, Yukon, Chatanika and Chena rivers. The folder is available free of charge from regional bureau offices, or from the Director, Bureau of Land Management, U.S. Department of the Interior, Washington, D.C. 20240.

3. SOUTHWESTERN ALASKA

In its administration of the Chugach National Forest, near Anchorage, the U.S. Forest Service has proposed some 600,000 acres on the western side of Prince William Sound, from Point Decision to Cape Puget, as the **Nellie Juan Wilderness,** a pristine terrain of islands, muskegs, meadows, glaciers, and mountain peaks, replete with wildlife. In common with other southeastern Alaska seashores its marine embayments teem with whales, whose black backs arch with ponderous grace above the waves, and sea otters, seals, and porpoises. Access by sea is perhaps easiest, but roads do approach the wilderness from Anchorage, fifty miles to the northwest.

🌲 A considerable portion of the Kenai Peninsula, due south of Anchorage, is taken up by the **Kenai National Moose Range,** 1,730,000 acres in area. Parts of it are commercially developed or open to exploration for oil and gas, and the Sterling Highway runs through it, but the rest is a wilderness of glaciers, mountains, and valleys—the latter forested with spruce, birch, and aspen. In the higher elevations live Dall sheep, mountain goats, marmots, and ptarmigan. Thousands of moose occupy the lowlands, and waterfowl, in season, feed and rest on the tidal flats. Cross-country hikers may also see black and brown bears, wolves, wolverines, coyotes, caribou, beaver, muskrat, mink, lynx, and weasels, but these animals are usually few and far apart and not to be expected on every acre crossed.

Once inhabited by the Kenaitze Indians, the region is now a recreation mecca for hundreds of thousands of outdoor enthusiasts every year. Campgrounds are available, and from them visitors may literally spread out in all directions. To the waters go fishermen in pursuit of rainbow, Dolly Varden, and lake trout, and four species of salmon, all of which spawn here. Many streams and lakes are suitable for canoeing. To the woods and mountains go naturalists, photographers, berry-pickers, or anyone seeking solitude. In winter the frozen landscape attracts cross-country skiers, and offers opportunities for dog-team travel and ice-fishing. The glaciers are immense, and the mountainous terrain both stark and picturesque. Kenai, a dramatic and accessible segment of Alaskan wilderness, will doubtless suffer from pressure for public use in excess of what the wilderness can absorb. The

Blue Grouse.   *Twayblade (orchid family), Sitka spruce forest.*

peninsula is already marred by oil fields. As in other wilderness areas, some restraints on human uses may have to be imposed. Food, supplies, and lodging may be obtained at nearby towns and resort areas.

Information: Manager, Kenai National Moose Range, Box 500, Kenai, Alaska 99611.

🌲 The proposed 300,000-acre **Harding Icefield–Kenai Fjords National Monument,** less than a three-hour drive south of Anchorage, rises to more than 6,000 feet and includes a 700-square-mile ice cap. Glacial features abound. The coast and islands are often battered by severe oceanic storms, but the area has its serene aspects—sandy beaches at the heads of fjords, quiet coves, and dense coastal forests of spruce and hemlock. Access is by paved road from Anchorage, two-and-a-half hours away, or by air or boat.

🌲 Two roadless islands in Cook Inlet are part of the **Tuxedni National Wildlife Refuge,** 120 miles southwest of Anchorage. Chisik Island (6,439 acres) and Duck Island (six acres) are remote and primitive. Their greatest value is as a breeding site for large colonies of black-legged kittiwakes, horned

34

Harbor seal, Glacier Bay National Monument, Alaska.

puffins, common murres, pigeon guillemots, and glaucous-winged gulls. There is a small spruce forest of 200 acres, but the rest of Chisik Island is covered mostly with grass, alder, and various shrubs. Foot travel is impractical because of dense vegetation. The beach can be utilized but is dangerous to hikers and can be impassable at high tide. Public visitation is not encouraged because of the high concentrations of nesting birds—a highly fragile community. Persons who genuinely wish to visit the Tuxedni wilderness should obtain specific recommendations from the refuge manager. The nearest accommodations are at Homer or Kenai.

Information: Manager, Kenai National Moose Range, Box 500, Kenai, Alaska 99611.

🌲 The proposed 2,610,000-acre **Lake Clark National Park** embraces the southernmost tip of the Alaska Range and the northernmost parts of the Aleutian Range, scarcely a hundred miles from Anchorage. The terrain is full of contrasts, from active volcanoes to active glaciers, and high peaks to level lowlands. There are even vegetational extremes, from alpine tundra to Sitka spruce forests. Along a coastal section are deep bays originally gouged out by glaciers. Lake Clark, forty miles in length, is the largest of numerous lakes. The region possesses three species of ptarmigan (white-tailed, willow, and rock), spruce grouse, trumpeter swans (which nest here), black and brown bears, Dall sheep, moose, and caribou. Until roads can be constructed, access will be principally by aircraft from Anchorage. Lodges are available and guide services operating throughout the area; charter flights may be hired to these points from Anchorage.

🌲 The proposed **Iliamna National Resource Range** of 2,850,000 acres should be a mecca for fishermen. In meadows, mountains, and valleys there are numerous streams; in addition, large bodies of water include Lake Iliamna, 640,000 acres in area. The region is the only designated Blue Ribbon Sport Fishery in Alaska. Species include pink, chum, king, and coho salmon, grayling, Arctic char, Dolly Varden, lake, and rainbow trout, and pike. Birds and mammals are also abundant. The area is located about 100 miles west of Anchorage, between Cook Inlet and Bristol Bay. Access is principally by air.

🌲 The proposed 2,740,000-acre **Togiak National Wildlife Refuge** is an important nesting area for seabirds and shorebirds, hundreds of thousands of which nest there every year. Salmon spawn by the million, and there are both land and sea mammals in abundance. The terrain varies from broad valleys to glacial lakes to steep-walled mountains. The area lies in the coastal ranges 400 miles west of Anchorage, and is scheduled to include Cape Newenham National Wildlife Refuge. There are no roads, so access is by boat on the rivers or by float plane.

🌲 Southwest of Cook Inlet the Alaska Peninsula stretches as a continuous arm of land for more than 500 miles. So rich is it in wilderness wildlife and scenic values that one of the largest units of the national park system, **Katmai National Monument,** 2,792,137 acres, is located on it. As yet, however, no roads reach out this far from Anchorage, 289 miles away, and access is by air or water via commercial airline, small boat, and charter plane. Within the monument is only one route, a primitive twenty-three-mile jeep trail that leads to an overlook from which to view the Valley of Ten Thousand Smokes. That valley's vents of steam have all but dissipated, but other remains of the 1912 explosion of Novarupta Volcano are evident, such as ash flows 300 feet deep and the collapsed caldera of Katmai itself. Indeed, the monument contains fifteen of the more than seventy-five major volcanoes of the Aleutian Range, and so it is a land of occasional geologic violence.

Nor is the weather very mild, except in summer, and even then high winds and rain can blow in from the sea. The williwaws are wild winds that may last a week and stir up eight-foot waves on inland lakes. Yet adverse weather seldom alters human use of Katmai; Eskimo, Aleut, and Athapascan cultures existed here in former times and remnants of villages may still be seen. Modern explorers, properly equipped and aware of where they are going, should seldom find the weather a serious obstacle.

Katmai's three distinctive habitats include the seacoast with its craggy cliffs, fjords, and offshore islands; the coastal mountains with their glaciated, ice-capped peaks; and the inland lake region. Especially suitable for wildlife are the interior habitats—forest, tundra, plunging streams, bogs, scattered lakes, meadows, marshes, alder thickets, patches of willow and cottonwood, and stands of birch and white spruce. On the lakes live loons, grebes, and gulls. The marshes provide ideal nesting habitat for ducks and whistling swans. For carnivorous mammals, such as foxes, lynx, and weasels, there is a natural meat supply consisting of hares, lemmings, mice, and ground squirrels. Perhaps most celebrated is the peninsula brown bear, a grizzly that weighs up to 1,500 pounds. It is often pictured taking salmon from Katmai streams.

Katmai is a productive habitat, and life seems to occupy every available niche from the slick, wet, rocky shores where seals and sea lions gather, to the upland tundra where ptarmigan live. Full national park status, and addition of 1,870,000 acres, principally for improving conservation of Alaska brown bears, have been proposed under the Alaska Native Claims Settlement Act. As for current visitor access, the King Salmon airport is served by commercial flights. Limited accommodations may be obtained inside and outside the Monument, but some are connected with package air tours operating from Anchorage. Boats and fishing equipment may be rented. Cross-country travel can be formidable due to large bodies of water. Backpackers should secure a backcountry use permit before starting a trip.

Information: Superintendent, Katmai National Monument, Box 7, King Salmon, Alaska 99613.

Southeast of Katmai, across the Shelikof Strait, lies Kodiak Island, of which two-thirds—1,815,000 acres—have been set aside as **Kodiak National Wildlife Refuge.** The island has not been appreciably altered by man, which means that the approximately 2,400 famed Kodiak brown bears, grizzlies that often attain 1,200 pounds in weight, can move freely through the kind of mountain environment in which their ancestors evolved. The streams are still pure and full of salmon, which bears pin to the gravelly bottom with their forepaws and eat at spawning time. During other seasons the bears are chiefly vegetarian, feeding on sedges, grasses, roots, and berries.

From forests of Sitka spruce to meadows to tundra, Kodiak Island's productive ecosystems contain numerous other mammals, including black-tailed deer, beaver, mountain goats, foxes, muskrats, weasels, and snowshoe hares. Although a few species such as the bear become less active in winter, others manage to get along; black-tailed deer, for example, roam the shores at low tide, feeding on kelp. All 800 miles of coastline within the refuge are a valuable sanctuary for wildfowl, and more than 200 pairs of bald eagles nest along the shoreline cliffs or in cottonwood trees. On offshore islands seabirds nest in colonies of thousands. Inland, the calls of loons resound from nearly every lake.

Travel by human beings through this lively environment is an extraordinary experience. Anglers after salmon may see a clumsy young Kodiak bear dashing downstream pouncing on fish that slip from its grasp. The earthen outlines of a few formerly inhabited Koniag Indian village sites remain. The refuge has no roads or maintained trails, which enhances its wilderness quality. In addition to backcountry exploration and camping, there are hunting and fishing pursuant to Alaska laws and regulations. The refuge is open to public use all year. Access is by daily air flights between Anchorage and the city of Kodiak. Anyone contemplating a summer visit should make early reservations for air flights and hotels. On Kodiak Island, local aircraft or fishing boats can be chartered to points in the interior or around the island. Guides are required for nonresidents wishing to hunt brown bear.

Information: Manager, Kodiak National Wildlife Refuge, Box 825, Kodiak, Alaska 99615.

The proposed **Aniakchak Caldera National Monument,** 440,000 acres, embraces 4,450-foot Aniakchak Volcano, on the Alaska Peninsula 160 miles southwest of Mount Katmai. The caldera, or summit crater, has an area of thirty square miles, and contains hot springs, boiling sulfur pools, steam vents, and colorful deposits of pumice and ash. Fed by "soda-flavored" springs, the Aniakchak River flows out of the crater through an opening in the east wall and down into the valleys below. Up this stream swim salmon to breed inside the crater, in Surprise Lake. Willows, lichens, and even orchids grow on the caldera floor. On the flanks of the volcano roam herds of caribou and there are brown bears, foxes, eagles, and other life typical of the peninsula. Access is by commercial flights or chartered aircraft to Port Heiden, on Bristol Bay, and thence by hired ground or water transportation.

🌲 When Vitus Bering, heading back to Siberia on his final, fatal trip of discovery to Alaska in 1741, landed in the Shumagin Islands (named after one of his men who died there), it was for the purpose of revitalizing his crew and taking on fresh water. But his naturalist, Georg Wilhelm Steller, thought far more of gathering plants that would arrest the rampant scurvy aboard. Clambering over one of the islands, Steller found whortleberry, crowberry, watercress, dock, and gentian. Ravens swooped overhead, ptarmigan ran from rock to rock. Small mammals barked at him or scampered out of his way. He watched ducks, auklets, and cormorants flying over, and gulls and guillemots clinging to rocky ledges above the beach. It was here that they saw their first sea lion; on account of its great size, Steller named it *Leo marinus*, lion of the sea, and it came to be known ultimately as Steller's sea lion. Thus are recorded a few eyewitness details by Alaska's first naturalist, when Alaska was all wilderness.

The Shumagins have changed, owing to subsequent fox and cattle raising, sea otter hunting, and other modifications of the environment, but Simeonof and a few islands in the eastern part of the group have been placed under federal protection. More than 25,000 acres of land and tidal waters have been designated the **Simeonof National Wildlife Refuge,** characterized by flat coastal lowlands, sandspits, white sand beaches, sloping shorelines, and small mountains, all covered by grasslands, salmonberry patches, dwarf willows, and heather. The original natural environment in this refuge is being restored, although cattle are allowed to graze on the island. Like Simeonof, the **Semidi National Wildlife Refuge,** 100 miles southwest of Kodiak Island, constitutes a home for North Pacific sea life. Semidi's islands, with a land surface of 8,422 acres, support numerous colonies of seabirds, an especially large colony of fulmars, and a sea lion rookery.

Both refuges are remote, reached only by chartered boats or planes. It amounts to an expedition to get to them, and special arrangements have to be made.

Information: Refuge Manager, Pouch 2, Cold Bay, Alaska 99571.

🌲 A combination of heath, mountains, seashore, rivers, lakes, lagoons, harbors, and wildlife at the tip of the Alaska Peninsula is preserved within **Izembek National Wildlife Range,** a 320,000-acre estuarine locality of enormous biological productivity—some say the most productive in Alaska. Beds of eelgrass, a fundamental food for waterfowl, cover two-thirds of the tidal flats, and the maritime climate has neither temperature nor precipitation extremes. These factors, plus others, make Izembek an ideal avian stopping point during migration, or a rich permanent residential area for wildlife. About 150,000 black brants, the total North American population of this species, use the lagoons in spring and fall. Sometimes shorebirds are so dense they appear as black clouds on the horizon, and harbor seals hauled out on a sandbar cover it like a living sealskin carpet. Caribou, wolves, bears, and numerous other species associate here in a complex ecological pattern.

Some of the military debris from World War II was never cleared away, but for the most part a wild environment persists. Though remote (600 air miles from Anchorage), Izembek is available for hunting, fishing (salmon and trout), boating, hiking, beachcombing, clam digging, camping, photography, and nature observation. Access is by sea, and boats may be chartered in Cold Bay. Food and lodging may be secured in Cold Bay.

Information: Manager, Izembek National Wildlife Range, Cold Bay, Alaska 99571.

🌲 A few miles west of Unalaska Island, far out in the Aleutian chain, are several spots of rock, born in fire and brimstone, which are being preserved more to benefit their wildlife occupants than for recreation by human beings. Although public use is permitted, restrictions are imposed if human activities threaten the natural ecosystem, especially during wildlife reproductive cycles. **Bogoslof Island National Wildlife Refuge** consists of two difficult-to-reach islands that are little more than jagged volcanic peaks likely to rise or sink during the next eruption. But murres, puffins, gulls, and other seabirds nest there in great numbers. Sea lions also arrive by the thousands to reproduce.

Information: Manager, Bogoslof Island National Wildlife Refuge, Pouch 2, Cold Bay, Alaska 99571.

🌲 The typical environment of sea lions, whether in Patagonia, the Galápagos, or the Aleutians, is frequently violent: crashing and thundering waves, gales that sweep across the sea with tons of water lashing at land and life, and individuals slashing at their neighbors' necks and leaving rivulets of blood. Yet life can also be serene, as witness the apparent bliss on the face of a sea lion sound asleep in the sun. Such images awaken a human appreciation of what is, to man, an alien environment. Little in the **Aleutian Islands National Wildlife Refuge** tempts human beings to establish settlements; there are only two villages in this vast domain of 200 islands with an aggregate area of 2,720,426 acres. The rocky outposts are better suited to colonies of sea lions, ducks, geese, gulls—millions of animals whose homes these islands were and are and who stay despite waves and storms.

The islands lie scattered in a gently curving arc that extends for a thousand miles into the North Pacific Ocean. Actually the tops of a submerged mountain chain, they are usually shrouded in fog, beset by stormy tides, or subjected to raging winds. Thus they support mostly dwarfed vegetation, and only a few land mammals (caribou, bears, wolves, wolverines, voles). West of Umnak Island there are no native land mammals except for Arctic foxes on Attu.

By far the greatest significance of the Aleutians is their hospitality to oceanic birds. The number of seabirds, even in winter, is phenomenal, and in summer they cling to cliffs by the millions, nesting in vast and noisy colonies. However, introduced foxes and rats have wrought havoc on certain species. The waters between Adak and Kiska islands are the primary home of once rare sea otters—which frequent beds of kelp. Human visitors to the Aleutians find access much more difficult than do mammals and birds; scheduled aircraft fly to only a few of the islands, and there are accommodations only at Cold Bay. Boats must beware of roaring gales and hidden rocks.

Information: Manager, Aleutian Islands National Wildlife Refuge, Pouch 2, Cold Bay, Alaska 99571.

4. SOUTHEASTERN ALASKA AND
ADJACENT CANADA

One of the most easily accessible wilderness areas in Alaska is **Glacier Bay National Monument,** reached by a short plane or boat trip fifty-five miles west from Juneau. Because of heavy precipitation in southeastern Alaska, much moisture collects as ice and snow, producing an immense glacier system. Moving up the bays and inlets one can see all kinds of them: valley glaciers, mountain glaciers, hanging glaciers, and floating chunks of ice on which seals bask in the sun. Or in whatever sun there is; the days are mostly cloudy, foggy, and rainy. Nevertheless, regardless of the weather, the clamor of kittiwakes (gulls) can be heard on their vertical cliffside nesting grounds, blue grouse may be seen with their young in forests of Sitka spruce, grizzlies can be observed as they pounce in the streams for fish, and snow-hung crags are revealed in fragmentary glimpses through cloud and mist.

The monument measures 2.8 million acres in area, nearly all of which is roadless, accessible only by boat, aircraft, or foot. The National Park Service operates a boat for daylong tours up the bay, but any boat is free to enter these wilderness waters. Care needs to be taken with regard to storms, and the tidal bore in Lituya Bay has claimed more than a score of lives. Beyond these possible perils, however, are great rewards, and park authorities can identify certain areas suitable for nonmotorized boats. To camp in a lonely vale in summer, when the night is scarcely two hours long, and hear the distant boom of cracking, calving ice that breaks from the glacier fronts and slides into the sea is a unique wilderness experience. Visitors will find so many things to see and do that it will be impossible to "keep up" with nature. And because the days are so long, the tendency is to keep going until exhaustion sets in.

This pristine region rises to 15,300 feet elevation on the summit of Mount Fairweather, a horizontal distance of less than fifteen miles from the sea. Actually it is not quite pristine; mining claims still exist, all legal until Congress moves to extinguish them or to designate the area as a national park.

Attempting to see Glacier Bay in a day, or even beginning to understand it in a short time, is futile, like trying to encompass all of Alaska in a weekend. It is a challenging wilderness, far from civilization, but not very far, where men can try their skills and endurance to the limit. Lodging and camping are available in the monument; Glacier Bay Lodge, in Bartlett Cove, is open from about May 15 to September 15. National Park Service rangers can provide up-to-date information on weather and ice conditions, localities where wildlife may be seen, and other planning data. A tour boat makes regular trips out into the bay. Visitors can arrange to be left at a certain place in the monument and later retrieved at the same or another location. A full range of accommodations and services, rental equipment, and charter craft is available in Juneau.

Information: Superintendent, Glacier Bay National Monument, Box 1089, Juneau, Alaska 99801.

One of the several areas being studied by the U.S. Forest Service for wilderness classification is that around **Russell Fiord,** a long arm east of Yakutat Bay and the gigantic Malaspina Glacier. This 227,000-acre study area possesses unusual beauty and demonstrates the tremendous abrasive power of recent glacial action. Hubbard Glacier is said to be the most active in Alaska. Deep forests contrast with blue waters of the fjord, polished rocks of the mountaintops, and glacial ice. The area is home to the unusual glacier bear as well as other wildlife.

Just after the turn of the century three groups of islands in southeastern Alaska were set aside especially for seabirds: **Forrester Island National Wildlife Refuge, Hazy Islands National Wildlife Refuge,** and **St. Lazaria National Wildlife Refuge.** All are closed to hunting and fishing by human beings. Thousands of birds swoop from the rocky walls and dive into the sea or patrol the rippling surface for anything that moves. The refuges shelter cliff-nesting species such as murres, puffins, auklets, gulls, and cormorants. Because of their small size, difficulty of access, and the delicate colonies of birds, more is to be gained by merely approaching and observing these islands than by actually disembarking and climbing on them. Hazy Islands, in the open sea, are virtually inaccessible. St. Lazaria, at the entrance to Sitka Sound, may be reached by small boat.

Information: Area Supervisor, Alaska Wildlife Refuges, 813 D Street, Anchorage, Alaska 99501.

Given the extraordinary beauty and richness of southeastern Alaska, it is not surprising that in Tongass National Forest, the largest federal forest (16 million acres), there should be a number of areas worthy of wilderness designation. Several sites have been identified as having unusual potential. The **Tracy Arm** area, forty miles south of Juneau, takes in a sweep of landscape from deep forested fjords and massive glaciers that meet the sea to snow-covered peaks. Except for tourists viewing it from sightseeing vessels, it has been visited by few people other than the Sumdum tribe of Tlingit Indians. The boom of calving ice still echoes across the waters and into remote forests. As their ancestors have for untold centuries, mountain goats leap on the upland crags, bald eagles soar like white specks on the icy breeze, wolves wander through the woods, salmon swim in the glacier-fed streams, and seals relax on floating ice in the fjords.

🌲 Another proposed wilderness in Tongass National Forest is that of **Granite Fiords,** thirty-five miles northeast of Ketchikan. This encompasses the glacier-carved fjords of Rudyerd Bay and Walker Cove, clothed in forests of spruce, hemlock, and cedar. In places there are muskegs, meadows fringed with willow, alder, and cottonwood, and high, snowy ridges. Large animals such as bears and deer share this undisturbed domain with smaller species, including beaver, mink, marmots, weasels, and blue grouse. Both Granite Fiords and Tracy Arm are accessible by water or air, but, as true wilderness, they have no facilities or trails.

🌲 The Wrangell and St. Elias Mountains of southeastern Alaska are so immense, so little known, and so inaccessible that it is hard to compare them with other mountain ranges. In this area is the greatest concentration of peaks over 14,500 feet in North America. Mount St. Elias, on the United States-Canadian boundary, reaches 18,008 feet. These uplands capture the heavy concentrations of moisture that blow in from the sea and as a result possess some of the largest glaciers on the continent, including Bering Glacier, nearly a hundred miles long, and Malaspina Glacier, 850 square miles in area and up to 2,000 feet thick. The first time one sees them from afar, these imposing peaks are breathtaking and the wonder is that the range was not made into national parks, forests, and wilderness areas long before this. Now a **Wrangell-St. Elias National Park** of 8,640,000 acres and a neighboring Wrangell Mountains National Forest of 5.5 million acres have been proposed.

One problem is access, and a human visitor without wings is unlikely to see very much of the Wrangell or St. Elias mountains. Still, some roads lead into the broad interior valley of the Copper River. Prospecting and mining for copper and silver, as well as logging, hunting, grazing, burning, and other surface manipulation, have badly altered some of the natural landscapes and disturbed the delicate ecological balance. Hydroelectric dams have also been proposed—which raises the threat of widespread man-made flooding. But the region is ecologically diverse, from coastal rain forests to tundra, and the volcanic landscape includes scenic cliffs, pinnacles, steam vents, and hot springs. The area is adjacent to Canada's Kluane National Park.

Access is by road from the Alaska Highway and off the routes that connect Anchorage, Fairbanks, and Valdez. Aircraft, including those equipped with floats or skis, provide additional access. Splendid views of the mountains may, of course, be obtained in clear weather from many miles away.

🌲 A number of Alaska rivers within existing or proposed federal areas are scheduled for addition to the national wild and scenic rivers system. Several other sizable river corridors have been proposed. Among them are the **Yukon-Charley National Rivers,** 1,970,000 acres near the eastern border of Alaska; **Fortymile National Wild and Scenic River,** 375 miles of stream course in an area of 320,000 acres, located along the Alaska-Canada border; **Birch Creek National Wild River,** 135 miles and 200,000 acres, between Fairbanks and Circle; **Beaver Creek National Wild River,** also 135 miles and 200,000 acres, located north of Fairbanks; and **Unalakleet National Wild River,** sixty miles and 104,000 acres, nearly 400 miles northwest of Anchorage. All of these areas have remote and more or less pristine environments, dramatic settings, and significant wildlife populations.

Proposals are also being made for enlarging existing wildlife refuges, and the establishment of additional island sanctuaries. Among the new areas are the **Aialik Peninsula National Wildlife Refuge,** 16,440 acres on the southern coast; **Barren Islands National Wildlife Refuge,** 10,000 acres on the southern coast; **Shumagin Islands National Wildlife Refuge,** 10,950 acres on the Alaska Peninsula; and **Chukchi Sea National Wildlife Refuge,** 24,500 acres on the northwest coast.

🌲 The St. Elias Mountains reach their culmination in Canada, and just over the border from Alaska is Mount Logan, 19,850 feet, second-highest peak in North America. It rises from one of the world's largest nonpolar systems of ice fields, and is in the midst of some of the finest remaining wildlife resources on the continent. This is **Kluane National Park.** To travelers along the Alaska Highway, one of the most vexing sections is that near Kluane Lake, 100 miles west of Whitehorse in Yukon Territory. It is vexing in the sense that off to the south rise the front peaks of the range, so tempting yet virtually inaccessible to men. Soon, however, access to these windswept uplands may be eased, at least to a small degree, because the Canadian government has withdrawn 5,440,000 acres in the heart of the region for establishment of the park. Thus, in due course, some form of access and facilities may be installed here.

45

Of course, much of the park will remain pure wilderness, as it should, containing natural ecosystems too valuable to disturb. The St. Elias Mountains extend through the area, blocking the passage of moist Pacific air and thus absorbing immense amounts of moisture that feed the fields of snow and glacial ice. In places, sand dunes have accumulated from powdery dust released by melting ice, especially the Kaskawulsh Glacier. Tundra vegetation, including colorful flowers and dwarf birch trees, thrives at altitudes between 4,000 and 5,000 feet, while lower down are valleys filled with white spruce and other conifers. Large populations of ptarmigan and golden eagles still live here, and even the bluebird nests in the Kluane area. Numerous Dall sheep and moose live in the park. Mountain goats, wolves, wolverines, and grizzly bears are less often seen, if only because they tend to shy away from man's presence and seek the more isolated areas.

The park is in the process of development and persons planning a trip to it should inquire about the current status of access, food, and lodging. Good accommodations are available in Whitehorse and on the Alaska Highway, which runs for eighty miles along the northern boundary of the park.

Information: Director General, Parks Canada, Department of Indian and Northern Affairs, 400 Laurier Avenue West, Ottawa, Ontario K1A 0H4.

The South Nahanni River, in the southwest corner of the Northwest Territories, runs through one of those rarities in North America today—a true wilderness. It flows from tundra-covered mountains into the Liard River, not far from the boundary of Yukon Territory, in an environment replete with mineral thermal springs, a 300-foot-high cataract called Virginia Falls, the narrow constriction of Hell's Gate, three canyons up to 4,000 feet deep, sheer cliffs, wide gravel deltas, limestone caves, lakes, meadows, spruce and poplar forests, eroded sandstone arches and pedestals, and abundant wild flowers that include mint, asters, and orchids. This region of extraordinary contrasts is the newly established **Nahanni National Park,** a scenic wildlife paradise of 1,177,600 acres, where caribou, wolves, deer, and black and grizzly bears roam.

Athapascan tribes were probably the first transient visitors in the region, followed by trappers and prospectors of European descent. The park lies ninety miles southwest of Fort Simpson, on the Mackenzie River, which has regular air service from Edmonton, Alberta, 650 air miles to the south. At this writing, the park is inaccessible by road, but a new route under construction between Ft. Simpson and Ft. Liard will pass near the southern boundary. The only access into the park is by boat; outfitters are located in the area.

Information: Director General, Parks Canada, Department of Indian and Northern Affairs, 400 Laurier Avenue West, Ottawa, Ontario K1A 0H4.

PART II
The Northwest

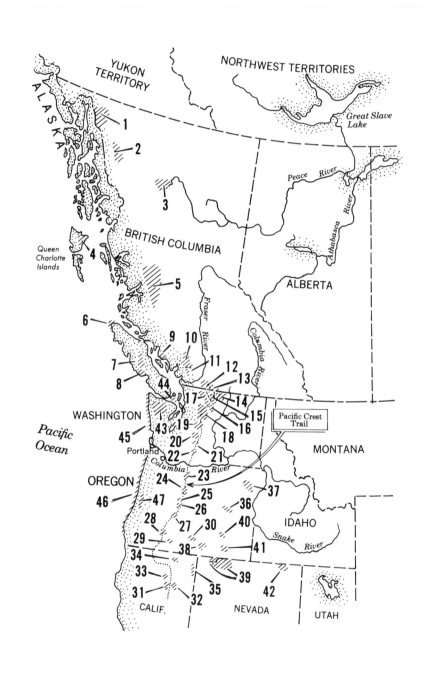

1. WESTERN BRITISH COLUMBIA

1. Atlin Provincial Park, British Columbia
2. Mount Edziza Provincial Park and Recreation Area, British Columbia
3. Tatlatui Provincial Park, British Columbia
4. Naikoon Provincial Park, British Columbia
5. Tweedsmuir Provincial Park, British Columbia
6. Cape Scott Provincial Park, British Columbia
7. Strathcona Provincial Park, British Columbia
8. Pacific Rim National Park, British Columbia
9. Desolation Sound Provincial Marine Park, British Columbia
10. Garibaldi Provincial Park, British Columbia
11. Golden Ears Provincial Park, British Columbia
12. Manning Provincial Park, British Columbia
13. Cathedral Provincial Park, British Columbia

2. CASCADE MOUNTAINS

14. Pasayten Wilderness, Washington
15. Ross Lake National Recreation Area, Washington
16. Lake Chelan National Recreation Area, Washington
17. North Cascades National Park, Washington
18. Glacier Peak Wilderness, Washington
19. Alpine Lakes Wilderness, Washington
20. Mount Rainier National Park, Washington
21. Goat Rocks Wilderness, Washington
22. Mount Adams Wilderness, Washington
23. Mount Hood Wilderness, Oregon
24. Mount Jefferson Wilderness, Oregon
25. Mount Washington Wilderness, Oregon
26. Three Sisters Wilderness, Oregon
27. Diamond Peak Wilderness, Oregon
28. Crater Lake National Park, Oregon
29. Mountain Lakes Wilderness, Oregon
30. Gearhart Mountain Wilderness, Oregon
31. Lassen Volcanic National Park, California
32. Caribou Wilderness, California
33. Thousand Lakes Wilderness, California

34. Lava Beds National Monument, California
35. South Warner Wilderness, California

3. EASTERN OREGON, WASHINGTON, NEVADA

36. Strawberry Mountain Wilderness, Oregon
37. Eagle Cap Wilderness, Oregon
38. Hart Mountain National Antelope Refuge, Oregon
39. Charles Sheldon National Antelope Range and Refuge, Nevada
40. Malheur National Wildlife Refuge, Oregon
41. Steens Mountain Recreation Area, Oregon
42. Jarbidge Wilderness, Nevada

4. PACIFIC COAST

43. Olympic National Park, Washington
44. San Juan Wilderness, Washington
45. Washington Islands National Wildlife Refuge, Washington
46. Oregon Islands Wilderness, Oregon
47. Oregon Dunes National Recreation Area, Oregon

49

1. WESTERN BRITISH COLUMBIA

Forty miles north of Juneau, just over the Alaska-Canada boundary, is a land of glaciers, bare rock surfaces, lakes, forests, and inlets. These are the Tagish Highlands, iced and deiced in the past million years and now being vegetated with the familiar succession of lichens, mosses, heather, willow, aspen, birch, spruce, and lodgepole pine. The government of British Columbia, a province larger than California, Oregon, and Washington combined, has selected a 575,000-acre section of this terrain and established it as **Atlin Provincial Park.** The land is still wild, its most prominent residents being cinnamon and grizzly bears, foxes, deer, mountain goats, and caribou. The park is so new (1973) that few trails yet lead into it, and access is only by means of water—across Atlin Lake. The jumping-off point nearest the park is the community of Atlin, reached by driving sixty miles south of Jakes Corner, on the Alaska Highway. Obviously, visitors must bring their own food, lodging, and supplies. But they will find themselves as though at the end of the world; the only music is wild music—waterfalls, the wails of loons, the chatter of gulls and terns, the songs of thrushes, the call of a lonely wolf. Fully a third of the park is ice: Llewellyn Glacier alone covers 274 square miles and neighboring Willison Glacier covers thirty-nine square miles. Before attempting to visit this remote area it would be well to obtain data on the latest stage of developments within the park. Contiguous with it is the 95,000-acre **Atlin Recreation Area.**

Information: Director, Parks Branch, Department of Recreation and Conservation, Parliament Buildings, Victoria, British Columbia.

🌲 In mid-1972 the British Columbia government conferred park status on 326,000 acres of unusual volcanic terrain in the Tahtlan Highlands, between the Stikine and Iskut rivers. But there was an interesting touch: The site was also surrounded by a buffer zone of 249,000 additional acres of lakes and woods to be used for recreational purposes. The entire unit is known as the **Mount Edziza Provincial Park and Recreation Area.** Mount Edziza, at 9,143 feet, is part of a volcanic system that began erupting four million years ago and kept on erupting nearly to the present time, as Tahtlan and

51

Tsimshiam Indian lore appears to verify. Ash falls, lava flows, cinder cones, and volcanic craters are the legacy of sometimes catastrophic violence in this region. At present, however, there are solitude, glaciers, forests, large lakes, and typical wildlife such as caribou, grizzly bears, mountain goats, and sheep. Access is by air or via the old Telegraph Trail, a difficult route from the Cassiar Highway. There is no land access from Telegraph Creek. The Stewart-Cassiar Highway, Route 37, passes twelve miles east of the eastern boundary, but there is no access road to the park. Actually, the inner park is scheduled to be treated as a wilderness area with little development—an admirable plan for sites of such marked geologic interest.

Information: Director, Parks Branch, Department of Recreation and Conservation, Parliament Buildings, Victoria, British Columbia.

Tatlatui Provincial Park, 261,500 acres in the Skeena Mountains of northern British Columbia, is so new (1973) and remote that it is accessible only by air and there is no developed trail system in it. Nor is there food and lodging even nearby; the coastal town of Prince Rupert is 170 air miles to the southwest. Nevertheless, for persons who can manage to get there, perhaps up the Finlay and Firesteel rivers, the wilderness experience should be remote enough to satisfy anyone. Magnificent lakes that mirror the Tatlatui Range are surrounded by dense woods of spruce and fir combined with thickly vegetated meadows including lupine, larkspur, monkshood, and Jacob's ladder. The streams are lined with birch and aspen. Bird and mammalian life is abundant, and the streams have rainbow trout.

Information: Director, Parks Branch, Department of Recreation and Conservation, Parliament Buildings, Victoria, British Columbia.

Forty miles west of the western shore of British Columbia lie the Queen Charlotte Islands, where 179,500 acres of wild wide beaches, spits, lagoons, sand bluffs, lakes, meadows, muskegs, meandering streams, and plains of stunted pines have been set aside as **Naikoon Provincial Park.** The shores teem in spring and fall with birds along the Pacific Flyway—cormorants, murres, guillemots, gulls, and oyster catchers, and the log-strewn sandy beaches lure human hikers and beachcombers. Occasionally, deer, bears, elk, and other mammals are sighted. Bald eagles may be observed frequently in their soaring search for carrion. The park may be reached from access points on Graham Island's main road, which connects the towns of Queen Charlotte and Masset. Picnicking, camping, and fishing are permitted in the park, but food and lodging must be secured in communities outside. The park's full range of services and facilities has not yet been completely developed, but even when it has, visitors will find that most of the land will be left in its natural state.

Information: Director, Parks Branch, Department of Recreation and Conservation, Parliament Buildings, Victoria, British Columbia.

🌲 The largest park in British Columbia, 2.4 million acres, is **Tweedsmuir Provincial Park,** a distant and virtually undeveloped wilderness that should be visited only by persons experienced in remote area travel. Route 20 goes through the park but the nearest large town where a full range of food and accommodations may be secured is Williams Lake, 229 miles by gravel road to the east. Burns Lake is closer, but the traveler must cross an artificial lake to get to the park, and this is so fraught with potential wind, storm, and floating debris hazards that nothing short of a large, well-powered vessel should be utilized. Access from the west at Bella Coola is also shorter, but Bella Coola is reached by sea only after negotiating some 400 miles of the Inside Passage north of Vancouver. And even when one arrives in the park, there are no supplies, food, gasoline, lodging, or local rescue crews. Perhaps as much as anywhere else in North America, the wilderness visitor is on his own.

Nevertheless, food and lodging may be found at settlements nearby and en route to the park; good maps are available, licensed guides may be hired, and the park is endowed with numerous lures for the hardy outdoorsman. An exception to the general rule of no hunting in North American parks is that Tweedsmuir is a hunting reserve, where moose, mountain caribou, mule deer, black and grizzly bears, mountain goats, and other species may be taken in accordance with regulations. (Two roadless tracts comprising about a third of the park are identified as nature conservancy areas where all natural resources are conserved in their natural state.) Fishing is permitted on lakes and streams, the catch being several species of salmon and trout.

A visitor prepared for all kinds of weather should have little trouble from the elements. Winters are long and sometimes severe, with heavy snow in the mountains; summers may be wet or dry, warm or cool, or a combination of these. But such variations, the hazards, remoteness, and other factors appeal to wilderness travelers, and in a park so large there are pronounced variations in topography and natural features. Eutsuk Lake alone is fifty miles long. One of the many streams plummets 1,200 feet in the spectacular but seldom seen Hunlen Falls. The bird life varies from eagles and ospreys to hummingbirds; grouse and ptarmigan inhabit the uplands, waterfowl the lakes, and other species the woods and open grasslands.

The Coast Mountains form the western boundary of the park, and

Monarch Mountain, on the south, rises to 11,950 feet. Glaciers contrast with alpine meadows filled with summer flowers. Lower forests are dominated by Douglas fir, cedar, and hemlock. Higher up are spruce and pine, and along the waterways grow cottonwood. Canoeing, with caution, is suggested by provincial authorities for certain lake chains.

A few trails lead from road or boat access points into the interior, but other routes, as well as campsites, must be selected by the traveler. Two campgrounds are located on Route 20: Burnt Bridge, thirty-two miles east of Bella Coola, and Atnarko River, fifty miles east of Bella Coola. The nearest food and accommodations are at Tweedsmuir Lodge on the Atnarko River.

Information: Director, Parks Branch, Department of Recreation and Conservation, Parliament Buildings, Victoria, British Columbia.

🌲 On the northwest tip of Vancouver Island, the British Columbia government has established **Cape Scott Provincial Park,** with forty miles of scenic coast, and fourteen miles of beaches from Nissen Bight to San Josef Bay. The environment is one of rocky headlands contrasted with placid lagoons, and crashing surf as well as sandy beaches and peaceful forests and meadows. At times there are violent winds, heavy rains, and raging seas. The highest point is Mount St. Patrick, 1,383 feet above sea level. On the lakes, surrounded by luxuriant woods of hemlock pine, spruce, huckleberry, and fern, anglers may try their skill on cutthroat trout. Provincial authorities are conserving most of the park's 37,200 acres in its natural state—a continuing home for wild animals from seals and sea lions on the windswept shores to deer, bears, and mountain lions in the uplands. Access is by road to a point five miles east of San Josef Bay, and thence into the park by trail. Hiking and camping are permitted, but food and lodging must be secured in Port Hardy or other communities en route.

Information: Director, Parks Branch, Department of Recreation and Conservation, Parliament Buildings, Victoria, British Columbia.

🌲 The rugged mountains of central Vancouver Island have been incorporated into **Strathcona Provincial Park,** more than 500,000 acres of scenic wilderness. From the perpetually snow-clad peaks that rise to 7,219 feet, meltwaters leap and cascade down past wild-flower gardens, and through thick forests of red cedar, fir, hemlock, spruce, and pine. Ponds and lakes are numerous, and in places there is good trout fishing. The highest waterfall in Canada, Della Falls, which drops 1,443 feet in three sets of cascades, may be approached by trail in the southern part of the park. Deer and elk are often seen in open places. Squirrels may be observed frequently but bears, wolves, wolverines, and mountain lions are less abundant.

The park, being largely roadless and with few developments, is a paradise for wilderness hikers. The trail system is being expanded and, with careful planning, hikers may spend weeks traveling through the park. Well-marked trails are available for one-day hiking trips. Some routes, however, are ill-defined, and so good maps and extra survival gear are advisable. Only experienced mountaineers with proper equipment should attempt the hazardous rocky slopes or venture out onto glaciers and snowfields. Access is via Route 28, between Campbell River and Gold River. Limited camping is available in the park. Additional campsites, as well as food and lodging, may be secured outside the boundaries and in nearby communities. There is good skiing in the winter.

Information: Director, Parks Branch, Department of Recreation and Conservation, Parliament Buildings, Victoria, British Columbia; or Regional Supervisor, Miracle Beach Provincial Park, R.R. 1, Black Creek, British Columbia.

The western shore of Vancouver Island, composed of sandy and gravelly beaches, rocky headlands, tidal pools, and sea caves, is replete with a rich biosystem. Barnacles, mussels, and limpets cling to the rocks despite the pulling power of thunderous waves. In tidal pools live species too numerous to mention—sponges, urchins, and stars among them. Seabirds and sea lions occupy secluded coves and islets. And nearly everywhere, strung over rocks or washed up in strands along the shore, are seaweeds. Gray whales come to feed offshore in summer, and on outer banks live halibut, salmon, cod, and other forms of aquatic life. In this environment the Canadian government is establishing **Pacific Rim National Park.** Of the projected 96,000 acres in three sections, including a cluster of ninety-eight islands, only the Long Beach section is open as of 1974. It consists of a narrow coastal plain with a dramatic background of mountains that rise to more than 7,000 feet. Western red cedar is the principal tree in the dense interior forests. Toward shore grow spruce, hemlock, and fir, with an almost impenetrable undergrowth of ferns and shrubs. Though birds and mammals are not abundant in such thick forests, thousands of migratory birds use the rivers, lakes, and shores.

The climate is generally mild, summer and winter, but visitors should always be prepared for cool rain and fog. Trails in the park are being expanded, and a campground is now available. There are conducted trips in the park, self-guiding nature trails, evening programs, and other educational facilities and services. Swimming and picnicking are done at Kennedy Lake, and some of the streams afford trout fishing. Access to the Long Beach section of the park is via Route 4 from Parksville, which is nearly a hundred miles north of Victoria. Food, lodging, and supplies may be obtained in nearby Ucluelet and Tofino.

Information: Superintendent, Pacific Rim National Park, Ucluelet, British Columbia.

🌲 Wilderness enthusiasts who like to cruise among wild islands will appreciate British Columbia's **Desolation Sound Provincial Marine Park,** which covers 14,100 acres in the Georgia Strait area, ninety nautical miles northwest of Vancouver. The park is located on the south shore of Desolation Sound, and incorporates the Gifford Peninsula. It has forty miles of irregular shoreline with a few sheltered coves and anchorages. The waters are warm enough in summer, both at the shore and on inland lakes, to allow for swimming. On the mainland, the park's forests of cedar, fir, and hemlock flourish on mountains that reach 4,000 feet elevation. Access at present is by water only; the nearest road reaches to Lund, six miles south on the east coast of the Malaspina Peninsula. There are no developed campgrounds, but wilderness camping is permitted. The nearest food, lodging, and supplies are at Lund. The 6,300-acre **Desolation Sound Marine Recreation Area** is contiguous with the park.

Information: Director, Parks Branch, Department of Recreation and Conservation, Parliament Buildings, Victoria, British Columbia; or Regional Supervisor, Porpoise Bay Provincial Park, Sechelt, British Columbia.

🌲 Forty miles northeast of Vancouver are the steep mountains, ice fields, glacial lakes, and coniferous forests of **Garibaldi Provincial Park.** But even though this area is near civilization, it should be pointed out that the park covers 484,000 acres and much of it is roadless and trailless. Visitors who go into the interior go strictly on their own. However, short trips are possible. Visitors can drive to the Rubble Creek parking lot, hike into the Garibaldi Lake–Black Tusk Meadows area (about three hours), spend most of the day, and hike out (one and a half hours). Much the same is true for the Cheakamus Lake area.

The landscape is volcanic. Mount Garibaldi, rising to 8,787 feet, is adorned, like other park ridges, with glaciers. At lower elevations the rock is well concealed by dense vegetation. Some trails follow waterways lined with alder, birch, and cottonwood. Away from the trails and deep in forests of hemlock, cedar, and fir, a hiker has to contend with underbrush of salal, salmonberry, and the viciously thorny devil's club. Such difficulty of passage is seldom encountered at high elevations, where meadows blossom in summer with heather, anemone, lily, lupine, and other wild flowers.

The best time for a summer visit is late July, August, and early September. Ski areas have been developed at Whistler Mountain, outside the park, and at Diamond Head, and the season can extend from November through June. Fishing is permitted. Campgrounds are available inside the park and at smaller parks not far away. Along Route 99 and the British Columbia Railway, which approach the western boundary through spectacular scenery from Vancouver, are hotels, motels, and tourist facilities. Several short trails on the west side of the park serve visitors who can spend only a day or two.

Information: Director, Parks Branch, Department of Recreation and Conservation, Parliament Buildings, Victoria, British Columbia; or Regional Supervisor, Alice Lake Provincial Park, General Delivery, Brackendale, British Columbia.

From the southern boundary of Garibaldi Provincial Park another wild area extends due south, an arrow-shaped unit named **Golden Ears Provincial Park,** after the prominent twin-peaked mountain between Gold Creek and Pitt Lake. Located in the Coast Mountain Range, thirty miles east of Vancouver, this park of 137,000 acres has characteristics similar to Garibaldi—snow-covered peaks, streams, lakes, and forests of Douglas fir, hemlock, western red cedar, cottonwood, and alder. Other than deer and bears, there are not many large mammals; birds and smaller mammals are much more in evidence. Access is via Haney, on Route 7. A paved road leads to the southwestern end of Alouette Lake, where there are parking places, picnic areas, two campgrounds, boat-launching ramps, a swimming beach, and hiking trails. In Alouette Lake and other park waters, anglers may seek steelhead, coastal cutthroat, Kokanee, and Dolly Varden. Trips deeper into the park should be planned with the park's staff. Motels, hotels, and tourist facilities are available in Haney and other nearby communities.

Information: Director, Parks Branch, Department of Recreation and Conservation, Parliament Buildings, Victoria, British Columbia; or Regional Supervisor, Golden Ears Provincial Park, Box 7000, Maple Ridge, British Columbia.

Along the Canada–United States boundary, 140 miles east of Vancouver, is **Manning Provincial Park,** 176,000 acres in the Cascade Mountains, richly carpeted with wild flowers in summer, especially at alpine elevations.

Camp in Pasayten Wilderness, Washington.

Pacific Crest Trail in Three Sisters Wilderness, Oregon.

Pinesap (heath family), Three Sisters Wilderness, Oregon. (right)

In marshes at lower levels live muskrats, beaver, and perhaps occasionally a moose. Black bears are common but not dangerous unless molested. The park offers good opportunities for exploration and scientific observation. Self-guiding nature trails introduce the visitor to several habitats in the region, and nature walks and evening talks are provided by the park staff in summer. Longer trails enable hikers to go out for a few hours, a day, or several days. One trail leads up Lightning Creek to Strike, Flash, and Thunder lakes. Another goes up Castle Creek to Monument 78 on the international boundary where it connects with the Pacific Crest Trail, a 2,350-mile route to Mexico. Both the Skagit and Similkameen rivers originate in the park, and along them are campgrounds and trails. Route 3 follows both rivers, providing easy access to the heart of the park. Lodging is available within the park at Manning Park Lodge, which is open all year. Other accommodations are available outside the east and west entrances. Winter activities in the park include skiing, tobogganing, and ice skating.

Information: Director, Parks Branch, Department of Recreation and Conservation, Parliament Buildings, Victoria, British Columbia; or Regional Supervisor, Manning Provincial Park, Manning Park, British Columbia.

🌲 Twenty miles east of Manning Provincial Park, and connected to it by trail, is **Cathedral Provincial Park,** an alpine wilderness of 18,000 acres. It protects subalpine lakes and meadows and the surrounding sawtooth mountains, which reach an elevation of 8,622 feet on Lakeview Mountain. Trails lead into various sections of the park, where anglers can try for cutthroat and Kamloops trout. The park is located eighteen miles southwest of Keremeos, which is on Canadian Route 3. Entry to the center of the park is by trail. Wilderness travelers may camp within the park; a developed campground is located at the park entrance on the Ashnola River. Resort accommodations are available just outside the entrance and on Quiniscoe Lake in the park.

Information: Director, Parks Branch, Department of Recreation and Conservation, Parliament Buildings, Victoria, British Columbia; or Regional Supervisor, Okanagan Lake Provincial Park, Box 318, Summerland, British Columbia.

2. CASCADE MOUNTAINS

The kingfisher utters a raucous shout and plunges into a mountain stream. A mule deer bounds across open meadows. The skyline gleams with rows of pointed, snow-covered mountains. Winds strum the needles of twisted conifers on Tatoosh Buttes. Snow settles among the freshly blooming lilies and paintbrushes—in the middle of August. Through transparent waters of placid lakes the cutthroat trout get in each other's way.

Such are some of the sights, sounds, and contradictions of the Cascade Mountains, and specifically the **Pasayten Wilderness,** an area of 505,524 acres along the Canadian border in Okanogan National Forest. Virtually every wilderness environment in the Cascades is here; there is a composite of granite, lava, marble, gneiss, schist, and other types of rock on which to build a foundation for contrast, and glaciers have swept the land in at least three stages. The ice scoured basins where lakes now exist and tore away rock from the crests, resulting in sheer-walled peaks and sharp ridges; or it overrode rocks and smoothed them. It carved out U-shaped valleys like that of the Pasayten River's west fork and left the tributaries "hanging," their waters coming down over cliffs or tumbling through side canyons. On melting, the ice deposited bouldery moraines. Four peaks, the highest 9,066 feet, still have ice fields, and during much of the year they seem to be gripped in another glacial age.

But on a summer trip into the Pasayten country—despite cold days now and then and perhaps a snowfall for which the traveler should be prepared—there is anything but a cold and forbidding environment. The approach up Eightmile Creek, for example, scarcely introduces the new-comer to the Cascades because he cannot see the distant mountains and gets no hint of the grandeur or the deep, dense forests to come. Indeed, it takes half a day's hiking, once having entered the wilderness, for a visitor to transfer from willow, alder, and shrubby habitats along stream courses to deep coniferous forests at higher elevations. Even at the end of the first day one still cannot see the crest of the Cascades unless he climbs into the Tatoosh Buttes or another high point and looks to the west. It is a boxed-in feeling, although some peaks are visible, but eventually the hiker camps at high

60

elevation and gets a wide view of the whole range. To the west are naked peaks, sheer cliffs, and rock-strewn slopes weighted down with clinging blankets of ice or snow, all in contrast to the ubiquitous wild flowers.

This summer profusion of flowers is a trademark of the Cascade Range. No matter how many snowbanks yet must melt, or whether the temperature takes a nightly plunge to freezing, the scarlet gilia sends forth vividly colored inch-long trumpet flowers. The higher slopes turn purple with acre after acre of lupine, punctuated with scarlet paintbrush. On closer examination, the traveler sees also senecio, twinflower, phlox, moss campion, bluebells, violets, larkspur, shooting star and other species. The Columbian tiger lily and the monkshood are specialties of the area. In addition to magenta fireweed, so often seen in Alaska, the yellow fireweed grows here. All is a challenge for photographers, who would be well advised to carry more film than they expect to need. With patience it is not too much to expect to see bears, coyotes, mountain lions, bobcats, porcupines, and mountain goats, some of the more common mammals. Or in the case of resident birds the photographer can try for Canada geese, grebes, loons, seven species of hawk, nuthatches, wrens, the melodious thrushes and bluebirds, colorful warblers, and the brilliant western tanager.

Trails in the Pasayten Wilderness lead mostly along streams, and reach many of the nearly 100 lakes. They pass through open forests of ponderosa pine, streamlining willows and birches, groves of aspen, spruce, and fir, and where creeping juniper hugs the slopes. The Pacific Crest Trail winds among mountain summits and beside watercourses along the western boundary to Monument 78, its northern terminus on the boundary between Canada and the United States. A few place names, such as Tungsten Creek and Scheelite Pass, suggest the presence of minerals. Copper and gold exist in small quantities. Dunite, consisting principally of olivine, occurs locally. There are also magnetite, garnet, calcite, fluorite, and serpentine; indeed, outside the boundaries are mines that have been economically profitable. Also outside are campgrounds in the national forests, lodges and other accommodations, and commercial outfitters who lead parties into the wilderness. The Pasayten area is especially suitable for setting up camp and hiking out on daylong forays. Permits are required for overnight stays and the use of horses, mules, or burros. Visitors should take their own fuel for fires.

Access is chiefly through Winthrop, Washington, on routes up the Methow River valley, the Chewack River valley, and Eightmile Creek. Accommodations and supplies may be secured in and around Winthrop.

Information: Supervisor, Okanogan National Forest, Okanogan, Washington 98840.

🌲 The heart of the North Cascades is composed of hundreds of mountain peaks and ridges to which cling glaciers, ice caps, ice falls, snowfields, and giant aprons of ice, snow, rock, and dust. The durable granites and related rocks of which these mountains are composed have held out longer against erosion than the softer lavas of the southern Cascade Range, and as a result the terrain consists of many sharp peaks and connecting knife-edge passes. Over the millenniums the relentlessly grinding ice has also taken its toll, scooping out valleys as deep as 8,500 feet, plucking out cirques, shearing off ridges, and carving canyons. All this would not have been possible without the immense amounts of moisture that flow in from the Pacific Ocean, forty miles to the west, and rise to precipitate as snow. The result is a spectacular, jumbled, forested, lake-dotted terrain now protected by Act of Congress and administered in four contiguous units: **Ross Lake National Recreation Area, Lake Chelan National Recreation Area,** and the north and south units of **North Cascades National Park.** Their combined area is 674,000 acres.

The principal difference between these units is that the recreation areas, centered around deep, elongated lakes, emphasize more intensive-use activities such as boating, fishing, and hunting, whereas the national park units are dedicated to preservation of wilder scenes where no hunting is allowed. All units have remote areas with high wilderness values and in all of them the beauty and solitude of the range are protected. Altogether they possess some 350 miles of trails, which lead through dense rain forests on western slopes and open, sunny woods on the east; over high passes, near glaciers, beside lakes, and along rivers and creeks. The major concentrations of glaciers are in the Picket Range, around Eldorado Peak, and on Mount Shuksan. In travels through these wild areas, a hiker is most likely to see deer, black bears, and mountain goats. Less common are grizzly bears, moose, mountain lions, and wolverines. During winter, bald eagles fly over the Skagit River, where they feed on salmon. The scene comes alive in summer with typical Cascade wild flowers. The range is of special interest to naturalists and photographers because of the widely differing ecosystems. Even when shrouded in mists, the forest and peaks—or what can be seen of them—may be pictured with telling effect. The lakes in their valleys bear considerable resemblance to fjords along the southeast Alaska coast.

Camping in the backcountry is by permit only. Open fires are prohibited in alpine and subalpine zones. Visitors may bring in horses, though horses are permitted only on certain trails, or may hire local outfitters to arrange a trip and supply their needs, including guides. Fishing for eastern brook trout, cutthroat trout, and Dolly Varden is in accordance with Washington state regulations. Mountain climbers will find every degree of difficulty, from easy to extremely difficult slopes, and are warned by the National Park Service to use modern gear, apply safety practices, and register with a park ranger in advance of all climbs. Boat trips and plane flights are available for sightseeing.

There are several campgrounds in the recreation areas (some accessible by boat rather than trail) and in adjacent national forests. Food and lodging are available in small communities locally; a full range of tourist supplies may be obtained only after two- to three-hour drives from the park. Access is via State Route 20, and by boat from the south, up fifty-five-mile-long Lake Chelan. Another approach is State Route 542 east of Bellingham. The north unit of North Cascades National Park lies along the Canada–United States boundary, approximately ninety miles in an air line northeast of Seattle.

Information: All four units are administered by the Superintendent, North Cascades National Park, Sedro Woolley, Washington 98284.

🌲 The **Pacific Crest Trail,** designated as a National Scenic Trail by Act of Congress in 1968, follows mountain ranges for 2,350 miles between Canada and México. In Oregon and Washington it is complete to the extent that a hiker can find the route on maps and follow the entire length; however, sizable segments are on roads, highways, and substitute trails some distance removed from the planned ultimate location. As such the trail affords a continuous footpath of 850 miles between the California boundary near Mount Shasta and the Canadian border at Monument 78, on the southern edge of Manning Provincial Park, British Columbia. This trail links several areas formally classified as wilderness, for in following the crest of the Cascade Range it skirts the slopes of such peaks as Mount Jefferson, Mount Hood, and Mount Adams. But it also enters other wild parts of national forests, as well as national parks. The environment through which the trail passes is spectacular indeed; a hiker finds himself either among volcanic peaks that rise from the horizon around him, as in Oregon and southern Washington, or among ice-covered ridges and massive mountains, as in the North Cascades. Rich forests envelop him at lower levels, a product of the abundant moisture of the region. Snow piles up to great depths in winter, which means that long segments of the trail are buried most of the year. The best time to hike is between July 1 and November 1, though local rangers should be consulted for up-to-the-minute details. In general, the trail environment is characterized by glaciated peaks, high passes, lava flows, streams, lakes, forests, and wild flowers. Along the route are shelters, campsites, campgrounds, and access to resorts or villages with conventional lodging. Good maps and guidebooks may be purchased for different sections of the trail. (For information on the California portion of the trail see page

104.) Permits are required for entry into wilderness areas along the route. Information: Regional Forester, Pacific Northwest Region, U.S. Forest Service, Box 3623, Portland, Oregon 97208; and Regional Forester, California Region, U.S. Forest Service, 630 Sansome Street, San Francisco, California 94111.

🌲 Sometimes the word "wilderness" evokes a vision of ice-covered peaks, dense forests, and hidden valleys so remote that they seem untouched by man. Nowadays, many types of terrain other than mountains have been set aside as wilderness, but that classical definition lives on, and applies to few places better than the Glacier Peak region of northwest Washington. Indeed, the forests and reflections of Image Lake are frequently utilized to typify the solitude and serenity of the United States wilderness system. A wealth of resources made this area valuable commercially, but the highest use of the land was eventually deemed to be wilderness recreation in a natural environment, and thus was established the **Glacier Peak Wilderness** in 1960.

Within its 464,240 acres are abundant glaciers, some covering large areas, some tucked into crevices, some clinging to nearly sheer walls. Dome and Glacier Peak have the most but fields of ice are scattered throughout the area, and their melting gives rise to a number of rivers, including the Suiattle. Just to the north and east of the wilderness boundary are the scenic Stehekin River and Lake Chelan.

A visit requires certain precautions, because even though the elevations are not extreme (Glacier Peak is 10,451 feet above sea level), the latitude and climatic pattern combine to make the environment unpredictable. The passes, filled with heavy winter snows, are usually open in July or early August, and may reasonably be counted upon to stay open through October. Still, the nights can be cold above tree line, and flurries of snow may be expected at any time of the year. Summers have frequent thunderstorms, with lightning a danger on exposed high ridges. So anyone hiking the Pacific Crest Trail—of which sixty-seven miles pass through the heart of the Glacier Peak Wilderness—or the other numerous paths in the area, should be well equipped for cold and violent weather.

The hiker or horseback rider may choose from more than twenty trails, although a few places are not safe for horse use. Trails lead across mountain slopes, over passes, and along ridges with extraordinary views of the North Cascades; or they pass beside gushing streams or on the meadows near meandering creeks. In upper regions the trails pass stands of white-bark pine and subalpine larch. Below tree line grow rich rain forests of fir and western hemlock. Flowers abound in open places. Lakes lie in ice-gouged basins, clear and blue, or gray-green with glacial silt.

There are many access routes to the Glacier Peak Wilderness, including up the Stehekin River road from Lake Chelan; by boat across Lake Chelan; by road up the White River on the south; and by the Suiattle River on the west. Commerical outfitters are located on some of the major valley approaches. Campsites have been designated within the area, and a number of simple shelters exist on major trails. Food, supplies, lodging, and major campgrounds are available in the vicinity. A wilderness permit is required for overnight visitors to the Glacier Peak Wilderness, and sizes of parties are limited.

Information: Supervisor, Mt. Baker National Forest, Bellingham, Washington 98225; and Supervisor, Wenatchee National Forest, P.O. Box 811, Wenatchee, Washington 98801.

🌲 Between Glacier Peak and Mount Rainier is a large land mass unusual for the Cascades—it is not dominated by an outstanding volcanic cone. These central Cascades of Washington reach no higher than 9,415 feet, but they are endowed with hundreds of lakes, a legacy of deep snows that accumulate in depths of up to thirty feet each year. The heart of this region has been kept relatively undisturbed for years by the U.S. Forest Service, which at this writing is proposing a 285,193-acre protected area to be called the **Alpine Lakes Wilderness.** Trails provide access to some of the 700 lakes here, and pass through mountain meadows, regions of sparse alpine fir and larch, fields with heather and snow lily, and deep forests of giant fir and hemlock. The Pacific Crest Trail passes through the area. Views from the high places are remarkable: forested slopes rising abruptly from the shores of lakes, steep cliffs, scattered remnants of glaciers, and scenes of soaring volcanic cones in the distance. The biotic habitat, like most ecosystems, is in an active state, bearing the brunt of natural fires, insect attacks, and other alterations. Yet its tranquillity appeals to persons seeking solitude. Attractive navelike forest glades and the roaring music of waterfalls characterize much of the wilderness experience here. Campgrounds are available in the surrounding national forests and accommodations can be obtained in nearby communities. Access is via forest roads and trails; U.S. Route 2 passes to the north, and Interstate 90 to the south.

Information: Supervisor, Snoqualmie National Forest, 1601 Second Avenue, Seattle, Washington 98101; and Supervisor, Wenatchee National Forest, Box 811, Wenatchee, Washington 98801.

🌲 Highest peak in the Cascade Range is Mount Rainier, 14,410 feet, and owing to an abundance of inflowing moist air from the Pacific Ocean it is endowed with up to eighty feet of snow in winter and smothered with twenty-six active glaciers, more than any other U.S. peak south of Alaska. This means a mecca for mountain climbers, and the trip to the summit can be exhilarating, but with thousands of persons attempting the climb each year, restrictions have had to be imposed by the National Park Service. For the mission of **Mount Rainier National Park** is to preserve in its natural state some of the finest remaining Cascade natural areas and to meet human recreational needs in accordance with the capacity of these fragile ecosystems.

The mountain lies most of the year under a blanket of snow, and even in July there may be eight-foot drifts remaining in sheltered places. But then, if to make up for lost time, the vegetation explodes into a sea of color. During June, in shaded bogs, the skunk cabbage sends up its large yellow flowers. Then the open meadows become densely packed with fawn lily, marigold, pasqueflower, lupine, paintbrush, gentian, and other species, a flowering mass that reaches its peak in late July and early August. After that the colors of autumn begin to show, and in September the reds of huckleberry, maple, and mountain ash are at their richest.

The volcanic ridges show evidence of numerous volcanic eruptions, intense glaciation, and mud flows that devastated wide swaths of forest. The mountain is quiet now, but the summit crater still has spots of warmth and there is little telling when Rainier will launch another series of lava flows.

Downslope, the forests are cathedrallike, with interlaced evergreen branches filtering the rays of the sun and reducing illumination to a kind of twilight. Great trunks rise from a tropiclike luxuriance where fallen trees, moss-covered, lie in the process of decay. It is an environment dominated by grand fir, Douglas fir, western red cedar, western hemlock, and bigleaf maple, nourished by heavy amounts of fog and rain. A hiker prepares for any eventuality of weather, and accepts what comes. In this frame of mind, he is set to take off on the Wonderland Trail, a ninety-mile route that circles the mountain, passing Indian Henry's Hunting Ground, Mowich Lake, Carbon and Winthrop glaciers, Sunrise, Ohanepecosh Park, Stevens Canyon, and Longmire. Altogether, the park has 300 miles of trails, some of which lead into surrounding national forests. Camping spots have been designated in the backcountry and a use permit is required. Size of groups is limited. Since bears, raccoons, and other animals have been relatively unmolested here for decades, they have developed a tolerance for man and a special interest in the food he carries, which means that a hiker's edible supplies had better be stored in something strong at night or suspended out of reach.

Mount Rainier is also a photographer's and scientist's wilderness. The glaciers, though fraught with peril for persons who approach too closely, are nonetheless picturesque, and most have icy caves. The contrasts between high cliffs of lava or ice and rich rain forests are fully explained in exhibits, self-guiding trails, public lectures, tours, and evening programs. Most of these, and most of the campgrounds, food, lodging, and supplies within the park are available in summer only. However, between December and April there are winter sports activities at Paradise; the Sunshine Point campground, at the Nisqually entrance, is open all year. In summer, anglers may fish without a license in lakes and streams, but must make themselves aware of park fishing regulations. No hunting is allowed and no motorized vehicles are permitted on trails. The park, which contains 235,400 acres, is located nearly a hundred miles southeast of Seattle. Access is via state routes 123, 165, 410, and 706. U.S. Route 12 passes a short distance south of the southern boundary.

Information: Superintendent, Mount Rainier National Park, Longmire, Washington 98397.

Between Mount Rainier and Mount Adams lies the **Goat Rocks Wilderness,** named for bands of mountain goats that inhabit its lava crests. These animals are quite at home among the rocky crags where they feed on grasses, lichens, and clumps of moss. The higher elevations are also attractive to elk because cool summer breezes help to keep away insects, and because succulent grasses grow on meadows in the intermontane basins. Elevations within the wilderness range from 8,201 feet on Mount Curtis Gilbert down to 2,905 feet on Glacier Lake. Coyotes, deer, and bears live here and occasionally a mountain lion is seen. Hikers hear the whistling marmot and the shrieking pika in rocky terrain. Fishing for trout and hunting for goats, elk, and deer are allowed in accordance with Washington State game laws.

Within the 82,680 acres of the Goat Rocks Wilderness are eighty-five miles of trails for hiking and horseback riding. The Pacific Crest Trail winds through the heart of the wilderness, and side trails from it lead down into the Cowlitz, Tieton, and other drainages as well as along alpine ridges and through lower-elevation forests. Views may be had into the Klickitat River drainage, but that is in the Yakima Indian Reservation on the southern edge of the wilderness and is not open to public entry.

A considerable portion of the central mountain summits of the wilderness is an Arctic-alpine rock and glacier zone where only the hardiest perennial plants, like deep blue Lyall lupine, can grow. This, of course, is dramatic terrain, with Cascade volcanoes visible in the distance. Descending, the hiker enters a zone of high meadows, dashing streams, and flower fields of lupine,

Aerial view of Lassen Peak, Lassen Volcanic National Park, California.

heather, phlox, and other species, with occasional clumps of alpine fir and mountain hemlock. Below that, the trails pass through a more dense vegetation consisting mainly of Pacific silver fir, noble fir, Alaska yellow cedar and western white pine, with an understory of such plants as blueberry and boxwood. Through the branches of trees a hiker gets views of lakes and river valleys with the overpowering presence of Mount Rainier and other volcanoes beyond.

Heavy snow blankets this wilderness each winter, so heavy that the trails may not be entirely snow-free until August. Although motorized vehicles, such as snowmobiles, are not permitted, visitors may enter the area via the White Pass chair lift and travel by ski or snowshoe cross-country to Hogback Mountain. Storms can come up suddenly, summer and winter, and the U.S. Forest Service advises hikers to carry warm clothing at all times in order to prevent overexposure and loss of body heat.

U.S. Route 12 passes the northern boundary of the wilderness, sixty miles west of Yakima. Accommodations and food are available in nearby communities, and campsites may be secured in adjacent national forests.

68

Upturned root, Three Sisters Wilderness, Oregon.

Sword fern, Hoh River Rain Forest, Olympic National Park, Washington.

Thistle, Lassen Volcanic National Park, California.

Information: Supervisor, Gifford Pinchot National Forest, Box 449, Vancouver, Washington 98660; and Supervisor, Snoqualmie National Forest, 1601 Second Avenue, Seattle, Washington 98101.

♣ Mount Adams (12,326 feet) and Mount St. Helens (9,677 feet), both in the state of Washington, are two of the most attractive peaks in the Cascade Range. Almost classical in shape, isolated, seemingly adrift in a sea of forest, they stand boldly on the horizon, visible for miles. On Mount Adams has been established the 32,400-acre **Mount Adams Wilderness.** The peak is adorned with glaciers, below which are lava crags and flows, alpine meadows, lakes, and forests of hemlock, fir, pine, spruce, and larch. A favorite pastime of hikers is the gathering of wild blackberries and huckleberries, especially in old burned-over areas on the north side of the mountain. The Pacific Crest Trail provides foot access along the alpine western side of the mountain, but is snow-free only during the summer and early autumn. Good maps are available from the U.S. Forest Service.

National forest campgrounds are provided on the western side and near the southern boundary of the wilderness, and campgrounds on the Yakima Indian Reservation are located just outside the southeast corner. Several forest roads permit a close approach to the mountain, particularly from State Route 141 at Trout Lake. Accommodations may be obtained in nearby forest areas.

Information: Supervisor, Gifford Pinchot National Forest, Box 449, Vancouver, Washington 98660.

♣ Indian legend has it that an ancient chieftain, with whom the Great Spirit had become displeased, was turned into a mountain because he constantly quarreled. And even after becoming a mountain he kept on showing anger by throwing out rocks and fire. Mount Hood has indeed thrown out a great deal of lava, and the ancient forests on its sides have also been devastated by slides of mud, ice, and stone. The mountain still emits a little gas and steam, and perhaps even a speck of ash from time to time, but the chieftain must be sleeping for the mountain is currently quiet. It sharply pierces the Oregon sky, not far south of the Columbia River, and to preserve a portion of the upper mountain environments, the **Mount Hood Wilderness** of 14,160 acres was established on its northern and western slopes.

The summit, at 11,235 feet, is not a particularly easy climb, but it is highly popular. Groups also ascend in winter, which is potentially perilous on account of rapid changes in weather. An easier hike is the Timberline Trail, a 37.6-mile route that is usually clear of snow by mid-July and weaves in and out of alpine and forested areas clear around the mountain. This trail should be taken in easy stages, given the variations of 3,000- to 7,000-feet elevation, and persons planning the mountain circuit should allow seven days for the trip. The wilderness area has several access trails and a few primitive shelters, but much of its steep terrain is covered by glaciers. Easiest access is from Timberline Lodge, less than two miles from the southern boundary, where food and lodging may be obtained. Campgrounds are available in surrounding forests. One major highway approach to the mountain is U.S. Route 26, fifty miles east of Portland. Oregon State Route 35 skirts the eastern slope of the mountain. Some of the best photography is possible during early morning, when the sky is apt to be clear, the waters of lakes tranquil, and the nightly mists evaporating among the crags and shadows. In autumn, bright red fruits of mountain ash provide a colorful foreground for views of the other volcanoes in the distance.

Information: Supervisor, Mount Hood National Forest, Box 16040, Portland, Oregon 97216.

Volcanic rocks in the **Mount Jefferson Wilderness** are composed of fine crystals and glass, spread out in flows and jumbles that still retain the structures produced in ancient explosive periods. Most of the area is underlain by andesite and basalt typical of the Cascade Range. Some lava was hardened in the central conduits of volcanoes and has eroded into spirelike peaks, e.g., Three Fingered Jack and Mount Jefferson itself, 10,497 feet at the summit. The lower slopes are composed of pumice and glacial debris with forests of mountain hemlock, and subalpine, silver, and noble fir.

There are 150 lakes here, and 160 miles of trails, including a portion of the Pacific Crest Trail. Altogether, 99,600 acres of volcanic plateau country have been included in the wilderness; parts of it are challenging to mountain climbers, all of it is challenging to photographers, and nearly half of the lakes have fish. Campgrounds are available on all sides, and excellent maps may be secured for extended hikes.

Access is by U.S. Route 20 on the south, Oregon Route 22 on the west, and forest roads at other points. The nearest major town is Redmond, thirty-four miles to the east. Salem lies sixty-five miles to the west.

Information: Supervisor, Deschutes National Forest, 211 East Revere Street, Bend, Oregon 97701; Supervisor, Willamette National Forest, Box 10607, 210 East Eleventh Avenue, Eugene, Oregon 97401; and Supervisor, Mount Hood National Forest, Portland, Oregon 97216.

🌲 Adjoining the Three Sisters Wilderness on the north, and generally similar to it in natural characteristics, is the **Mount Washington Wilderness,** which contains 46,116 acres. Largely composed of typical Cascade lava flows, it is covered by several hiking routes, including the Pacific Crest Trail, and may be reached from either Oregon Route 242, or a forest road south from U.S. Route 20–126. Mount Washington has an elevation of 7,794 feet. Campgrounds and scenic points of interest exist outside the boundaries, and food and lodging are available in nearby communities or the cities of Bend, to the east, and Eugene, to the west.

Information: Supervisor, Willamette National Forest, Box 10607, 210 East Eleventh Avenue, Eugene, Oregon 97401; and Supervisor, Deschutes National Forest, 211 East Revere Street, Bend, Oregon 97701.

🌲 Forty-five miles due east of Eugene, Oregon, three volcanic mountain peaks constitute the backbone of the Cascade Range: the North Sister, elevation 10,094 feet; the Middle Sister, 10,053 feet; and the South Sister, 10,354 feet. They and the land around them, consisting of lava flows, glaciers, flowering meadows, hundreds of mountain ponds and lakes, high forests of alpine fir and mountain hemlock, and low forests including Douglas fir, pine, and western red cedar, have been protected as the **Three Sisters Wilderness.** The rocky summits of South and Middle Sisters are not considered difficult to climb, but the North Sister ascent is fairly difficult, even in good weather. The peaks are relatively free of ice and snow between July and October. Broad, open slopes, with only occasional patches of trees, give to the upper regions a high, wide, and lonesome aspect, but deer, elk, coyotes, mountain lions, grouse, and other animals live there. Downslope, with increasing density of trees, live martens, bears, and bobcats.

One can detect differences in the more moist western slopes, where deep forests of Douglas fir abound, and the drier eastern slopes, with their mountain hemlocks and lodgepole pines. Indeed, the discerning naturalist will come upon many workings of the wild ecosystem, such as white pines killed by mountain pine beetles. The meadows spring to life each summer with larkspur, heather, arnica, columbine, lily, snow plant, mimulus, and shooting star. In a few places, forest dells echo with the music of waterfalls and cascades. Geologically, the Three Sisters area appears to have been the site of more volcanic activity in the last few thousand years than any other part of the Cascades.

Within the 199,902 acres of this wilderness are 240 miles of trails, including fifty miles of the Pacific Crest Trail. Large sections of terrain are trailless, and the hiker can go off on his own; however, the good weather of summer could be deceptive, for snowstorms can often blow up unexpectedly. Any rock climbing, says the U.S. Forest Service, should be done in groups of four or more, with proper equipment, first-aid supplies, and high-energy food. From spring through mid-August, the many lakes spawn swarms of mosquitoes; protection against them should be carried. For anglers, the lakes are supplied with rainbow, brook, and cutthroat trout, and, in a few high places, golden trout.

Campsites are numerous in national forests surrounding the Three Sisters Wilderness and food and supplies are available in nearby towns. Eugene lies eighty miles to the west on U.S. Route 126 and Bend about twenty-five miles due east.

Information: Supervisor, Deschutes National Forest, 211 East Revere Street, Bend, Oregon 97701; and Supervisor, Willamette National Forest, Box 10607, 210 East Eleventh Avenue, Eugene, Oregon 97401.

🌲 When John Diamond climbed the Cascade Crest in 1852, searching for a route across the mountains, he made his way through roadless, trailless, tracts of hemlock, pine, and fir inhabited only by deer, elk, bears, and other wild animals. From the summit of one peak, at 8,744 feet, surrounded by patches of ice, snow, and tumbling ridges of bare volcanic rock, he could look northwest toward the headwaters of the Willamette River, and north and east where forests and lakes spread out into the interior. Today, in much the same way, a hiker can enter the **Diamond Peak Wilderness** of 36,637 acres, and with the help of a few trails, pass through a domain that looks much as it did in Diamond's day. The same kinds of mammals and birds are there, the same quiet and solitude, the same hazards of getting caught in a summit storm. One modern advantage is the ability to take a camera and capture on color film the panoramic views and the close-ups of lupine, penstemon, paintbrush, and mimulus flowers on the meadows.

Access is far more easy than it was in pioneer days. The wilderness lies sixty miles southeast of Eugene, off Oregon Route 58. Food and lodging may be obtained nearby, and campgrounds are available in surrounding national forests. The Pacific Crest Trail passes through the eastern part of the wilderness.

Information: Supervisor, Willamette National Forest, Box 10607, 210 East Eleventh Avenue, Eugene, Oregon 97401; and Supervisor, Deschutes National Forest, 211 East Revere Street, Bend, Oregon 97701.

🌲 There is no blue like the blue of Crater Lake, perhaps because the water is so deep—1,932 feet—or at times so tranquil, reflective, and seemingly translucent. Its purity, naturalness, and the wilderness values surrounding the volcano in which it is located have been protected for three-quarters of a century as **Crater Lake National Park,** a rectangular unit of 160,290 acres. A rim road now circles the five-mile-wide crater, far above the lake, and a village was erected years ago on the edge of the abyss. But one still gets a feeling of wilderness, and contemplating the immensity of explosions that once blew this mountain apart gives man a feeling of smallness. Short trails lead along the rim, and the Pacific Crest Trail passes around the western slope of the mountain.

Most of the time, the rim area, at an elevation of 7,000 feet, lies beneath the fifty feet of snow that fall each year, and sometimes the roofs of village buildings scarcely begin to appear until June. Winter itself confers on the landscape a special attractiveness, when deep-blue waters contrast with green coniferous foliage and pure white snow. But as a consequence the summers are short. Displays of phlox, knotweed, monkeyflower, paintbrush, lupine, penstemon, aster, and other species, though exceedingly colorful, do not endure for long. The forest, composed of mountain hemlock, fir, and pine, is home to deer, elk, bears, bobcats, foxes, coyotes, jays, and nutcrackers. Some of the best times to observe this wildlife, as well as to see the lake in its mirrorlike moods, is early in the morning. Occasionally, visitors are disappointed by fog, which obliterates the lake, the crater, and all but the nearest trees.

Naturalist facilities, services, and publications help make the complex geology and ecology of the region understandable. The park can be reached from the south, over State Route 62, which is open all year. The north entrance road is open from July to October; the lodge, cafeteria, campgrounds, stores, and other facilities are open from mid-June to mid-September. However, a coffee shop does operate on winter weekends and holidays. During summer, fishing is permitted without a license, though subject to detailed regulations. For overnight backcountry travel a permit must be secured.

Information: Superintendent, Crater Lake National Park, Crater Lake, Oregon 97604.

The **Mountain Lakes Wilderness,** of 23,071 acres, located forty miles south of Crater Lake, is indeed a high country with numerous blue lakes in a glacially scoured terrain with high mountains all around. The larger lakes are stocked with trout, and deer may be seen among groves of fir and hemlock. Hiking trails reach all quadrants but since most of the wilderness is above 6,000 feet elevation, hikers should be prepared for frosty weather, no matter what the season. Snow ordinarily blankets the ground from mid-October to late June. Mosquitoes are thick following snowmelt. Thundershowers are frequent in July and August. Access is via forest roads and trails from Oregon Route 140; campgrounds are located at Lake of the Woods, three miles west, and elsewhere in the vicinity. Food and lodging may be obtained at private resorts in the vicinity, or at Klamath Falls, fifteen miles to the southeast.

Information: Supervisor, Winema National Forest, Post Office Building, Klamath Falls, Oregon 97601.

Fifty miles in an air line northeast of Klamath Falls, Oregon, lies the **Gearhart Mountain Wilderness,** 18,711 acres of lava domes, cliffs, and slopes, with occasional meadows and lakes. The waters of Blue Lake, situated in a glacially formed depression, are always clear and cold, and since there is no surface inflow or outflow, the lake must be part of a subterranean water distribution system. The andesitic lava in this wilderness has been cracked and eroded into pillars, palisades, pedestals, and other photogenic features, all easily accessible by trail on one-day hiking or riding trips. Gearhart Mountain, the highest point, reaches an elevation of 8,364 feet. Forest roads from near Bly, on State Route 140, or Lakeview, on U.S. Route 395, lead to the wilderness boundaries. Campgrounds are available in the adjacent national forest, and food and lodging in nearby communities.

Information: Supervisor, Fremont National Forest, Box 551, Lakeview, Oregon 97630.

In all the violent volcanic history of the Cascades, few eruptions have been witnessed by men, who came too late—or nearly too late. Early Indians may have seen some spectacular explosions. But in 1914, Lassen Peak, fifty miles east of Redding, California, began a series of eruptions that lasted for seven years and blanketed the landscape with superhot steam, incandescent lava, and layers of cinders and ash. More than 100,000 acres of this relatively fresh landscape have been designated **Lassen Volcanic National Park,** and supplied with roads and trails to the most interesting features. Some of the landscape is still alive, as it were, for boiling water or subterranean steam issue from hot springs, fumaroles, and sulfur vents. Such sites, wherever encountered in the park, are potentially hazardous and should be approached with care; in developed thermal areas, visitors must keep on trails.

Lassen Peak itself, a chaotic jumble of crags and technically a plug dome, rises to 10,457 feet. The rest of the park is a wilderness of cinder cones and lava flows covered sparsely with pines, firs, aspens, willows, alders, shrubs, and wild flowers. Among the hundreds of resident animals are deer, chipmunks, and golden-mantled ground squirrels. Fishing is permitted in designated areas. As in all national parks, hunting is prohibited. During half of the year the park is inundated by snow, which may in places accumulate to depths of twenty feet. Most of this melts by June, producing plentiful water for the scattered lakes—a phenomenon rather rare in young volcanic areas where the soil is porous and water usually sinks out of sight.

The Pacific Crest Trail passes through the eastern part of the park; altogether there are about 150 miles of trails. These lead to such places as Boiling Springs Lake, Fantastic Lava Beds, Painted Dunes, and the summit of Lassen Peak. Self-guiding trails provide on-site details about natural features. In winter, because of the generally ideal snow conditions, the park is excellent for cross-country skiing. All camping and backcountry use at any season is subject to specific regulations, which should be secured in advance.

Access is via California routes 36, 44, and 89. Food, supplies, lodging, and campsites are available in summer. Winter access is limited, depending on snow conditions, and fewer facilities are available at that season.

Information: Superintendent, Lassen Volcanic National Park, Mineral, California 96063.

🌲 Adjacent to the eastern boundary of Lassen Volcanic National Park is the **Caribou Wilderness,** 19,080 acres of volcanic terrain composed of cinder cones, small peaks, and barren, rocky areas. The wilderness is studded with lakes, and since many of these are surrounded by trees they offer good camping sites and, where stocked, good fishing. Trails enter the area from three sides. Some of the lakes may be reached on a short hike from the Rocky Knoll and Silver Bowl campgrounds, accessible on good country roads twenty-six miles northwest of Susanville, off California State Route 44. Trails lead through forests of Jeffrey, lodgepole, and western white pine, red fir, and hemlock. Horseback riders must pack in their own horse feed.

Information: Supervisor, Lassen National Forest, 707 Nevada Street, Susanville, California 96130.

🌲 Eight miles northwest of Lassen Volcanic National Park, off California routes 44 and 89, is the **Thousand Lakes Wilderness,** a volcanic area punctuated by cinder cones. Magee Peak reaches nearly to 9,000 feet elevation and may be ascended by trail. The wilderness gets its name from lakes and ponds in pockets of lava. Fishing is good in the major lakes. Patches of woods are chiefly ponderosa pine, fir, and sugar pine. The U.S. Forest Service recommends short trips into this relatively small wilderness. Cars can be left at various road endings near all four sides of the area. Horseback riders must pack in their own horse feed. Campgrounds are available not far away, along Route 89. Food and lodging may be secured in and near Lassen Volcanic National Park.

Information: Supervisor, Lassen National Forest, 707 Nevada Street, Susanville, California 96130.

🌲 Lava flows and lava tube caves offered the Modoc Indians a considerable advantage against United States troops during the fierce but brief Modoc War of 1872–1873. The Modocs knew the rough and jumbled terrain far better than the soldiers did and so eluded them, but not before taking numerous lives. Today the maze of passageways in Captain Jack's Stronghold may be explored at leisure, as can the numerous lava tubes (decorated with lavacicles, sulfur deposits, and patches of ice), cinder buttes, jagged flows, spatter cones, and wild forests of the region. In **Lava Beds National Monument,** thirty miles from Tulelake, in northeastern California, 46,239 acres of relatively recent eruptive rock (some only 300 years old) have been placed under permanent protection.

On the freshest flows very little vegetation has taken root; at other places the fragrant fernbush thrives in the merest soil; finally, the oldest volcanics support broad fields of sagebrush and juniper or mature open forests of ponderosa pine. Though passage for human beings is difficult across the most jumbled lava flows, neither deer nor pronghorn seems to have much trouble. The lava beds are in fact a paradise for most life forms, what with millions of tiny holes and complex subsurface passageways. Rodents, rattlesnakes, rabbits, and squirrels are only a few of the resident species, and for all the handy passages of escape they must still beware of hawks and owls. Altogether, the lava beds are remarkable for their variation of natural features. Geological aspects dominate, but a wealth of wild flowers and abundance of birds exist throughout the region during summer. And for autumn, one need only note that the northern boundary of the monument is contiguous with Tule Lake National Wildlife Refuge, where millions of waterfowl gather during periods of migration, the largest concentrations of ducks and geese on the continent.

The monument is reached on good roads leading south or west from California Route 139. Camp and picnic sites are open summer or winter, but food, lodging, and supplies must be secured in nearby towns. Wilderness hikers should bear in mind that there is no surface water at Lava Beds.

Information: Superintendent, Lava Beds National Monument, Box 867, Tulelake, California 96134.

🌲 Twenty miles east of Alturas, California, the **South Warner Wilderness,** an isolated southern spur of the Cascade Range, preserves 68,507 acres of alpine peaks, canyons, glacial lakes, and richly vegetated mountain meadows. Eagle Peak, in the southern section of the wilderness, rises to 9,906 feet. The Summit Trail extends along ridge tops at a 9,000-foot contour for more than fifteen miles, affording fine views of mountain scenery as well as distant alkaline lakes, lava beds, and volcanic country. Other trails link lakes and streams within the wilderness and connect with hiking routes or forest roads within the Modoc National Forest. U.S. Route 395 parallels the wilderness on the west. A permit is required for entry.

Information: Supervisor, Modoc National Forest, 441 North Main Street, Alturas, California 96101.

Hoh River Rain Forest, Olympic National Park, Washington.

3. EASTERN OREGON, WASHINGTON, AND NEVADA

In eastern Oregon, two miles southeast of Canyon City, begins an elongated, east-west area of 33,000 acres called the **Strawberry Mountain Wilderness.** It is a region of long ridges, rounded mountains, crystal-clear lakes, and forests composed of pine, fir, and other species. Bears, grouse, deer, and elk are among the principal animal residents, and from July through early September the meadows and hillsides burgeon with wild flowers. The highest summit is Strawberry Mountain at 9,038 feet, easily reached by trail. Access is via forest roads on nearly all sides; these are generally clear of snow from mid-July to early November. Campgrounds exist on adjacent forest lands, and food and lodging may be secured at communities along U.S. Route 26, which passes less than ten miles north of the wilderness.

Information: Supervisor, Malheur National Forest, 139 Northeast Dayton Street, John Day, Oregon 97845.

Mountains in northeast Oregon are quite unlike the lava peaks and plateaus of the Cascade Range in the western part of the state. Durable, light-colored granite, marble, and limestone prevail, so that a hiker feels closer to the Rocky Mountains. Traveling through the **Eagle Cap Wilderness,** in the Wallowa Mountains, he ascends through ponderosa pine, spruce, and Douglas fir, comes out of deep canyons and rocky valleys onto meadows and thinning woods of alpine fir and whitebark pine. There the weather is cold and severe in winter, and most trees lose their struggle to live. Higher yet, the mountains are bald, and on the summits—Eagle Cap reaches 9,595 feet—little more than rock and ice exists. But there are also views of a wide wilderness (293,735 acres) composed of jumbled peaks, icy lakes, and glacier-scoured valleys.

Snow is usually gone between July and November, when many parts of the wilderness may be reached on a network of trails. Wildlife consists of deer, elk, bear, coyote, pika, porcupine, grouse, jay, and others—including the

79

world's entire population of the rare Wallowa gray-crowned rosy finch. Wild flowers, best in July and August, include lupine, lily, bluebell, buttercup, heather, gilia, and phlox.

Alas, these attributes have been so appealing that hordes of human beings have swarmed into the area and threatened its fragile ecological equilibrium. For that reason, the U.S. Forest Service has had to impose restrictions on public use, in accordance with instructions of the Wilderness Act to preserve the area in its natural state. These restrictions involve the limitation or exclusion of horses in certain areas, prohibition of camping near trails or the shores of lakes and streams, reduction in size of visiting groups, and necessity for registration upon arrival.

Eagle Cap Wilderness lies thirty miles in an air line northeast of Baker, and is accessible on forest roads. Interstate 80N and Oregon routes 82 and 86 are the nearest main highways. Campgrounds are available near the trailheads at the wilderness boundary; food and lodging may be obtained in nearby towns and villages.

Information: Supervisor, Wallowa-Whitman National Forest, Box 907, Baker, Oregon 97814.

🌲 In few places can better evidence of man's concern for wildlife be found than in southern Oregon and northwestern Nevada. There was little such concern originally: The uniquely American pronghorn survived for twenty million years of geologic history only to be reduced almost to extinction within fifty years by the impact of domestic livestock and man and his guns. We may never again possess great herds like those that roamed the grasslands, but at least some fragments of the primitive ecosystems have been reserved, and their location is based not on the desires of man but on the needs and habits of the animals. **Hart Mountain National Antelope Refuge,** in Oregon, was established in 1936 to conserve pronghorn breeding grounds. But the animals have to move out of the mountains, owing to a harsh winter climate, and the lands to which they go, in northwestern Nevada, were established as the **Charles Sheldon National Antelope Range and Refuge.** Altogether, these reserves encompass 818,933 acres at the western edge of the Great Basin Desert, and are home to more than 2,000 pronghorns.

The refuges have values other than pronghorn protection grounds. Hart Mountain, for example, is a massive fault-block ridge rising to 8,065 feet elevation with steep cliffs and precipitous canyons on one side and hills covered with grass and sagebrush on the other. It has numerous springs, streams, and intermittent lakes, and is populated by deer, bighorns, coyotes, bobcats, and an abundance of other animals. Hiking is allowed into the remote parts of the refuge, but overnight wilderness camping is authorized only by a permit, which is obtainable at refuge headquarters. There is limited rock collecting, hunting, and fishing. A campground may be found three miles south of headquarters, and visitors may follow a self-guided twenty-mile auto-tour route in the refuge. Hart Mountain, though fairly remote, is accessible via county roads from U.S. Route 395 and Oregon Route 140. Gasoline and supplies may be obtained at Plush, twenty-five miles to the southwest, or at Adel, forty-five miles to the south. Lodging and accommodations are available at Lakeview, sixty-five miles to the southwest.

In the Sheldon area, located in the northwestern tip of Nevada, the topography is made up principally of high and dry tablelands, rolling hills, valleys, canyons, and rims of lava. There are few trees, mostly patches of aspen, juniper, and mountain mahogany. Roads lead into the refuge from all directions. Lakeview, Oregon, lies sixty-eight miles to the northwest; Cedarville, California, is forty-three miles to the southwest.

Information: Manager, Sheldon-Hart Mountain National Antelope Refuges, Box 111, Lakeview, Oregon 97630.

One of the most important breeding and resting areas for migratory birds traveling the Pacific Flyway is the **Malheur National Wildlife Refuge,** thirty-two miles southeast of Burns, Oregon. Because of wildlife-management structures and practices, such as dikes, fences, low-flying aircraft, grazing, water diversion, and drainage, very little of the refuge's 180,850 acres is true wilderness. However, the salt-encrusted bed of Harney Lake, having been unsuited to agriculture or hunting, has been left alone, more or less, for hundreds of years, and so represents a fairly wild area of about 30,000 acres. It certainly is different from most other wilderness areas, what with gleaming white alkali flats, small clumps of vegetation sparsely scattered, a few warm springs, and varying quantities of shallow water. The water contains numerous small invertebrates that attract large flocks of ducks and shore-birds—some of them even nesting when water is abundant. The greatest number of bird species can usually be observed in mid-May. Access is via State Route 205. Food and lodging are available in Burns.

Information: Manager, Malheur National Wildlife Refuge, Burns, Oregon 97720.

South of the Malheur National Wildlife Refuge, upstream along the Donner und Blitzen River in southeastern Oregon, Steens Mountain rises to an elevation of 9,733 feet—the highest point in Oregon that can be reached by car. The fault-block mountain rises abruptly, providing visitors with notable views of deserts, lakes, rolling foothills, deep canyons, and dramatic escarpments. Men also come to hunt for deer, pronghorn, sage grouse, quail,

81

dove, and partridge, and to fish for trout in the lakes and streams. Unfortunately, the fragile mountain ecosystems have been deteriorating from overuse and the Bureau of Land Management, which administers much of the mountain and vicinity, has proposed a **Steens Mountain Recreation Area** of nearly 200,000 acres, where careful management of human use would lead to perpetuation of the natural values people seek there. A great deal of the mountain is still reasonably wild by virtue of its inaccessibility, but hikers willing to leave the roads and climb into difficult terrain will be rewarded. The mountain slopes are covered with sagebrush, juniper, aspen, and fir at successively higher levels, and are replete with twenty-seven perennial streams fed by heavy winter snows. Bighorn sheep occupy some of the less severely disturbed areas, and an estimated 14,000 mule deer inhabit the mountain. Picnicking and camping sites are available, but the mountain is rather remote and a full range of tourist facilities must be sought in Burns, the nearest town of substantial size, eighty miles to the north. The road to the summit of Steens Mountain is closed above the 5,000-foot level from approximately November through May.

Information: State Director, Bureau of Land Management, Box 2965, 729 Northeast Oregon Street, Portland, Oregon 97208.

In northern Nevada the **Jarbidge Wilderness** protects high mountain terrain on the boundary between the Columbia Plateau and the Basin and Range Province. The Jarbidge River flows north toward the Snake and Columbia rivers and the Mary's River drains south into the Humboldt. Mountain peaks in this wilderness are the Matterhorn, which reaches 10,839 feet elevation; Jarbidge Peak, 10,789 feet; and Square Top, 10,687 feet. Much of the higher land is grassy or barren, but there are scattered stands of aspen, alpine fir, and limber pine at lower levels. Wildlife includes deer, pronghorn, coyote, mountain lion, bobcat, badger, and raccoon. Fishing is reported excellent in lakes and streams. Trails reach into the heart of this 64,667-acre wilderness, and some of them are steep and rugged. Access is via forest roads and trails, and there are campgrounds and picnic sites on surrounding forest lands. The area is seventy-five miles north of Elko, Nevada, and the majority of the roads are secondary gravel. Twin Falls, Idaho, is 78 miles northwest of the wilderness, and the majority of the roads are paved. Limited food and lodging are available near the wilderness. State Route 51 passes to the west and U.S. 93 to the east.

Information: Supervisor, Humboldt National Forest, Elko, Nevada 89801.

82

4. PACIFIC COAST

The earth as a greenhouse of rich and abundant vegetation is nowhere more superbly illustrated than in western British Columbia and Washington. The Amazon jungles scarcely compare with it in sheer luxuriance, and only a few places, such as the montane oak and orchid forests of central Costa Rica, the mountain vegetation of Ecuador, or the Canary Island cloud forests of Tenerife, are comparably dense. None is as delicate as the temperate rain forest of **Olympic National Park,** where under benign winds and gentle rain, seventy kinds of lichen flourish, where ferns overlap so densely on the forest floor that a hiker sinks halfway to his knees, and where trees grow from the fallen trunks of other trees. The rainfall that sustains this extraordinary productivity amounts to more than 140 inches a year, the wettest climate in the conterminous United States. The soft blanket of growth seems to absorb all outside sounds, and the hiker becomes more acutely aware of dripping water, the chatter of squirrels, the voices of birds. In thick mats of sphagnum moss he can search through lacy leaves for slugs, insects, and a lower layer of life that most people miss. Overhead, giant Sitka spruce and western hemlock dominate the forest; Douglas fir and western red cedar are also common, with the "gaps" filled in by maple. All this is festooned with hanging curtains of clubmoss, and ferns seem to grow everywhere, both high and low. In few places is the color of green so vivid; photographers can have a field day, but should take a tripod because the prevailing light is usually at low levels.

The rain forests are broken by wide, gravelly valleys through which course streams that originate either in springs or in high mountain glaciers. The Olympic Mountains, a massif of sedimentary strata, rise out of the dense woods to treeless, snow-packed, glaciered summits, of which the highest is Mount Olympus, 7,965 feet. Altogether, there are sixty glaciers in the park, fed by seaborne moisture that leaves the low rain forests and rises to precipitate as snow on the peaks. High-elevation meadows may also turn literally white and yellow when lilies bloom in the spring. Flower displays are best in mid-July.

Such environmental variation across the park's 897,000 acres provides remarkable opportunity for the wilderness hiker. He can roam the fifty miles of wild Pacific beaches with their jumbled piles of driftwood; explore tidal pools; make circle tours of some of the loveliest lakes in the West; or climb into valleys where every cliff seems to have a waterfall. The chances of seeing Olympic elk depend on how well the hiker knows their habits and where to look for them. Other mammals he may see include deer, raccoons, beaver, bobcats, marmots, and bears.

Spur roads provide several points of vehicular access to the park from U.S. Route 101, which loops around the Olympic Peninsula and thus nearly surrounds the park. But the roads do not penetrate very deeply, so this is essentially a wilderness park, endowed with more than 600 miles of trails. A hiker can make base camp in the several campgrounds, or in motels and hotels of surrounding communities, and take short hikes of a day's duration into the park's habitats, wet or dry, low or high. Or he can mount an expedition to roam the wild mountains for days. Information is available from park rangers and naturalists, museums, nature trails, wayside exhibits, guidebooks, and interpretive publications.

Information: Superintendent, Olympic National Park, 600 East Park Avenue, Port Angeles, Washington 98362.

🌲 Between Canada's Vancouver Island and the northwest coast of Washington, a series of islands, islets, and rocks barely above the sea lie scattered like pieces of a jigsaw puzzle. The largest masses of land in this San Juan Archipelago have been occupied for years, and some smaller islands have been equipped with Coast Guard stations or navigational markers. Many are forested. About eighty islands and islets still retain their original values, however, and are being designated as the **San Juan Wilderness**. Although their combined area is 355 acres, their relative isolation by open water gives them aspects of wilderness. The principal islands are Matia, Puffin, Colville, Bare, and Buck. Since these and numerous rocky islets are home to thousands of birds, mainly seabirds such as glaucous-winged gulls, it is more desirable for visitors to observe them from a boat. Some of the other resident species include cormorants, tufted puffins, pigeon guillemots, auklets, and oyster catchers. In some cases, intricate tidal pools exist, and along the shores or in the harbors may be seen porpoises, seals, and whales. For such activities as camping, picnicking, and hiking, there are adjacent mainland sites developed by the U.S. Department of the Interior and the Washington State Parks and Recreation Commission. Food and lodging are also available on the mainland.

Information: Manager, Willapa National Wildlife Refuge, Ilwaco, Washington 98624.

 Down the outer coast of Washington and Oregon lie numerous offshore islands, rocks, reefs, and spires. Some have been combined into the **Washington Islands National Wildlife Refuge,** which extends along a hundred miles of the coast of Washington State, and others in the **Oregon Islands Wilderness,** which includes more than sixty islands. Most of these rocky protrusions are precipitous and surrounded by surf treacherous to man. But man is not the user of the islands; hundreds of thousands of colonial seabirds such as glaucous-winged gulls, auklets, puffins, common murres, and Leach's petrels nest here, and seals and sea lions occasionally occupy the sea-washed shores. Rainfall is heavy and fog abundant, the temperature remaining generally between 35° and 65°. Human use is restricted; it is nearly impossible or fruitless to land on the islets anyway. One can approach them by boat, taking care to stay far enough offshore to avoid disturbance of birds or mammals, or observe them from viewpoints on the mainland.

Information: Manager, Washington Islands National Wildlife Refuge, Ilwaco, Washington 98624; and Refuge Manager, Box 208, Route 2, Corvallis, Oregon 97330.

Valentine Cave, Lava Beds National Monument, California.

🌲 A broad area of seacoast, sand dunes, forests, rhododendron patches, and other natural features on the Oregon coast south of Florence was established in 1972 as the **Oregon Dunes National Recreation Area.** Although set aside principally for outdoor recreation, where hunting, fishing, and trapping are among the pursuits authorized, the Congressional Act (PL 92-260) also instructs the Secretary of Agriculture to examine the recreation area for possible wilderness values. By March, 1975, the Secretary must report to the President, in accordance with the provisions of the Wilderness Act, his recommendation as to the suitability or nonsuitability of any part of the area as wilderness. If his report is favorable, then Congress would presumably establish a wilderness under existing procedures. In the meantime the management of the area is under the U.S. Forest Service. Access is via U.S. Route 101. Campsites are available. Accommodations may be secured in nearby communities.

Information: Supervisor, Suislaw National Forest, Box 1146, Corvallis, Oregon 97330.

PART III

The Far West

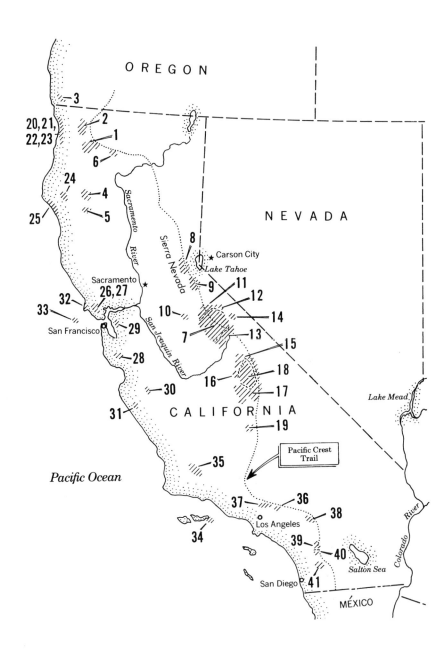

OREGON

20, 21,
22, 23

3

2

1

6

24

4

5

25

Sacramento River

Sierra Nevada

NEVADA

8

Carson City

Lake Tahoe

Sacramento

26, 27

9

11

12

32

10

14

33

7

13

San Francisco

29

San Joaquin River

15

28

16

18

30

17

Lake Mead

31

CALIFORNIA

19

35

Pacific Crest
Trail

Pacific Ocean

37

36

38

34

Los Angeles

39

40

Salton Sea

Colorado River

San Diego

41

MÉXICO

1. NORTHERN MOUNTAINS

1. Salmon–Trinity Alps Primitive Area, California
2. Marble Mountain Wilderness, California
3. Kalmiopsis Wilderness, California
4. Yolla Bolly–Middle Eel Wilderness, California
5. Snow Mountain Wilderness, California
6. Castle Crags State Park, California

2. SIERRA NEVADA

7. Yosemite National Park, California
8. Desolation Wilderness, California
9. Mokelumne Wilderness, California
10. Calaveras Big Trees State Park, California
11. Emigrant Wilderness, California
12. Hoover Wilderness, California
13. Minarets Wilderness, California
14. Devils Postpile National Monument, California
15. John Muir Wilderness, California
16. High Sierra Wilderness, California
17. Sequoia National Park, California
18. Kings Canyon National Park, California
19. Dome Land Wilderness, California

3. CALIFORNIA COAST

20. Jedediah Smith Redwoods State Park, California
21. Del Norte Coast Redwoods State Park, California
22. Prairie Creek Redwoods State Park, California
23. Redwood National Park, California
24. Humboldt Redwoods State Park, California
25. King Range National Conservation Area, California
26. Muir Woods National Monument, California
27. Mount Tamalpais State Park, California
28. Big Basin Redwoods State Park, California
29. Mount Diablo State Park, California
30. Pinnacles National Monument, California
31. Ventana Wilderness, California
32. Point Reyes National Seashore, California
33. Farallon Island National Wildlife Refuge, California
34. Channel Islands National Monument, California

4. SOUTHERN MOUNTAINS

35. San Rafael Wilderness, California
36. Cucamonga Wilderness, California
37. San Gabriel Wilderness, California
38. San Gorgonio Wilderness, California
39. San Jacinto Wilderness, California
40. Mount San Jacinto Wilderness State Park, California
41. Agua Tibia Primitive Area, California

89

1. NORTHERN MOUNTAINS

In the vast domain of Cascade volcanoes it is surprising to discover a mountain range composed not of cinders but of gabbro, granite, and marble. Approaching the Salmon Mountains and Trinity Alps of northern California, one can imagine oneself in Alaska or heading for the Sierra Nevada or the Rocky Mountains—or even approaching the Alps. But these are part of the Klamath Mountains, and although they are 200 miles from the Sierra Nevada, their rocks and geologic structure have striking similarities. Nor are they typical of other California coastal mountains; they have been sharply glaciated, and their snow-speckled, ice-hung summits reach close to 9,000 feet. The forest climbs as high as it can, thins to twisted, stunted specimens, and on the summits or bare rock shoulders, disappears. The valleys below, gouged out by movements of massive glaciers, lie free of ice, as though uncovered recently, and basins in them hold translucent lakes. Such is the **Salmon-Trinity Alps Primitive Area,** forty miles southwest of Mount Shasta. From sharp matterhorn summits, rock walls plunge as much as 4,000 feet into craggy canyons. The vegetation varies from chaparral (manzanita and scrub oak), on southern exposures, to maple and madrone on lower slopes, to fir and weeping spruce at higher levels.

Since Gold Rush days, many millions of dollars in precious metals have been mined in the Klamath Mountains, both in lode and placer deposits, and the remains of scattered diggings may still be found. Anglers will discover good trout-fishing in many of the mountain streams. Deer, bears, and small mammals may be encountered, and perhaps a bobcat now and then.

The Salmon-Trinity Alps Primitive Area, containing over 250,000 acres, is located forty miles northwest of Redding. An entry permit is required and party size is limited. Camping, food, and lodging are available nearby. Access is by forest roads and trails from all sides. California Route 3 is not far from the eastern boundary.

Information: Supervisor, Shasta-Trinity National Forests, 1615 Continental Street, Redding, California 96001; and Supervisor, Klamath National Forest, 1215 South Main Street, Yreka, California 96097.

Agua Tibia Primitive Area, California.

🌲 Not so raw or rugged is the **Marble Mountain Wilderness,** named for a mass of metamorphosed white limestone that caps an upland mass with a thickness of as much as 1,000 feet. The terrain is mostly gentle, well-forested, endowed with flower-strewn meadows, hidden lakes containing trout, and streams where steelhead and salmon run. Most streams drain into the Salmon, Scott, and Klamath rivers, a short distance beyond the boundaries. The rare weeping spruce is abundant. Columbian black-tailed deer inhabit the region. Bears occupy upper ridges in summer and move to lower elevations for winter retirement. Scenic, shaded trails reach into nearly all parts of this 213,363-acre wilderness. The Pacific Crest Trail passes along the eastern edge. Forest roads and trails provide access from all sides; California routes 3 and 96 approach the area from Yreka, twenty-five miles to the northwest. Campgrounds that can be used as starting points for wilderness trips are located in surrounding forests. The nearest food and lodging are in small towns nearby.

Information: Supervisor, Klamath National Forest, 1215 South Main Street, Yreka, California 96097.

🌲 The Klamath Mountains in the southwestern corner of Oregon are unusually interesting from a botanical point of view because so many pre-Ice Age plants seem to have taken refuge there. This situation, and even some of the plant genera, are remarkably parallel to the state of events in the Great Smoky Mountains of North Carolina and Tennessee. Several parts of Siskiyou National Forest have been set aside to preserve the natural habitat where such species as the weeping spruce, Sadler oak, Port Orford cedar, madrone, leucothoe, and rock rhododendron or Kalmiopsis grow. The latter is one of the oldest members of the heath family, and the species that grows here is the only one in its genus. The exceptional significance of this has been recognized in naming 76,900 acres of the most rugged part of the botanical area the **Kalmiopsis Wilderness.**

Remote and reached only on primitive mountain roads, this wilderness has no towering peaks or glacial lakes; its highest elevation is just over 5,000 feet. The trails within are also primitive, recommended for hiking rather than horseback riding. Old roads, once used in connection with chromium mining, may also be traversed, but most of the area is roadless and trailless. The persistent naturalist, seeking lady's slipper orchids, Darlingtonias or pitcher plants, Labrador tea, or any of the seventeen species of conifers in the area, will find himself clambering over "buckskin boulders" or peridotite, a dark-colored rock that decomposes into reddish soil, plus granite, diorite, and serpentine. If not careful, he will also clamber over rattlesnakes, which are common here. Yellow jackets and hornets are numerous, and poison oak is dense throughout the area. Given such extra hazards, the recommendations against traveling alone seem especially valid.

The wilderness is located thirty miles southwest of Grants Pass, and is reached by roads branching off U.S. Route 199 on the east and the coast highway, U.S. Route 101, on the west. The area is seventeen miles in an air line from the Pacific Ocean, though its aspect is generally dry and nearly devoid of lakes. Accommodations are available at Brookings and Grants Pass.

Information: Supervisor, Siskiyou National Forest, 1504 Northwest Sixth Street, Box 440, Grants Pass, Oregon 97526.

🌲 About thirty-five miles west of Red Bluff, California, rises a rugged terrain bounded by the North and South Yolla Bolly mountains. The name Yolla Bolly, derived from Wintun Indian words, means "high snow-covered peaks," and although most of these ridges are below 8,000 feet elevation, there is indeed snow on them, at least until June. Several rivers originate here, including the middle fork of the Eel River. Fortunately, these headwaters and their environs remain relatively undisturbed, and 111,091 acres have been set aside as the **Yolla Bolly–Middle Eel Wilderness.** The mountains are well vegetated, with a dense cover of typical chaparral (chamise, manzanita, mountain mahogany) on the lower slopes, and pine and fir forests higher up. Western white pines and Jeffrey pines grow on the uppermost summits. A relatively rare grove of foxtail pines occurs on South Yolla Bolly. With so much excellent shelter, there is an abundance of wildlife in the region, including many deer, bears, and smaller mammals. Hunting and fishing are permitted in season. The best month to visit is July, when the weather, flowers, streams, and other attractions are at their best. Motorized vehicles and equipment are prohibited—the sounds of nature have priority. Groups should be limited to fewer than ten persons. There are good trails and a number of possible loop trips. The map of Mendocino National Forest, available from the U.S. Forest Service, delineates numerous access trails to this wilderness. Food and lodging are available in the nearby communities of Covelo, Red Bluff, and Corning.

Information: Supervisor, Mendocino National Forest, 420 East Laurel Street, Willows, California 95988; and Supervisor, Shasta-Trinity National Forests, 1615 Continental Street, Redding, California 96001.

🌲 Forty miles south of the Yolla Bolly–Middle Eel Wilderness, and still within Mendocino National Forest, a portion of the wild country around

Snow Mountain, elevation 7,056 feet, has retained many natural values. The wildlife includes deer, bear, and mountain lion; there are snow-clad summits, rare plants, deep canyons—in short, a remote area with exceptional scientific value. Citizens groups have endeavored for years to get a **Snow Mountain Wilderness** established, and at this writing a bill for that purpose is before Congress. At public hearings on the proposed 37,000-acre area, citizens recommended that the unusual botanical growths and fragile slopes be kept inviolate for permanent human enjoyment. Forest roads follow much of the boundary of the area, and several trails cross it. The U.S. Forest Service has prohibited all trail bikes and other motor vehicles in the area. Whatever the outcome of the legislation, Snow Mountain's wild qualities seem likely to be perpetuated in some degree. Access is via various roads west of Willows or northeast of Ukiah. Food, lodging, and campgrounds are available in nearby forest lands or communities.

Information: Supervisor, Mendocino National Forest, 420 East Laurel Street, Willows, California 95988.

Upstream on the Sacramento River, in the shadow of Mount Shasta, lies **Castle Crags State Park,** whose granite eminences, pushed up by earth movements and sculptured by glaciation, rise to an elevation of more than 6,000 feet above sea level. The coniferous forest is unusually attractive, including sugar and ponderosa pines, Douglas fir, Port Orford and incense cedars, and rare Brewer's spruce, the latter with its characteristic weeping foliage. But all is not somber evergreen; among the deciduous trees are maples that put on dazzling displays of color in autumn, as well as azaleas, dogwoods, and ceanothus that bloom in spring. The park has an area of 4,351 acres. A 2.7-mile trail leads into the crags and to panoramic views of the surrounding countryside. Fishing is reported good both in the Sacramento River and its tributaries. Food, campsites, and a picnic area are available in or near the park, with accommodations obtainable in nearby towns.

Information: Superintendent, Castle Crags State Park, Castella, California 96017.

2. SIERRA NEVADA

The claims of its patrons may well be true. In all the 400-mile length of the Sierra Nevada, or perhaps in all North America, there is no greater concentration of outstanding scenic features or wilderness environments than in **Yosemite National Park.** Only in Venezuela, according to present knowledge, is there a waterfall higher than Yosemite Falls, which plunges 2,425 feet to the floor of the valley. For that matter, very few wilderness areas or parks have such a collection of major falls, which include Bridalveil, 620 feet; Ribbon, 1,612 feet; Cascade, 500 feet; Vernal, 317 feet; Nevada, 594 feet; and Illilouette, 370 feet—all more or less accessible by trail. A zigzag path leads up out of Yosemite Valley beside the roaring, seething spumes of Yosemite Falls; from this route, a hiker gains repeated panoramic views of Half Dome and the High Sierra, framed by boughs of oak or pine.

There is little the Sierra has that Yosemite hasn't. Tuolumne Meadows is claimed to be the largest montane meadow in the range. Three groves of giant sequoia trees lie within the park: Mariposa (with the celebrated but now fallen Wawona tunnel tree), Merced, and Tuolumne. The elevational range from 2,000 to 13,114 feet is divided by nature into five distinct zones of vegetation, and the wildlife ranges from ground squirrels to golden eagles.

Within the 761,320 acres of the park a network of 700 miles of trails has been constructed. Short trips lead up out of Yosemite Valley to Sentinel Dome, Glacier Point, and Vernal Falls. The high backbone of the park is traversed by the Pacific Crest Trail. Other footpaths lead into national forests, with which the park is surrounded. With the benefit of advance research, some hikers go out for weeks, wandering at random as John Muir did in his travels here. Others, whose time is more limited, select the outstanding destinations they most wish to see and follow a definite itinerary.

The granite gorge of the Tuolumne River, a wild, light-colored canyon, resounds with the roar of falling waters. Half Dome may be climbed with ease on the rounded side or scaled by professional climbers on the sheer north face. To scale El Capitan, a 3,500-foot vertical cliff, the first successful climbers took eleven days, suspended by ropes as they inched their way to the top. Mount Lyell calls for a climb over barren ground and tundra vegetation.

Yet, for all the breathtaking adventures, daring climbs, and stunning scenery, it is possible that some of the least expected sights or happenings will remain the longest in a hiker's memory. For example, the magenta flowers of penstemon seem all the more brilliant when growing in a crevice of high cold granite where no flowers at all may have been anticipated. Red columbines thrive in moss-lined, shaded dells. Or an open space among lodgepole pines may turn into a sea of purple when shooting stars burst into bloom. At lower elevations the greening slopes in spring become covered with millions of poppies, and the western redbud opens its pink and purple clusters. The most vivid color is that of snow plants, scarlet heaths that burgeon through mats of pine needles shortly after the snow has melted.

Both oak and aspen turn a striking yellow in autumn, and dogwood leaves are transformed into cinnamon brown. The waterfalls may be dry or much reduced, but deep winter snows, which turn each valley into something of an Arctic Elysium, replenish the water supply that renews the falls next spring. Even if he stays out in the wilderness for weeks the hiker seldom feels alone: He hears a constant chatter of Steller jays or the voices of marmots, and with the waterfalls and wind in the pines he never lacks a wild music. It is an explorer's park; with so many lakes and streams, so many canyons, so many meadows, even remnants of early mining in the high country, an outdoors-man can divide the park into quadrants or otherwise systematize his explorations and still not thoroughly examine everything. Photographic opportunities are almost limitless; for example, certain bare granite slopes were polished to a mirrorlike finish by glaciers, and it is a challenge to find the right angle and the right time of day in order to secure the best arrangement of light and shadow. During storms, this country is at its most dramatic.

Roads lead into Yosemite Valley, to Glacier Point, the redwood groves, Hetch Hetchy reservoir (focus of a conservation battle that John Muir lost), and up over Tioga Pass. However, attempts are under way to reduce or eliminate the adverse impact of the automobile in the park, so shuttle buses may eventually replace the private car, whose numbers became far more than the park could support. For complete planning details, the serious explorer should consult the maps of surrounding national forests: Stanislaus, Toiyabe, Inyo, and Sierra. He should also check at a ranger station or visitor center for current information and restrictions regarding backcountry travel. Food, lodging, camp and picnic sites, museums, outdoor exhibits, lectures, publications, and a full range of services are available. Access is by California routes 140 northeast of Merced, 41 north of Fresno, and 120 between Manteca and Leevining. The park is open year round although the Tioga and Glacier Point roads are closed in winter; a family ski area is located at Badger Pass. Cross-country skiing and snowshoeing are encouraged.

Information: Superintendent, Yosemite National Park, California 95389.

🌲 The **Desolation Wilderness,** near the edge of Lake Tahoe, is the northernmost wilderness that possesses landscapes characteristic of the Sierra Nevada. It consists of two parallel ranges, the Sierra Nevada main crest on the east and the summits of the Crystal Range on the west, separated by Rockbound Valley, a U-shaped glacial depression. The average altitude is 8,000 feet. The rocks are principally of the Sierra Nevada batholith, a mass of once-molten material from deep within the earth that welled up not quite to the surface some seventy million years ago. Now the granite has been "unroofed" by erosion and uplifted, so that it is exposed to ice, wind, and running water that slowly wear it away. Gold is present in the rocks but mostly too low in grade and too erratically distributed to be of much commercial value.

The surface features were modified by alpine glaciation. Ice plucked out large basins from the solid granite and in these cirques water has collected to form attractive mountain lakes. Altogether the wilderness has 130 lakes (the largest, unhappily, being a man-made reservoir). Where soil has accumulated, lodgepole pines, grasses, wild flowers, and other vegetation have managed to grow.

Trails and tent sites have been established within this 63,469-acre area, with campgrounds, food, and lodging offered in nearby forests, resorts, and communities. The wilderness has been heavily utilized for years and is crisscrossed with trails, many scarcely discernible. They are either not signed, or are poorly signed—indeed, one of the most common sights in this wilderness is that of a hiker holding a map and wondering where he is. This is not necessarily bad, because true wilderness never had signs; it is just that a hiker in this area should have a good topographic map (the Fallen Leaf Lake Quadrangle, available locally or from the U.S. Geological Survey, covers the area best), and even then he should resign himself to getting lost and allow enough time for it. If he finishes his hike too late in the day, he might have to stumble over difficult, bouldery terrain at night.

Access is off U.S. Route 50 on the south, and California routes 89 and 94 on the east.

Information: Supervisor, Eldorado National Forest, 100 Forni Road, Placerville, California 95667; and Manager, Lake Tahoe Basin Management Unit, U.S. Forest Service, 1052 Tata Lane, South Lake Tahoe, California 95705.

🌲 Fifteen miles due south of the Desolation Wilderness is another wild terrain that consists of massive granite domes and peaks with scattered Sierra junipers clinging to crags and crevices, silver pines, and patches of buckwheat whose flowers look like bright Sierra gold. The **Mokelumne Wilderness,**

50,400 acres, rises nearly to 10,000 feet, and the hiker shares it with deer, mountain lions, black bears, and other Sierra wildlife. Alpine lakes, flower-filled tundra, and meadows add to the attractiveness of the area. Wilderness travelers may find campsites along remote lakes, the Mokelumne River, and small streams, or within the shelter, such as it is, of fir, pine, and hemlock patches. The nearest main roads are California routes 4 on the south, and 88 on the north. Food and lodging are available in nearby communities.

Information: Supervisor, Eldorado National Forest, 100 Forni Road, Placerville, California 95667; and Supervisor, Stanislaus National Forest, 175 South Fairview Lane, Sonora, California 95370.

🌲 In addition to the giant sequoia trees of Yosemite, Sequoia, and Kings Canyon national parks, there are two groves preserved in **Calaveras Big Trees State Park,** reached on California Route 4, seventy-five miles northeast of Stockton. One tree has a diameter of twenty-two feet; some are more than 300 feet tall. Roads, trails, campgrounds, and other facilities exist in the area, but withal the aspect is a serene and peaceful one where nature dominates. One may hike in groves of sequoias, beneath sugar pines, with their twenty-four-inch-long cones, and under ponderosa pines, incense cedars, oaks, and maples. In spring, azaleas and dogwoods burst out in joint displays of color. The pileated woodpeckers and water ouzels are among the most interesting of the birds. Mammalian life includes deer, bears, porcupines, and raccoons. The park, containing 5,437 acres, is open all year. Lodging, food, and supplies may be obtained in nearby communities.

Information: Chief Ranger, Calaveras Big Trees State Park, Box 686, Arnold, California 95223.

🌲 Adjacent to the northern boundary of Yosemite National Park is the **Emigrant Wilderness,** a glaciated granite landscape of 97,020 acres, crossed by the Tahoe-Yosemite Trail. The hiker walks through typical Sierra landscapes composed of rounded granite domes and boulders, patches of dark volcanic rock, soft meadows, lodgepole pines and aspen, lakes of transparent emerald and clear streams; he passes patches of willow and wild currant, colorful displays of penstemon flowers, and rows of elderberry. Proceeding south from Sonora Pass, his only company at this elevation may be the raucous Clark nutcracker; other animals are likely to be more discreetly hidden. Lupine, fleabane, and small yellow monkeyflowers liven the otherwise open rocky terrain. At Emigrant Meadow and vicinity the route is that utilized in the 1850s by travelers on the main trans-Sierra trail, largely emigrants seeking gold in the then Eldorado of California. At Emigrant Pass, 9,650 feet, the Duckwall and Wash Train parties attempted, in October, 1853, to cross what was at that time virtually impassable terrain and unfortunately got caught in an unseasonable snowstorm. Several members of the group died before rescuers from Sonora could guide them to safety.

This wilderness lies at the northern end of the largest roadless area in California; trails to the south enter the heart of the High Sierra, preserved in parks, forests, and wilderness areas. Access is on California Route 108. Campgrounds, food, lodging, and supplies are available in nearby communities. This wilderness is popular and heavily used; hikers should avoid holiday and midsummer trips if possible.

Information: Supervisor, Stanislaus National Forest, 175 South Fairview Lane, Sonora, California 95370.

🌲 While Yosemite, Sequoia, and Kings Canyon national parks protect the high summits and some of the western slope of the Sierra Nevada, several adjacent wilderness and natural areas protect the precipitous east face of the Sierra block, which plunges from elevations around 14,000 feet down into Owens Valley and neighboring semidesert areas at about 4,000 feet. The **Hoover Wilderness,** for example, is a steep, almost treeless summit area of 42,779 acres on the eastern boundary of Yosemite National Park, just north of Tioga Pass. Replete with lakes and elegant scenery, the area offers splendid challenges to the hiker, but the trails are so high—8,000 to 13,000 feet—that only the hardy should attempt to climb very much in it. July and August are the only parts of the year that can usually be called summer, and severe storms may be experienced at almost any time. The lakes and streams are stocked with rainbow, brook, and golden trout.

Access is by roads leading west from U.S. Route 395 or north from California Route 120. Campgrounds are available in Inyo and Toiyabe national forests. Food and lodging may be obtained in Bridgeport, Leevining, and other places on Route 395.

Information: Supervisor, Inyo National Forest, 2957 Birch Street, Bishop, California 93514; and Supervisor, Toiyabe National Forest, Box 1331, Reno, Nevada 89504.

🌲 South of Tioga Pass, and adjoining nearly the entire eastern boundary of Yosemite National Park, is the **Minarets Wilderness,** including high peaks, sharp-pointed ridges, steep cliffs, and abundant lakes surrounded by alpine meadows. There is good fishing in the lakes and excellent terrain for experienced mountain climbers. The Pacific Crest Trail crosses the center of the area. Not only is the mountain scenery spectacular, but there also are views of the volcanic craters and lava flows (including obsidian flows or "glass mountains") in the valleys below. An excellent view of the Minarets can be obtained from California Route 203, at Minaret Summit, near Mammoth Lakes; this road also goes to Devils Postpile National Monument, a good jumping-off place for trips into the Minarets Wilderness. Other road approaches are California routes 120 through Tioga Pass, and 158 south of Leevining. Detailed maps showing the excellent trail system in this 109,484-acre wilderness may be purchased from the U.S. Forest Service. Food, lodging, supplies, and campgrounds are available nearby.

Information: Supervisor, Inyo National Forest, 2957 Birch Street, Bishop, California 93514; and Supervisor, Sierra National Forest, 1130 O Street, Fresno, California 93721.

🌲 Southeast of Yosemite, over the mountains and down into the Middle Fork of the San Joaquin River, lies a small reservation (798 acres) designed to protect a cluster of lava columns that looks like some bizarre stockade wall. At **Devils Postpile National Monument,** ancient lava flows cooled into multiple-sided columns, some of them sixty feet from base to top. Glaciers overrode the lava later, sheared off the top, and polished a cross-section of the columns, producing an unusual black "pavement" that looks as though it were designed by honeybees in a giant comb. The setting is a reasonably wild one; the Pacific Crest Trail passes through the monument, and a round-trip hike of 2.5 miles from road's end brings visitors to Rainbow Falls, which plunge 140 feet over dark basaltic cliffs into a green pool. Devils Postpile is reached over sixteen miles of country roads west of U.S. Route 395. A campground is maintained in the monument during the summer; food and lodging are available about two miles outside the boundaries.

Information: Superintendent, Yosemite National Park, California 95389.

🌲 Largest of the California wilderness areas administered by the U.S. Forest Service is an elongate region covering some of the highest and most precipitous portions of the Sierra Nevada. Named in honor of the famed naturalist, the **John Muir Wilderness** of 503,258 acres extends from the Devils Postpile south to Kings Canyon and Sequoia national parks, of which it adjoins most of the eastern boundaries. Included are special zoological areas devoted to California bighorn sheep, and the rugged east faces of many high peaks, including Mount Whitney (14,495 feet). The landscape is typical

Sierra Nevada: glaciers, treeless tundra, rocky gorges, hundreds of lakes, patches of coniferous woods, deep canyons, herds of mule deer. Fishing is best in lakes and streams from late August to late September. The Pacific Crest Trail, which here coincides with the John Muir Trail, extends through much of the northern portion of the wilderness; however, this trail is heavily traveled in August and should be avoided at that time. Other trails are integrated with networks in adjacent national parks and forests. Access is principally via roads that branch westward from U.S. Route 395 in the towns of Bishop, Big Pine, Independence, and Lone Pine. In these communities may be obtained food, supplies, and accommodations. Campgrounds are located on adjacent national forest lands. The tremendous popularity of wilderness areas in Inyo National Forest has made necessary entry permits, party-size limitations, and camping restrictions.

Information: Supervisor, Inyo National Forest, 2957 Birch Street, Bishop, California 93514; and Supervisor, Sierra National Forest, 1130 O Street, Fresno, California 93721.

A relatively small area of 10,247 acres on the western boundary of Kings Canyon National Park has been designated the **High Sierra Wilderness** by the U.S. Forest Service. Currently being considered for reclassification as the Monarch Wilderness, it is located at the junction of the middle and south forks of the Kings River, which flow in deep canyons separated by a rise known as Monarch Divide and Junction Ridge. The area is extraordinarily rugged, as suggested by the difference in elevation from the Kings River at 2,200 feet to a point on Monarch Divide, 11,081 feet, just a few miles away. The U.S. Geological Survey refers to the canyons of the Kings River here as some of the deepest in the United States. Such steep slopes and sheer cliffs almost preclude human use, and the area is nearly trailless. Crossing either of the forks of the Kings River is virtually impossible without a rope, and the Geological Survey team that studied the area in 1970 had to establish field camps by helicopter. Most of the rock is the familiar durable granite of the Sierra Nevada, but there are also marble, lava, and other types. The natural history in general is similar to that in the adjacent Kings Canyon National Park. Access is off California Route 180. The nearest food, supplies, and lodging are at Grant Grove in Kings Canyon National Park.

Information: Supervisor, Sierra National Forest, 1130 O Street, Fresno, California 93721; and Supervisor, Sequoia National Forest, 900 West Grand Avenue, Porterville, California 93257.

Giant redwoods, once abundant in much of the northern hemisphere, have slowly diminished over the millenniums and in North America remain only as the coast redwoods, growing from southern Oregon to south of San Francisco, and the giant sequoias or big trees, which survive in scattered groves only on the western slopes of the Sierra Nevada (except, of course, where they have been planted, which is now in many parts of the world). The best natural groves of each species have been preserved either by the United States government or the State of California, along with some sizable acreage of surrounding wilderness. In **Sequoia National Park,** the big tree concentrations cover only a small percentage of the 386,863 acres included within the boundaries. After observing such famed attractions as the General Sherman Tree (largest of living organisms), and the Giant Forest, a hiker may depart for the high country. The possible destinations and trail combinations seem infinite because this park is bordered on the north by Kings Canyon National Park and on most other sides by national forests. Thus virtually the whole Sierra is available for public use, though the higher the summits the shorter the summer.

It is typical Sierra country: wide valleys or narrow canyons, rounded granite cliffs and domes, extensive forests of lodgepole pine, alpine lakes, foaming cascades, high tundra, long-lasting patches of ice and snow, and summit peaks from which to view the deserts to the east. Mount Whitney, at 14,495 feet the highest peak in the contiguous United States, is a popular—at times too popular—destination. Deep in the interior of the park is the Kern River Canyon, an almost straight-line gorge more than twenty miles long, being cut into an old erosion surface that was uplifted by seismic activity. Few valleys in the Sierra are more spectacular.

Elsewhere in the high country one sees massive panoramas, barren except for snow and tundra, bald gray domes with scattered pines growing from crevices, sheer granite cliffs and splintered crags, chutes down which rocks and snow avalanche, lake after lake, waterfalls, intricate designs in the rock, meadows fringed with lodgepole pine, golden eagles with their seven-foot wingspread, pikas in rocky jumbles, yellow-bellied marmots, Belding ground squirrels, and other forms of life. Lower down live black bears and mule deer.

For full details, the park has wayside exhibits, self-guiding trails, museums, and interpretive talks. Maps (including topographic maps advisable for extended Sierra trips) are also available, along with books and booklets on the natural sciences and human history. Lodging, supplies, meals, and campsites are available within the park. Saddle horses and pack animals may be hired at several locations in and around the park. For travel in the backcountry, wilderness-use permits are required and may be obtained at ranger stations. Daily entrance limits are in effect on the major trails in an effort to protect the fragile high country from overuse.

Information: Superintendent, Sequoia National Park, Three Rivers, California 93271.

🌲 Adjoining Sequoia National Park on the north is **Kings Canyon National Park,** whose 460,331 acres have many of the same characteristics. However, very little of Kings Canyon is accessible by road. On California Route 180, fifty miles east of Fresno, there is an isolated section of it that encloses the Grant Grove of sequoia trees. But only at one other point does a road enter the park, the same Route 180, and then only for six miles along the south fork of the Kings River. This is gigantic scenery, however, and an ideal introduction to the typical terrain, much of it steep or vertical, of the Sierra Nevada. The road, open in summer only, leads past Cedar Grove, with its series of campgrounds, and Roaring River Falls, to areas where cars may be parked either daytime or long-term. The scenery in this valley is striking, but the high walls do not permit panoramic views of the rest of the park.

For that the hiker must climb—upstream eastward to Mist Falls, Paradise Valley, and beyond, or north to Granite Pass, Frypan Meadow, and other points of interest. Names such as Cirque Crest, Ragged Spur, Castle Domes, Pyramid Peak, and Hell for Sure Pass give some idea of what the terrain is like and what a hiker is in for. However, there are also Enchanted Gorge and Scenic Meadow. Hiking and horseback riding trails have been constructed in the park, but many large areas are also trailless. In addition to high peaks, some of which reach over 14,000 feet, there are glaciers, blue and green high-country lakes, and a jumble of canyons and streams. Accordingly, hiking in this park is a continuous adventure, because one can seldom predict what lies around the next bend. However, use permits and daily limits of hikers are in effect.

Perhaps the greatest surprise in these "eternal hills" is that they are not eternal at all, and the high-country trails lead past evidence of this. The Sierra Nevada is, in fact, being eroded, principally by the freezing and expansion of ice. Piles of frost-split rock lie all over the upper summits; cliffs are not only slabbing off but being undermined by freezing, a process called "frost-sapping." Ultimately gravity pulls this debris down to the rivers, whence it is taken away. The Sierra hiker gets intimately acquainted with all this evidence of erosion as he climbs among the peaks and canyons.

Food and lodging in the park are available only in the Grant Grove area. Access from Owens Valley, on the east side of the park, is limited; prospective visitors should consult park maps. No road crosses the Sierra in either Kings Canyon or Sequoia national parks.

Information: Superintendent, Sequoia and Kings Canyon National Parks, Three Rivers, California 93271.

🌲 Southernmost of the Sierra Nevada wilderness areas is a rocky domain with characteristics of the desert country: piñon pines, sagebrush, rabbit brush, and sharp-leaved Joshua trees. Because of the prevalence of typical domelike structures in eroded Sierra granites, it is called the **Dome Land Wilderness.** Located at the southern edge of the Kern Plateau it provides a view down the Kern River Valley, which cuts a deep and winding canyon on its way toward Bakersfield, seventy miles to the southwest. The south fork of the Kern River flows through the wilderness, which consists of 62,561 acres, and varies in elevation from 3,000 to 9,000 feet. It is roadless and has comparatively few trails, but the forest is largely open and parklike, and the various dome rocks provide good landmarks for cross-country hikers. An entry permit is required. The Pacific Crest Trail passes nearby.

The closest paved highway is California Route 178, at the southern end. Forest roads and trails approach the boundaries on all sides. Accommodations are mostly to the southwest, on Route 178. The nearest campgrounds are in Sequoia National Forest, outside the wilderness.

Information: Sequoia National Forest, 900 West Grand Avenue, Box 391, Porterville, California 93257.

🌲 The **Pacific Crest Trail** in California has not, at this writing, been completed, but temporary routes have been laid out and a well-equipped, experienced long-distance hiker can cover the entire distance—as some have already done. The trail passes mostly through national forests and national parks, parts of which have been given wilderness status. Even where this is

Desolation Wilderness, California.

Peeling bark, California madrone.

not the case, the terrain is usually wild, if only because it is so rugged and inaccessible. The southernmost few hundred miles, for example, ending up at the Mexican boundary, is a jumble of giant granite boulders, deep canyons, chaparral slopes, and pine-covered peaks, with occasional traverses of pastoral meadows. The trail can be blocked by snow as early as November in southern California; in the Sierra Nevada, the season of snow-free hiking is even shorter.

Nevertheless, the rewards are worth the effort, and day-use hikers as well as long-distance professionals can begin at numerous points where highways cross the trail. In northern California the path leads over volcanic terrain south of Mount Shasta to Lassen Volcanic National Park, thence through the Desolation and Emigrant Basin wilderness areas, Yosemite, Kings Canyon, and Sequoia national parks, along the Tehachapi Mountains with their abundant Joshua trees, eastward through the Transverse Ranges and the San Gabriel and San Gorgonio wildernesses, and finally south over the San Jacinto and Laguna mountains to México.

A single wilderness permit, obtained in advance from either a national park or national forest, will be honored along the entire declared route. A fire permit must also be obtained from a Forest Service office. Both permits are free. Various guidebooks to the Pacific Crest Trail have been published. Detailed route maps (at a nominal charge) and other information can be obtained from the U.S. Forest Service, Division of I & E, 630 Sansome Street, San Francisco, California 94111.

3. CALIFORNIA COAST

One of the most successful, though at times embattled, efforts of mankind to save a segment of the wild outdoors has centered around the redwood tree, whose ancestors used to grow throughout the northern hemisphere in a habitat now greatly diminished. The principal groves of Sierra Nevada specimens, the giant sequoias, were largely preserved in public parks. Down in the lowlands, along the humid shores of California and seldom more than thirty miles inland, grows the Pacific coast redwood. Though closely related to the giant sequoia, it is taller, not as massive or long-lived, and different in other ways. Its environment is decidedly a moist one: damp with drizzle, frequently fogbound, the relative humidity nearly always high. This tempers any extremes of climate that might occur, and the result is a habitat in quiet repose. Evidently the tranquil glades and nourishing soils have remained rather stable for thousands of years, and so a number of luxuriant groves have evolved. Where the lumberman's ax has been stayed, they still exist and some of the finest are in national and state reserves. California's state park system alone protects more than 100,000 acres of redwoods, with 250 designated memorial groves. The larger parks, with sufficient acreage to sustain a wilderness aspect, are listed here.

🌲 Northernmost is **Jedediah Smith Redwoods State Park,** less than twelve miles from Crescent City on U.S. Route 199. The park is rugged, with drier uplands as well as humid lowlands, and trails reach into a few parts of it. Some parallel and cross plunging whitewater streams. Some border the Smith River with its sandy beaches. Often the vegetation closes in above the trail, the light of the sun is filtered through layers of leaves, and only a soft light bathes the banks of ferns, the fallen trees, the masses of rhododendrons and huckleberries, the vivid azaleas and carpets of oxalis below. In this gentle environment the temperature ranges between 30° and 85°, a comfortable habitat for chipmunks, squirrels, raccoons, deer, and rarely, a bear or otter.

The dense, encompassing vegetation muffles the sounds of civilization and visitors find solitude here, yet there is seldom much silence. The Steller jay alone sees to that. One also hears the chattering of squirrels, pounding of pileated woodpeckers, songs of thrushes, and music of falling water.

106

The park's 8,852 acres are a tribute to man's resolve that these woods in their natural state mean more than commercial uses to which they could be put. The area is an amalgam of memorial groves purchased with thousands of donations, largely through the Save-the-Redwoods League, Garden Club of America, Daughters of the American Revolution, and other organizations. It may be visited at any time of year. Fishermen catch twenty-pound steelhead and thirty-pound salmon in winter, trout in autumn. Campsites are located along the Smith River. Food and lodging are available in Crescent City.

Information: Jedediah Smith Redwoods State Park, Drawer J, Crescent City, California 95531.

🌲 **Del Norte Coast Redwoods State Park,** located along the ocean six miles southeast of Crescent City, on U.S. Route 101, has an area of 6,375 acres. Noteworthy are flowering displays of rhododendron, azalea, Olympia lily, redwood sorrel, salal, trillium, and iris. Damnation Creek Trail leads through deep redwood forests to a small beach and tidal pools. The Last Chance Trail parallels the coast and provides access to views of the rocky shore. Other trails lead along Mill Creek or connect with hiking routes outside the park. Numerous campsites are available. Food and lodging may be obtained in Crescent City.

Information: Superintendent, Del Norte Coast Redwoods State Park, Drawer J, Crescent City, California 95531.

🌲 To read the names of Gold Bluff and Gold Bluff Beach, one would think that riches lay in the sands of **Prairie Creek Redwoods State Park.** Many searches have been made, but the riches that exist today are principally the delicate vegetation of Fern Canyon, the cathedrallike groves of redwoods more than 300 feet tall, herds of Roosevelt elk, natural gardens of wild flowers, and rushing streams with salmon and trout. More than twenty trails reach into parts of this 12,240-acre park. One is known as the Rhododendron Trail. Two reach the beach. The Revelation Trail is equipped with labels describing features along the way, and has a Braille guide for the blind. Several trails intersect with U.S. Route 101, which bisects the park. A campground, picnic area, and museum are located at park headquarters. Food, lodging, and supplies are obtainable in nearby communities.

Information: Area Manager, Prairie Creek Redwoods State Park, Orick, California 95555.

Joshua tree forest near Dome Land Wilderness, California.

🌲 An almost continuous corridor of redwoods has been preserved for approximately fifty miles south of Crescent City. It is composed of the three state parks described above, which are connected by isolated sections of **Redwood National Park.** This park was authorized by Congress in 1968 under Public Law 90-545, which provides that California may eventually donate its three state parks to the federal government and the whole will be administered as a single national park of 58,000 acres.

Redwood National Park offers several distinctive environments. The redwood forest, of course, is first in priority, and consists of nearly pure groves, one of which contains the tallest tree in the world, 367 feet. The park was also established to protect about thirty continuous miles of coast where marine life, including colonies of birds, seals, and sea lions, may be observed. A strip of scrub habitat, salted by sea winds, lies back from the coast. And then there are ugly open spaces where forests were clear-cut in the days of logging and must start their growth again.

U.S. Route 101 runs the length of the park, which is generally quite narrow. Nevertheless, from parking places along the road hikers can depart on coast or hill excursions. Camping is available in state parks, national forests, and private parks; lodging may be secured in motels along the major highways.

Information: Superintendent, Redwood National Park, Drawer N, Crescent City, California 95531.

🌲 The Avenue of the Giants is a major feature of **Humboldt Redwoods State Park,** thirty miles southeast of Eureka, California. Originally known as the Redwood Highway, the major access route was bypassed when U.S. Route 101 was relocated for high-speed traffic not far away. Now the old road is a leisurely scenic drive from which short walking trails lead into the forest. A visitor can readily get away from the roads because there are 42,318 acres in the park, and longer trails lead to Grasshopper Peak (elevation 3,381 feet), Bull Creek Basin, and Canoe Creek.

The giant trees have survived—or benefited from—extensive fires and floods for thousands of years, and today rise from dense fern beds and rich soil to heights of over 300 feet. The delicate calypso orchid grows in this environment, as do anemones, fairy lanterns, and sugar scoops. Where there are streams, the willow grows in association with bigleaf maple and red alder. Occasionally meadows are encountered, as well as forests of Douglas fir, madrone, laurel, and tan oak. Upstream logging and fires have opened the way for severe floods that damaged some of the groves, and the California Department of Parks and Recreation is undertaking the long and arduous task of restoration and stabilization. When the waters of streams are less violent, and fishing is best (usually in spring and fall), anglers seek out steelhead trout and king and silver salmon.

Now and then an osprey or golden eagle may be sighted. Black-tailed deer are often seen, and from time to time, coyotes, bobcats, skunks, and ringtails. The park has an abundance of poison oak and it behooves the traveler to know this plant well if he is going to spend much time among the redwoods. The poison oak can climb on these trees to a height of 150 feet. For on-the-spot scientific details, a nature trail has been established in the Founders Grove, and park rangers present informal programs during the summer. Self-guiding nature trails are also located in the Enoch P. French and Garden Club of America groves.

A hundred miles of hiking and riding trails have been developed in the park, and there are sites for camping and picnicking. Food and lodging may be obtained outside the park along U.S. Route 101 and in nearby communities.

Information: Manager, Dyerville Area, Humboldt Redwoods State Park, Box 100, Weott, California 95571.

🌲 The **King Range National Conservation Area,** on the California coast twelve miles southwest of Humboldt Redwoods State Park, encompasses an area of 50,000 acres and is administered by the Bureau of Land Management, U.S. Department of the Interior. It consists of steep mountain ridges, long segments of natural seashore, and mountain streams in a primitive setting of Douglas fir and other forest trees. From these mountain ravines and ridges the views down toward the coast and the blue Pacific Ocean are striking. Hiking, camping, and nature study are among the major uses. An abundance of black-tailed deer, wild pigeons, quail, and rabbits exists. The area is rugged and the slopes not only steep but thickly covered with underbrush. This presents difficult passage, and there are rattlesnakes to contend with, hence wilderness enthusiasts will find substantial challenges. But with normal precautions, and following the well-constructed trails, hikers should enjoy a visit to this scenic wild area. Food, lodging, and supplies are available in nearby towns. Roads within the area are narrow and unpaved. Access is off U.S. Route 101 forty miles south of Eureka.

Information: District Manager, Bureau of Land Management, 555 Leslie Street, Ukiah, California 95482.

🌲 **Muir Woods National Monument** contains only 500 acres, but it lies within **Mount Tamalpais State Park,** which has an area of 6,204 acres; both are included within the boundaries of the **Golden Gate National Recreation Area,** authorized in 1972. Recreation, in the larger area, will have priority but some of the land will remain in a natural state, so the wilderness values of deep redwood groves and primeval solitude can be sampled just fourteen miles north of San Francisco. Both parks are accessible via California Route 1. Muir Woods has six miles of trails that connect with the twenty-eight-mile system in Mount Tamalpais. In the sheltered valley of Muir Woods some of the redwoods reach a height of nearly 250 feet. The understory typically includes azaleas, tan oaks, laurels, and ferns, with wildlife that ranges from the black-tailed deer to secretive, harmless snakes, lizards, and salamanders.

Mount Tamalpais protects a predominantly coastal upland environment, and from the top of the mountain, at 2,604 feet, on a clear and fogless day, it is possible to see the Farallon Islands, twenty-five miles at sea, or the Sierra Nevada 200 miles to the east. The park has deep valleys and redwood groves, which contrast with the drier chaparral-covered ridges and slopes of oak and grassland. Muir Woods has no picnic or camping facilities; Mount Tamalpais has picnic sites and a group camping area. Accommodations and meals may be obtained nearby.

Information: Superintendent, Muir Woods National Monument, Mill Valley, California 94941; and Supervisor, Mount Tamalpais State Park, 801 Panoramic Highway, Mill Valley, California 94941.

🌲 On the western slope of the Santa Cruz Mountains, sixty miles south of San Francisco, is California's oldest state park, established in 1902 to protect superlative redwood groves in the Big Basin region. Known as **Big Basin Redwoods State Park,** it covers over 12,000 acres, and in its sheltered canyons are typical plants that have evolved along with giant redwoods: Douglas fir and huckleberry, wild lilac, hazelnut, thimbleberry, and the carpeting mosses, lichens, liverworts, ferns, and numerous other species tolerant of shade.

A fascinating aspect of this park is that only a few steps away from the humid vales are steep, semiarid slopes of chaparral. Trails lead from one ecosystem to another, past attractive waterfalls into utterly different forests of nutmeg, wax myrtle, madrone, and oak. The quiet hiker may see some of the park's opossums, weasels, and foxes, as well as more familiar squirrels, raccoons, and deer. Over forty miles of trails follow stream banks through redwood groves, lead up ridges, and pass scenic viewpoints overlooking Big Basin country and the blue Pacific Ocean beyond. A "Nature Lodge" contains exhibits on history and natural history, and a self-guiding trail leads through the oldest of the redwood groves in the park.

Access is over winding country roads off California Route 9, north of Santa Cruz. Campsites are available and may be reserved in advance. Numerous picnic sites are utilized on a first-come, first-served basis. Meals and accommodations may be secured in nearby communities.

Information: Supervising Ranger, Big Basin Redwoods State Park, Big Basin, California 95006.

🌲 Two small areas in the western mountains of California provide a hint of what this part of the state was like before the advent of agriculture and industry. One, within sight of San Francisco, is **Mount Diablo State Park,** 7,000 acres of steep chaparral and canyon environments. From its summit at 3,849 feet, a great deal of California is visible when the air is clear: Lassen Peak, the Sierra Nevada, the Santa Cruz Mountains, the Golden Gate. Due to the differences between sheltered and exposed terrain, the park has varied vegetation. Typical oak and grassland types prevail, but there are also digger pines, maples, sycamore, alders, and cottonwoods. The Coulter pine, so

111

familiar in southern California wilderness areas, reaches its northern limit here. The park protects numerous species of flowering plants—but the ubiquitous poison oak also abounds. Wildlife includes deer, squirrels, raccoons, skunks, foxes, and bobcats. The park has roads, trails, campsites, and picnic areas. It is reached off Interstate 680 at Danville. Accommodations are available nearby.

Information: Chief Ranger, Mount Diablo State Park, Box 258, Diablo, California 94528.

For the most part, California's coastal ranges are gently rolling, but a remarkable exception is in **Pinnacles National Monument,** where spires, cliffs, and jagged peaks have resulted from erosion of an ancient volcanic mass. The broken, weathered rocks are accessible on the delightful (unless the temperature is 100°) High Peaks Trail, which begins at the visitor center and winds for six miles in a loop to the Rim Trail, Moses Spring Nature Trail, Bear Gulch Caves, and back to the visitor center. This trail makes an ascent of 1,450 feet and provides broad views of the Pinnacles as well as the surrounding horizons and valleys. From Bear Gulch a trail climbs to the summit of Chalone Peak, 3,305 feet elevation. This is an all-day trip; it leads through dense chaparral, the common mixture of chamise, buckbrush, hollyleaf cherry, and manzanita. This is really a "fire forest" in that it is made and sustained by wildfires; at least it *was* a fire forest until men undertook to suppress the fires. This part of California, like the Sierra Nevada, has dry summers and sometimes high winds and if the "pygmy forest" is set ablaze it can produce horrendously hot conflagrations. But fires are normal and natural, as a rule; they help to open up the brush and stimulate new growth on which such animals as black-tailed deer can feed.

Another trail in the Pinnacles goes along the Balconies opposite Machete Ridge and along the west fork of Chalone Creek. All trails pass through wild-animal habitat, and the common species, in addition to deer, are foxes, raccoons, bobcats, rabbits, and bats. The birds most often seen are acorn woodpeckers, brown towhees, California quail, and turkey vultures. The best time to visit is spring, when wild flowers are at their best; but weekends, holidays, and above all, Easter vacation time, should be avoided because of the heavy crowds. In a typical California summer the rains cease, the skies clear up, and the sun sears the land to a toasted brown.

The Monument may be reached off California Route 25, about thirty-five miles south of Hollister. Camping and picnic places are available but no food or lodging. The nearest food and fuel are at Paicines, twenty-three miles north. Lodging is available at Hollister, thirty-five miles north or at King City, twenty-five miles south. A walk-in tenting ground on the west side of the Monument may be reached via a narrow, winding fourteen-mile drive off U.S. Route 101 from Soledad.

Information: Superintendent, Pinnacles National Monument, Paicines, California 95043.

From the Big Sur River to the crest of the Coast Range is a rich collection of environments preserved as the **Ventana Wilderness,** 98,112 acres located approximately twenty-five miles south of Salinas. Geologically, the Santa Lucia Range is part of a block of crystalline rocks along the edge of the San Andreas Fault. Though the lower slopes have little but chaparral, the higher elevations are favorable for pine and fir. However, on the western flank, closest to the sea, coast redwoods grow, the southernmost of the species, and it is interesting to observe the vegetative changes from one side of these mountains to the other. The wilderness area is drained by the Big Sur and Little Sur rivers to the southwest; the Carmel River to the northwest; and the Arroyo Seco, a tributary to the Salinas River, to the northeast.

According to a report by the U.S. Geological Survey,

Ventana is an anachronism in mid-20th century California. It is only a few hours drive from two major metropolitan areas, and it is almost within sight of two of the most heavily traveled highways in the State. The scenic coast highway (California Highway 1) parallels the primitive area at a distance of 2 to 5 miles, and U.S. Highway 101 lies in the Salinas River valley to the northeast. Thousands of people drive within 15 miles of the area each day, but despite its proximity to civilization, only a few hundred people penetrate more than a mile into it each year.

Nevertheless, use grows rapidly. A splendid system of trails has proven very popular, to the point where certain restrictions, such as fire closures, have had to be placed in effect, and it is thus incumbent upon prospective users to obtain a wilderness-use permit. Among the activities are hiking, camping, riding, hunting, fishing, photography, cave exploration, and observations of geological features and flora. Food, lodging, and supplies may be obtained in nearby communities.

Information: Supervisor, Los Padres National Forest, 42 Aero Camino Street, Goleta, California 93017.

Nearly all of the authorized 64,546 acres of **Point Reyes National Seashore** have been acquired for public use, and more than seventy miles of hiking trails are open. They lead to the edge of the sea, through woods, across grassy meadows, and up into the mountains. Several beaches are accessible, and at some of them tidal pools may be observed. Summer days can be wet, cold, and foggy, though hikers proceeding inland over Inverness Ridge are apt to find clearer air. Spring and autumn can be mild and pleasant. At times

Oak near San Rafael Wilderness, California.

vast beds of blue and yellow lupine cover the sloping meadows above the sea. Within the dense woods are majestic conifers that have won the battle against wind and salt. Being on the Pacific Flyway, Point Reyes often serves as a transit stop for wild migrants; over 300 species of birds, an unusually high number for North American wilderness areas, have been recorded here. Other animals are abundant, too, but perhaps the most distinctive and significant feature is geological. Point Reyes is, in effect, a product of the San Andreas Fault, and lies precisely where that thousand-mile-long fracture zone meets the sea. During the 1906 earthquake the Point Reyes Peninsula moved fifteen to twenty feet with respect to the other side of the fault, and in all its history may be offset as much as 350 miles from the rocks that were originally on the other side of the break.

So far, a splendid informational program has been inaugurated, and two self-guiding nature trails are available. Four hike-in campsites have been placed strategically in the trail system, and permits are required for their use. Horses and bicycles are permitted in certain places, but pets are not allowed on trails. The area is located thirty-two miles northwest of San Francisco on California Route 1. Food, lodging, and supplies may be obtained in communities along the approach routes.

Information: Superintendent, Point Reyes National Seashore, Point Reyes, California 94956.

The **Farallon Island National Wildlife Refuge,** twenty-eight miles west of San Francisco, consists of a series of precipitous rocks and islands lying on a northwest-southeast axis, ten miles wide. The islands, with a combined surface area of about 211 acres, have been proposed as a wilderness—except for the largest, seventy-acre Southeast Farallon Island, which contains a Coast Guard lighthouse manned by personnel from Point Reyes Bird Observatory. These islands provide vital nesting habitat for approximately 200,000 birds. They are closed to public use, but the auklets, petrels, gulls, murres, cormorants, guillemots, puffins, and other seabirds, as well as sea lions and elephant seals that haul ashore there can be viewed from boats cruising nearby. Vegetation is scant. The slowly disintegrating granite isles are perpetually pounded by wave action. Temperatures range from 40° to 60°, and the islands are often shrouded by fog. The nearest food, supplies, and lodging are at San Francisco.

Information: Regional Director, Bureau of Sport Fisheries and Wildlife, Box 3737, Portland, Oregon 97208.

🌲 Another nationally significant wild area off the southern California coast, between the latitudes of San Diego and Los Angeles, is in the Channel Islands, a group of mountain peaks once connected to the mainland but then submerged by crustal movements so that only the summits protrude above the sea. Several of the smallest islands have been set aside as **Channel Islands National Monument,** specifically Santa Barbara, a three-sided island one and a quarter miles across, thirty-eight miles west of San Pedro, and Anacapa, a strung-out group of islands five miles long, only ten miles from the mainland. Although the temperatures seldom fall to frosty levels, these are by no means balmy tourist isles; they are wild areas with steep, jagged cliffs, rocky shores, and crashing waves—the sort of milieu sought by mammals of the marine environment. No matter that channel seas may at times be rough and perilous to man and his boats; no matter that winds may blow in fierce and steady gales, or fog may clamp in a shroud around the headlands—to sea lions, these are the comforts of home, and fog or no fog, their barking seems never to cease. It comes out of the mist, and rises above the crash of waves. Gulls add to the cacophony, and indeed many seabirds nest on these islands, forming rookeries on ledges above the crashing surf. At times, sea elephants pull ashore, those massive marine mammals that roam the seas along the western coasts of the United States and México. Fur seals, sea otters, and other rare species may be seen from time to time. The Channel Islands constitute a major wildlife sanctuary where the animals are free to lead a noisy life undisturbed by man.

On the upper parts of the islands one may see hundreds of species of flowering plants in spring, a striking display led by the giant coreopsis, a sunflower. Evolution on these islands, cut off for so long from the mainland, has produced plant modifications of unusual scientific interest, species quite distinct from their continental relatives—a situation somewhat reminiscent of the fabled Galápagos Islands of Ecuador.

There is no public transportation to the islands, and no facilities have been constructed on them. However, visitors may camp on Anacapa if they have all the necessities to sustain themselves, including water and fuel. In these seas, visitors who bring their own boats should be experienced navigators. Mooring is a problem in heavy surf.

Information: Superintendent, Channel Islands National Monument, Box 1388, Oxnard, California 93030.

4. SOUTHERN MOUNTAINS

Despite the heavy pressure of population, many thousands of square miles in southern California still possess wilderness aspects. Along much of the United States–México boundary, and for more than a hundred miles north, the terrain is so rugged as to be nearly inaccessible. Immense granite boulders lie scattered across the jumbled peaks and ridges, and to get around them or climb between them often calls for more equipment than an ordinary hiker possesses. Roads go into remote areas—but only so far. Trails in the Cleveland National Forest and Cuyamaca Rancho and Palomar Mountain state parks reach farther into the wild ravines and along pine-covered ridges, but there are wide expanses with only primitive paths or none at all.

Within this setting have been established half a dozen prime wilderness areas, all of them within a two-hour drive of millions of people in and near the Los Angeles basin. All are on mountain masses and in summer their cool, dry, forested meadows contrast with the warmer lands below. In winter, most are suitable for cross-country skiing or snowshoeing. From each may be had broad views of vast arid lowlands—the Mojave Desert, the Anza-Borrego country, or seemingly endless tracts of Joshua trees. Because they rise so high out of superheated deserts, the change in vegetation is striking. On lower slopes grow cactus and perhaps creosote bush or ocotillo. In the middle is the major vegetative type that blankets nearly all of southern California, the chaparral. So dense and in places virtually impenetrable do the head-high chamise, oak, and manzanita grow, and so dry and volatile do they become after months of high winds, that the dread of residents and forest authorities is fire. The fury and intensity of these wildfires is well known, and because of the potential destruction, parts of the forests, including portions of wilderness areas, are closed to entry at certain times of the year.

Above the chaparral are forests of juniper, incense cedar, fir, and several species of pine, but by contrast with chaparral these woods are much more sparse and open.

Without exception, the wilderness areas of southern California are rugged and replete with cliffs, dead ends, box canyons, and similar pitfalls that could entrap unwary newcomers. The distances one can travel within them are considerable, and good maps are available, chiefly those of the U.S. Forest

Service. When completed, the Pacific Crest Trail will pass near or across these reserves, but at this writing most of the trail follows temporary routes such as mountain roads.

🌲 After the Wilderness Act was passed in 1964, the first new addition recommended by the President for inclusion in the national system was the **San Rafael Wilderness,** a dozen miles in an air line north of Santa Barbara. Coming up the Happy Canyon Road, off California State Route 154, east of Santa Ynez, one gets a wilderness feeling simply by traveling the narrow, winding dirt road through wild forests of digger pine and ravines that possess dense growths of oak and sycamore. This is the type of terrain that continues beyond the end of the road and up Manzana Creek. The San Rafael Mountains are mostly arid to semiarid, with dense pine pockets. On sunny slopes grow yucca and chaparral, while along streams are dense growths of sycamore, manzanita, and giant live oak.

Unlike the massive granitic ranges of southern California, the San Rafael Mountains are made up of thousands of feet of broken and folded sedimentary layers, chiefly sandstone, conglomerate, siltstone, and shale. Trails lead through the Sisquoc River Valley, along the San Rafael Mountain summits, into canyons, over the "Hurricane Deck," and across open flats, but there is one place from which trails and human entry are excluded: the Sisquoc Condor Sanctuary, part of the last refuge for California condors. Largest of soaring birds in North America, California condors have for a long time been fewer than a hundred in number. They nest in the Sespe Sanctuary, also in Los Padres National Forest, forty miles to the east, but they come to the Sisquoc area to bathe in a large natural pool near the brink of a waterfall. After bathing, this drop-off provides an ideal site from which they can take flight. In addition to condors, this wilderness is home to eagles, owls, hawks, bobcats, coyotes, and other carnivorous creatures that prey on mice and small mammals.

Although autumn can be delightful in this region if there is rippling water in the streams, the best time to visit is usually late winter and spring. In summer the canyons are hot and because of the volatile vegetation, the U.S. Forest Service closes the wilderness to entry—usually from July 1 of each year until the fire season ends in early November.

All sides of this wilderness are accessible by trail, but permits are required for entry. Food and lodging are available in the Santa Ynez and Santa Barbara areas.

Information: Supervisor, Los Padres National Forest, 42 Aero Camino Street, Goleta, California 93017.

🌲 The northern side of the Los Angeles Basin is walled in by the Transverse Ranges, so called because their east-west trend is contrary to the general run of mountains in California, and indeed North America. These rugged masses are broken only in a few places, such as at Cajon Pass. Human habitations have expanded in dense clusters to the bases of them—and then some. Roads reach on into the jagged canyons and most of the mountains are scarred by construction, housing developments, ski runs, and the like. Nevertheless, a few wild places provide relief from the crowded environments.

Within the San Gabriel Mountains are two wilderness areas, the 9,022-acre **Cucamonga** and the 36,137-acre **San Gabriel.** Persons who want to give their mountaineering skills and capacity for endurance a thorough test will find the trails few and the terrain demanding. Because the land is so preponderantly vertical, it mostly escaped human settlement and road construction, and anyone who threads his way among the cliffs and slanting ledges, tears his flesh on whitethorn bushes, rolls and falls on the abundant loose rock, or skins his knees on tumbled stream boulders will understand the naming of Devils Canyon. But to be so near great cities and yet so far removed, so quiet and serene, so undisturbed, renders the scratches and falls worthwhile.

These wilderness areas are readily accessible. The Mount Baldy winter sports area lies on the northwest border of the Cucamonga Wilderness. The Angeles Crest Highway (California State Highway 2) borders the north and west sides of the San Gabriel Wilderness, scarcely twenty miles from Hollywood. Entry permits are required. Food, camping, and lodging are available at various points in the Angeles National Forest.

For information on the San Gabriel: Supervisor, Angeles National Forest, 150 South Los Robles, Pasadena, California 91101; for information on the Cucamonga: Supervisor, San Bernardino National Forest, 144 North Mountain View Avenue, San Bernardino, California 92408.

 # 3 8

🌲 Northeast of San Bernardino lies the **San Gorgonio Wilderness,** 34,644 acres of bold summit terrain that thrusts eastward like the prow of a ship gliding into the Mojave Desert. It is the highest wilderness in southern California, its summit reaching 11,502 feet. The mountains possess nearly pure forests of piñon pine at medium elevations, and trails lead past colorful Sierra junipers into high coniferous forests of sugar, Jeffrey, and lodgepole pines. The canyons and meadows are remote and enticing but water is not always available, a fact that hikers should note in advance. Among the mammals are deer and bighorn. As in all these southern ranges, the California jay and acorn woodpecker are among the most prominent birds.

Access is from the east through Joshua tree country, from the south up Whitewater Canyon, and via California Route 38, which skirts the northern boundary of the wilderness. A wilderness permit is required and may be obtained from the district ranger (address below). The fire danger is often acute, and visitors who wish to build fires must appear in person at the ranger station. Portable backpack stoves are recommended anyway because of the scarcity of fuel. Moreover, owing to the threat of heavy impact from overuse, the number of visitors admitted at any one time is subject to limitation. Food, lodging, and camping are available in San Bernardino National Forest.

Information: District Ranger, Mill Creek Ranger Station, San Bernardino National Forest, Route 1, Box 264, Mentone, California 92359.

In the San Jacinto Mountains, between Hemet and Palm Springs, are two wilderness areas, one within the other. The **San Jacinto Wilderness,** part of the San Bernardino National Forest, consists of 21,955 acres covering the rough-and-tumble summits of this granitic mountain mass. As is the case at San Gorgonio Wilderness, the fire danger is high and visitors should pack in their own small stoves. Fire permits may be obtained by mail or at the district ranger station (address below). Likewise, the number of visitors admitted to the wilderness is subject to control. The other area, **Mount San Jacinto Wilderness State Park,** administered by the California Department of Parks and Recreation, contains 13,521 acres. From one point of view, these summits, which reach up to 10,831 feet, are some of the most easily accessible in North America because the Palm Springs Aerial Tramway, the largest and longest single-lift passenger tramway in the world, reaches an elevation of 8,516 feet on the eastern side. However, there are much less mechanized ways to approach the quiet uplands. California State Route 243 cuts over the lower west shoulder of the San Jacinto Mountains and from forest campgrounds in secluded places hikers can take off on trails that lead to San Jacinto Peak, Tahquitz Peak, meadows, river basins, and rich coniferous forests.

An especially prominent feature of these mountains is the northeast face, one of the steepest and highest escarpments in North America. Within a horizontal distance of five miles the cliffs and ridges plunge from nearly 11,000 feet to less than 1,000 in San Gorgonio Pass.

Wilderness-use permits are required for both the state and national areas. The nearest accommodations are along Route 243 and in Palm Springs.

Information: District Ranger, San Jacinto Ranger District, San Bernardino National Forest, Box 518, Idyllwild, California 92349; and Superintendent, Mount San Jacinto Wilderness State Park, Box 308, Idyllwild, California 92349.

Hikers along Manzana Creek, San Rafael Wilderness, California.

*Yosemite Valley in winter, Yosemite
National Park, California.*

Lodgepole pine cones.

🌲 Southernmost in California is the **Agua Tibia Primitive Area** on the western flank of an upland massif where the famed Palomar Observatory was built. At the higher elevations, around 6,000 feet, the relatively humid coniferous forests are pleasantly cool, the tree-roofed ravines well cushioned with bracken ferns. Woods on the ridges seem uneven and disheveled because of the presence of big-cone Douglas fir, which sends its branches out in seemingly helter-skelter fashion. But as a hiker descends he soon departs from heavy forest and enters the ubiquitous chaparral. At the lowest levels he comes to gorges with boulders brought down by mountain floods and lined with sycamore trees and different kinds of oak. The lower portions of the area are accessible on California State Highway 71-79. Campgrounds, food, and lodging are available at several points around the Agua Tibia Mountains, but a permit is required to enter the primitive area.

The Agua Tibia Primitive Area contains 25,995 acres, but when the fire hazard is high, very little of it is open to public use. The annual fire closure runs from July 1 to the first good fall rains, generally in November or December. It is thus, in effect, a winter-use region. Actually, more than half of the area has been fire-free for over a century, which has allowed a rich and superlative vegetation to develop. The chaparral, usually kept in a dwarfed condition by fire and other adverse elements, here reaches optimum growth, and the ceanothus, red shank, and manzanita approach tree dimensions. The variation from top to bottom in this wilderness is of great interest to botanists and ecologists. Mammals include mountain lions, bobcats, and coyotes. The Palomar region (*paloma* means "pigeon" in Spanish) is home to a large population of wild band-tailed pigeons.

Information: Supervisor, Cleveland National Forest, 3211 Fifth Avenue, San Diego, California 92103.

Yucca leaves, Lone Pine Canyon,
Pacific Crest Trail, California.

PART IV

The Southwest

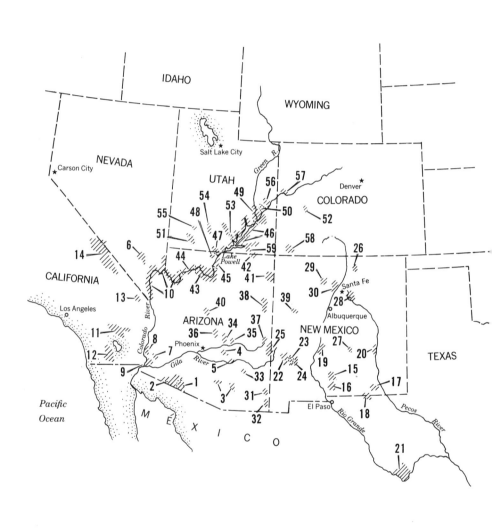

1. DESERT LOWLANDS

1. Organ Pipe Cactus National Monument, Arizona
2. Cabeza Prieta National Wildlife Range, Arizona
3. Saguaro National Monument, Arizona
4. Superstition Wilderness, Arizona
5. Aravaipa Canyon Primitive Area, Arizona
6. Desert National Wildlife Range, Nevada
7. Kofa Game Range, Arizona
8. Needles Wilderness, Arizona-California
9. Imperial National Wildlife Refuge, Arizona-California
10. Lake Mead National Recreation Area, Arizona-Nevada
11. Joshua Tree National Monument, California
12. Anza-Borrego Desert State Park, California
13. Providence Mountains State Recreation Area, California
14. Death Valley National Monument, California-Nevada
15. White Sands National Monument, New Mexico
16. San Andres National Wildlife Refuge, New Mexico
17. Carlsbad Caverns National Park, New Mexico
18. Guadalupe Mountains National Park, Texas
19. Bosque del Apache National Wildlife Refuge, New Mexico
20. Salt Creek Wilderness, New Mexico
21. Big Bend National Park, Texas

2. DESERT UPLANDS

22. Gila Wilderness, New Mexico
23. Gila Primitive Area, New Mexico
24. Aldo Leopold Wilderness, New Mexico
25. Blue Range Primitive Area, Arizona–New Mexico
26. Wheeler Peak Wilderness, New Mexico
27. White Mountain Wilderness, New Mexico
28. Pecos Wilderness, New Mexico
29. San Pedro Parks Wilderness, New Mexico
30. Bandelier National Monument, New Mexico
31. Chiricahua National Monument, Arizona
32. Chiricahua Wilderness, Arizona
33. Galiuro Wilderness, Arizona
34. Mazatzal Wilderness, Arizona

35. Sierra Ancha Wilderness, Arizona
36. Pine Mountain Wilderness, Arizona
37. Mount Baldy Wilderness, Arizona
38. Petrified Forest National Park, Arizona
39. Grants Lava Flow, New Mexico

3. CANYONS

40. Sycamore Canyon Wilderness, Arizona
41. Canyon de Chelly National Monument, Arizona
42. Monument Valley Tribal Park, Arizona
43. Grand Canyon National Park, Arizona
44. Grand Canyon National Monument, Arizona
45. Marble Canyon National Monument, Arizona
46. Glen Canyon National Recreation Area, Arizona-Utah
47. Paria Canyon Primitive Area, Utah-Arizona
48. Vermillion Cliffs Natural Area, Arizona
49. Canyonlands National Park, Utah
50. Dead Horse Point State Park, Utah
51. Zion National Park, Utah
52. Black Canyon of the Gunnison National Monument, Colorado

4. HIGH PLATEAUS

53. Capitol Reef National Park, Utah
54. Bryce Canyon National Park, Utah
55. Cedar Breaks National Monument, Utah
56. Arches National Park, Utah
57. Colorado National Monument, Colorado
58. Mesa Verde National Park, Colorado
59. Grand Gulch Primitive Area, Utah

1. DESERT LOWLANDS

The Basin and Range country, a physiographic province curving 700 miles from New Mexico to Nevada, consists of broad, shimmering valleys bordered by elongated mountain ridges. The climate is hot—120° in summer shade—and dry, for rain, if it falls at all, seldom equals more than ten inches annually. Yet life is abundant, especially in public reserves where men pose little threat to natural ecosystems. The cactus wren, atop a giant saguaro, calls in a sing-song chatter at dawn. Coyotes bark in nightly chorus. Peccaries scurry among the shadows. Mesquite, paloverde, ironwood, cottonwood—the forest is different, but forest it is, as complex ecologically as luxuriant tropical woods. Of paramount interest are natural adaptations to environmental extremes, including leaves reduced to spines, seeds remaining dormant for years, and animal avoidance of midday heat.

Man is not so well adapted, and must take his life-support paraphernalia with him: food, map, head covering, and most importantly, at least a gallon of water per person a day. July, August, and September are the months of extremely hot conditions, and midday hours should be devoted to less than strenuous exercise.

🌲 **Organ Pipe Cactus National Monument,** covering 330,874 acres, is crossed by U.S. Route 85 between Ajo, Arizona, and the Mexican border. Access to this region was pioneered by Spanish soldiers and Jesuit missionaries on their way from México to California in the sixteenth and seventeenth centuries. Their routes are now but lonely trails in the desert. Modern roads reach only to idyllic oases such as Quitobaquito Spring, where hooded orioles, white-winged doves, and vermilion flycatchers sing in thorny groves of mesquite.

Two loop roads penetrate this richly vegetated wilderness. The Ajo Mountain Drive, a twenty-one-mile, one-way loop to the east of the visitor center, provides an introduction to wild desert country and leads past the Bull Pasture trail, which ascends into the Ajo Mountains. The Puerto Blanco Drive, a thirty-five-mile circuit west of the visitor center, leads to the

127

Saguaro National Monument, Arizona.

Dripping Springs trail, from which may be had commanding views of the Puerto Blanco Mountains and surrounding desert; it then goes on to Quitobaquito Spring (a good place for an evening picnic), and to the edge of the vast Cabeza Prieta wilderness, beyond the Growler Mountains. From this drive there is also a road up into the Senita Basin, site of unusual cactus forests and the starting point for hikes into the south side of the Puerto Blanco Mountains. A hiker makes his way through the multitrunked organ-pipe cactus, saguaro cactus, barrel and other types of cactus, ocotillo, paloverde, and ironwood, to name a few of the plants. The flowering period, which may be spectacular from March on into the summer, is a good time to visit, but winter is the more popular season because of the mild climate. The openness of the terrain invites cross-country hiking, but it is a good idea to check the proposed route with a park ranger before setting out. There is a campground. but no food or lodging in the Monument. Accommodations may be obtained in Ajo or at the México–United States border area.

Information: Superintendent, Organ Pipe Cactus National Monument, Box 38, Ajo, Arizona 85321.

🌲 West of Organ Pipe Cactus National Monument lies the much larger **Cabeza Prieta National Wildlife Range,** covering 860,000 acres in the southwestern corner of Arizona. Early explorers called the road through it "El Camino del Diablo," the Devil's Highway, and well they might. Hundreds of luckless souls perished along it for lack of water, food, or other supplies. But desert life, if not human life, is admirably adapted to extremes of heat and drought. This last large expanse of relatively undisturbed lower Sonoran desert in the U.S.A. is home of the rare Sonoran pronghorn as well as of deer, desert bighorns, peccaries, thousands of white-winged doves, and associated desert wildlife. A few Jeep roads penetrate the range, but access is limited. And although numerous unimproved trails exist, one of the values of this wilderness is that a hiker can see for miles, and so can strike out across country to enjoy a feeling not far different from that of the early explorers. Maps are a requisite for safety, however, and the scarcity of water governs all human activity.

Good roads surround this wilderness: Mexican Route 2 on the south, and U.S. Route 85 on the east and Interstate 8 on the north. However, care must be exercised in entering Cabeza Prieta and vicinity because much of the refuge is still used for military aerial rocket bombing and gunnery practice; visitors are admitted to certain parts of the range only by permission and when rockets and missiles are not being fired.

Joshua tree in Joshua Tree National Monument, California.

Fluted side of saguaro cactus.

Ocotillo at sunrise, Anza-Borrego Desert State Park, California.

There are no food, lodging, or potable drinking water facilities within the range. Campsites are available in Organ Pipe Cactus National Monument nearby.

Information: Manager, Cabeza Prieta National Wildlife Range, Box 1032, Yuma, Arizona 85364.

Saguaro National Monument preserves unusually dense stands of giant saguaro cactus, though there are also woods of juniper, oak, and piñon pine, and upland forests of aspen, fir, and ponderosa pine. Within the elevational range of 2,700 to nearly 9,000 feet are ecosystems of desert, grassland, and mountain. It doesn't take the hiker long to notice that on arid flats he walks among creosote bush, whereas on the banks of sandy washes (usually dry) he finds the going more difficult because of the greater density of plants like mesquite and paloverde. One good flood can nourish these streamside thickets through months of drought and ovenlike temperatures. Up on the rocky slopes the saguaro cactus seems more abundant and healthy, but the higher one goes the less he sees of desert plants. Animal life is abundant in this protected area, and a common recollection is of Gambel quail calling and skittering through the brush.

Exhibits and self-guiding trails point out the relationships between plants and animals in the several environments, and rangers provide additional information on trails in the Rincon Mountains. There are two sections to this monument, the headquarters unit seventeen miles east of Tucson, and the Tucson Mountain unit, fifteen miles west of the city, off Arizona Route 86. Nearby is the outstanding Arizona-Sonora Desert Museum. The monument acreage is 78,986. There is picnicking but no camping; Pima County's Tucson Mountain Park, west of the city, has campgrounds.

Information: Superintendent, Saguaro National Monument, Box 17210, Tucson, Arizona 85710.

Ninety miles north of Saguaro National Monument lies the **Superstition Wilderness,** an area of 124,140 acres within Tonto National Forest. The Superstition Mountains, a rugged rhyolite lava range that reaches a maximum elevation of 5,057 feet, can be seen for miles. No roads enter it, but many explorers have gone into this wild and rugged country. Some have sought the legendary Lost Dutchman Mine—and never returned. The real treasure of the Superstitions, however, is solitude, valleys filled with flowering cactus, hidden springs, natural bridges, deep canyons, towering cliffs, the conspicuous volcanic monolith of Weaver's Needle, and the quail, coyotes, bobcats, mountain lions, roadrunners, band-tailed pigeons, and other inhabitants. The region can be violent, what with floods from summer thunderstorms, and also searingly hot. Yet most of the year it is a pleasant desert wilderness accessible on a network of excellent trails. Springs exist, though they are sometimes difficult to locate; for maximum security sufficient water should be carried to sustain a hiker during his entire trip. All trash, of course, should be packed out; small backpack stoves should be utilized in lieu of making wood fires.

Paralleling the northern boundary of this wilderness is the rugged Apache Trail (Arizona Route 88). U.S. routes 60, 70, 80, and 89 pass through nearby Apache Junction, which is thirty-two miles east of Phoenix. A booklet, entitled "Superstition Wilderness Guidebook," was published in 1971 by Dr. Michael F. Sheridan, 2526 North Fifty-sixth Street, Phoenix, Arizona 85008. It contains maps, trail data, and scientific information. The most popular approaches are from Route 88, turning off 5.4 miles northeast of Apache Junction, or from Dons Camp, reached on a side road that leaves Routes 60-70-80-89 at a point eight miles southeast of Apache Junction. Primitive roads provide access to the more isolated and picturesque eastern portion of the wilderness.

Food, supplies, and lodging are available in nearby communities; campgrounds are located on Canyon and Apache lakes, to the north of the Superstitions. Maps and informational folders are available from the U.S. Forest Service.

Information: Supervisor, Tonto National Forest, Federal Building, 230 North First Avenue, Phoenix, Arizona 85025.

The **Aravaipa Canyon Primitive Area,** administered by the Bureau of Land Management, U.S. Department of the Interior, lies in the Gila River Basin sixty-five miles northeast of Tucson, Arizona. It is an unusually attractive deep wilderness gorge with that rarity of desert phenomena—a perennial stream. Flanking the water are cottonwood, ash, walnut, and sycamore trees, whose leaves turn bright orange or gold in autumn. On the rocky slopes grow more arid plants such as saguaro cactus. The canyon is alive with birds, and is visited by mule deer, peccaries, mountain lions, and coyotes. Nearly eight miles of the canyon have been preserved by the government, and private groups are protecting additional portions. Hiking trips of one of two days may be enjoyed within this area; horses can be used, but not motorized vehicles. The area has a recommended stay limit of three days and two nights, with a daily limit of fifty visitors. These restrictions are subject to evaluation and adjustment based on impact of visitor use on the natural features. The hiker's trash is neither burned nor buried here—it is packed out. Access is from Arizona Route 77 on the west and Arizona Route 70 on the east. Accommodations are available in nearby towns. An information center is located at Klondyke, Arizona, about eleven miles southeast of the boundary.

Information: District Manager, Bureau of Land Management, 1707 Thatcher Boulevard, Safford, Arizona 85546.

🌲 It seems incongruous that animals the size of bighorns (up to 225 pounds) exist in deserts where food and water are scant. They entered this region about 300,000 years ago, when apparently the climate was favorable. Now the environment seems to have grown more dry, but bighorns have adapted by nibbling on shrubs and grasses and staying near water holes. Nevertheless, they need substantial room in which to roam without interference from men and domestic or foreign sheep, so several wild places have been set aside in order to sustain the ecosystems in which they thrive. The **Desert National Wildlife Range,** in southern Nevada, was established in 1936, when the bighorn population in this territory had dwindled to 300. Under protection and management the numbers increased to more than 1,700 in the late 1950s; the current population is estimated to be between 500 and 1,000.

Many live in the Sheep Range, due north of Las Vegas. The entire refuge, containing 1,588,379 acres, extends more than eighty miles to the north and fifty miles to the west of Las Vegas. It is composed of elongated desert mountain ranges that seldom receive more than ten inches of rain a year. Yet there is variation in vegetation up to the highest elevation of 9,920 feet, and thus the number of animal species varies. Mule deer, coyotes, foxes, mountain lions, and more than 245 species of birds have been observed.

U.S. routes 93 and 95 border parts of the refuge, and there are primitive roads over which visitors are permitted to drive; but off-road travel is prohibited. No camping or accommodations are available; food, supplies, and lodging may be obtained in Las Vegas.

Information: Manager, Desert National Wildlife Range, 1500 North Decatur Boulevard, Las Vegas, Nevada 89108. .

🌲 An Arizona refuge for the desert bighorn is the 660,000-acre **Kofa Game Range,** a rugged mountain region forty miles north of Yuma. Travel within the refuge is better suited to bighorns than men, although some of the trails can be negotiated with four-wheel-drive vehicles. The range is accessible from the north and west over primitive roads that branch away from U.S. routes 60 and 95. There are no food or lodging facilities. Of special interest is a canyon that contains the only native palm trees (*Washingtonia*) growing wild in Arizona. Wild burros roam throughout the range. Inquiries about travel in remote areas should be made before starting out.

Information: Manager, Kofa Game Range, Box 1032, Yuma, Arizona 85364.

🌲 Along the Colorado River many miles of original habitat have been submerged under reservoirs created by man. In the Havasu and Imperial national wildlife refuges, the wildlife and recreational aspects are managed to conserve the remaining natural values of this elongated desert oasis. The surrounding region is one of cattail marshes, narrow canyons, giant saguaro cactuses, and sharp-pointed desert peaks. These last are foci of the proposed **Needles Wilderness,** a 17,116-acre section of the Havasu refuge where the Colorado River winds through Mojave Canyon beneath the Needles, a series of volcanic pinnacles. The habitat is strictly Sonoran desert, and one of the hottest parts of the U.S.A., yet home to quail, white-winged doves, roadrunners, desert bighorns, and feral burros. In marshes along the river's edge rails, waterfowl, and other wildlife find respite from the dryness of the desert.

Most of the wilderness is in Arizona but a small segment lies across the Colorado River in California. It is approached on Interstate 40 and Arizona State Route 95. Food and lodging are available in Needles, fifteen miles to the northwest.

Information: Manager, Havasu National Wildlife Refuge, Needles, California 92363.

🌲 **Imperial National Wildlife Refuge** stretches out for some thirty miles along both sides of the Colorado River behind Imperial Dam, and includes desert uplands. A proposed wilderness of 14,470 acres would provide a home for wild waterfowl, particularly wintering Canada geese of the Great Basin flock. Recreational activities in the refuge include fishing, hunting, boating, photography, and wildlife observation. Accommodations are available in the Martinez Lake area and in Yuma and vicinity. Access is off U.S. Route 95.

Information: Manager, Imperial National Wildlife Refuge, Box 1032, Yuma, Arizona 85364.

🌲 **Lake Mead National Recreation Area,** 1,912,692 acres in Arizona and Nevada, contains approximately a hundred miles of Arizona's Grand Canyon, on the Colorado River. East of Pierce Ferry lies a wild and exceedingly rough canyon and plateau country with few trails. Access can be had by boat along the river, and hikers may proceed up some of the side streams, being careful to take water, protection from the sun, maps, and food if they go very far. Auto access to the recreation area is off U.S. routes 91 in Nevada and 93 in Arizona. Accommodations are available from Boulder City to Las Vegas, Nevada, the latter thirty miles to the west.

Information: Superintendent, Lake Mead National Recreation Area, 601 Nevada Highway, Boulder City, Nevada 89005.

🌲 Both the Lake Mead region and **Joshua Tree National Monument,** the latter in California, contain large forests of a giant yucca known as the Joshua tree, a member of the lily family. That this plant grows to forty feet and produces large clusters of creamy-white flowers in so dry a climate is striking evidence of adaptation to environment. There are other examples, such as native California fan palms. More than 200 species of birds have been sighted within the Monument, and hikers on the trails early in the morning have a chance of seeing them, as well as bighorns, badgers, deer, coyotes, and other mammals.

The monument's 558,184 acres vary in elevation from about 1,000 to 6,000 feet. We thus find two distinct ecosystems, High Desert and Low. From several vantage points can be obtained panoramic views of the Coachella Valley, Salton Sea, and Santa Rosa Mountains. Roads and trails, including self-guiding nature trails, reach some of the more interesting features in the monument. For example, massive boulders of light-colored quartz monzonite not only provide dramatic surroundings for hikers but are geologically significant and offer a field day for artists and photographers. The California Hiking and Riding Trail passes through the area. Two-mile trails lead to the Fortynine Palms Oasis and the Lost Horse Mine Stamp Mill; a four-mile trail goes into Lost Palm Canyon. Museums explain ecological and geological aspects of the scene. Accommodations are available on or near California Route 62, in and near Twentynine Palms. The south entrance of the monument may be reached from Interstate 10, approximately thirty miles east of Indio.

Information: Superintendent, Joshua Tree National Monument, Twentynine Palms, California 92277.

🌲 California, possessor of an immense state park system, concisely sums up in an information folder the significance of its largest park:

When Butterfield Overland Mail coaches from St. Louis sped through the desert over the southern route toward Pueblo de Los Angeles in the 1850's, the hot lowlands and rugged mountains that are now part of the half-million-acre **Anza-Borrego Desert State Park** stood as the one, final barrier in the vast Colorado Desert. Beyond were cool ocean breezes, abundant fresh water to wash away the dust, and comfortable accommodations. Stagecoach passengers were only too happy to pass through this arid wilderness as quickly as possible.

Today, this very vastness and desolation are the desert's greatest attraction. Less than three hours from the major metropolitan centers of southern California, the park's isolation, magnificent vistas, and clear star-studded nights unspoiled by the lights of nearby cities draw over a half-million visitors annually. During the winter and spring, when the park receives its greatest use, the desert wildflowers bloom in a profusion of color, and temperatures during the day range in the 70's and 80's.

The park is a fine example of original desert, replete with bighorns, jackrabbits, coyotes, roadrunners, rattlesnakes, and other members. of a relatively undisturbed desert ecosystem. It is also a mecca for sightseers because of the scenic variety: sculptured badlands, seeps and springs with migratory birds, canyons with sheer walls, oases fringed with palms, the botanical oddity of "elephant trees," dry lakes and washes, historic trails, rugged mountains and gorges, and panoramic views into the Salton Sea basin.

Though reasonably wild, the park is penetrated by numerous access routes, mostly "Jeep roads" and trails into desert mountains and canyons. One road has been designated the Borrego–Salton Sea Self-guiding Automobile Tour, a twenty-five-mile round trip that begins near park headquarters. Another is the Southern Emigrant Trail Self-guiding Automobile Tour, which emphasizes the historical aspects of the region, chiefly the Butterfield Stage Trail. The best time to be out, considering coolness and clear air, is dawn. Camping is available at several locations, mostly in primitive sites without water or shade but accessible by auto. From such points one may explore more deeply into the wilder portions of the southern California desert, less than ninety miles east of San Diego. Good maps and informational folders and books are available from the park.

In addition to camping, picnic areas are provided. At Borrego Springs, in the heart of the park, may be obtained food, supplies, and lodging. Access is via routes 78, S1, S2, and S22. Interstate 8 passes the southern end of the park.

Information: Manager, Anza-Borrego Desert State Park, Borrego Springs, California 92004.

🌲 In the heart of the Mojave Desert, but mercifully at elevations of 3,400 to 7,171 feet, lies the **Providence Mountains State Recreation Area,** 5,280 acres that include part of the rhyolitic Providence Mountains. Vast desert stretches administered by the U.S. Bureau of Land Management lie adjacent, so that the visitor's vision is sometimes stretched across eighty-five miles of more or less wild desert ridges and valleys to the Hualapai Mountains in Arizona.

From gentle slopes on which grow cactus, creosote bush, and cholla, the rock-filled landscape rises to high crags where piñon pine predominates. Indeed, the productive ecosystem in these desert hills consists of several woody species such as juniper and scrub oak. Considering the grass as well as herbaceous cover it is obvious that the natural flora constitutes a rich base for small mammals, including ground squirrels, rabbits, and rodents. These in turn are a source of both food and water for such predators as coyotes, foxes, bobcats, and snakes. Nor is the bird niche vacant, for the arid flats and escarpments, especially at dawn and dusk, resound with the notes of piñon jays, cactus wrens, roadrunners, white-crowned sparrows, and others. A nature trail is located near headquarters.

Underground water has dissolved from limestone layers a number of caverns in which stalactites and stalagmites have been formed. The temperature within the subterranean passages remains at a constant 65°. Tours are conducted daily. The recreation area, located in a "lonesome triangle" of sparsely populated desert, has only a limited number of campsites, though other camping is available on nearby Bureau of Land Management terrain. Travelers should carry sufficient food, water, and gasoline for their round trip. The area lies eighty miles in an air line east of Barstow, and is twenty-three miles north of Interstate 40, near Essex.

Information: Manager, Providence Mountains State Recreation Area, Box 1, Essex, California 92332.

🌲 The driest and hottest part of the Basin and Range Province, **Death Valley National Monument,** has an elevation of 282 feet below sea level near Badwater, and a record temperature of 134° F. In summer the valley is like a furnace during the hottest part of the day, though visitors can explore in relative comfort from dawn to about 11:00 A.M. Winter is better, but the valley is worth a visit in any season. Hundreds of species of wild flowers bloom in spring, including the daisy, orchid, paintbrush, milkweed, evening primrose, snapdragon, poppy, buckwheat, lupine, and aster. Creosote bush and desert holly grow in the gravelly washes. Aquatic vegetation and animals—pupfish, invertebrates—thrive even in warm, saline spring waters.

A few miles away, the land rises to Telescope Peak, elevation 11,049 feet. As a result of this variation in altitude, and the immensity of the Monument (over 2 million acres), Death Valley is a place of numerous ecosystems and destinations of interest, including jagged salt flats that stretch for miles, broad regions of sand dunes, winding canyons, colorful rock cliffs, and historic sites. Although the average annual rainfall is less than two inches, cloudbursts occasionally cause flash floods that wash out roads and trails. Usually, however, Death Valley is a Shangri-la of serenity in which to experience the desert's wildness and vastness.

The valley is reached from the north and east over U.S. Route 95, and from the south and west over California state routes 127, 178, and 190. The lowlands and surrounding mountains are accessible by roads and trails; in addition, the openness of the terrain invites cross-country hiking. A special time for photographers is early morning or late afternoon when the sand dunes near Stovepipe Wells are in bold relief. Good maps and booklets are available at Monument headquarters. Camping is permitted. Accommodations may be obtained in and near the valley.

Information: Superintendent, Death Valley National Monument, Death Valley, California 92328.

🌲 In New Mexico, the Chihuahua Desert extends from Texas and México northwesterly in two lobes, one up the Pecos River and the other up the Rio Grande almost to Albuquerque. The region is characterized by creosote bush–covered plains and by occasional limestone peaks and promontories. A unique section lies in **White Sands National Monument,** where windblown dunes of pure gypsum have accumulated over an area of 176,000 acres, the world's largest gypsum desert. Particles of calcium sulfate, transported by rain and snowmelt waters from gypsiferous strata in the mountains, arrive at Lake Lucero, where evaporation releases them to the winds. In such a gleaming white environment, certain animals (lizards, pocket mice) have evolved into whiter shades than usual, an asset in escaping detection by soaring hawks.

The best times to visit are dawn or sunset, when shadows are long, the dunes accentuated, the air cool, and animals apt to be moving about. Visitors at midday hours should wear sunglasses to protect their eyes from glare. A road leads partway into the dune area; after that a hiker strikes out on his own, and the trails he makes are as temporary as the wind. Photographic opportunities are limitless, not only because of artistic dune patterns, but because of other features such as yuccas perched on pedestals, and the tracks of animals. There are no campgrounds. Visitors may picnic, but food and lodging must be obtained outside the Monument. The White Sands are located on U.S. routes 70 and 82, fifteen miles southwest of Alamogordo, where hotels, motels, trailer parks, and camping areas are available.

Information: Superintendent, White Sands National Monument, Box 458, Alamogordo, New Mexico 88310.

🌲 Within the White Sands Missile Range, New Mexico, and subject to security regulations, 57,215 acres have been set aside as the **San Andres National Wildlife Refuge.** It protects a desert ecosystem that includes deer, mountain lions, and several kinds of quail. Bighorn sheep, once perilously low in population, have not only increased in numbers but moved out to repopulate adjacent areas. The refuge is closed to public use except during periodic deer-hunting seasons. It was considered for study under the Wilderness Act but the matter was dropped because of primary jurisdiction of the military and secondary jurisdiction of other government agencies. There are no campgrounds or accommodations. Access is via county roads north of Las Cruces.

Information: Manager, San Andres National Wildlife Refuge, Box 756, Las Cruces, New Mexico 88001.

🌲 Nearly a hundred miles southeast of White Sands National Monument rise the Guadalupe Mountains, part of an ancient curving reef of marine limestone in which huge caves have been dissolved. Within the 46,753 acres of **Carlsbad Caverns National Park** are more than sixty caves, though aside from the main, well-visited caverns, public entry into most is limited chiefly to scientific and educational researchers. Above ground, the winding canyons reveal features of geologic, ecologic, and aesthetic interest. Depending on how well a visitor has studied the geology of the ancient reef he may recognize teepee structures, ripple marks, bedding planes, and fossil fragments. The crystalline limestones contain inclusions of red chert and fossil remains of more than 200 invertebrate life forms older than 200 million years.

Intricate associations of Chihuahuan Desert flora and fauna have evolved in these canyons. The most conspicuous plants are Texas sotol, lechuguilla, cactus, and ocotillo—yet the delicate canyon ecosystems also include walnut trees, oaks, grass, moss, and ferns. A hiker who takes the time to explore not only the desert plateaus but the backcountry portions of this park, and on up into the wilderness regions of Lincoln National Forest and Guadalupe Mountains National Park, will understand that there is far more here than caves. Detailed information is available on hiking trails, plant and animal life, caverns, prehistoric Indians, and other features.

Hikers must plan their trip carefully and carry at least a gallon of water per person per day because there is no safe and reliable water in the backcountry. They should also carry their own fuel since deadwood is reserved for wildlife habitat. Trash must be packed out.

Access is via U.S. Route 62-180, 140 miles east of El Paso, Texas, or 27 miles south from the city of Carlsbad, New Mexico. Food and lodging are available near the park and in the city of Carlsbad.

Information: Superintendent, Carlsbad Caverns National Park, 3225 National Parks Highway, Carlsbad, New Mexico 88220.

It will be some time before public-use facilities are constructed at **Guadalupe Mountains National Park,** which was established late in 1972. However, for persons willing to rough it, the park is open to public use. Hikers will find fifty-five miles of rugged but scenic trails in the 77,500-acre park, which encompasses the four highest points in Texas (up to 8,751 feet). A relict forest of ponderosa pine, limber pine, and Douglas fir grows in the high country. Some canyons within the park shelter exceptional segments of original ecosystems, along with exposed cross-sections of the ancient Captain Reef and its associated rock formations. A minor road leads south into the park from Lincoln National Forest. It would be wise to consult the superintendent for updated information on new developments and facilities, as well as a current bibliography that would facilitate reading about this area before arrival.

Backcountry camping is limited to designated sites, which are rotated periodically to prevent wearing out of the landscape. Wood fires and the use of native fuels are not permitted but containerized fuel stoves may be used. There are no safe, dependable sources of water in the backcountry, and what springs and seeps there are have a critical value for wildlife, hence human beings must locate wilderness camps far away from them. The absence of water imposes a limit on how far a hiker can go in this rugged terrain and how long he can stay; practical experience has shown that a gallon of water per person per day is required in the Guadalupe Mountains during most seasons of the year. That in turn suggests that a three-day backpacking trip is about all that can be undertaken by most persons. In addition, though the Guadalupes look peaceful, there can be cold wintry days, severe electrical storms, flash floods, and high winds at different times of year.

Access is via U.S. Route 62-180. No accommodations are available in the park; the nearest concentrations of lodging facilities are at El Paso, Texas, 110 miles to the west, Carlsbad, New Mexico, 55 miles to the northeast, and at Van Horn, Texas, 65 miles to the south. There is a small campground in the park.

Information: Superintendent, Guadalupe Mountains National Park, 3225 National Parks Highway, Carlsbad, New Mexico 88220.

🌲 About seventy-five miles south of Albuquerque, above Elephant Butte Reservoir in central New Mexico, lies **Bosque del Apache National Wildlife Refuge.** Most of its 57,200 acres are dry desert with sparse vegetative cover, but nearly a fourth of the area protects river bottomlands along the Rio Grande. The name of the refuge means "Apache forest" and refers to cottonwood groves along the Rio Grande. It is less a wilderness than a managed sanctuary for ducks, geese, Gambel quail, and sandhill cranes, and there are dikes, canals, and water-control structures. Nevertheless, several sections are roadless, and for persons fascinated by birds, of which 284 species have been recorded here, the refuge has unusual value. There is a prehistoric Indian pueblo on a volcanic mesa. The nearest accommodations are at Socorro, New Mexico. Access is by refuge roads eight miles south of San Antonio.

Information: Manager, Bosque del Apache National Wildlife Refuge, Box 278, San Antonio, New Mexico 87832.

🌲 The 23,189 acres of **Bitter Lake National Wildlife Refuge,** on the Pecos River eleven miles northeast of Roswell, New Mexico, are a haven for thousands of ducks and geese, chiefly mallards, American widgeons, pintails, and canvasbacks. As many as 70,000 sandhill cranes roost on the refuge during winter. There are also such shorebirds as plovers, avocets, and stilts. Despite high salt concentrations in the waters, certain lakes are open to fishing and good catches of channel catfish and white bass are often reported. No boats are permitted. Picnic areas are available but overnight camping is limited to supervised youth groups. About a third of the refuge has been designated the **Salt Creek Wilderness.** The environment is a desert one, with salty lakes, gypsum sinks, grasslands, scaled quail, jackrabbits, and coyotes. No vehicles of any kind are permitted, nor are fishing, picnicking, or camping allowed. Public use on the wilderness part of the refuge is limited to persons walking or on horseback. Food and lodging can be secured in Roswell. Access is on U.S. Route 70.

Information: Manager, Bitter Lake National Wildlife Refuge, Box 7, Roswell, New Mexico 88201.

🌲 The Big Bend country of Texas, located in an elbow of the Rio Grande, was badly damaged by overgrazing and other excesses during pioneer days, but in 1944, **Big Bend National Park,** now containing 708,221 acres, was established. Grazing, shooting, and man-induced erosion were halted, and the terrain has begun to revert to original Chihuahuan Desert, endowed with plants unfamiliar to most Americans—drooping juniper, madrone, sotol, lechuguilla, Spanish dagger. Few desert locales are as dramatic. Deep canyons, whose walls enclose the Rio Grande in cool shadows, rise as much as 1,500 feet above the river. Sand whips along the banks and catches in deep dunes that fill cliff cul-de-sacs. A good river boatman can manage to float with ease through these gorges, providing he gets from rangers an up-to-the-minute assessment of the capricious Rio Grande and the rocks within it. Permits are required for float trips.

A rugged and impressive hike is the seven-mile ascent from the Chisos Basin to the South Rim, through the steep, forested Chisos Mountains. This leads to a high promontory from which a sizable portion of Texas and México may be seen, though the Rio Grande lies hidden in its canyons, 6,000 feet below. The view lingers long in memory, an almost primeval vista veiled in light-blue haze. The contrast between cool patches of aspen above and cactus lands below is one of the greater values of Big Bend's wilderness. Among the animals in these mountains that do not occur naturally anywhere else in the United States are the Colima warbler and the Carmen white-tailed deer.

Access to Big Bend National Park is principally by automobile, either from Marathon, 69 miles away over U.S. Route 385, or Alpine, 100 miles distant over Texas Route 118. Several roads approach from México but there is no bridge across the Rio Grande into the park. Visitors may engage in hiking, horseback riding, boating, fishing, and camping. The clear desert air improves photographic opportunities. The four-mile Lost Mine Trail has points of interest described in a trail booklet. Other trails and old roads may be explored. Food, lodging and supplies are available in the park.

Information: Superintendent, Big Bend National Park, Texas 79834.

2. DESERT UPLANDS

The higher the elevation, the less we see of desert environments. The mountains are cooler, more moist, and more densely covered with vegetation. Some are inundated by ten feet or more of snow in the winter. A good example, with its mean elevation 8,000 feet and its highest point nearly 11,000 feet above sea level, is the **Gila Wilderness** in New Mexico, the first such area set aside (1924) in the national forest system. A popular way of reaching it is over a paved but sharply curving road, New Mexico Route 15, that leads through pine-scented forests and rugged woodlands for forty-four miles north of Silver City. At the end of the road is Gila Cliff Dwellings National Monument and the Gila Visitor Center, operated jointly by the Forest Service and the National Park Service. A score of other approach routes exist, intersecting access trails to other portions of the wilderness, but to enter the wilderness a visitor must leave his vehicle altogether. At Gila Hot Springs and several other access points pack outfits can be secured for extended trips into the volcanic canyon country. Visitors are requested to register at trail entrance points.

In deep and sinuous gorges of the Gila River the hiker is immersed in wildness where the silence is broken by the chatter of a kingfisher or of wind in the alder leaves. He sees stream impoundments superintended by half a dozen beavers, or raccoons probing at the water's edge. The canyons are confined, however, and popular with visitors. To find more solitude and wide-open places, one should climb to the higher areas where quail and turkeys roam, and tassel-eared Abert squirrels clip twig-ends of pines, their favorite diet. The upper-echelon chain of predation includes black bears, bobcats, coyotes, and mountain lions, the latter stalking mule deer whenever they can. Merriams elk inhabited the area until the early 1900s before becoming extinct. Rocky Mountain elk have been successfully planted to replace them, but the herd has been continuously plagued by infestations of bloodworm, which reduces the number of calves that survive.

One of the most refreshing experiences in this wilderness is breaking out on a promontory and gazing over hundreds of square miles of tumbled terrain, broken by deep, narrow gorges, decorated with rocky spires and broad flats covered with pines, and almost entirely free of human occupation. The Gila

Wilderness contains the most extensive area of ponderosa pine forest in the world under continuous management as wilderness. That is a tribute to forester Aldo Leopold, who here pioneered the concept of public wilderness, and whose written thoughts (*Sand County Almanac, Round River*) urged Americans to save and multiply such areas.

The Gila Wilderness contains 429,506 acres, once land over which Geronimo and his Apache warriors rode. The wilderness is bounded on the north, east, and south by the **Gila Primitive Area,** containing 135,978 acres. Portions of the Gila Primitive Area and other contiguous lands have been recommended for addition to the Gila Wilderness. Limited accommodations are available nearby.

Information: Supervisor, Gila National Forest, 301 West College Avenue, Silver City, New Mexico 88061.

In the Gila National Forest is the **Aldo Leopold Wilderness,** containing 188,179 acres. From its high peaks may be gained wide views of southwestern New Mexico. The landscape consists of deep canyons, narrow ridges, mesas, escarpments, box canyons, steep talus slopes, and heavy forests of pine, spruce, white fir, Douglas fir, and juniper. Burned-over places have been invaded naturally by squawbush, locust, and manzanita. Early human occupation by Apache Indians, the U.S. Cavalry, and a few prospectors hunting for gold and silver left little more than footprints. All that remains of this era are a few rotting log cabins. Access is via New Mexico routes 61 and 90 east of Silver City, New Mexico.

Information: Supervisor, Gila National Forest, 301 West College Avenue, Silver City, New Mexico 88061.

In the tangled, gullied, pine-clad mountains of western New Mexico and eastern Arizona lies the **Blue Range Primitive Area,** twenty-three miles north of Clifton, Arizona. Here rises the Mogollon Rim, romanticized in Zane Grey's novels, an escarpment from which to view broken terrain, deep canyons, jagged ridges, and dense coniferous vegetation. A hiker in a single day can climb from semidesert to mountain peaks 9,000 feet in elevation, past sunburned lava pinnacles and gray cliffs into patches of wild rose, lupine, and fern. Some trails border musical mountain brooks where Apache Indians roamed; some enter historic canyons where—who knows?—horse thieves might have hidden to avoid pursuing posses. Within the 117,239 acres of this wilderness one can get lost literally and figuratively. There are no developed recreation sites and no jarring reminders of civilization (except jet aircraft overhead). All motorized equipment is prohibited, as in most wilderness areas. The opportunities are excellent for seeing bobcats, mountain lions, deer, bears, the celebrated tassel-eared Abert squirrels, Arizona gray squirrels, and such colorful birds as acorn woodpeckers. The wildlife has been little disturbed by human hunters because of the remoteness and difficult nature of the terrain, and because there is good hunting elsewhere in the region.

U.S. Route 666 passes along the western boundary of the area. Accommodations may be obtained in nearby towns.

Information: Supervisor, Apache National Forest, Box 640, Springerville, Arizona 85938.

🌲 The **Wheeler Peak Wilderness,** twelve miles northeast of Taos, New Mexico, in the Carson National Forest, contains only 6,051 acres but it includes the highest point in New Mexico, Wheeler Peak, 13,161 feet. Therefore, alpine tundra is common, and the surrounding scenery consists of rugged mountains whose shoulders and lower slopes are enclosed with thick coniferous forests, aspen patches, and carpets of grass. Trails follow streams to lakes and cross over the high elevations.

The wilderness is approached on forest roads off New Mexico routes 3 and 38. Several campgrounds are located nearby along the Rio Hondo and Red River. Food, supplies, and lodging may be obtained in Taos, Questa, and Red River. Wilderness-use permits may be obtained at ranger stations in Taos or Questa.

Information: Supervisor, Carson National Forest, Box 558, Taos, New Mexico 87571.

🌲 Another fairly small New Mexico wilderness is found in the Lincoln National Forest in the southern part of the state. Here the 31,000-acre **White Mountain Wilderness** includes environments ranging from desert grasslands and low, juniper-covered hills to the higher slopes of ponderosa pine, then higher still a mixed forest of spruce and fir, finally rising to a subalpine flora at 11,000 feet. Because of the abrupt transition from one zone to another, botanists have found this an excellent place to study the effects of altitudinal changes on the vegetation. In the forests mule deer and black bears are occasionally seen, as are smaller mammals such as coyotes, porcupines, skunks, raccoons, mountain lions, and foxes. Hikers may also spot wild turkeys, scaled or Gambel's quail, and band-tailed pigeons. During some parts of the year, water in many of the streams may have ceased flowing, so it is best to check on this at local ranger headquarters before entering the wilderness.

Access is from Carrizozo south on State Route 37, turning west on side roads, or north from Alamogordo on U.S. Highway 70, turning east on side roads. There are campgrounds just outside the wilderness on both east and west sides of the national forest. Food and supplies may be obtained at Ruidoso, Capitan, or Carrizozo. A small museum in the national forest near the wilderness attests to the fact that a bear cub named Smokey once lived nearby.

Information: Supervisor, Lincoln National Forest, Box 840, Alamogordo, New Mexico 88310.

🌲 Access to the **Pecos Wilderness,** at the southern end of the Sangre de Cristo Mountains near Santa Fe, New Mexico, is by foot and horseback only; there are no roads, hotels, stores, or developed campsites. The wilderness covers 167,416 acres, in which the waters of the Pecos River begin to flow. Truchas Peak, 13,102 feet, second highest in New Mexico, dominates the area. Wildlife is abundant and includes turkeys, grouse, bighorns, elk, deer, bears, and mountain lions. The wilderness hiker may wander along 150 miles of streams, past springs and cascades, and up to high-country lakes. Too many visitors could result in the familiar confrontation between people and fragile wilderness, in which case restraints on human travel may be put into effect. Certain popular sites have in the past suffered trampling, trash accumulation, pollution, and other temporary damage.

Approaches to the wilderness are over State Route 63 from the south and routes 3 and 76 from the north. Developed campsites are available in both Carson and Santa Fe national forests. Food and lodging may be secured in Pecos and Santa Fe, just outside the forest boundaries. Wilderness entry permits may be obtained at ranger stations in Pecos, Las Vegas, Espanola, and Santa Fe.

Information: Supervisor, Santa Fe National Forest, Box 1689, Santa Fe, New Mexico 87501; and Supervisor, Carson National Forest, Box 587, Taos, New Mexico 87571.

🌲 The **San Pedro Parks Wilderness,** New Mexico, was set aside in 1931 to preserve high, moist plateau country in the Santa Fe National Forest. Its summits are characterized by patches of spruce and open meadows, through which flow clear mountain streams. Along the trails, hikers and horsemen may observe wild turkeys, grouse, bears, deer, and elk.

145

This 41,132-acre area, located approximately fifty-five miles in an air line northwest of Santa Fe, is reached from roads that branch off state routes 44 and 96. Campgrounds are available in the surrounding Santa Fe National Forest, and accommodations may be obtained in Cuba, New Mexico. Entry permits are available at ranger stations in Cuba, Coyote, or Santa Fe.

Information: Supervisor, Santa Fe National Forest, Box 1689, Santa Fe, New Mexico 87501.

🌲 A hiker comes away from **Bandelier National Monument** with the feeling that this wilderness has a little of everything: volcanoes, canyons, Indian ruins, ceremonial caves, rock carvings, waterfalls, mountain peaks, beaver dams, dense forests, clear air, and solitude. Its 29,661 acres are composed of consolidated volcanic ash (tuff) and basaltic lava ejected thousands of years ago when fifty cubic miles of molten material spewed out on the surface to form the Pajarito Plateau. The lava and ash are part of a fifteen-mile-wide volcanic crater, the rim of which forms the Jemez Mountains. Out of this compressed ash-turned-to-stone the Indians carved cave dwellings or constructed apartmentlike community housing. They occupied these between the thirteenth and sixteenth centuries, and several are of immense size; Tyuonyi Ruin has about 400 rooms. Most of the monument is wilderness, and most of its features are accessible only by trail. To hike in Bandelier, one must be in good physical condition because much of the walking is up and down; the elevation ranges from 6,000 feet to over 8,500 feet. Yet the effort is worthwhile, not only for the scenic views and ancient ruins, but for the dry climate, bright sun, and silence. Highlights of wilderness travel include the gorges of Alamo Canyon; the Rio Grande and White Rock canyons; Frijoles Canyon and its waterfalls; Alamo, Hondo, and Lummis canyons; Painted Cave; the Stone Lions Shrine; the Indian ruins of San Miguel and Yapashi; Boundary Peak; and Santa Fe National Forest, which forms the western and northern boundary.

The monument, forty-six miles west of Santa Fe, may be reached on New Mexico Route 4. It is a place to plan a trip carefully, obtain topographic maps and a backcountry-use permit, and consult with park rangers. Lodging and food are available from May 1 through September 30, and a campground is open all year.

Information: Superintendent, Bandelier National Monument, Los Alamos, New Mexico 87544.

🌲 Of Arizona's desert uplands, none possesses a more unusual fauna than the Chiricahua Mountains. Some of the wildlife is Mexican in origin, and the

View from Font's Point, Anza-Borrego Desert State Park, California.

ranges of certain species reach their northern limits here. In **Chiricahua National Monument,** thirty-five miles southeast of Willcox on Arizona Route 186, coatimundis were first sighted in appreciable numbers in the 1950s, and have become fairly common. How many jaguars roam these mountains is difficult to say because the species is scarce; perhaps there are no more at all. A hiker on trails in rhyolite lava canyons may find exotic and colorful birds, including the coppery-tailed trogon and harlequin quail. All of which is in addition to a more conventional fauna that includes skunks, white-tailed

147

deer, peccaries, and black-headed grosbeaks. Among the plants not widely found north of here are Mexican piñon, madrone, Schotts yucca, and Apache pine.

Hiking is the prime way to enjoy these mountains. In Chiricahua National Monument well-constructed trails lead to fantasylike destinations born of volcanic eruptions. The southern portion of the Monument, a rhyolite plateau, has been eroded into pinnacles, spires, serrated ridges, and balanced rocks. Short self-guiding trails serve as an introduction to the natural history of the Chiricahuas, and longer trails lead to the Heart of Rocks, Echo Canyon, Sara Deming Canyon, and Rhyolite Canyon. Historic Fort Bowie and Apache Pass lie a short distance to the north. Campsites are available in the Monument as well as in Coronado National Forest.

Access to the Monument is via side roads off U.S. routes 80, 666, and Interstate 10. The nearest food and lodging may be secured at Portal, Rodeo, Willcox, or Douglas, Arizona.

Information: Superintendent, Chiricahua National Monument, Dos Cabezas Star Route, Willcox, Arizona 85643. *Sky Island*

Weldon Heald

🌲 Whereas Chiricahua National Monument lies mostly on the lower slopes of the mountains, below 7,300 feet, the **Chiricahua Wilderness,** ten miles to the south, ranges from 6,100 to 9,797 feet. This provides protection to some of the highest ridges in the Chiricahua Mountains, and by means of primitive trails leading into rugged canyons and through aspen groves, the hiker will find himself on a high mountain "island" in the midst of the desert. He will also encounter Douglas fir, so common in the Pacific Northwest, spruce, red columbine, and Gambel oak. Coatimundis are only occasionally seen here. Black bears may be observed now and then, as well as deer and foxes, but bobcats and mountain lions are rare. Among the birds are creepers, ravens, bluebirds, and six kinds of hummingbirds.

The area is accessible via forest roads off U.S. routes 666, 80, and Interstate 10. Campgrounds are available on approach roads. The nearest accommodations are in Rodeo and Portal.

Information: Supervisor, Coronado National Forest, 130 South Scott Street, Box 551, Tucson, Arizona 85702.

🌲 Within the boundaries of Coronado National Forest lies a desert-mountain primitive area, the **Galiuro Wilderness,** about forty-five miles northwest of Willcox, Arizona. This lava range, with broken cliffs and terraces, supports dense scrub vegetation that renders passage challenging, if not difficult.

Primitive roads approach from the north and east, and desert trails lead into the heart of the area.

In and around the Galiuros, much of the mountain region of central Arizona remains fairly wild, so difficult of access that human settlers and hunters have not been able to get in very easily. Wilderness hikers who make their way to the heart of it will find chaparral (oak and other shrubs),

Desert holly, Death Valley National Monument, California.

communities of piñon pine and juniper, cool forests of ponderosa pine, distant views of desert and upland, Indian ruins, wild turkeys, mountain lions, isolation, and quiet. Sometimes in winter or spring the canyons have tumbling streams. No campgrounds are available in the wilderness or closer than forty miles by road. Food and lodging are available in Willcox.

Information: Supervisor, Coronado National Forest, 130 South Scott Street, Box 551, Tucson, Arizona 85702.

🌲 Besides the Superstition Mountain Wilderness, three other wild areas have been set aside in Tonto National Forest. They are exceptionally rugged and rise to the elevations higher than those reached in the Superstitions. One is the **Mazatzal Wilderness,** 205,137 acres, thirty-five miles north of the Superstitions. Located in the northern part of the Mazatzal Range, and approached by Arizona Route 87 north from Phoenix, this region is exceedingly difficult to traverse. The hiker must negotiate narrow, steep-walled canyons, or climb over naked ridges that rise to 7,800 feet. This has been a fairly effective barrier to human settlement, and the resident wildlife seems to be relatively intact. From high points one sees the desert, other ranges of central Arizona, and the storied Tonto Basin. Trails cross the eastern and northern parts of the area. Food and lodging are available only in nearby towns and villages.

Information: Supervisor, Tonto National Forest, Federal Building, 230 North First Avenue, Phoenix, Arizona 85025.

🌲 Across the Tonto Basin, thirty-five miles southeast of the Mazatzal Wilderness, is the **Sierra Ancha Wilderness,** 20,850 acres in mountains so steep and pitching that parts of them are accessible to little more than ravens or mountain sheep. To reach this wilderness, a traveler goes approximately ninety miles east of Phoenix and then takes Arizona Route 288. This, as well as more primitive roads, approaches the boundary closely, but access thereafter is step by step, or hand over hand. Accommodations are available in communities on the approach routes.

Information: Supervisor, Tonto National Forest, Federal Building, 230 North First Avenue, Phoenix, Arizona 85025.

🌲 The **Pine Mountain Wilderness,** on the boundary between Prescott and Tonto national forests, fifty miles north of Phoenix, is approached on

Interstate 17 or Arizona Route 87, but these roads do not come very close. For thirty-four years the 19,569-acre area was administered by the U.S. Forest Service as a "primitive area," so its deep canyons, flat-topped mesas, and steep terrain are in a reasonably wild state. There are eighteen miles of trails, but no developed campsites, food, or lodging in or near the area.

Information: Supervisor, Tonto National Forest, Federal Building, 230 North First Avenue, Phoenix, Arizona 85025.

🌲 Early explorers more than a century ago called the **Mount Baldy Wilderness,** west of Alpine, Arizona, a perfect landscape and true solitude, undefiled by the presence of man. Thanks to the U.S. Forest Service, this description is still apt. Though easy to get to—Arizona Route 273 comes to within a mile of the boundary—there is a sense of remoteness typical of the White Mountains. On the border between Apache National Forest and the Fort Apache Indian Reservation, this wilderness was and is essentially aboriginal country, and that part of Mount Baldy within the reservation is being preserved in a primitive state by the Apaches themselves, thus effectively enlarging the nearly 7,000 acres of the designated wilderness.

On volcanic Mount Baldy, hikers may ascend to 11,590 feet, observing for themselves the same scenes that pioneer scouts called a harmonious blend of mountain, forest, valley, and stream. Two main trails lead to the summit of the mountain. One follows the east fork of the Little Colorado River and is four and a half miles long. The other follows the west fork and is five miles long. One-day hiking and horseback trips are conducted into the wilderness, with most visitors returning to campgrounds outside the boundary. No motorized equipment is permitted, summer or winter.

The forest through which one ascends Mount Baldy is Canadianlike, composed of Douglas, white, and corkbark fir, blue and Engelmann spruce, and white and ponderosa pine. Trails occasionally traverse open meadows, which are ringed with quaking aspen trees. These different environments support grouse, turkeys, squirrels, rabbits, deer, elk, wildcats, and other animals in a cool setting where the skies are nearly always clear. The U.S. Forest Service provides information, exhibits, and naturalist-conducted hikes at the nearby Big Lake Information Center. There are several campgrounds in the vicinity; food and lodging may be obtained in the nearby communities of Greer, Springerville, and Alpine.

Information: Supervisor, Apache National Forest, Box 640, Springerville, Arizona 85938.

🌲 **Petrified Forest National Park,** east of Holbrook, Arizona, is almost entirely devoid of living trees. Most of the park, 50,260 acres, has been set aside as true wilderness, so wide open that no trails are necessary. This is the heart of the Painted Desert, a landscape of highly colored hills and valleys where a hiker can see for miles. The soil of sand and clay, with scant moisture content, supports a sparse vegetation of yuccas, sunflowers, cactuses, asters, and paintbrushes, to mention the more colorful species. The vegetation supports small mammals such as cottontails, jackrabbits, and squirrels, and they in turn are food for bobcats and coyotes. Even the tree-loving porcupine manages to get along here. So the Painted Desert is a functioning ecosystem not nearly as desolate as it appears. It also abounds in fossils, including petrified wood, and the remains of prehistoric Indian cultures, none of which can by law be disturbed; these objects constitute interesting discoveries as one explores the bizarre hills.

This wilderness is one of the most accessible; Interstate 40 passes through the park, and paved roads lead nearly to the boundaries of the designated wilderness units. Folders, maps, and booklets are available. Picnic sites, food, souvenirs, and supplies may be obtained. The park is closed at night, hence no camping or accommodations are available. Holbrook, twenty-seven miles away, has a full range of facilities and services for travelers. Use of the wilderness is subject to reservations, permit, and specific regulations.

Information: Superintendent, Petrified Forest National Park, Holbrook, Arizona 86025.

🌲 A large series of lava flows in the Mount Taylor region, southwest of Grants, New Mexico, is currently being reviewed for establishment as a protected area. Known as **Grants Lava Flow,** the area is ranked as one of the classic examples of recent extrusive volcanism in the United States. Present are pressure ridges, cinder cones, fumaroles, ice caves, and some extraordinary fresh-appearing lava flows. The area under study covers some 120,000 acres, sections of which are extremely rough lava, giving the name "El Malpais," Spanish for "bad country." At this writing, however, the question of which federal agency or agencies will eventually administer the area is not resolved. Most of the land is currently under the Bureau of Land Management, U.S. Department of the Interior.

3. CANYONS

Canyons are distinctive habitats; to the hiker they represent a confined environment with limited vision ahead, and the mystery of what lies around the next bend can be one of the most compelling of wilderness lures. They are distinctive also because of the shelter they give to vegetation and wildlife; indeed some plants such as the Douglas fir remain as relict species in canyons where all their plateau neighbors have been eliminated for hundreds of miles around by changing climatic conditions. For all their immensity and beauty, however, the most memorable sight might be a redbud tree in full bloom in a red-rock amphitheater. Though mostly arid, they often possess idyllic springs that filter through beds of moss and fern and orchid.

🌲 The **Sycamore Canyon Wilderness** is typical. Eroded into the southern edge of the vast Colorado Plateau, the canyon itself is reached over a gravel road twelve miles north of Clarkdale, Arizona. Sycamore Creek south of Parsons Spring is clear, cool, often ponded in deep pools, and supports a dense vegetation of sycamores, willows, alders, head-high yellow columbines, wild grape tangles, and banks of grass and watercress. The trail along Sycamore Creek weaves in and out of this humid environment, at times passing through arid open patches of mesquite and cactus that grow away from the influence of the stream. One minute the hiker observes a black phoebe at the water's edge, and the next sees the bright yellow flash of a hooded oriole as it swoops into a catclaw bush. Such goings-on delay the perceptive naturalist, and a prospective trip into this canyon should be planned on a time-delay rather than a hurry-up basis.

The trail in the canyon leads upstream, and if the hiker climbs high enough he emerges on the lava-capped plateau near the town of Williams—having traveled from an elevation of 3,600 feet, in typical desert surroundings, to 7,000 feet, where a cool forest of ponderosa pine and alligator juniper prevails. The red, white, and yellow rock formations through which he passes are identical to strata comprising the walls of the Grand Canyon, not far north.

No roads or tramways mar the solitude of this 49,575-acre wilderness, and visitors take advantage of the delightful riparian groves or rocky coves to make their camps. However, within the area of year-long stream flow no camping is allowed, only day-use activities such as fishing, swimming and sightseeing. North of Parsons Spring, camping is permitted with a stay limit of fourteen days. Biological observations are especially rewarding in this cliff-bound oasis, and one is struck by the bright plumages of such birds as the all-red Cooper's tanager and the blue grosbeak. Sycamore Canyon is a sanctuary for action—swimming, climbing, photography—or inaction, depending on the mood of the moment. Food and lodging are available at various places in the Verde Valley.

Information: Supervisor, Coconino National Forest, Box 1268, Flagstaff, Arizona 86001.

🌲 At **Canyon de Chelly National Monument,** near Chinle, Arizona, the gorges are cut into deep red De Chelly sandstone, the walls often sheer and smooth for hundreds of vertical feet. This is in the heart of Indian country, that of the Pueblo cliff dwellers of the past, whose thousand-year-old ruins remain in hidden recesses, and that of the modern Navajos. The monument was proclaimed with the consent of the Navajo Tribal Council, and the Indians retain all title to the land. Some continue to live in the canyons and pursue their normal activities—hence a nonresident must inquire at Monument headquarters and obtain a guide and permit before embarking upon any extended hikes or four-wheel-drive trips among these canyons and plateaus. As the lands are not public, the rules of free access to national park lands do not apply. Guide service may be arranged for at the visitor center. Visitors may travel freely down the White House Trail, which provides an opportunity to observe the inner-canyon environment and some of the ruins. Roads on the north and south rims have numerous overlooks that provide scenic views of the canyons and cliff dwellings. But other than this it would be advisable to hire a guide for trips to remote points of interest.

Camping, accommodations, exhibits, self-guiding trails, and four-wheel-drive tours are available in this 83,840-acre area. Access is via Arizona Route 63 and a side road from Chinle.

Information: Superintendent, Canyon de Chelly National Monument, Box 588, Chinle, Arizona 86503.

🌲 Sixty air miles northwest of Canyon de Chelly is another scenic locality that owes its prominence, at least in part, to the red De Chelly sandstone.

The Navajo Tribal Park Service, recognizing the extraordinary values of wild and colorful lands within the Navajo Indian Reservation, is developing a system of reserves, of which first and foremost is **Monument Valley Tribal Park,** located astride the Arizona-Utah line. It is accessible on a side road that branches off U.S. Route 163 at a point twenty miles north of Kayenta, Arizona. From a visitor center that contains exhibits, crafts, and observation terraces one gets an exceptionally fine view of the valley, with its celebrated monoliths, The Mittens, in the foreground. A fourteen-mile dirt road takes visitors into the heart of the park, past Navajo hogans, sheer crimson cliffs, the Totem Pole, reddish sand dunes, and observation points from which the valley never looks the same. Limited accommodations are available near the park and at Kayenta.

Information: Chairman, Navajo Tribal Parks Commission, Window Rock, Arizona 86515.

The largest and best-known gorge in the Southwest, if not in the world, is the Grand Canyon, preserved in **Grand Canyon National Park, Grand Canyon National Monument, Marble Canyon National Monument,** and Lake Mead National Recreation Area. Color and stratification, from Precambrian times near the earth's beginnings, to relatively recent times, are outstanding, but immensity is the most impressive feature. The elevational range in this region, from the bottom of the canyon at 2,400 feet to the summit of the San Francisco Peaks, fifty miles to the southeast, is such that six of the world's seven life zones are represented, from the near-tropics to the Arctic. Shaped like a giant bowl, four to eighteen miles wide, the Grand Canyon contains springs, seeps, waterfalls, and cascades as much as 1,000 feet high, plateaus, mountains, caves, alcoves, and the Colorado River, which is now somewhat tamed because of dams upstream.

In this vast wilderness—the combined area totals 897,935 acres—are hundreds of miles of trails. Travel through piñon-juniper-ponderosa-pine forest on the south rim, or spruce-fir-pine forest on the higher north rim, is an exhilarating experience. Tassel-eared squirrels leap among the trees. Canyon wrens clamber singing down the sheer rock faces. Bright glades of blue lupine liven the forest shadows. Below the rim are cactus flats, fern-covered springs, old mines, the Havasupai Indian village, and a hundred unexpected natural worlds.

Within the canyon, nineteen trails have been constructed by man—perhaps even more—some dropping as much as 6,000 feet to the Colorado River at the bottom. The Kaibab and Bright Angel trails are maintained for use by men and mules. Other trails are maintained to minimum standards for

Colorado River and Canyonlands National Park
from Dead Horse Point State Park, Utah.

wilderness hiking. These attract people who descend into remote and
seldom-visited parts of the canyon. High temperatures and the unreliability
of springs are only a few of the hazards faced. A worthwhile wilderness jaunt
here requires careful planning, because the margin for error or miscalculation
can be rather small. Climbing *out* of the canyon is an arduous task even if
nothing goes wrong. The National Park Service has available trail maps,
park folders, a guide to wilderness trails, and other descriptive data. All trails
are subject to reservation and hikers should check on registration requirements prior to the start of trips. In addition, there are books and booklets for
sale on geology, flora, history, and prehistory. Campgrounds are available on
the north and south rims of the main canyon, at the Monument, within the
canyon at Bright Angel and Havasu canyons, and in the adjacent Kaibab
National Forest. Food, lodging, supplies, and services may be obtained in and
near the park.

Information: Superintendent, Grand Canyon National Park, Grand
Canyon, Arizona 86023.

🌲 Upstream from the Grand Canyon are spectacular gorges along the Colorado River. One of them, Glen Canyon, has been inundated by a reservoir, but back away from the shoreline and the motorboats are parts of the **Glen Canyon National Recreation Area,** Arizona-Utah, that have wilderness values. For example, the Waterpocket Fold, one of the most famous geologic features of the Southwest, is partly preserved in the recreation area, and it is a place of quiet canyons, sheer cliffs, and exceedingly colorful terrain. (See also Capitol Reef National Park.) But beyond virtually any arm of the reservoir, the explorer can penetrate wilderness for as far as he likes, and come upon unusual sights, such as Rainbow Bridge and Navajo Mountain. Miles of dry stream beds lead into remote corners where patches of willow, cottonwood, and saltcedar provide a contrast to the red sandstone cliffs. Much of the landscape is simply unvegetated "slick rock," and on the hiking trails there is a great deal of up-and-down travel. Altogether the recreation area contains 1,226,880 acres.

Access is via U.S. Route 89, and Utah routes 95, 273, and 276. Facilities and services available include: campgrounds, picnic sites, marinas, restaurants, camp stores, and limited lodging. The nearest accommodations are at Page, Arizona, or Hanksville, Utah.

Information: Superintendent, Glen Canyon National Recreation Area, Box 1507, Page, Arizona 86040.

🌲 The U.S. Bureau of Land Management has designated an 18,909-acre section in Paria Canyon, on the Arizona-Utah border, as the **Paria Canyon Primitive Area.** The backpacker finds himself in singularly beautiful red-rock canyons as much as 1,500 feet deep and as little as twelve feet wide. A natural arch in Wrather Canyon is 200 feet high. According to the Bureau of Land Management, a backpack trip down the canyon normally requires at least five days to reach Lees Ferry landing on the Colorado River if the adventurer spends any time exploring side canyons and browsing among rocky ledges for remains of Indian encampments. Horses will encounter difficulty with soft sand through portions of the canyon—such as the narrows, but other areas are conducive to trail riding. The bureau also suggests a one-day hiking descent into Wire Pass via Goblin's Stairwell, thence north up the Buckskin Dive through Kaibab Grotto back to the entrance road, a total of six miles. Travelers in deep canyons should, of course, remain alert to the possibility of flash floods; and in fact, the canyon is closed during July and August, the major flash-flood season. Although animals are not abundant, there are deer, bobcats, bighorns, mountain lions, and songbirds in the canyons. Water is available from springs and from the Paria River, though care should be taken

Monument Valley Tribal Park, Utah-Arizona.

to treat it for drinking purposes. Registration at the head of the canyon is required before entry.

In this remote area there are no amenities. Access is forty-three miles east of Kanab, Utah, off U.S. Route 89.

Information: State Director, U.S. Bureau of Land Management, Federal Building, Phoenix, Arizona 85025.

🌲 For thirty miles en route to Lees Ferry and the Colorado River or on their way to the north rim of the Grand Canyon, travelers across Arizona's House Rock Valley skirt the Vermillion Cliffs, a thousand-foot precipice of colorful rock layers. The blackbrush-covered plain over which U.S. Route 89-A passes leads up to this great red wall, which has been designated the **Vermillion Cliffs Natural Area** by the U.S. Bureau of Land Management. The purpose of thus setting aside 50,495 acres is to assure that scenic values of the cliffs will be protected. Exhibits, picnic sites, and other facilities are planned. The nearest accommodations are east toward Lees Ferry or west at Jacob Lake.

Information: State Director, U.S. Bureau of Land Management, Federal Building, Phoenix, Arizona 85025.

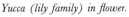
Yucca (lily family) in flower.

Dawn in Goblin Valley, near Capitol Reef National Park, Utah.

🌲 **Canyonlands National Park** was established in 1964 to preserve a vast region of canyons, and more than canyons: pinnacles, needlelike spires, upheaved domes, fractured valleys, arches, richly colored cliffs, Indian ruins, and a flora and fauna characteristic of elevated arid regions. There are a few trails and Jeep roads, beyond which getting lost is quite easy. The Green and Colorado rivers meander through deep-red sandstone mazes as though entrapped, and finally join near the Land of the Standing Rocks. Canyonlands National Park is so large, 337,258 acres, and intricate that years would be required to explore it all. In summer the heat of the sun focused into box canyons turns them into veritable open-air furnaces, and the scarcity of water simply doubles the jeopardy for hikers. In spring or autumn the environment is more hospitable. For less hardy wilderness hikers the Canyonlands can be enjoyed without having to undertake a major expedition. Short forays from access routes near Monticello and Moab can be taken into the park, which is approached via U.S. Route 163. Although the park has campgrounds, all food and supplies must be obtained outside the park, and are available in neighboring towns. Accommodations may be secured in Moab and Monticello.

Information: Superintendent, Canyonlands National Park, 446 South Main Street, Moab, Utah 84532.

🌲 **Dead Horse Point State Park** preserves a portion of the high rim on the edge of the Canyonlands. It is reached by proceeding north from Moab on U.S. Route 163 for fifteen miles, then turning west over twenty-two miles of paved road. Early morning is best for a visit because the haze is apt to be less. A few hungry antelope ground squirrels and Say chipmunks have learned that man is a dispenser of food so campers or picnickers may have company at their tables. The park has an information center. The nearest food, lodging, and supplies are in Moab.

Information: Utah State Division of Parks and Recreation, Salt Lake City, Utah 84116.

🌲 A region of large canyons and immense sandstone towers is **Zion National Park,** in southwestern Utah. Its 147,035 acres consist of the Kolob Terrace with sheer scarlet walls that stretch human belief, deeply cut tributaries of the Virgin River, heavily forested plateaus, and white rock domes so cracked and layered that they have a checkerboard effect. Numerous trails, easy and strenuous, long and short, reach such destinations as The Narrows (where canyon walls literally close in overhead), Angels Landing, Emerald Pools, Weeping Rock, and Kolob Arch. The West Rim and East Rim trails require a good deal of exercise to traverse, but the views are eminently compensating. The park and nearby communities provide full services and facilities. Access is on Utah Route 15.

Information: Superintendent, Zion National Park, Springdale, Utah 84767.

🌲 By contrast to the Utah red-rock country is **Black Canyon of the Gunnison National Monument,** eleven miles east of Montrose, Colorado, where the Gunnison River has cut through very old, dark-colored rock. Though somber in color, this narrow gorge is one of the most dizzying in the Southwest, its cliffs in places virtually sheer for more than 2,000 feet. At the narrowest point the canyon walls are only 1,300 feet apart. Some walls are patterned with bands of granite and gneiss, neatly sheared by the abrasive power of tumbling stream boulders. The downstream western end is less precipitous than the main canyon, but it is still rough enough to provide a challenge for serious hikers. Climbing into or through the canyon requires considerable exertion and in some cases technical climbing experience. Although access is limited, hikers can descend to the river on a primitive trail from Gunnison Point. Entering by means of the river requires fording, clambering over rocks, and negotiating steep walls. In all cases, it is wise to discuss with a park ranger the current condition of the routes. Camping permits are required for all overnight trips. Less strenuous hikes may be taken along the rims, both of which are easily accessible and have campgrounds.

The Monument's 13,690 acres contain twelve miles of this canyon. Access is by means of side roads off U.S. Route 50 on the south and Colorado Route 92 on the north.

Information: Superintendent, Black Canyon of the Gunnison National Monument, Box 1648, Montrose, Colorado 81401.

Double Arch, Arches National Park, Utah.

4. HIGH PLATEAUS

In few places has so much of the world's land surface—some 150,000 square miles—been lifted so high with as little disturbance as the Colorado Plateau. In places the rock strata have been raised to more than 10,000 feet elevation, and although occasionally bent, warped, and broken, they still convey a scenic horizontality of layer on layer. Erosion, of course, commenced as soon as the strata were exposed to weather, and the "remnant landscape," now in the process of disintegration, contains shapes and forms that stimulate human sensibilities. The region is mostly cool and well forested; it has arid aspects because of low rainfall or because runoff from snowmelt and cloudbursts seeps into porous lava layers and drains away. Still there are numerous streams, and even a few pleasant lakes here and there.

🌲 One of the most pristine portions of the Colorado Plateau, long accessible only by dirt road but now reached over paved Utah Route 24, is **Capitol Reef National Park.** Though it has no "reefs," except in the sense of rocky barriers to human travel, it does have prominent light-colored domes that look like capitol buildings, set in mazes of red cliffs and canyons. This park preserves the Waterpocket Fold, an immense doubling up, or flexure, of colorful rock layers along a 150-mile front. Now breached by erosion, the upfolded rocks are cut into domes, spires, pinnacles, gorges, and multiple-hued cliffs. There are even natural bridges.

Although the road goes through the Fold where the Fremont River has cut a passage, very little else is accessible by automobile in this geologic wonderland. The pine and sagebrush country is a boon to naturalists who strap on packs and head out into the red-rock wilderness. They hike through copses of juniper, mountain mahogany, and buffalo berry, start up deer and rabbits, observe foxes, wildcats, eagles, hawks, owls, reptiles, and a host of other wild animals. The geologic phenomena are some of the finest of their type, and the great cliffs with "desert varnish" or sandstone crossbedding make it seem as though nature had sculptured an endless variety of friezes and bas-reliefs. And all this is spread over an area of 241,865 acres.

Weeks could be spent poking into the hidden corners of Capitol Reef, but it is not an easy land, and careful preparations should be made. Labyrinthine passages, box canyons, and high ledges are potentially perilous. But with the advice of park rangers, excellent exploration trips can be worked out in detail. Shorter trips are also available and travelers should consult or purchase maps at the headquarters visitor center. Campgrounds and accommodations are available in or near the park.

Information: Superintendent, Capitol Reef National Park, Torrey, Utah 84775.

The high plateaus of southern Utah are capped in places by pink, yellow, orange, and red rocks that were laid down in relatively recent lake environments and then uplifted by earth movements. Presently at elevations of 8,000 to 10,000 feet, these rocks have eroded into bright cliffs and vivid escarpments visible for a hundred miles or more in southern Utah and northern Arizona. They also stand out in contrast to somber forests of spruce and fir, or neighboring black lava rocks. Being soft and friable, the layers weather into bizarre topographic forms. The two most spectacular concentrations, preserved in **Bryce Canyon National Park** and **Cedar Breaks National Monument,** may be reached by paved roads, except when temporarily blocked by heavy snows in winter. A network of trails allows explorers to walk the rims or descend into canyons that look like enclaves of red stone goblins. It is some of the most unusual hiking terrain in the Southwest and these are perhaps the most brilliantly colored canyons anywhere. Surroundings so vividly orange and in such varied shapes will delay most hikers and especially the photographer.

Cedar Breaks is especially known for mountain meadows richly filled with wild flowers, among them columbine, bluebell, gentian, larkspur, lupine, and Indian paintbrush. In the cool forests live Steller jays, mule deer, marmots, weasels, badgers, porcupines, squirrels, and chipmunks—to name a few of the more conspicuous species.

Exhibits, self-guiding trails, and camping are available in both areas, as well as additional opportunities to explore wild places in the surrounding Dixie National Forest. Access to Bryce Canyon is via Utah Route 12, and to Cedar Breaks a short distance north of Utah Route 14. Accommodations are available at Bryce Canyon and in nearby towns.

Information: Superintendent, Bryce Canyon National Park, Bryce Canyon, Utah 84717; Cedar Breaks National Monument is under the administration of the Superintendent, Zion National Park, Springdale, Utah 84767.

🌲 In eastern Utah, the reddish-brown Entrada sandstone has been rather uniformly cracked on a massive scale and the result is a series of deep, narrow canyons separated by little more than narrow walls, or "fins." Many of these walls, growing thinner with erosion, have been breached, with the resultant formation of a great number of sandstone arches, the largest concentration in the world. These natural sculptures, protected in **Arches National Park,** provide extraordinary destinations for hikers. It is only one and a half miles, for example, from a parking area, up gentle slick-rock slopes, through juniper-sprinkled washes, and out to the edge of a sandstone amphitheater to Delicate Arch, sixty-five feet high. From another parking point, one may walk through the Devils Garden and see several arches, including Landscape Arch, the world's longest at 291 feet.

In addition to hiking among arches, one can go up desert streams, over reddish sand dunes, through deep canyons, past balanced rocks, and beside flower-lined springs. By keeping a sharp lookout, travelers can see scarlet flowering cactuses, flights of magpies, beaver tracks in sandy stream beds, and—who knows?—perhaps an arch that has never been seen by man.

The size of the park is 73,233 acres. It is entered from U.S. Route 163 four miles north of Moab. There is a campground in the park but no lodging; Moab has excellent motels.

Information: Superintendent, Arches National Park, 446 South Main, Moab, Utah 84532.

🌲 Throughout much of its course, the Colorado River and its tributaries have carved canyons and valleys of diverse character from the horizontal rock layers of southwestern plateaus. West of Grand Junction, Colorado, near U.S. Route 50 and Interstate 70, a massive rim of sandstone lies eroded into pinnacles, coves, and cliffs on a gigantic scale. Years ago a twenty-two-mile scenic road was constructed in the forest along this escarpment, and 17,669 acres of the most picturesque terrain set aside as **Colorado National Monument.** This northeast edge of the Uncompahgre Plateau provides a high point from which to look down into a broad agricultural valley and white cliffs beyond. The rim rock itself represents a bold succession of strata from the earliest geologic eras. The first-known skeleton of the amphibious dinosaur *Brachiosaurus*, perhaps the largest reptile (up to fifty tons) that ever lived, was excavated near here.

Hiking through this dry woodland, one can examine red fin walls, caves, and towering monoliths, explore hidden canyons, and get a firsthand glimpse of the ecology of a semiarid upland. Within the ecosystem are towhees, piñon jays, canyon wrens, foxes, coyotes, porcupines, and deer, all circulating within a dense forest of piñon, juniper, cactus, yucca, sagebrush, mountain mahogany, and serviceberry. Wild flowers are conspicuous and during much of the summer great clumps of yellow rabbitbrush bloom.

Trails pass through both mesa and canyon environments, and there are ample self-guiding trails, exhibits, and publications to provide an understanding of the natural history. The Monument has one campground and two picnic areas; lodging may be secured in Grand Junction and nearby communities. Permits are required for overnight wilderness travel and no wood fires are permitted.

Information: Superintendent, Colorado National Monument, Fruita, Colorado 81521.

Mesa Verde National Park, at 6,000 to 8,600 feet elevation in southwestern Colorado, has thousands of fragile and irreplaceable prehistoric Indian sites. For that reason, backpacking and wilderness camping are prohibited. Even hiking is restricted and persons found away from developed areas or designated trails, or entering cliff dwellings when not accompanied by a uniformed National Park Service employee will be subject to penalties provided for in Title 36 of the Code of Federal Regulations. However, more than thirteen miles of trails have been specifically designated as hiking trails, and these lead to scenic viewpoints, canyon rims, deep gorges, and dense woods. Roads provide access to ruins and other points of interest. To a large degree this forested tableland remains as it was when the early Indians lived here, a plateau covered with piñon pine, juniper, ponderosa pine, and oak. Though subjected to heavy snows and cold winters, it is a rich forest, and the Indians found in it what they needed: food from vegetation and wildlife, clothing from animal skins, and medicines from various natural sources. They found shelter in overhangs, which also provided protection from enemies and cold winter winds.

Each canyon, promontory, and hidden glade has its secrets. Undoubtedly there are prehistoric ruins as yet undiscovered; the sites or structures known reach a density in places of 100 per square mile.

Trails in this 52,074-acre park enable hikers to explore the mesas and descend into canyons. Campgrounds, food, and lodging are available, and a full range of outdoor opportunities is provided in the nearby San Juan National Forest. Museums and guided tours also exist within the park, and road access has been provided to the major ruins such as Cliff Palace. The park is reached on a spur road that leads south of U.S. Route 160 near Cortez, Colorado.

Information: Superintendent, Mesa Verde National Park, Colorado 81330.

🌲 A proposal has been made, and the U.S. Bureau of Land Management is studying it, to establish a 384,000-acre "archeological wilderness" in the Grand Gulch–Cedar Mesa area of Utah. As of this writing, the bureau has designated 26,629 acres as the **Grand Gulch Primitive Area.** The idea is to associate the long-gone primitive human activity of those days with the still intact rugged physical setting in which it took place. The belief is that such wilderness areas where man evolved in harmony with nature are significant evidence of human interaction with environmental systems and should be preserved in a special manner. In such a milieu, modern man might be able to experience some of the problems faced by primitive man. All of which could lead to a new dimension of understanding of both man and environment.

In any case, considering the extensive remains of early human cultures, visitors could learn a great deal about life in primitive times, for example, uses of plants and animals, needs for tools and weapons, creativity, and interaction with other tribes. The area consists of arid plateaus dissected by erosion, escarpments of crossbedded sandstone, giant alcoves, deep, twisting canyons, slick-rock domes, springs, and a vegetative cover of juniper, yucca, piñon pine, sagebrush, mountain mahogany, oak, and numerous other species. This abundance of plants is very likely to have been utilized extensively by the Indian occupants, who are referred to in archeological terms as the Anasazi. The Indians must also have hunted deer, bighorns, rabbits, and the other abundant mammals, as well as birds and reptiles on the mesa and in the canyons.

Indians occupied the area from about A.D. 100 to nearly 1300. No one knows how many lived here at any one time, but the number of identifiable sites that remain—cliff dwellings, burial grounds, granaries, surface ruins, and the like—amounts to a concentration of thirty to sixty per square mile. In addition, there are numerous pictograph panels, some of them now delicate and fragile.

Obviously this whole proposed wilderness with its overlay of prehistoric values, is worthy of careful consideration, whatever its density is to be. One certainty is that, in accordance with the Antiquities Act, the archeological sites must be preserved. The area remains relatively inaccessible. No camping or accommodations exist; approach is via Utah routes 95 and 261.

Information: District Manager, Bureau of Land Management, 284 South First West, Box 1327, Monticello, Utah 84535.

PART V

The Rocky Mountains

1. CANADIAN ROCKIES AND ADJACENT RANGES

1. Banff National Park, Alberta
2. Kootenay National Park, British Columbia
3. Yoho National Park, British Columbia
4. Glacier National Park, British Columbia
5. Mount Revelstoke National Park, British Columbia
6. Jasper National Park, Alberta
7. Hamber Provincial Park, British Columbia
8. Willmore Wilderness Park, Alberta
9. Rocky Mountains Forest Reserve, Alberta
10. White Goat Wilderness, Alberta
11. Siffleur Wilderness, Alberta
12. Ghost River Wilderness, Alberta
13. Mount Robson Provincial Park, British Columbia
14. Muncho Lake Provincial Park, British Columbia
15. Stone Mountain Provincial Park, British Columbia
16. Kwadacha Wilderness Provincial Park, British Columbia
17. Carp Lake Provincial Park, British Columbia
18. Bowron Lake Provincial Park, British Columbia
19. Wells Gray Provincial Park, British Columbia
20. Mount Assiniboine Provincial Park, British Columbia
21. Kokanee Glacier Provincial Park, British Columbia
22. St. Mary's Alpine Provincial Park, British Columbia
23. Monashee Provincial Park, British Columbia
24. Okanagan Mountain Provincial Park, British Columbia
25. Top of the World Provincial Park, British Columbia
26. Elk Lakes Provincial Park, British Columbia
27. Waterton Lakes National Park, Alberta

2. NORTHERN ROCKIES

28. Bob Marshall Wilderness, Montana
29. Scapegoat Wilderness, Montana
30. Mission Mountains Primitive Area, Montana
31. Cabinet Mountains Wilderness, Montana
32. Glacier National Park, Montana
33. Selway-Bitterroot Wilderness, Montana
34. Humbug Spires Primitive Area, Montana
35. Anaconda-Pintlar Wilderness, Montana
36. Salmon River Breaks Primitive Area, Idaho
37. Idaho Primitive Area, Idaho
38. Hells Canyon–Seven Devils Scenic Area, Idaho
39. Sawtooth National Recreation Area and Wilderness, Idaho
40. National Bison Range, Montana
41. Gates of the Mountains Wilderness, Montana

3. MIDDLE ROCKIES

1. Yellowstone National Park, Montana–Wyoming–Idaho
2. Spanish Peaks Wilderness, Montana
3. Bear Trap Canyon Primitive Area, Montana
4. Absaroka Primitive Area, Montana
5. Beartooth Primitive Area, Montana
6. Bighorn Canyon National Recreation Area, Montana-Wyoming
7. North Absaroka Wilderness, Wyoming
8. Washakie Wilderness, Wyoming
9. Teton Wilderness, Wyoming
10. Grand Teton National Park, Wyoming
11. Glacier Primitive Area, Wyoming
12. Bridger Wilderness, Wyoming
13. Popo Agie Primitive Area, Wyoming
14. Cloud Peak Primitive Area, Wyoming
15. Red Rock Lakes National Wildlife Refuge, Montana
16. Craters of the Moon National Monument, Idaho

17. High Uintas Primitive Area, Utah
18. Dinosaur National Monument, Utah-Colorado

4. SOUTHERN ROCKIES

19. Eagles Nest Wilderness, Colorado
20. Flat Tops Wilderness, Colorado
21. Rawah Wilderness, Colorado
22. Mount Zirkel Wilderness, Colorado
23. Rocky Mountain National Park, Colorado
24. Maroon Bells–Snowmass Wilderness, Colorado
25. West Elk Wild Area, Colorado
26. Powderhorn Primitive Area, Colorado
28. Wilson Mountains Primitive Area, Colorado
29. Weminuche Primitive Area, Colorado
30. Great Sand Dunes National Monument, Colorado
31. Uncompahgre Primitive Area, Colorado

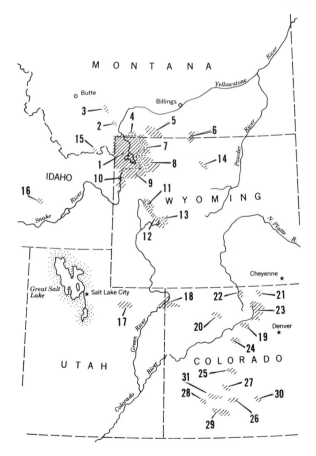

1. CANADIAN ROCKIES AND
ADJACENT RANGES

The sheer immensity of the Canadian Rockies and the size of wilderness areas preserved within them strikes visitors as an extraordinary anomaly in the Industrial Age. But Canada began to conserve its pristine scenery rather early, and **Banff National Park** was established in 1887 as the first Canadian national park. It has grown in size to 1,640,960 acres, and when considered with the contiguous Jasper, Yoho, and Kootenay national parks, and provincial parks and reserves, the total of connected reservations is well over 6 million acres, or more than 10,000 square miles, larger than Massachusetts.

From this it may be concluded that a vast amount of Canada's wilderness remains intact. True, Jasper, Banff, and Yoho national parks are bisected by a transcontinental railway; the Trans-Canada Highway goes through Banff, Yoho, and Glacier; and there are townships and tramways in some of the most scenic locations. Nevertheless, the wilderness (including bears and bighorn sheep) comes right down to the edge of these developed centers, which means that a hiker departing for the interior can be assured of getting into wild country soon after leaving his point of departure.

A splendid system of 700 miles of trails in Banff, most of them following stream courses beneath towering mountain ranges, is open for public use. The streams themselves present attractive displays, especially where they plunge over rocky terraces in torrential cascades. Some are glacial outwash streams gritty and colored by sediments. Some are so vigorous they leave wide gravel valleys through which the water flows in a braided pattern. In places water issues as hot springs, or is frozen in tons of ice that cling like blue-white cascades to the cliffs. Some glacial lakes, such as Lake Louise, are emerald green, some are milky blue, others almost gray. The hiker is never very far from water, in one form or another.

Nor from wildlife, though he may not find it as readily discernible as the ubiquitous streams and falls. Water ouzels, which spend their time either near or under the water, may be difficult to hear above the roar of falls, but should be looked for on the smaller tumbling streams. Ducks and geese may be found on lakes; warblers, thrushes, and kinglets in the forest canopy;

Avens, Jasper National Park, Alberta.

creepers and nuthatches on trunks of trees; and golden eagles among high, rocky crags. But perhaps the species most often remembered after travels through this region are Clark's nutcrackers, Canada jays, and magpies. The hiker is likely to encounter bears, moose, deer, elk, and bighorns in the Canadian Rockies, in addition to smaller residents such as squirrels, marmots, chipmunks, and porcupines. It takes a sharp eye to spot mountain goats on high-elevation terraces or rocky ledges because they may at first appear to be patches of snow. Newcomers could also have difficulty spotting the pikas, little hares of the high country, even though they hear their piercing call among the piles of rock. Distances are so vast in these Canadian wilds, and the natural features so profuse, that binoculars should be high-priority equipment. For observation of grizzly bears and the rarer wolverines and mountain lions, it may be necessary to reach remote locations in the mountains, and the advice of wardens should be solicited.

Canada's Rocky Mountain wilderness poses some real challenges to human visitors, not only because of hiking distances, but because of elevations (some peaks rise to more than 11,000 feet), sudden weather changes, sheer cliffs of naked rock, and vast ice fields. Hikers intending to make overnight trips into the backcountry or to leave the trails and climb in any mountain areas must register with park authorities. Persons interested in less arduous excursions will find campgrounds, cabins, nature trails, conducted trips, and opportunities for canoe trips, horseback rides, and short hikes. The park is open all year, with peak visitation in July and August.

Excellent highways provide automobile access to points from which hikers may launch their explorations into the wild country. Food and lodging are available at Banff townsite, Lake Louise, and other locations within the park. Information: Superintendent, Banff National Park, Banff, Alberta.

🌲 West of Banff National Park, on Canadian Route 93, is an elongated wilderness astraddle the Vermilion and Brisco ranges. Lying on the western slope of the Rocky Mountains, it is endowed with glaciers, hot springs, and most of the floral and faunal features found in Banff. This is **Kootenay National Park,** 347,580 acres of rugged mountain country clothed with evergreen forests. Lodgepole pine, Douglas fir, and western red cedar grow in the lowlands, while Engelmann spruce and alpine fir survive where conditions permit on the higher slopes. Actually, the forests are not as simply composed as that; there are aspen, birch, alder, juniper, and other species as well, with a shrub layer including blueberry and rhododendron. Summer wild flowers are particularly noteworthy in Kootenay, not only in the green valleys but at high elevations where summer is brief.

Trails lead through valleys of the Kootenay and Vermilion rivers and up a number of important side streams. Hikers and climbers with stamina to challenge the mountain peaks, one of which rises to more than 11,000 feet, must register and obtain details from the park superintendent. While the main visitor season is between late May and early October, the park is open all year and rewarding wilderness experiences are possible during every month.

In addition to alpine lakes, glaciers, and flower-strewn river valleys, Kootenay offers other scientific and recreation resources: Marble Canyon, a narrow gorge of great depth; the Ochre Beds, deposits colored by iron-impregnated spring waters; and Radium Hot Springs, which flow at a rate of 475,000 gallons a day at a temperature of 113°F. Like most hot springs, including those at Banff and Jasper, these have certain dissolved salts and a slight trace of radioactivity. Any potential therapeutic values depend on so many factors that positive medicinal values cannot be stated with certainty. In any case, a swim in the pools, where the temperature has been cooled to more tolerable levels, is a delightful experience among these mountains.

No hunting is permitted in Canadian national parks, but anglers can try their luck at taking trout from the lakes and streams. Maps, folders, booklets, and literature on the natural history of the Canadian Rockies are available at various points in the parks and surrounding towns. The park is 107 miles north of Cranbrook, British Columbia. Camping and accommodations are available in the park.

Information: Superintendent, Kootenay National Park, Radium Hot Springs, British Columbia.

In many ways, **Yoho National Park** is one of the most idyllic and magnificent of Canada's mountain wilderness areas. Certainly days could be spent in various localities contemplating the shifting shadows as they flow across massive landscapes of mountains, lakes, and streams. "Breathtaking," and "majestic," though clichés in our day, apply to Yoho as much as to any wilderness in North America. The Cree Indians, when they saw this terrain, uttered a single word: *"Yoho!"* which means "How wonderful!"

The park encompasses 324,480 acres on the "roof of the Rockies," with Banff National Park on the east and Kootenay National Park on the south. The Trans-Canada Highway and the Canadian Pacific Railway run through it, but there are 150 miles of improved trails by which to get away from civilization. Networks of trails fan out from scenic points of interest, and reach pure lakes set amid tall spruce and rugged glaciated mountain ranges. One circle of high-altitude hiking may be enjoyed over the Opabin Plateau,

173

around the base of Mount Schaffer to Mary Lake, and return. Another footpath climbs beside Seven Veil Falls and follows a turbulent stream to the attractive green Lake Oesa, cradled among high peaks and delicately colored glaciers; the return is back down a series of switchbacks from Wiwaxy Gap to Lake O'Hara. The views in all directions from these outings are unusually panoramic. However, portions of the routes require mountain-climbing techniques and climbers should not venture without proper ropes and ice axes.

This is only a sample of the high-country hiking in Yoho. Lower-altitude hiking is also enjoyable, and park authorities recommend the Ottertail, Otterhead, and Amiskwi river valleys. One of our favorite rivers is the Kicking Horse, a vivid blue-green stream of glacial origin that starts in the mountains of Yoho and soon after leaving the park joins the Columbia River. Along its broad and grassy banks grow shrubs of cinquefoil decorated with handsome yellow blooms in summer. A visitor can while away hours watching Columbian ground squirrels appearing at the doors of their multiple-exit burrows, barking fierce, sharp, piercing notes, and running to other exits, or creeping out and feeding on the riverside meadows. These antics may be as captivating as watching the more celebrated bears, moose, and mountain goats. And all the while, high overhead, framed by the soft green branches of stately firs, are the mountains that seem to soar as high as the moon.

Yoho has geological interest, too. Ancient Cambrian muds hardened into massive layers of rock that were ultimately lifted thousands of feet above sea level. This part of the Canadian Rockies is a classical open-air textbook in several fields of physical and historical geology, and hence a mecca for naturalists and hikers curious about the history of this planet.

The difference in relief within Yoho National Park—nearly 8,400 feet from the lowest to highest points—accounts in part for the massive mountain spectacle. But there are other spectacular features as well: Takakkaw, Wapta, Twin, and Laughing falls; eroded clay pinnacles called hoodoos; ice fields and cliff glaciers; tundra flower beds; and, of course, an extensive Rocky Mountain fauna. No wonder the Indians cried *"Yoho!"*

Accommodations and campgrounds are available in the park, and details about wilderness trips, including park maps, may be obtained from the park staff. As in other Canadian national parks, protection of landscapes and visitors is provided by park wardens. The area is open in winter, but accommodations and services are limited at that time.

Information: Superintendent, Yoho National Park, Field, British Columbia.

174

🌲 In the Selkirk Range of British Columbia, fifty miles west of Yoho, lies **Glacier National Park** (not to be confused with Glacier National Park, Montana), a place almost classic in its arrangement of lofty mountains draped with snow at high levels and dense coniferous forests below. Coming in on the Trans-Canada Highway or the Canadian Pacific Railway, a human being feels overwhelmed by the immensity of the mountains. The park is well named because it has huge glaciers and snowfields that are the envy of alpinists. The Illecillewaet Glacier, particularly, is impressive: it drops more than 3,500 feet from the snow mass in which it originates, and is altogether ten square miles in area. A steep trail leads to it from the highway. Other trails lead into flower-filled valleys, over high ridges, and near cataracts. Given the size of the area, 333,440 acres, it is easy to imagine the wilderness values, but here the trails are not excessively long and on some trails a hiker may go out and return in a single day. Other trails provide more extended outings.

Campgrounds and accommodations are available within the park.

Information: Superintendent, Glacier National Park, Revelstoke, British Columbia.

🌲 Twelve miles west of Glacier, also on the Trans-Canada Highway, is the 64,000-acre **Mount Revelstoke National Park,** on the western slope of the Selkirk Mountains. A zigzag sixteen-mile road leads from the town of Revelstoke to the mountain summit, from which clear views are to be had of the Monashee and Selkirk ranges, and the valleys of the Columbia and Illecillewaet rivers. More than fifty miles of trails have been constructed, the most popular leading from the summit of Mount Revelstoke to Millar, Eva, and Jade lakes. Vegetation is colorful and luxurious in the meadows in summer, and panoramic views from the trails are framed by sharp-pointed spires of spruce and fir.

There are no campgrounds or accommodations within the park, but the city of Revelstoke has a full range of facilities.

Information: Superintendent, Mount Revelstoke National Park, Revelstoke, British Columbia.

🌲 Between the townsites of Banff and Jasper a scenic highway extends through breathtaking valleys and passes of the Canadian Rockies for 179 miles, entering **Jasper National Park** near the famed Columbia Icefield. Jasper itself is one of Canada's larger parks, 2,688,000 acres, and like the others in these massive mountains is endowed with glaciated peaks,

175

picturesque lakes, roaring rivers, waterfalls, canyons, and quiet woods of Douglas fir, whitebark and lodgepole pine, three kinds of spruce, subalpine fir, aspen, and birch. In summer the park becomes a colorful locale of wild flowers; on high-altitude meadows along the Icefields Parkway, it is easy to observe elephant head and red and yellow paintbrush. Higher yet, hikers have a chance of seeing tundra species in bloom, including heather and forget-me-not. Since Jasper adjoins the central plains of Canada, it also possesses prairie species, such as pasqueflower.

The essential fact for anyone entering Jasper's wilderness is that distances are vast and altitudes vary considerably. Moreover, the park lies about 50° north latitude. Not only must a hiker be prepared for any eventuality of changing weather, he must sustain himself over trail distances of many miles. Of course, there are short trail outings in the vicinity of Jasper townsite—to lakes, camp and picnic sites, Maligne River Canyon (an extremely narrow gorge more than 150 feet deep with walls less than ten feet apart in some places), swamps, bogs, muskegs, dense spruce forests, berry patches, the Miette and Athabasca rivers, and photogenic views of mountains and valleys. But the more hardy hiker, longing for an extended wilderness experience, may follow some of the 700 miles of trails that lead along meandering or cascading streams and over mountain passes. One recommended trip is that to the Tonquin Valley with its Amethyst Lake and Ramparts above. The most overwhelming aspect of these Canadian mountain parks is their geology, for at every hand are cliffs whose strata have been upturned, dramatic reminders of the millions of years required to produce such terrain. Fossils help to measure eons of time that have transpired since they were living creatures in an ancient sea. And the energy required to lift these millions of tons of rock from sea level to 12,000 feet was so great that we have few standards for measurement or comparison. Thus the peaks defy a hiker in more ways than one, and he returns from the wilderness with a new perspective on the relation between man and time.

Some other points of interest in Jasper are accessible by road. On Mount Edith Cavell one gets not only a close-up look at glaciers and glacial terrain, but at Clark's nutcrackers and other birds cavorting nearby in the firs. Maligne Lake, with its quiet emerald waters, tree-lined shores, and mountain backdrop, is one of the most photogenic wilderness lakes in North America. On the eastern side of the park, Miette Hot Springs discharge 125,000 gallons of water a day at temperatures as high as 129°F. The public may swim in a pool filled by these waters, and perhaps nearby observe bighorns that frequent the area.

Hiking and horseback riding are the principal ways of getting into the wilderness; canoes are also welcome but boats with motors are limited or prohibited on most waters. Campgrounds and private lodgings are available within the park, which is accessible on Canadian routes 16 and 93 as well as the Canadian National Railway. In winter the park is suitable for cross-country wilderness skiing; commercial skiing facilities are also available. Two adjacent areas, **Hamber Provincial Park** of British Columbia (see page 178) and the **Willmore Wilderness Park** of Alberta, serve as effective enlargements of the park's wilderness domain. Actually, the province of Alberta is setting up an immense **Rocky Mountains Forest Reserve** along the eastern side of the Canadian Rockies from Jasper south for nearly 300 miles to Waterton Lakes National Park. Although published details are not available at this writing, the reserve includes the **White Goat Wilderness, Siffleur Wilderness,** and **Ghost River Wilderness** on the eastern boundaries of Jasper and Banff national parks.

Information: Superintendent, Jasper National Park, Jasper, Alberta T0E 1E0. For information on Alberta provincial wilderness areas: Director, Provincial Parks Division, Lands and Forests, Natural Resources Building, 109th Street and 99th Avenue, Edmonton, Alberta, T5K 2E1.

🌲 Another provincial wilderness, this one contiguous with the western boundary of Jasper National Park, is the 515,000-acre **Mount Robson Provincial Park,** in British Columbia. As seen from below, Mount Robson reaches 12,972 feet with all the majesty of a giant iceberg rising stolidly from a tumultuous sea. The park is one of the most rugged in the Rockies, with jagged peaks and ridges, precipitous canyons, steep forests, and tumbling cataracts. A great deal can be seen by short walks of a few minutes from Canadian Route 16, which passes through the center of the park. The Fraser River, Robson Falls, and Rainbow Canyon and Falls—the latter a 1,000-foot cascade—are examples. But for the more ardent wilderness-seeker, there are longer trails deep into—or high up into—the backcountry, where as many as fifteen glaciers may be observed, or to such places as the Valley of a Thousand Falls. Mount Robson itself is a substantial challenge for adept and experienced alpinists. Berg Glacier contributes blue-white chunks of ice into the waters of Berg Lake. Caribou may be seen in the high basins, and deer, elk, mountain goats, and bears can be observed at many points in the park. Ptarmigan and grouse are common, and in August the open places have patches of dwarf huckleberries full of fruit. The forests are spruce, fir, pine, birch, and other species. Trout exist in park waters, but fishing is not particularly good in the glacial lakes. Campgrounds and accommodations are available in the park, as well as natural history displays.

Information: Director, Parks Branch, Department of Recreation and

Conservation, Parliament Buildings, Victoria, British Columbia; or Regional Supervisor, Mount Robson Provincial Park, Red Pass, British Columbia.

🌲 A few miles along the crest of the Canadian Rockies south of Mount Robson Provincial Park is **Hamber Provincial Park,** accessible only by trail from Route 93 between Jasper and Banff townsites. The park is bounded on three sides by Jasper National Park and protects similar mountain terrain. There are no facilities in this 60,585-acre park; the nearest food, lodging, and supplies are in Jasper National Park.

Information: Director, Parks Branch, Department of Recreation and Conservation, Parliament Buildings, Victoria, British Columbia.

🌲 Two undeveloped parks along the Alaska Highway are worthy of mention: **Muncho Lake Provincial Park,** 218,461 acres, at Milepost 456; and **Stone Mountain Provincial Park,** 64,000 acres, at Milepost 390 (distances northwest of Dawson Creek, British Columbia). Their scenery and other resources are typically Rocky Mountain—soaring cliffs, high peaks, deep canyons, dense forests, trout-filled lakes, and abundant wildlife that includes mountain sheep, mountain goats, caribou, and grizzly bears. Muncho Lake lies at an elevation of 2,683 feet, but the heavily forested mountains rise around it to some 7,000 feet. The deep blue and green waters contain lake trout, grayling, and other species of interest to fishermen. At Muncho Lake there are camping facilities, accommodations, food, supplies, boat rental, and commercial outfitters who will guide sightseeing, hunting, and fishing parties into the wilderness. The Alaska Highway passes along the east side of Muncho Lake, and directly through the heart of Stone Mountain Park. In the latter area the highest point on the Alaska Highway (4,218 feet above sea level) is reached at Summit Lake, where food and lodging are available. West of that point can be seen erosional pillars of sedimentary rock and the scenic gorge of McDonald Creek.

Information: Director, Parks Branch, Department of Recreation and Conservation, Parliament Buildings, Victoria, British Columbia.

🌲 Fifty miles south of the Alaska Highway and Stone Mountain Provincial Park is the **Kwadacha Wilderness Provincial Park.** No roads lead to it; no food or lodging are available in or near it. In other words—it is remote and virtually untouched, a true wilderness of 414,000 acres. It encompasses headwaters of the Tuchodi, Muskwa, Warneford, and North Kwadacha rivers, the Lloyd George Icefield, and upheaved mountains that rise to 9,750 feet. Among the mammals in their native habitat are timberwolves, grizzly bears, elk, wolverines, caribou, moose, black bears, and mountain goats.

Information: Director, Parks Branch, Department of Recreation and Conservation, Parliament Buildings, Victoria, British Columbia.

🌲 **Carp Lake Provincial Park,** a short distance west of the Canadian Rockies, contains 47,800 acres, a third of which is water. The main features are Carp Lake, War Lake, and an interconnecting navigable waterway. There are also other waterways and wild islands so that this park, when fully developed, will be oriented principally to water recreation: boating, canoeing, fishing, and swimming. Sand beaches and deltas are common. The forest is mostly lodgepole pine mixed with spruce and aspen. The nearest community with food and lodging is McLeod Lake, on Route 97. Access to the park is via gravel road between McLeod Lake and Fort St. James, to the southwest. The eastern part of Carp Lake is reached over a private logging road. The park itself is presently undeveloped.

Information: Director, Parks Branch, Department of Recreation and Conservation, Parliament Buildings, Victoria, British Columbia.

🌲 There is no other wilderness in North America quite like **Bowron Lake Provincial Park,** in the Cariboo Mountains seventy miles east of Quesnel, British Columbia. Its principal attraction is an almost rectangular chain of lakes (Kibbee, Indianpoint, Isaac, McLeary, Lanezi, Sandy, Babcock, Spectacle, and Bowron), which constitutes a loop waterway of seventy-three miles. The Cariboo and Bowron rivers are utilized for part of this distance, and since there are fewer than six miles of portages in the entire distance, the circuit is a canoeist's paradise, especially in September when the insects are reduced and the deciduous trees along the shores are turning color. The route can be navigated between the first part of June and the end of October.

The scenery is stunning, for the route circles a series of mountain ranges (McCabe Ridge, McLeod Peaks, Tediko Peaks, Mowdish Range, and Needle Point Ridge) that rise to 8,200 feet. The upper valleys and peaks are decorated with snow, the lower slopes covered thickly with spruce and alpine fir, with lesser amounts of western hemlock and western red cedar. In places the canoes glide through marshes that are favorite feeding grounds of moose, or past beaver dams where the builders may be at work. Indeed, the quiet passage of canoes does very little to disturb wildlife, and the chances of seeing waterfowl, or bears feeding on salmon, are good. Kamloops trout inhabit all

179

the lakes and streams, and there are also Dolly Varden, kokanee, and Rocky Mountain lake trout; however, the angler's success depends on locality and time of season, and local inquiry might improve the chances for success. There is no hunting in this park because the entire area is a wildlife sanctuary; however, a cameraman can leave his canoe and try photographing caribou, mountain goats, and grizzly bears in the high country. He can also capture the placid mirror lakes of early morning, or the thundering white spectacle of Cariboo Falls, eighty feet high, without venturing very far from his canoe.

Running the circuit is best clockwise because one travels with the water flow. There are several shelters and campsites around the loop; travelers should have their own complete wilderness gear, which, along with canoes, can be rented near the park (arrangements that should be made before arrival). No horses, dogs, cats, or firearms are permitted, and the only road into this 304,000-acre wilderness covers a negligible distance in the vicinity of headquarters. Few hiking trails exist. In most of the park, groups of more than six persons are prohibited. While the circumnavigation of lake and stream routes in this park may seem an idyllic enterprise, it can be dangerous. Park authorities require all visitors traveling the circuit to register at the information center before departing and to check out on returning. Furthermore, they warn: Anyone contemplating taking the circuit trip should come to the park well prepared and well equipped. While it is true that many canoeists with only limited experience have successfully completed the circuit, good physical condition and good equipment are essential. Since Bowron Lake Provincial Park is essentially an undeveloped wilderness, users of the waterway can expect to experience conditions similar to the hazards and hardships of pioneer travel. At least a week, and preferably 10 days, should be allocated to make the trip. It is quite common to be stormbound for several days.

Access is via Route 26 east of Quesnel. Food, lodging, supplies, and campgrounds are available in the vicinity of park headquarters; advance reservation of accommodations and rental equipment is advisable.

Information: Director, Parks Branch, Department of Recreation and Conservation, Parliament Buildings, Victoria, British Columbia; or Regional Supervisor, Bowron Lake Provincial Park, Box 33, Barkerville, British Columbia.

🌲 Unless a traveler goes into the Canadian Rockies specifically for winter activities, he faces a paradox: the wilderness areas are so huge and complex and the summer season so short. **Wells Gray Provincial Park** covers more

Columbian ground squirrel,
Yoho National Park,
British Columbia.

Bighorn ram, Jasper
National Park, Alberta.

Bison, Yellowstone National Park, Wyoming.

than 1.3 million acres, and has few roads or facilities to mar the natural scene. Yet the summer season scarcely begins until July, and by late September the valleys are gold with autumn color. Nor is it easy to visit this park, most of which must be done by backpacking along trails. Yet all these aspects make Wells Gray attractive from the wilderness point of view; the best advice is to plan a trip carefully and make the most of whatever time is available. Perhaps the ideal is to hire licensed guides in the park, but it is possible to explore on one's own.

The park is located in the Cariboo Mountains, 240 air miles northeast of Vancouver. It is distinctly a wilderness of mountain waters because it has five major lakes, all narrow and up to sixteen miles long. In addition, there are connected strings of lakes, and several networks of streams, including nearly all of the upper drainage of the Clearwater River. In consequence, the park is replete with more than a dozen waterfalls of more than routine interest, and is a mecca for anglers and canoeists, although a few waterways are so dangerous that provincial park authorities brand them unsafe for navigation. They do recommend a sixty-four-mile round trip on Clearwater and Azure lakes. Most lakes and streams provide good fishing, with excellent possibilities of seeing grizzly bears, moose, deer, and caribou. Contrary to the policy in most world parks, hunting is permitted here on a limited basis. Half of the park, however, is designated as a Nature Conservancy Area where all natural resources are preserved in their native state. Clearly, the scenic and wilderness values are most impressive at Wells Gray: deep forests of Douglas fir and western red cedar, alpine tundra, glaciers, volcanic craters, lava flows, deep canyons, mineral springs, and a fluctuating population of birds.

Park headquarters may be reached over a gravel road twenty-five miles north of Canadian Route 5 near Clearwater. A dirt road then extends farther into the park to Clearwater Lake. The park may also be reached over gravel road and trail from Blue River, on Route 5, to the east end of Murtle Lake; or by fifty-five miles of gravel road from Route 97 to Mahood Lake. Limited supplies, food, and lodging are available near park headquarters, on the south shore of Mahood Lake, and on approaches to the park. For campers there are several campgrounds within the park.

Information: Director, Parks Branch, Department of Recreation and Conservation, Parliament Buildings, Victoria, British Columbia; or Regional Supervisor, Wells Gray Provincial Park, Box 297, Clearwater, British Columbia.

🌲 Between the southern tips of Banff and Kootenay national parks is a 96,500-acre wedge of land containing famed Mount Assiniboine, a Matterhornlike pyramid that reaches 11,870 feet above sea level. This wedge is preserved by the British Columbia government as **Mount Assiniboine Provincial Park**, a wilderness of jagged peaks, shining glaciers, sparkling lakes, and alpine meadows. The only developments in the park are trails, and the administrative intent is to save the area for wild-land recreation. Accordingly, authorities encourage hiking, fishing, wilderness camping, climbing the several spectacular peaks, and cross-country skiing in winter. With regard to mountain climbing, provincial officials warn that only experienced mountaineers, properly roped and equipped with ice axes, should attempt it or should venture onto glaciers and snowfields. No over-the-ground or over-the-snow vehicles are permitted. Good maps are available.

There are several access routes. One is by trail from the junction of the Vermilion and Simpson rivers, near Route 93 about thirty-five miles north of Radium Hot Springs, British Columbia; this trail proceeds over Ferro Pass to Lake Magog, within the park. Another trail from near Canal Flats on Route 93–95 follows the Cross and Mitchell rivers into the park. From the Alberta side there are rough roads and trails out of Canmore, leading over Assiniboine Pass or via Marvel Lake and Wonder Pass. Limited access is also available from the Sunshine Ski Village near Banff. Guides are available. Accommodations may be obtained at Mount Assiniboine Lodge or in the town of Banff.

Information: Director, Parks Branch, Department of Recreation and Conservation, Parliament Buildings, Victoria, British Columbia; or Regional Supervisor, Wasa Lake Provincial Park, Box 118, Wasa, British Columbia.

🌲 Indians knew the landlocked salmon that spawned in the waters of the Rocky Mountains as *kokanee,* or "red fish." The name has since been applied to other features, including Kokanee Glacier, located in the Selkirk Mountains of British Columbia, eighteen miles northeast of Nelson. From the glacier, at 9,000 feet elevation, waters flow downhill to Kokanee Lake and Kokanee Creek, in which the familiar red fish spawn and live. Much of the 64,000 acres surrounding this site remain almost as wild as when the early Indians came, a region of colorful glacial lakes enclosed among rugged granite peaks. Such is **Kokanee Glacier Provincial Park,** most of which lies above 6,000 feet. As a result, the park is inundated by heavy snows in winter and not released from them until July, and even then the highest peaks remain enclosed in ice and snow. Barren slopes, cliffs, and rock slides characterize the mountains down to the shores of many lakes, or there are grassy meadows and patches of alpine coniferous trees. Dwarf huckleberry and dwarf azalea also flourish.

183

The creeks tumble down to erode broad valleys where forests of Engelmann spruce, lodgepole pine, hemlock, larch, and western red cedar grow. The visitor who hikes the trails along streams through these environments, past waterfalls or over passes all the way up to the glaciers, can station himself on a prominent point and, with binoculars, see some of the caribou, bears, or mountain goats that live here, or hear the notes of pikas, marmots, ground squirrels, and birds. Anglers will find the lakes stocked with cutthroat trout, with fair to good fishing dependent upon the season.

The park is undeveloped, except for a gravel road that leads to the central area. Access to all boundaries is possible via dirt roads, which connect with park trails. The nearest main routes are 3A and 6. Wilderness camping is permitted within the park, but there are no developed campgrounds; these may be found in Kokanee Creek Provincial Park, twelve miles east of Nelson. Food and lodging are available not in the park but in Nelson, Kaslo, Slocan City, New Denver, and other nearby communities.

Information: Director, Parks Branch, Department of Recreation and Conservation, Parliament Buildings, Victoria, British Columbia; or Regional Supervisor, Kokanee Creek Provincial Park, R. R. 3, Nelson, British Columbia.

🌲 A high wilderness thirty miles northwest of Kimberley, British Columbia, has been preserved as **St. Mary's Alpine Provincial Park,** 22,600 acres in a rugged, glaciated granite setting. Although there are bears, caribou, deer, mountain goats, and other mammals, wild animals are not abundant. Neither are fish, with the exception of those in Spade Lake and White Creek. Access is by trail from logging roads west of Kimberley, where food and lodging may be obtained.

Information: Director, Parks Branch, Department of Recreation and Conservation, Parliament Buildings, Victoria, British Columbia.

🌲 A few miles south of Kootenay National Park is a small reserve of 19,800 acres on the Top of the World Plateau, protecting alpine flower displays of meadow cinquefoil, golden fleabane, paintbrush, and other typical Rocky Mountain flowers. This is **Top of the World Provincial Park,** situated between the Hughes Range to the west and the Van Nostrand Range to the east, with Mount Morro forming the highest point—9,553 feet—in the park. Although birds are not too prevalent in this high-altitude park, the larger mammals are present: bears, mountain goats, elk, deer, and bighorns. Trout and char weighing up to eight pounds have been taken from Fish Lake. Of geologic interest are limestone beds containing Silurian and Devonian marine fossils. The intention of British Columbia authorities is to retain the wilderness atmosphere of this park. Consequently, access is by trail only from nearby country roads. The nearest food and lodging are in Kimberley, British Columbia, thirty miles to the southwest on Route 95-A, and other nearby communities.

Information: Director, Parks Branch, Department of Recreation and Conservation, Parliament Buildings, Victoria, British Columbia.

🌲 South of Banff National Park, in a high mountain setting of sharply eroded peaks, glacial lakes ideal for canoeing, streams with crystal-clear waters, and strands of coniferous trees that seem to flow down the mountain slopes, the British Columbia government has set aside 13,900 acres as **Elk Lakes Provincial Park**. It is a subalpine landscape with glaciers that pour icy meltwaters into the Elk Lakes. Marmots and pikas inhabit the more barren upper slopes, and the park has a full complement of larger mammals typical of the Rocky Mountains. Also common are such birds as jays, ravens, crows, hawks, and eagles. Access to the park is north from Sparwood, on Route 3, via sixty-five miles of paved and country roads. The nearest accommodations are at Fernie and vicinity.

Information: Director, Parks Branch, Department of Recreation and Conservation, Parliament Buildings, Victoria, British Columbia.

🌲 In the Monashee Mountains, between the Shuswap River and Arrow Lake in southern British Columbia, lies the 18,566-acre **Monashee Provincial Park**. It lies to the west of the Canadian Rockies and is actually a part of the Columbia Mountains. Mount Revelstoke National Park is not far to the north. High glaciated peaks rise near the park, thus adding spectacle to the scenic lake, forest, and mountain aspects of the region. Monashee is a remote wilderness park and, like most other British Columbia provincial parks, relatively inaccessible. It may be reached by gravel road to Rainbow Lakes and then by trail into the park. The nearest community is Lumby on Provincial Route 6.

Information: Director, Parks Branch, Department of Recreation and Conservation, Parliament Buildings, Victoria, British Columbia.

🌲 In the area of Okanagan Mountain and Squally Point, on Okanagan Lake in southern British Columbia, a 25,500-acre park has been established to protect the natural beauty and ecological values of this lake and forest region. **Okanagan Mountain Provincial Park** consists of rugged bare rocks, sheer cliffs, and deep gorges, as well as seven miles of shoreline on Okanagan Lake. As the park is developed on an intended wilderness theme, facilities are expected to be limited, although a network of trails is likely to make some of the scenic viewpoints and natural features accessible to hikers. Provincial Route 97 passes along the western side of Okanagan Lake, but only country roads approach the park south from Kelowna and north from Penticton.

Information: Director, Parks Branch, Department of Recreation and Conservation, Parliament Buildings, Victoria, British Columbia.

🌲 At the southern end of Alberta, and the southernmost wilderness in the Canadian Rockies, is **Waterton Lakes National Park,** twenty-five miles west of Cardston, Alberta. Its 129,980 acres constitute an abrupt transition from open prairie to rugged glaciated mountain ranges nearly 10,000 feet high. As such it offers wide contrasts which may be observed on the more than 100 miles of trails that reach into the interior. Several short excursions can be taken to places of interest in the vicinity of Waterton Park townsite. Medium-length trails reach wilder terrain. For example, a lakeside trip of five miles leads up Hell Roaring Canyon past waterfalls and through a natural tunnel to Crypt Lake, on the Canada–United States border. Auto access to points farther into the park—Red Rock Canyon, Cameron Lake—provides opportunities to reach other wilderness valleys and ridges. Trails also lead southward into the wild mountains of Glacier National Park, Montana. At high altitude may be found lakes of extraordinary beauty, some stocked with trout. The park is replete with cirque lakes, U-shaped gorges, hanging valleys, and other glacial phenomena. By contrast, in the area to the northeast lies more open prairielike terrain with occasional desertlike badlands.

On the prairies grow maple, alder, birch, willow, and cottonwood. In the mountains are fir, spruce, and pine. Black and grizzly bears inhabit the park, as do bighorns, moose, and mountain goats. It is not uncommon to see a coyote loping across a meadow, a golden-mantled ground squirrel skittering up an open slope, a ruffed grouse slipping through the woods, or ducks and swans on lakes. As in most of the Rockies, the wildlife here offers opportunities for photographers. In addition, the summer wild flowers constitute handsome picture subjects.

Visitors wishing details on fishing, boating, mountain climbing and other activities to which certain restrictions apply should write in advance or call at the park information center in Waterton Park townsite. Picnic areas, campgrounds, and accommodations are available. The park is reached via Montana State Route 17 from the south and Canadian routes 5 and 6 from the north and east. Sightseeing launches carry visitors south on Waterton Lake into Glacier National Park, Montana.

Information: Superintendent, Waterton Lakes National Park, Waterton Park, Alberta T0K 2M0.

2. *NORTHERN ROCKIES*

From a distance it is sometimes easy for inexperienced persons to imagine the wilderness as antihuman, especially in the Northern Rocky Mountains, where enormous ridges and valleys dwarf men to insignificance. There are also stories—much embellished—of grizzly bears, which make the land seem far more hostile than it is. The frigid winters, with their hip-deep snows and temperatures fifty or sixty degrees below zero, also produce an imaginary scene that seems like something on far-off Saturn, where life as we know it appears to be nonexistent.

Some truth exists in all of this, except that the Northern Rockies are no more antihuman than urban environments. Superhuman they are, however, and the cliffs of Cambrian sandstones are so immense and ancient that they are difficult to comprehend. The wildlife is well adapted to the environment, and some of the animals certainly do possess greater strength than human beings. Once accepting this, and accepting that in the wilderness man is not the dominant factor of life, we are ready for some extraordinary experiences.

🌲 Two weeks in the **Bob Marshall Wilderness** of Montana provide a good introduction to typical sights and sounds of the Northern Rockies. The first night out comes a warm mountain wind and, beyond the nearest ridge, a crashing storm whose furies illuminate the sky with orange flashes and fill the valleys with echoing rumbles of thunder. Next morning the meadows are wet, and the sun strikes them to reveal lilies, gentians, paintbrush, shooting stars, senecios, and forget-me-nots. Mile after mile we pass dense concentrations, and dozens of species, clutching the banks of streams or climbing the slopes of valleys. Sego lilies, beargrass, harebells, vetch, aster—we make a list, but it soon becomes too long, and there are lesser-known species that we do not recognize.

Frequently, mountain goats are seen on the ledges, or marmots in the rock piles. Higher up we hear the shrill, high notes of pikas. Deer wander not far from camp, seeming to ignore our presence. It is August, and the nights grow colder, but grouse do not seem to mind. We ascend from forests of lodgepole pine to high alpine slopes where little but alpine forget-me-nots and shooting

Bowron Lake Provincial Park, British Columbia. Courtesy British Columbia Department of Recreation and Conservation.

stars grow, and there see elk—some beginning their rutting ceremonies even now. Mountains and ridges lie in all directions, punctuated with patches of snow and ice that will not melt this year. The land appears barren and the ridges naked, but that is only if we forget the alpine grass and flowers that clothe the uplands.

Each day brings something new. From the summits we look out over a vast wild land of 950,000 acres intended to be kept forever as wilderness. In this collection of jagged peaks and forested valleys the south fork of the Flathead River originates. Over sixty miles of the Continental Divide wind through the area. There are fossil outcrops, ice caves, pioneer homestead sites, and glacier-fed lakes to be examined. Coming down, we follow a water ouzel and her chicks until they submerge in the cascading torrent and disappear. We swim and share the mountain pools with water snakes. The endless display of flowers goes on: larkspur, clematis, rose, strawberry, geranium, lupine, dwarf dogwood. . . . One day we walk through dense groves of Douglas fir and lodgepole pine, the next across open meadows with ponderosa pine. Often we are dominated by the Chinese Wall, a sedimentary rock rampart a thousand feet high and twelve miles in length. That night the northern lights play throughout the sky from rim to rim where camp is made.

The last days seem almost like a dream; the canyons through which we descend are richly vegetated in different shades, and at times we feel as though coasting along on a restless sea of green. At every hand comes the music of rivulets, miniature waterfalls, dripping seeps—clear water so abundant that we need not carry a canteen. There are regrets, of course; the days too short, the trip too abrupt, the cutthroat trout that got away when we were fishing on the Flathead River. But the audio and visual images appear to be so strongly engraved that they will not soon disappear.

188

Grand Teton National Park, Wyoming.

Entry points into the Bob Marshall Wilderness lie within two hours of easy driving from Kalispell, Missoula, Helena, or Great Falls, Montana. Outfitters are available and the U.S. Forest Service has maps and excellent advice about a variety of trips that can be taken into the remote interior.

In the end, a newcomer may be converted much as was Bob Marshall himself, a youthful New York forester who in the 1930s became a prime mover in the national inventory and classification of roadless areas. "For me," he wrote, "and for thousands with similar inclinations, the most important passion of life is the overpowering desire to escape periodically from the clutches of mechanistic civilization. To us the enjoyment of solitude, complete independence, and the beauty of undefiled panoramas is absolutely essential to happiness."

Campgrounds are available in the surrounding national forests, and food and lodging in Kalispell and Missoula.

Information: Supervisor, Lewis & Clark National Forest, Federal Building, Great Falls, Montana 59401; and Supervisor, Flathead National Forest, 290 North Main, Kalispell, Montana 59901.

🌲 Bordering the Bob Marshall Wilderness on the east and south is the **Scapegoat Wilderness,** sixty miles northwest of Helena, Montana. This 240,000-acre area was won in 1972 by embattled conservationists after a prolonged effort to preserve prime natural habitat for grizzly bears. It consists of scenic mountain terrain along both sides of the Continental Divide—one of the longest roadless stretches of the Divide—including numerous high points that rise above 7,500 feet, with sheer cliffs and high-mountain snowfields. The area is characterized by plunging streams, quiet lakes, and narrow valleys filled with grassy meadows and wild flowers. As a sanctuary for Rocky

189

Mountain mammals it has few equals; black and grizzly bears, mountain lions, bighorns, mountain goats, deer, elk, and wolverines are a few of the resident species. The environment is principally alpine and subalpine, headwaters for parts of the Columbia and Missouri river systems.

Campgrounds are available on surrounding national forest lands, and accommodations in nearby communities. The town of Lincoln lies eleven miles from the southern boundary. Access is via U.S. Route 287, State Route 200, secondary roads, and trails.

Information: Supervisor, Lewis & Clark National Forest, Federal Building, Great Falls, Montana 59401; Supervisor, Helena National Forest, 616 Helena Avenue, Helena, Montana 59601; and Supervisor, Lolo National Forest, 2801 Russell Street, Missoula, Montana 59801.

🌲 About fifteen miles west of the Bob Marshall Wilderness lies the Mission Range, a remarkable mountain mass composed of very old layers of sediments broken and uplifted so that they now dip slightly eastward. Along this inclined fault block, a narrow stretch of rugged terrain thirty miles long and one to seven miles wide has been set aside as the **Mission Mountains Primitive Area,** containing 73,861 acres. The western boundary is not only the crest of the range, but also the eastern edge of the Flathead Indian Reservation. Elevations range from 5,600 to 9,000 feet above sea level, and while the upper parts have only a sparse vegetation, they are very scenic, what with glacier-filled cirques, crystal lakes, snow-capped peaks, knifelike ridges, waterfalls, cascading streams, and massive layered cliffs.

Farther down, the forest becomes more dense, mostly Engelmann spruce mixed with fir, western red cedar, hemlock, western larch, and pine. The rare subalpine larch also grows here. In these woods can frequently be heard the song of the varied thrush. Ptarmigan and several species of grouse are among the scores of bird species that visit the mountains. Like other parts of the Northern Rockies, the Mission Mountains support both mule deer and white-tailed deer. Black and grizzly bears may be seen occasionally. Among other mammals are mountain lions, mountain goats, moose, mink, bobcats, lynxes, beaver, foxes, and coyotes.

In summer the Mission Mountains are a haven for hikers. The goal may not often matter so much; the opportunity for fishing, photography, sketching, nature study, or simply relaxation in a pine-scented environment of natural beauty and wild solitude is ample reason for entering this wilderness. July, August, and September are the best months, otherwise hikers may have to contend with snow, ice, and swollen streams. In winter the mountains are buried in a massive blanket of snow, ideal for cross-country skiing.

Entry is mainly from the east. Montana Route 209 between Kalispell and Missoula provides access to the Swan River Valley; gravel roads then lead to the wilderness boundary. Developed campgrounds may be found in the Flathead National Forest outside the wilderness. A full range of food and lodging is available in communities around the area—but at some distance; Missoula is sixty miles to the south and Kalispell fifty miles to the north.

Information: Supervisor, Flathead National Forest, 290 North Main Street, Kalispell, Montana 59901.

Near the Idaho line, not far from the attractive Pend Oreille Lake, lies the **Cabinet Mountains Wilderness,** Montana, a series of picturesque naked peaks rising from dense forests containing giant white pine and western red cedar trees. Among the peaks, snow-clad and brushed with icy winds most of the year, are glacial basins holding alpine lakes. Trails lead through this 94,272-acre area from all sides, with initial approaches made on U.S. routes 2 and Alternate 10. As elsewhere in the Northern Rockies, the photographic opportunities are varied: cliffs and shadows, lake reflections, twisting streams, remote waterfalls, and—with a little luck and persistence—mountain goats and other animals. Among the activities permitted are hiking, rock climbing, hunting, and fishing. Horses are not encouraged because of their impact on the wilderness. Campgrounds are available in the adjacent national forests. The towns of Libby, Troy, Noxon, and Trout Creek are nearby.

Information: Supervisor, Kootenai National Forest, 418 Mineral Avenue, Libby, Montana 59923.

Glacier National Park, Montana (not to be confused with Glacier National Park, British Columbia), famed as a place of trails, has more than 700 miles of them, leading through some of the most spectacular land forms in North America. The unusual beauty and immense scale compare with Banff and Yoho national parks in Canada, a compliment indeed. At a time when the world was younger and evidently far more violent, enormous layers of rock in this region were thrust over other layers for as much as thirty miles horizontally. Although such massive movements no doubt took place over many millenniums, the scale of geologic overthrusting is difficult for human beings to comprehend. The thick, uplifted strata have eroded into picturesque contours, and a heavy blanket of glaciers in the recent past has carved the landscape into sharp peaks, broad valleys, and scattered basins that hold magnificent lakes.

Most of this is accessible by trail, and a hiker may find it difficult to choose among such superlative destinations as Avalanche Basin, Sperry Glacier,

191

Gunsight Pass, Iceberg Lake, Going-to-the-Sun Mountain, the Garden Wall, Morning Eagle Falls, Two Medicine Lake, Swiftcurrent Valley, and the adjoining Waterton Lakes National Park in Canada. He might like to see them all at once, but would need years to know the park thoroughly, and even then would have difficulty covering every one of its 1,013,129 acres. There is so much to see and do. Great beds of wild flowers adorn the meadows, valley slopes, and terraces near tumbling streams. The beargrass (not a grass but a lily) raises its tall stalk and cream-colored flower heads as though it were a trademark of Glacier. The ubiquitous paintbrush mingles in places with avalanche lilies, gentians, and larkspur. The delicate purple clematis clings to the trunks of pines. Wild hollyhock lines some of the roads and trails with its flower stalks. Altogether more than a thousand species of plants are known from Glacier National Park. Guides to them, as well as to geology, trails, and other features, are available for purchase at the St. Mary and Logan Pass visitor centers, at park headquarters in West Glacier, and at hotels and communities nearby.

Although much of the scene may be viewed from an automobile or on conducted tours by launch, the person who penetrates the wilderness on foot is more apt to see black and grizzly bears, mountain goats, coyotes, lynxes, mountain lions, and any of the fifty other species of mammals in the park. In addition, more than 200 species of birds have been recorded, and the flight of a golden eagle, against the backdrop of great stratified cliffs, is a sight to remember. The hiker, rather than the motorist, enjoys pure scents from the highest forests of spruce and fir, reaches the greatest number of fifty glaciers within the park, is startled by a sudden flight of grouse, hears the delicate distant song of the thrush, or comes across fossils embedded in rock beside the trail—evidence of life across the ages.

Accommodations are plentiful around the park, and hotels and motels still remain within it. Hikers can walk to Sperry and Granite chalets for an overnight stay (space should be reserved well in advance), and there commune with mountain views and mountain goats. West Glacier, the principal southern entrance to the park, is reached by rail and by U.S. Route 2. On the eastern side of the park, continuing on to the Canadian boundary, is U.S. Route 89. Campgrounds are available in and around the park.

Information: Superintendent, Glacier National Park, West Glacier, Montana 59936.

One of the largest wilderness areas in the lower United States begins a few miles southwest of Missoula, Montana. It rises into the Bitterroot Mountains and crosses over into Idaho, where it takes in large sections of the Lochsa and Selway river drainage basins. This immense collection of cliffs, high peaks, steep valleys, lakes, coniferous forests, and pure mountain streams, covering 1,240,605 acres, is preserved as the **Selway-Bitterroot Wilderness.** It is accessible from all directions, mainly via U.S. routes 12 and 93.

Inside, one gets a feeling of vastness that Chief Joseph and his people must have felt when they lived among the mountains and which doubtless impressed upon Lewis and Clark the immensity of the American West. Some names applied to geographic features suggest a colorful, distant past: Indian Creek, Saddle Gulch, Wahoo Pass, and Sneakfoot Meadows. However, as far as naming goes, there seems to have been an unusual predilection toward commemorating animal life, and goats in particular, including Goat Ridge, Goat Creek, Goat Lake, Goat Mountain, Goat Roost. A few examples of other species in topographic names illustrate the variety of wildlife inhabiting the range: Eagle Point, Wapiti Creek, Otter Butte, Mink Peak, Wolf Point, Grizzly Saddle, Fox Park, Elk Ridge, and Fish Lake.

Most points of interest are accessible, or at least approachable, on a comprehensive network of trails. Trips by canoe or raft down the wild Selway River are recommended. Detailed recreation maps may be obtained from the U.S. Forest Service. Campgrounds are common around the edges of the wilderness. Food and lodging may be secured in Hamilton, six miles to the east.

Information: Supervisor, Bitterroot National Forest, 316 North Third Street, Hamilton, Montana 59840; Supervisor, Lolo National Forest, 2801 Russell Street, Missoula, Montana 59801; Supervisor, Nezperce National Forest, 319 East Main, Grangeville, Idaho 83530; and Supervisor, Clearwater National Forest, Route 3, Ahsahka Road, Orofino, Idaho 83544.

In the **Humbug Spires Primitive Area** the Bureau of Land Management has designated 7,041 acres of western Montana, near the town of Divide, as a preserve for scenery and wildlife. The scenery is composed of granite pinnacles partly clad in open coniferous forests. These are not only photogenic, but the sheer, vertical surfaces constitute a challenge for rock climbers. Nine of the spires rise 300 to 600 feet above their surroundings. Another has overhangs on all sides. In addition there are fifty other spires, some easy climbs for beginners, others of moderate or extreme difficulty. It is wild-area climbing, which calls for caution on the part of mountaineering individuals or groups because rescue services have not been fully developed.

No specific walking trails have been designated, which allows the wilderness hiker freedom to roam as he pleases. He may encounter bears, deer, and elk, residents of the Mount Humbug area. Or he may meet seasonal inhabitants, such as moose and bighorn sheep.

Camping in primitive locations is permitted; visitors may obtain water from Moose Creek, Lime Gulch, and the tributaries of Tucker Creek, but it should be treated before being used for drinking. The Humbug Spires Primitive Area is located twenty-five miles south of Butte, Montana. U.S. Route 91 passes through Divide, west of the site. Several more primitive roads approach the area from all sides.

Information: Director, Montana State Office, Bureau of Land Management, Federal Building, Court House, 316 North Twenty-sixth Street, Billings, Montana 59101.

🌲 In the Anaconda Range west of Butte, Montana, rise the Pintlar Peaks, named for a pioneer settler and trapper in the Big Hole River country who blazed trails and explored the area. Today, much of this mountain vastness remains unsullied by the agriculture and industry that surround these uplands, and 157,803 acres have been set aside as the **Anaconda-Pintlar Wilderness.**

Each year, when the buttercups, shooting stars, spring beauties, and pasqueflowers emerge from soil that is moistened by melting ice, the high country renews itself as it has every year for millenniums. After severe winters (the elevation is close to 10,000 feet) lakes and streams seem cleaner and more pure than ever, if that is possible, and the vegetation fairly springs forth, as though to grow furiously and reproduce before the short summer season is over.

As a result, the aspect is one of freshness, cleanliness, pure air, and complex natural beauty. This can be said of most wilderness areas, of course, but in the Anaconda-Pintlar area, nature has endowed the scene with Sierralike crests of crystalline granite, folded and faulted sedimentary strata, gouged-out alpine basins, scoured valleys, and glacial moraines. Deep snow, not all of which melts each year, provides water for the spruce-fringed lakes; it also, with the help of springs, feeds a network of streams that cascade on their way to the Big Hole, Bitterroot, and other rivers.

Many miles of wilderness paths lead along these streams, providing access to nearly all parts of the area, and seldom is a hiker more than two or three miles from another trail. He is also surrounded by animal life but unless he is unusually perceptive, takes his time, and uses binoculars, it is likely that he will be seen by more creatures than he sees. The ubiquitous Clark nutcrackers, Steller jays, Canada jays, marmots, and pikas make themselves heard as they chatter or screech at intruders. But to see coyotes and mountain goats may take some careful observation, and the hiker should count himself very lucky if he observes a bobcat, lynx, or marten. Nevertheless, the signs are all around, and if he knows how to recognize tracks of lions, pine bark chewed by porcupines, nests of eagles, and burrows of Columbian ground squirrels, he will have a keener awareness of the intricate structure of the ecosystem. It is instructive to observe natural processes in undisturbed wilderness areas where pine-killing beetles are as important as flower-pollinating wasps.

The best times for wildlife observations are early morning and late evening. Good photographs may be taken at such times, also, including views from the summits, when shadows enhance the relief of distant mountain ranges. A recommended hike is that along the Continental Divide, forty-five miles of open panoramas, invigorating thin air, alpine lakes, and picturesque peaks. Fishing, hunting, riding, climbing, and camping are some of the other recreational uses here. As in all wilderness areas trash must be packed out rather than burned or buried; if feed for horses is taken in it must be processed or pelletized feed, or baled hay certified as being free of noxious weed seeds.

Access is by roads connecting U.S. routes 93 and Alternate 10, and Montana routes 38 and 43. Developed campgrounds exist around the wilderness, and food and lodging may be secured in nearby towns.

Information: Supervisor, Bitterroot National Forest, 316 North Third Street, Hamilton, Montana 59840; Supervisor, Deerlodge National Forest, Federal Building, Butte, Montana 59701; and Supervisor, Beaverhead National Forest, Box 1258, Dillon, Montana 59725.

🌲 Some of the most rugged and scenic water trips in North America are to be had on the Salmon River. This stream originates in the Sawtooth Mountains of central Idaho, starts flowing north, then heads west, picks up three major north-flowing tributaries—the East Fork, Middle Fork, and West Fork—and eventually goes on to the Snake River for a total distance of 425 miles. The upstream portions have eroded so deeply into an immense and ancient mass of granite that the resulting gorges are claimed by Idahoans to be deeper than any in North America. For 180 miles of its course, the Salmon flows through V-shaped canyons more than a mile deep. One eighty-mile section is so rough that the stream drops nearly a thousand feet in elevation, earning it the name "River of No Return." In the most rugged parts of this vast domain, two wilderness areas border the river.

The **Salmon River Breaks Primitive Area** stretches along forty miles of white water and deep gorges between Riggins and North Fork, Idaho, and protects 216,870 acres of deeply eroded terrain. The river itself is not included within the wilderness, and is therefore open to motorboats, which sometimes make the trip upstream. There are foot and pack bridges that allow crossings to the south bank of the river, and a few pieces of private property along the stream. By and large, however, a float trip down the river in rubber raft, kayak, or flat-bottomed barge is done in reasonably wild surroundings. A trail follows the river much of the way, and side paths lead up into the primitive area at several points. Consequently, persons making the trip downstream may enter the Salmon River Breaks backcountry and explore it in detail.

Among the features of interest along the river or in the wilderness are old mines and cabins, waterfalls, hot springs, scenic lookouts, Indian writings, and the historic Nez Perce Trail. Obviously, the terrain is better suited to bighorn sheep and eagles than to human beings, and hiking up out of deep gorges calls for a measure of strength and endurance. The river itself has dozens of stretches of rapids, some quite turbulent and hazardous. Inexperienced boatmen need to bear in mind that human lives have been lost in ill-prepared attempts to negotiate this "River of No Return." Persons unfamiliar with the river can get into dangerous falls and rapids without warning and learn too late that there is no opportunity to beach their boat. They may be in very deep trouble indeed if their supplies and equipment plunge to the bottom of the river. Also, as the U.S. Forest Service says, "the amateur should remember that chances of rescue in case of upset are poor." Other hazards are forest fires and rattlesnakes.

Nevertheless, a float trip through this gorge, and explorations in the Salmon River Breaks from campsites along the river, can result in a first-class wilderness experience. Careful preparations should be made to help insure safety throughout. Detailed maps of the river, and of the primitive areas on both sides of it, are available from the U.S. Forest Service. Rangers operating river patrols can offer helpful suggestions. They must be advised of routes and schedules before a party departs on a river trip, and can be contacted at ranger stations on the approaches to the river. Pack and riding horses, as well as guides, are available from commercial outfitters. Boating, hunting, and fishing are subject to Idaho state regulations.

Access to the upstream end of the primitive area is via forest roads from North Fork, Idaho, and U.S. Route 93 south of Missoula, Montana. Developed campgrounds are located on national forest lands outside the boundaries; food and lodging may be secured in nearby communities.

Information: Supervisor, Bitterroot National Forest, 316 North Third Street, Hamilton, Montana 59840; and Supervisor, Nezperce National Forest, 319 East Main, Grangeville, Idaho 83530.

🌲 The **Idaho Primitive Area,** a reserve of 1,232,744 acres on the south side of the Salmon River, is a maze of peaks, ridges, and canyons, partly forested, at elevations between 8,000 and 10,000 feet. It has 1,600 miles of trails, many along streams and in deep canyons, others on ridges and high points. These make accessible such interesting destinations as Quis Quis Hot Springs, Pistol Hot Springs, Papoose Lakes, Indian paintings and writings, cliff dwellings, Box Canyon, Rainbow Mountain, Monumental Rock, Phantom Meadow, old mines and placer camps, and the Middle Fork of the Salmon River.

The Middle Fork was designated by Congress in 1968 as part of the National Wild and Scenic River System, and since it flows through a primitive area, motorboats and motorized terrain vehicles are prohibited. Once declared impassable, the Middle Fork flows through some of the deepest gorges in North America, over numerous falls and rapids, for eighty miles within the Idaho Primitive Area to its junction with the Salmon. Along the lower part of the route rise the Bighorn Crags, a broken, lake-studded upland, well served by trails, that is regarded as among the most wild and rugged mountain ranges in the northwestern United States.

Numerous camping spots for boaters have been designated along the Middle Fork, and from many of them trails lead up side creeks or canyon walls and out into the wilderness. For most of the distance, a riverside trail parallels the Middle Fork. The stream itself, by virtue of a swift current, abundant falls, and seething white rapids, is an exciting place for float trips, but no place for a novice boatman. Amateurs can find themselves surging through rough and dangerous waters before they know it and the chances for quick rescue in case of disaster in these wild canyons are pretty slim. The only recommended types of river craft are large rubber rafts, kayaks, or specially constructed wooden float boats. First-aid equipment for injuries, poison ivy, and rattlesnake bite should always be at hand. Numerous licensed outfitters and guides are available for hire. Boating permits are required and refuse must be packed back out.

The presence of mineral veins and hot springs attests to the geologic fascination of this region. The most ancient rocks are quartzites, slates, and schists hundreds of millions of years old. These have been invaded by younger upsurging masses of molten rock now hardened into light-colored biotite granite. Above that, in places, are flows of volcanic tuff and lava even younger in age.

The rocks and crags may seem at first a formidable and even forbidding place for animal life, but the ecosystems are varied, and there are open flats, grassy meadows, wide sandbars, and dense forests. Bighorn sheep and mountain goats thrive in the more inclined places, while elsewhere live mule and white-tailed deer, elk, bears, moose, foxes, coyotes, and other species. Naturalists will find the mountains replete with birds, including grouse, and displays of summer wild flowers. All in all, this area ranks as one of the most interesting and magnificent wilderness areas in North America.

There are seventeen major entrances into the Idaho Primitive Area, providing access from all sides. Secondary roads approach from U.S. Route 93 on the east and Idaho state routes 55 on the west and 21 on the south. Developed campgrounds may be found on neighboring forest lands. Food and lodging are available in nearby communities.

Information: Supervisor, Payette National Forest, Forest Service Building, McCall, Idaho 83638; Supervisor, Challis National Forest, Challis, Idaho 83226; and Supervisor, Salmon National Forest, Box 729, Salmon, Idaho 83467. Boating information may be obtained from the Idaho Outfitters and Guides Association, Box 95, Boise, Idaho 83701.

🌲 While hunting in the volcanic mountains and deep canyons of what is now western Idaho, an Indian brave became lost, so legend has it, and met a devil. Fleeing, he met another, and another, until he encountered seven before returning home. Hence the name of the Seven Devils Range, which hovers high over the Snake River. The drop in elevation from the top of these mountains down across the basalt cliffs and terraces to the river is close to 8,000 feet in just over six miles of horizontal distance, reminiscent of the 9,800-foot drop on the north side of California's San Jacinto Mountains over a horizontal distance of seven miles. Besides such vertical spectacles, this canyon country contains grass-carpeted plateaus, valleys filled with pine, spruce, fir, and larch, and a wildlife population of mountain lions, mountain goats, deer, elk, bears, and bobcats. The region is so scenic that 130,000 acres of it has been set aside by the U.S. Department of Agriculture as the **Hells Canyon–Seven Devils Scenic Area,** and includes twenty-six miles of the Snake River about three hours' drive north of Boise, Idaho. The Eagle Cap Wilderness of northeastern Oregon lies less than fifteen miles to the west.

Hikers may reach the "devils" and other rocky crags on trails into the high country, and indulge in wilderness camping. Boatmen may gain access to wild canyons along the river. Anglers have forty mountain lakes in which to try for cutthroat, Dolly Varden, brook, and rainbow trout; other species include white sturgeon, chinook salmon, catfish, crappies, bass, and perch. Hunting is also allowed in season. The gorge has been severely damaged by an artificial reservoir and the roar of motorboats detracts from the naturalness of the area, but numerous trails allow the hiker access to more remote and quiet terrain. Some of the Snake River downstream is still wild, and float trips are permitted in accordance with Idaho and Oregon regulations. In May and June the river is not safe, however, because of high water from spring runoff.

The Scenic Area is accessible via Idaho State Route 71, Oregon State Route 86, and low-standard dirt roads. Camping and picnic sites are available along the shores of the reservoir and at more distant points in the adjacent national forests. Food and lodging may be secured in communities beyond the perimeters of the forests.

Information: Supervisor, Wallowa-Whitman National Forest, Main and Auburn Streets, Baker, Oregon 97814; Supervisor, Nezperce National Forest,

319 East Main, Grangeville, Idaho 83530; and Supervisor, Payette National Forest, Forest Service Building, McCall, Idaho 83638.

🌲 The **Sawtooth National Recreation Area and Wilderness** contains a total of 754,000 acres, located about forty miles northwest of Sun Valley, Idaho. It was established by Act of Congress on August 22, 1972, and placed under the administration of the Forest Service, U.S. Department of Agriculture. However, the act also required the Secretary of the Interior to undertake a study of the area, plus the adjoining Pioneer Mountains, for potential as a unit of the national park system, and report back to Congress by the end of 1974. Many parts of the recreation area, particularly the White Cloud Peaks and Boulder Mountains, have wild and scenic aspects, but 216,000 acres, located in the Sawtooth Range itself, have been specifically classified as wilderness. One of the most picturesque approaches is off U.S. Route 93 on a spur road to Redfish Lake, which forms an attractive foreground for views of the Sawtooth Range, whose sharp-edged peaks reach well over 10,000 feet above sea level. Numerous trails lead into the wilderness from Sawtooth Valley, along the east side, as well as from other scenic access points. These paths follow clear mountain streams from lake to lake and over basin divides into remote valleys where solitude, forest, wildlife, and disintegrating mountain peaks are the dominant aspects of the environment. Especially interesting are the redfish themselves, brightly colored landlocked salmon called kokanee, which may easily be observed in the transparent waters. Not far away, chinook and sockeye salmon can be seen spawning at the end of their 800-mile migratory swim upstream from the sea.

Accommodations and food may be obtained at nearby resorts and towns. Permits are required for use and occupancy of the wilderness; visitors should also obtain details on other applicable regulations before departing for the backcountry.

Information: Supervisor, Sawtooth National Forest, 1525 Addison Avenue East, Twin Falls, Idaho 83301.

🌲 Not all of the wild places in the Northern Rockies are mountainous; the **National Bison Range** is a 19,000-acre tract of hill and prairie country in the Flathead Valley of Montana. Access, however, is restricted; visitors may enter only along a nineteen-mile self-guiding tour route. This limitation arises from the unpredictable nature of bison, which can charge human intruders without warning. Yet even though visitors have to stay near their vehicles, a visit to this wildlife refuge eminently justifies the efforts and limits. Between 300 and 500 bison are kept on the range. From the tour route, observations may also be made of deer, elk, bighorns, pronghorns, and waterfowl on streams and ponds. The familiar bunchgrass, a fescue, grows on open slopes, while the streams are lined with snowberry, hawthorn, and cottonwood. May and June are the best months for wild-flower observations. Facilities are available for picnicking but not camping. Access is via Moiese on Montana Route 212. Missoula is forty-five miles to the south.

Information: Refuge Manager, National Bison Range, Moiese, Montana 59824.

🌲 When Captain Meriwether Lewis and his party moved up the Missouri River on July 19, 1805, they came to a series of limestone cliffs that seemed especially spectacular in comparison with the prairies to which these pioneers had become accustomed. "A most sublime and extraordinary spectacle," Lewis called it. For more than five miles the expedition passed perpendicular sedimentary beds that rose to heights of 1,200 feet. Some of the upturned strata stood out like knife-edge walls, and since the area between them was smoothly eroded, they inevitably took on the name Devil's Slide. On each side of the river lay folded fossiliferous limestones whose walls plunged directly into the river and allowed no place for camping; the party was obliged to continue after dark before stopping for the night. "This extraordinary range of rocks," wrote Lewis in his journal, "we called the Gates of the Rocky Mountains."

Today, the **Gates of the Mountains Wilderness,** of 28,562 acres, has been established near this site, though the scene that captivated Lewis has been modified by reservoir waters behind Holter Dam. Trails provide access that Lewis didn't have, and present-day explorers can examine such places as Refrigerator Canyon, so narrow that in places the sun never reaches the bottom. They may also see foxes, coyotes, bobcats, badgers, weasels, and mountain lions. Deer are plentiful and, along with mountain goats, grouse, and wild turkeys, are sought by hunters when the season is open. Since the peaks in the wilderness do not reach higher than 8,000 feet, they are well vegetated, from grassy hills and flowered vales to stands of fir and pine.

Trails reach throughout the wilderness, but water is scarce in places. Rainfall sinks into the limestone and drains away through cracks and fissures; this results in springs and seeps but it is still a good idea for hikers to carry canteens. Campsites are available near the boundaries.

Access is from U.S. Route 91 via boat across the reservoir, or by secondary roads and trails. Tourist facilities are available in and near Helena, sixteen miles to the south.

Information: Supervisor, Helena National Forest, 616 Helena Avenue, Helena, Montana 59601.

3. MIDDLE ROCKIES

Despite the peaceful look of the terrain today, the high country in and around **Yellowstone National Park** has undergone extremely violent convulsions. Volcanic upheavals and outpourings, aged more or less than a million years, left the landscape in a smoking jumble that has not yet cooled. Thousands of steaming springs give surface evidence that red-hot lava is not very far below, and the explosive eruptions of geysers like Steamboat show that violence is not entirely over. In Yellowstone's wilderness, far from the crowds, can be found secluded pools of boiling water, simmering creeks, and steam eruptions that give uniqueness to this land and a certain peril to men or beasts who venture out on delicate crusts in the thermal basins. It is a world most tourists never see.

The grizzly's world is an example. Up around 8,000 feet, on treeless rolling meadows where there are elk to bring down in spring and roots to dig up in fall, these powerful bears live mostly a solitary life, except when mother and cubs are together. The only animal they try to avoid is man, an unpredictable intruder whose habits they have not yet become accustomed to. For all its strength, however, the grizzly is king of nothing, rather a part of grassland life communities that include the elk and bison.

The moose's world is of streams, specifically marshy meadows such as those along the Yellowstone River, where willow is common. Bighorns occupy lava ledges and summits at high elevations. Mule deer move in and out of forests. Black bears live in the woods, bald eagles overhead, swans on ponds, pelicans on lakes, pronghorns on prairies, and wolves and mountain lions wherever they can survive. Yellowstone is clearly a wildlife paradise, one of those rare domains in which every species of wild animal known to have been there a century and a half ago is still there. As the oldest national park in the world (1872), it represents a wilderness that has been allowed to develop largely on its own. Thus it is about as close to being pristine as any terrain this side of Alaska. More than a thousand miles of trails make nearly all of the wild environments accessible to men. Some of the more interesting wilderness trips are as follows.

A day's hike up Mount Washburn, covering about three miles and reaching 10,243 feet elevation, provides the most all-inclusive panoramic view of the park and a chance to see pikas and bighorns at close range. Up Avalanche Peak, another day's hike, the route climbs to 10,566 feet, where the terrain is rocky and rough and a summer storm likely to be frigid. Several remote geyser basins are accessible by trail. From road's end at Lone Star Geyser it is approximately seven miles over an obsidian-strewn trail to Shoshone Geyser Basin, a busy and complex thermal area that takes hours to explore. Another trail leads nine miles from the park road, near Lewis Lake, to Heart Lake Geyser Basin, a place of brilliant blue pools, hissing eruptions, and bright-orange algal terraces. From Heart Lake, incidentally, an angler once pulled a forty-two pound Mackinaw trout.

Longer trips are especially appealing because they allow a more thorough appreciation of Yellowstone's wilderness values. One section is attractive for its waterfalls; by traveling through Idaho to the Southwestern corner of the park—to Cave Falls and then to the Bechler Ranger Station—it is possible to take off by foot or horseback into the Bechler River country. This leads across marshy flats where sandhill cranes sing their quivering notes, through forests of pine and fir, and across some of the clearest, purest streams in the West. The route passes several cascades—Colonnade (102 feet), Ouzel (230 feet)—but there are dozens of off-trail falls that are worth the effort to reach, though time is required to negotiate steep ravines and sprawling lava talus slopes that sometimes separate them from the trail. Eventually the Bechler River trail climbs over the Madison Plateau and comes out at Old Faithful.

Perhaps the wildest trip is that up the Yellowstone River into what is known as Thorofare Country, thence west across Two Ocean Plateau, up over Big Game Ridge, down Harebell Creek, and into the Snake River drainage. At least five days should be allowed for such an extended journey—and more if any side explorations are contemplated. The wild-flower gardens in summer are striking, though frost can appear on the meadows in early morning. At high points, alpine flowers thrive, and even in the melting snowbanks red algae grow. Among other interesting features in Yellowstone's wilderness are petrified tree trunks still standing after millions of years.

Books, booklets, and guides are available to describe the trails of Yellowstone, the flora, fauna, history, and geology. The park is open all year, and even though most of the roads are blocked by snow, winter use is increasing; certain places are accessible by car or snowmobile, and the sight of steam clouds rising from snow-covered terrain, at temperatures below zero, is dramatic as well as incongruous. In winter great numbers of elk can be seen along the road between Mammoth and the northeast entrance, and bison and bighorns are usually easily observed.

Campgrounds, picnic areas, and accommodations are available within the

park, which is reached via U.S. routes 89, 287, 14, 20, 191, and 212, and
Idaho State Route 47.
Information: Superintendent, Yellowstone National Park, Wyoming
82190.

🌲 The **Spanish Peaks Wilderness** of Montana (not to be confused with the
Spanish Peaks of southern Colorado) is located off the northwest corner of
Yellowstone National Park. Its 63,300 acres include snowy peaks, glacial
lakes, waterfalls, and wild-flower meadows in the Madison Mountain Range,
a complex of ancient granite, gneiss, schist, and other types of rock, much of
which has been broken and folded. There are a few volcanic rocks and some
glacial deposits.

The Peaks get their name from a Crow Indian phrase that means "canyon
where the Spaniards stop," referring to a time about 1836 when the Indians
came upon a half-dozen Spanish trappers in this area. The elevations in the
wilderness are moderately high; more than two dozen peaks exceed 10,000
feet, and the highest is Gallatin Peak, 11,015 feet. Consequently, the terrain is
raw and rugged, the ridges sharpened by glacial action, the cliffs underlain
with steep talus slopes where rocks have avalanched, and boulders have been
strewn in natural disarray. But gentle flower-laden meadows surround the
sparkling lakes, and a hiker may photograph, fish, or simply relax and watch
the clouds go by. Below 9,000 feet grow forests of lodgepole pine, Douglas fir,
and spruce interspersed with parklike vales of grass and herbaceous plants.
The wildlife resembles that in Yellowstone: moose, elk, deer, bighorns, bears,
coyotes, mountain lions, badgers, beaver, foxes, and numerous small mammals. The woods and meadows possess their typical resident or migratory
birds, and the streams and lakes abound in trout.

Accommodations are available at Bozeman, twenty-five miles to the
northeast. Access is by U.S. routes 191, which skirts the eastern boundary,
and 287 on the west. The area is popular and heavily used by hikers.

Information: Supervisor, Gallatin National Forest, Box 130, Bozeman,
Montana 59715.

🌲 Along the Madison River, thirty miles west of Bozeman, Montana, and
a two-hour drive northwest of Yellowstone National Park, the Bureau of
Land Management has established the **Bear Trap Canyon Primitive Area,** a
nine-mile-long gorge in the Madison Range. Steep grassy or forested slopes,
canyon walls, high crags, and sparkling waters characterize this 1,500-foot-
deep passage. A trail runs the length of it, along the edge of a river that has

been designated by the Montana Stream Classification Committee as a "Blue Ribbon Trout Stream." The Madison and its tributaries are indeed known for their angling potential, principally brown and rainbow trout, and through this canyon fishermen can hike and try their luck from the bank, or they can float downstream. In the latter case, they should be experienced boatmen because of the presence of extremely hazardous rocks and rapids. Terrestrial wildlife apt to be encountered include deer, coyotes, and bobcats. Hawks, ospreys, and eagles nest among the rocks; ducks and geese nest along the river.

A campground is located at Red Mountain, near the northern end of the primitive area, off Montana State Route 289. To walk or float downstream, one should approach the southern end of the gorge via U.S. Route 287 south of Norris, proceeding past Ennis Lake to the starting point at a power plant on the Madison River. Food and lodging are available in Bozeman and vicinity.

Information: Director, Montana State Office, Bureau of Land Management, Federal Building, U.S. Court House, 316 North Twenty-sixth Street, Billings, Montana 59101.

🌲 A 64,000-acre "extension" of the Yellowstone wilderness has been set aside along the park's northern boundary. This is the **Absaroka Primitive Area,** abundant with moose, black and grizzly bears, elk, deer, bighorns, mountain goats, and much other wildlife. It is especially noted for its summer wild-flower displays. The landscape consists of three main mountain divides lying in a north-south direction. The uplands are mostly open grassy plateaus with elevations ranging above 9,000 feet. They lack the steep rocky characteristics of the Absaroka Mountain Range outside the boundaries. The main drainages within the primitive area are Buffalo, Slough, and Hellroaring creeks. Trails lead into the backcountry not only from Yellowstone National Park, but from Jardine, Mill Creek, and Boulder River. The nearest accommodations are at Gardiner, Mammoth, and Cooke City.

Information: Supervisor, Gallatin National Forest, Box 130, Bozeman, Montana 59715.

🌲 By the time one drives to the top of the Beartooth Mountains, on U.S. Route 212 between Billings, Montana, and Yellowstone National Park, Wyoming, he feels as though he has reached the lower levels of the stratosphere. The rock is solid granite, and to the north, in the **Beartooth Primitive Area,** walls and ridges of it seem to scrape the sky. Twenty-five peaks rise above 12,000 feet. Indeed, Granite Peak, at 12,799 feet, is the highest mountain in Montana. At such elevations, snow and ice can cling to the shady sides of the peaks all year, and there are times when some of the high, secluded lakes are scarcely free of ice before autumn sets in.

But life persists even in the coldest regions, and the snow itself may nourish red algae that in summer give some snowbanks a reddish watermelon color. The weather may be frigid and frequently dangerous to hikers who are ill-prepared, but the unexpected is part of a wilderness experience. There is room enough—230,000 acres—to "get lost" for days at a time. The area has more than 300 lakes and hundreds of waterfalls. The remoteness, the stark aspects, the boulder-strewn meadows, the delicate alpine flowers—all provide continuous contrasts, but the alpine areas are beginning to deteriorate from visitor use, so restrictions are coming into effect.

Trails allow access from the Stillwater River, East and West Rosebud rivers, Red Lodge Creek, Rock Creek, and the Cooke City area, just outside the northeast corner of Yellowstone National Park. However, large areas within the wilderness are trailless, and good maps, available in local stores, should be carried. The mountains have some extraordinary opportunities for challenging rock climbs for the summer or winter mountaineer. Rock walls and numerous difficult peaks are suitable for the technical climber. Precautions should be taken when exploring glaciers or attempting to ascend steep cliffs. Though winter is a spectacular time to climb into these uplands, it is also highly dangerous because of the exposure factor, and even professional explorers have suffered death and disaster on these uncompromising peaks. Forest rangers can provide full details, warnings, and suggestions.

Accommodations, summer and winter, are available at Cooke City and Red Lodge, but deep snows often close the roads to conventional vehicles between October and Memorial Day. Snowmobiles may help in the approach, but they cannot be taken into the wilderness itself.

Information: Supervisor, Custer National Forest, 2601 First Avenue, North, Billings, Montana 59103; and Supervisor, Gallatin National Forest, Box 130, Bozeman, Montana 59715.

🌲 **Bighorn Canyon National Recreation Area,** in Montana and Wyoming, is located on and around Bighorn Lake, a seventy-one-mile-long reservoir behind the Yellowtail Dam. The recreation area also includes approximately twelve miles of the Bighorn River below the dam—and on this portion float trips are becoming popular. On the lake, access may be had by boat to deep canyons, plateaus, and mountains. The region is semiarid, with growths of juniper, mountain mahogany, sumac, and buffalo berry. At higher elevations grow pine, fir, and spruce. The wildlife species resemble those of Yellowstone National Park, 125 miles to the west: deer, bears, elk, coyotes, and other natural species, but here too are wild horses and introduced partridges. Geologically, the area presents a variety of highly colored sedimentary and volcanic formations ranging in age from Paleozoic to Cretaceous. Launching ramps, campsites, picnic areas, and some supplies are available. Hiking in this vertical terrain is difficult because there are no designated trails, and proposed routes should be discussed with park rangers. The recreation area is bordered by the Crow Indian Reservation, into which entry is prohibited without permit. During storms, floods should be watched for in side canyons. The nearest food and accommodations are in Hardin, Montana, and Lovell, Wyoming. Access is by U.S. Route 14-A and Montana Route 313.

Information: Superintendent, Bighorn Canyon National Recreation Area, Box 458, Fort Smith, Montana 59035.

🌲 Off the northeast boundary of Yellowstone National Park lies the **North Absaroka Wilderness,** 353,103 acres of rough volcanic terrain that has dramatic peaks rising to more than 12,000 feet. The landmark Pilot and Index peaks rise along the northeast boundary. There are glaciers, standing petrified trees, and a natural bridge. The area possesses few lakes, but streams are abundant and many miles of trails lead along them. A number of trails have been constructed over passes in the Absaroka Range to connect with the Yellowstone trail system to the west. Trails also lead north, east, and south into other parts of Shoshone National Forest, so that the opportunities for wilderness trips of several weeks or months are extraordinary. Trout fishing in the streams of deep canyons is a sport with spectacular settings. Mountain mammals include black and grizzly bears, bighorns, elk, deer, mountain goats, coyotes, and possibly wolves. The mountains were home to Shoshone Indians, and Chief Joseph of the Nez Perce once took haven here.

Ten-day limitations have been placed on occupancy of a single campsite. Horse numbers are limited to thirty per party and people to twenty per group. Organized groups must acquire a permit before entering.

Automobile approaches are via U.S. routes 14, 16, and 20 on the south, and 212 on the north. Campgrounds are available along these routes. Food, lodging, and supplies may be secured at nearby resorts and villages. The town of Cody lies about twenty-five miles to the east.

Information: Supervisor, Shoshone National Forest, Box 961, Cody, Wyoming 82314.

🌲 The **Washakie Wilderness,** adjoining Yellowstone National Park on the southeast, is reached via U.S. Route 26-287 from the south, Wyoming Route 120 from the east, or U.S. Route 16-20 from the north. A combination of the former South Absaroka Wilderness and Stratified Primitive Area, this unit encompasses the southern reaches of the Absaroka Mountains, an accumulation of thousands of feet of volcanic rock extruded through numerous vents. Erosion has dissected these layers and is in the process of crumbling them to dust. For the most part this is high country, the average elevation being 10,000 feet. Terrain above that is largely devoid of dense vegetation; only along the streams and lower slopes, and deep in canyons, does much spruce or fir or lodgepole pine endure. The barren gray-brown landscape seems like a topographic system on the moon, but hikers find the rocks more jumbled and sharp-edged here. Like the astronauts, they soon get powdered with dark-brown dust, especially if they have to slide down slopes of volcanic ash and cross over tilted talus fields. But the high ramparts of volcanic debris, the pinnacles, buttes, towers, and deeply etched canyons make the effort worthwhile.

Ancient ash falls, incidentally, smothered living forests and as a result numerous fragments of fossilized wood, ferns, and other forms of life lie scattered about; remains of tree trunks, still standing after millions of years, can be seen at the head of Frontier Creek.

The soaring peaks and volcanic layers provide a dramatic backdrop for hikers entering the 679,520 acres of the Washakie Wilderness, but there are also gentle and less conspicuous aspects that can be as memorable as mountains. Diminutive pikas, for example, relatives of the rabbit, rapidly store away food all summer, and the hiker hearing their piping calls among the rocky crags can count it as a genuine wilderness experience. The same is true of watching hawks or coyotes pouncing on gophers, or pine squirrels gathering seeds, or beavers stripping a riverbank of saplings. Such interlocked systems of life occur everywhere and the size of Washakie means that fragile ecological relationships are likely to be continuously renewed despite severe winters, drought, or any other environmental setbacks they may receive. A considerable amount of wildlife traffic comes and goes through these hills, especially when herds of elk migrate to and from the high country. Other large mammals include the bighorn, moose, deer, black bear, and grizzly.

Over a hundred miles of crystal-clear streams and more than sixteen lakes lie within the wilderness boundary, but because of the high elevations and scarcity of nutrients in many waters, fishing is only good in certain places. Hiking, riding, backpacking, and other activities may be engaged in, and commerical packers and outfitters are available.

Information: Supervisor, Shoshone National Forest, Box 961, Cody, Wyoming 82314.

🌲 The Thorofare trail in Yellowstone National Park meanders in and out of the **Teton Wilderness,** an immense 563,500-acre area along the southern boundary of the park. Administered as part of Teton National Forest, it consists of high mountain meadows replete with deer and elk in summer, tranquil lakes, forests of lodgepole pine, deep canyons, roaring waterfalls, and mountain peaks that rise to 12,165 feet. Part of it, like Yellowstone, is volcanic country, but without the massive concentration of thermal phenomena. The western half consists of sandstones, shales, limestones, and gold-bearing conglomerates. Wildlife, including bears, moose, bighorns, beaver, wolves, ospreys, sandhill cranes, and trumpeter swans, is similar to that of adjacent wilderness areas. But there is one feature of unique interest: Two-Ocean Creek, which begins on the Continental Divide and splits in such a way that waters from one branch flow eventually into the Atlantic Ocean and waters from the other flow into the Pacific.

A hiker climbing into the Teton Wilderness passes meadows adorned with purple beds of monkshood flowers. Even at high elevations, tundra flora covers the ground. In the lakes and streams are abundant cutthroat trout. More than 400 miles of trails have been established in this wilderness, which is accessible from U.S. routes 26, 89, and 287 along the southern and western boundary. Accommodations and campgrounds are available in nearby parks, forests, and communities.

Information: Supervisor, Bridger-Teton National Forest, Jackson, Wyoming 83001.

🌲 From most high points in the northwest corner of Wyoming, the bold, soaring summits of the Teton Range may be seen on the horizon. Their rocks, being principally granite, are far more durable and have resisted the ravages of erosion, including glaciation, much more than volcanic layers of the Absaroka Mountains or the Yellowstone lava plateaus. As a result, their sawtoothed ridges have been a beacon to mountain climbers for decades, and at present thousands of mountaineers attempt to scale them every year. Most succeed. They pit themselves against the challenges posed by nature: rough configuration of landscape, and sometimes severe conditions of weather.

Yet in **Grand Teton National Park,** the wilderness may be discreetly utilized by man without the necessity of climbing a cliff or rolling up in a down-filled sleeping bag. At lower elevations, trails lead through dense coniferous forests at the edge of Jackson Hole—a pioneer name for the extensive sagebrush-covered basin beneath the mountains. The park has 220 miles of trails, arranged in a highly scenic network. The most popular trails are those around Jenny Lake, at the foot of the mountains, which are easy to negotiate and lead into spectacularly scenic locales. Through forests of lodgepole pine, spruce, and fir, these well-constructed and well-maintained routes lead to such places as Hidden Falls, Inspiration Point, Paintbrush Divide, and Lake Solitude. Above the forests and in alpine tundra terrain are cliffs, ledges, glaciers, crystal-clear mountain lakes, and—in late July and early August—broad fields of wild flowers, especially in Alaska Basin. The Skyline Trail reaches nearly to 11,000 feet elevation. Other trails lead around Leigh Lake and String Lake, at the foot of the mountains. The Paintbrush Trail is especially good for seeing wild flowers, including blue columbine and mountain gentian. Trails reach out from the Berry Creek and Whitegrass ranger stations, Colter Bay, Taggart Lake, Lupine Meadow, and other points. Inquiries must be made and permits obtained at ranger stations with regard to extended hikes or scaling of peaks. Dangerous snow and ice conditions prevail much of the year.

Float trips on the Snake River, offered by commercial outfitters, are conducted in pontoonlike rubber rafts that hold up to twenty people. The river is generally placid though the strong current carries rafts at a rapid rate. The waters are cold and clear. In places, branches of coniferous trees have dipped to the water's edge, and logs have fallen along the shore. Passengers frequently have some striking views of the Teton Range. Closer at hand lie meadows, marshes, and woods, and it is not unusual to see moose among the willows or a bald eagle perched on some tall tree above the stream. Several trips are conducted daily in summer, with competent naturalist-guides describing the phenomena along the way. A Snake River float trip is one of the easiest ways for persons who are not strong hikers to enjoy a wilderness experience.

Although Grand Teton National Park is of modest size (310,443 acres) it protects a thirty-mile segment of the highest and most precipitous parts of the Teton Range, which rise in broad granite cliffs and spires to an elevation of 13,770 feet. Views of Jackson Hole and the lakes below are panoramic and dramatic. The scene is perhaps most striking in late September, when long lines of aspen and cottonwood trees turn yellow, gold, and orange in the autumn sun. Winter temperatures can drop as low as forty degrees below zero, but winters are mostly exhilarating and delightful, and ski touring is a common pastime at this season.

Since the park is well developed to cater to recreational needs, the list of opportunities is substantial: horseback rides, wilderness picnics, swimming, boat trips on Jackson Lake, hiking tours, self-guiding trails, and museums. There is a comprehensive selection of published material relating to the history and natural history of the region. Food and lodging are available in and near the park.

Information: Superintendent, Grand Teton National Park, Moose, Wyoming 83012.

🌲 Several wild areas have been preserved in the rugged granite and limestone reaches of the Wind River Mountains, between Jackson and Riverton, Wyoming. In the **Glacier Primitive Area** (not to be confused with Glacier National Park, Montana, Glacier National Park, British Columbia, or the Glacier Peak Wilderness of Washington) is the highest point in Wyoming—Gannett Peak, 13,804 feet—and seven additional summits above 13,000 feet. It is generally cool, or even freezing, in summer, which is to be expected, considering the forty-four active glaciers that cover nearly 8,000 acres, and the icy, tumbling, silt-laden streams that issue from them. These streams flow first through rugged gorges nearly devoid of vegetation, and then into cliff-walled valleys containing stands of spruce, pine, and fir. More than thirty lakes and fifty miles of streams are suitable for sport fishing.

Jagged granite peaks, high plateaus of broken rock, and alpine meadows characterize the Glacier Primitive Area. Mammals and birds are abundant, among them deer, elk, moose, bears, bighorns, coyotes, wildcats, grouse, eagles, and ptarmigan. Nature study and photography are prime activities in this environment. Opportunities also exist for mountain climbing, camping, hunting, horseback riding, and hiking. However, only about eighty miles of hiking routes have been constructed; the southern and western portions of this 182,510-acre wilderness are largely trailless, and visitors either take off on their own, or avail themselves of services offered by commercial packers and outfitters. Main access is via U.S. Route 26-287, with food and lodging available in nearby communities.

Information: Supervisor, Shoshone National Forest, Box 961, Cody, Wyoming 82314.

🌲 Not only is the **Bridger Wilderness** roadless, there are places in it that have received the designation "trailless areas." This is a commendable administrative action for a segment of the Wind River Mountains that Jim Bridger, Kit Carson, William Sublette, Captain Bonneville, and John C. Frémont first explored with few or no trails available. Today the Bridger Wilderness stretches for ninety miles along the Wind River Range, and in its 383,300 acres are nearly every conceivable type of mountain terrain: glaciated peaks, sharp ridges, cirque basins, glaciers, hundreds of icy lakes, spring-fed streams, canyons, and tree-lined valleys. The highest point, Gannett Peak, 13,804 feet, lies on the boundary with the Glacier Primitive Area. It is rough country not only because of the jumbled rocks and dizzying cliffs, but because of the unpredictable weather, freezing temperatures, severe electrical storms, and clouds of mosquitoes in early summer.

The extraordinary scenic views amply compensate for these not unusual "hardships." Wildlife, from moose and mountain lion to grouse and grayling, inhabit the region. However, sheep and cattle are permitted to graze during summer. Hikers have a wide choice of routes through the wilderness because there are 550 miles of trails. Specific restrictions apply to human entry into this wild domain, and it is thus advisable to secure the latest details before planning a trip. Though most use is by backpacking, commercial outfitters may be hired to lead horseback trips. Access is mainly through five entry points along the southwest boundary, on roads leading off U.S. Route 187. Short hikes from these points to scenic lakes helps to make the Bridger a "family wilderness"; beyond are the rugged peaks that challenge long-distance hikers. Upper trails are usually free of snow by mid-July. Food and lodging may be obtained in nearby towns.

Information: Supervisor, Bridger-Teton National Forest, Jackson, Wyoming 83001.

Adjacent to the Bridger Wilderness on the east lies the **Popo Agie Primitive Area** of 70,000 acres. It is likewise a remnant of beautiful, mostly undisturbed alpine terrain along the flank of the Wind River Range, with a high point of 13,225 feet. The upper peaks and ridges are sharply cut by glaciation, which also resulted in "plucked-out" basins called cirques. Collected waters from snow and melting ice flow down deep glaciated canyons. All is not rugged terrain, however, because the glaciers did not etch their way everywhere and some ridge tops are flat or gently rolling. Most of the rock is granite, and since the area is largely above tree line, the naked rocks stand out as bold cliffs and sawlike ridges, with occasional talus slopes and patches of ice and snow.

But on rock-filled glacial moraines, patches of lodgepole and limber pine, spruce, and fir grow. Hiking, fishing, hunting, and mountain climbing are major uses of the area, which is accessible over gravel roads from Wyoming State Route 131 southwest of Lander. Food and lodging are available in nearby towns.

Information: Supervisor, Shoshone National Forest, Box 961, Cody, Wyoming 82314.

One hundred and forty miles northeast of the Wind River Range lie the Bighorn Mountains, an isolated but spectacular uplift in the midst of rolling

Wyoming prairies. The uppermost point, Cloud Peak, rises to 13,165 feet and around it are sweeping ridges, basins, and boulder-strewn vales of durable granite and gneiss, rocks that resist even the most forceful ravages of glaciation. As a result, the **Cloud Peak Primitive Area** is a rough, high mountain vastness, although some of the mountain peaks appear to be beveled off because they were once part of an eroded plain that was uplifted when the mountains rose millions of years ago.

Down from these bare rock areas, we encounter cliffs of dolomite, forests of lodgepole pine and Engelmann spruce, and rolling slopes of open grassland and sagebrush. "During June and July," according to a U.S. Geological Survey report, "these open parks display a striking array of wild flowers, the colors of which, augmented by green grassy slopes and majestic grandeur of the mountain background, lend an air of lyrical beauty to the primitive area."

Hikers may share this domain with the abundant deer and elk; trails provide access to remote sections, at least after the heavy snows of winter have melted. Even then the weather can be severe, and snow may be expected in any month of the year.

Cloud Peak, between the towns of Worland and Sheridan, is approached first on U.S. routes 14, 16, or 87, then on secondary roads through Bighorn National Forest. The wilderness encompasses 137,000 acres, including lakes and streams suitable for fishing. Campgrounds are available nearby; accommodations may be reserved in surrounding towns.

Information: Supervisor, Bighorn National Forest, Sheridan, Wyoming 82801.

About fifty miles west of Yellowstone National Park is another sanctuary important to the restoration of trumpeter swans, the **Red Rock Lakes National Wildlife Refuge.** On this 40,000-acre refuge, near the headwaters of the Missouri River, the trumpeters increased from fewer than fifty birds in 1935 to hundreds twenty years later. They are still wary but may be photographed from mid-July through August. However, nesting is a delicate process and the birds have prior rights, so advance information on access, road conditions, hunting, fishing, camping, and special regulations should be obtained. Thousands of other birds either nest in or pass through the refuge, including whistling swans, sandhill cranes, herons, curlews, and numerous ducks. Many species of hawks also inhabit the region. Moreover, because of the varied habitats—marshes, lakes, streams, and upland forests— there are numerous mammalian residents, including moose, elk, deer, and pronghorns. Photographers are especially attracted to the refuge in July, when wild flowers abound. Accommodations are available at Lima and West Yellowstone, fifty miles away.

Information: Manager, Red Rock Lakes National Wildlife Refuge, Monida Star Route, Lima, Montana 59739.

🌲 Man now knows that the craters on the moon are considerably smoother in contour than he had originally imagined. But in the early days he applied moon names to cratered volcanic landscapes on earth which were, roughly speaking, out of this world. Such was **Craters of the Moon National Monument,** Idaho, set aside as a unit of the national park system in 1924 and designated, in part, as wilderness in 1970. It may seem a little strange, at first glance, to apply such distinguished national attention to a landscape so obviously—to use the old clichés—impassable, barren, and desolate. But the fact is that Craters of the Moon, like most or all volcanic areas, deserves none of these appellations. It is certainly not barren nor desolate. More than 300 species of plants are native to these lava flows and black cinders. Some are unusually adapted to live on waterless cinder dunes: the dwarf buckwheat, though scarcely four inches tall, has a root that penetrates as deeply as four feet. The natural carpets of dwarf monkeyflower that bloom on the cinders—a vivid mass of purple—extend as far as the eye can see. The plant occupants range from lichens, ferns, and mosses to whole groves of limber pine. The secret, of course, is that these plants, like desert plants, are variously adapted to the specific environmental conditions under which they grow. Even so, to persons accustomed to vegetation in more humid climes, it will seem a little strange to see white, snowlike clumps of buckwheat growing on such freshly erupted rock.

The rock itself, product of many fiery explosions, possesses extraordinary forms. The lava seethed or burst out and either flowed away freely or was pushed along the surface. The result has been congealed cascades of smooth rock in many designs, or formidable jumbles so sharp they defy easy passage. On trails across this bizarre landscape the hiker will also encounter lava tubes and other tunnels, ice caves, volcanic monoliths, natural bridges, fragments of crater walls, spatter cones, cinder dunes, ejected bombs of hardened lava, vents and rift zones, and molds of trees enveloped by lava. In other words, it is as distinctive an environment as the craters of the moon.

The wilderness portion has neither firewood nor water. Campgrounds are available but not accommodations; the town of Arco lies twenty miles to the northeast on U.S. Route 26.

Information: Superintendent, Craters of the Moon National Monument, Box 29, Arco, Idaho 83213.

🌲 Southernmost of the Middle Rockies are the Uinta Mountains, fifty miles east of Salt Lake City, Utah. Though most mountain ranges in North

America extend from north to south, the Uintas defy that trend. They stretch from the Wasatch Mountains due east out of Utah into Colorado—a distance of 150 miles. Geologically, they are part of a broad, gentle arch with nearly flat-lying older rocks in the center and more steeply dipping younger rocks along the margins. Topographically they are divided into two rather different-appearing sections, the west and the east, each containing a unit of the national wilderness preservation system.

The western section of the High Uintas has the greater elevations, including Kings Peak, 13,528 feet, the highest point in Utah. These uplands of rolling treeless peaks and stratified ridges carved by glaciation into picturesque shapes are still largely wild and primitive, and 240,717 acres of them have been set aside as the **High Uintas Primitive Area.** Up in this thin, clear air the hiking can be rough on account of jumbled, sharp-edged, frost-riven fields of rocks, called felsenmeer. The patches of ice and snow that may impede progress, even late in the spring, are merely indicative of a prior ice-age history. Judging from the great walled basins that drop away from the summits into steep canyons, the glaciers that once occupied this range were enormous. Some are believed to have been more than twenty miles long. The sea of glacial ice that engulfed all but the highest summits is virtually outlined by the surrounding moraines, deposits of boulders that were left when the ice thawed and melted. Because of all this, a hiker in the High Uintas sees a "deranged" terrain—sheard-off peaks, truncated spurs of ridges, hanging tributary canyons from which a few falls and cataracts plunge, and glistening surfaces of rocks smoothly polished by the abrasive movement of ice. Since then, eroding streams have cut spectacular canyons on their way to adjacent valleys.

Today the Uintas are no longer smothered by glacial ice. Below 11,000 feet, in fact, they are clothed with dense coniferous forests. Broad meadows separate these forests, and dwarf willows grow beside meandering, transparent streams. Lakes are abundant. As for wildlife, elk range the mountains from end to end. Moose live mostly on northern slopes. Mule deer occupy brushy slopes at lower levels. Smaller mammals, as well as birds, are abundant and often seen by alert observers.

Trails reach into nearly all sections of this wilderness. Roads approach closely on the south and west, principally Utah Route 150, and numerous campgrounds provide base points from which trips into the mountains can be commenced. For accommodations there are ranches, resorts, and lodges in the surrounding area, and at these places visitors may also arrange for horses, guides, and equipment.

Information: Supervisor, Wasatch National Forest, 125 South State Street, Salt Lake City, Utah 84138; and Supervisor, Ashley National Forest, Vernal, Utah 84078.

🌲 The eastern half of the Uinta Mountains differs from the western half in having a lower profile and in possessing colorful sandstone canyons made spectacular by sharply bent and folded strata. An immense concentration of dinosaur bones originally justified the establishment of **Dinosaur National Monument,** in northeastern Utah and northwestern Colorado, but so impressive were the adjacent river gorges and high plateaus that the monument boundaries were enlarged and—difficult practice in cattle country—grazing was scheduled for a slow phase-out. Once there were proposals to flood the canyons, and bitter battles ensued, but Dinosaur stands as a landmark in the alteration of public policy from reclamation to conservation. Now wilderness is winning out, and the 206,662 acres of the Monument will eventually be almost as wild as they were originally.

The remoter portions are difficult of access. To be sure, one can drive over comfortable roads from U.S. Route 40, near Vernal, Utah, to the quarry of dinosaur bones and to scenic overlooks. There are also a few primitive roads within the Monument. But to cross the wild, roadless juniper-covered plateaus takes sustained effort and the carrying of one's own life-support equipment. To climb down dizzying slopes and precipitous canyon walls calls for courage as well as ropes and technical training. A float trip down the Green and Yampa rivers is perhaps the easiest access to this wilderness, but such popular pastimes have to be restricted lest too many travelers damage the fragile river domain. In the words of the National Park Service, "Between the extremes of total preservation and unbridled use lies a realistic carrying capacity." The boat trip, in addition, is potentially dangerous, and visitors who wish to float down the rivers must have a permit from the Monument superintendent or be accompanied by a guide who has one.

Split Mountain Canyon, the Gates of Lodore, Island Park, Echo Park, Steamboat Rock—the names recall an era of pioneer exploration that began with John Wesley Powell's audacious voyage downstream in 1869. Today there are box canyons to be explored, broad "benches," rocky crags with bighorns and mountain lions, and pictographs and other evidence of occupation by early man. Beyond the Monument lie open lands administered by the Bureau of Land Management. Campgrounds within the Monument are scheduled to be- eliminated if sites are developed outside the boundary. Primitive campsites in the interior should suffice for travelers who spend a few days or a few weeks in this high, open wilderness. Extended trips should be well planned in advance. Winter travel is encouraged, though high-elevation approach roads may be closed by snow between October and May. There are nature trails, exhibits, and publications. Food and lodging may be obtained in Vernal, Utah, and other nearby points.

Information: Superintendent, Dinosaur National Monument, Dinosaur, Colorado 81610.

4. SOUTHERN ROCKIES

No other collection of mountains south of Canada has peaks as consistently high as those in Colorado. Indeed, of the fifty highest summits in the United States, including Alaska, twenty-eight are in Colorado. This segment of the Cordillera, that great backbone of North America, has few of the sweeping, uptilted layers of rock so prominent in the Canadian Rockies, or vast outpourings of lava like those in the Yellowstone region of the Middle Rockies. In these mountains, touches of the desert mix with touches of the subarctic, a kind of crossroads situation that accounts for arid forests at low elevations, tundra patches at higher levels, and occasional masses of summit rock scraped bare by glaciers. But in common with the rest of the Rockies, these wilderness areas possess the ingredients of solitude and natural beauty that qualify them for special protection.

🌲 No wilderness area in Colorado is nearly as large as those of greatest size in the Middle or Northern Rockies. This is somewhat of an irony because Colorado, most populous of the Rocky Mountain States, certainly has a need of them. Such were the sentiments expressed at hearings during establishment of the **Eagles Nest Wilderness,** sixty miles west of Denver. Eagles Nest contains approximately 128,000 acres, and in the midst of mountains roaded, logged, mined, grazed, farmed, and urbanized, it is a valuable prize indeed.

It consists, for the most part, of the highest and roughest parts of the Gore Range, a hard-rock mass of escarpments, ridges, deep valleys, and sharp-tipped mountains. Seventeen peaks within the boundaries rise above 13,000 feet. Nearly half of the wilderness is made up of bare rock, grass, and the waters of lakes and streams. The rest is coniferous forest or shrub domain. So rugged and inaccessible is it that trails cross only at either end and a hiker exploring between them should be well-equipped and experienced in the disciplines of wilderness travel. These mountains can test the mettle and survival capacity of human travelers. For the less hardy visitor, easier trails and terrain may be found at lower elevations. The grassy meadows on lower slopes are some of the deepest, densest, and richest in North America. Yellow buckwheat and scarlet gilia are the principal contenders for dominance during mid-July. In somewhat more sheltered vales, blue columbine and wild roses grow luxuriously. The air is alive with yellow warblers flying to and from their nests in willow thickets, sapsuckers chattering, robins exploring in the sagebrush vales, bluebirds hunting insects, and veeries trilling deep in the woods.

Altogether more than a hundred miles of trails lead through these uplands of ancient, broken rock and from them hikers have a chance to see mountain goats and bighorn sheep, elk, deer, bears, mink, and other mammals. Above Eagles Nest Mountain, 13,397 feet, the sight of a soaring golden eagle gives special meaning to this wilderness. Campgrounds and accommodations are available nearby and outfitters can assist on hiking, riding, fishing, and hunting trips. Trails are usually free of snow between June and October, though the higher mountains may not be snow-free until July. Primitive roads reach toward the wilderness from access routes off U.S. routes 6, 24, and 40, Interstate 70, and Colorado routes 9 and 131.

Information: Supervisor, White River National Forest, Federal Building, Ninth and Grand Avenue, Glenwood Springs, Colorado 81601.

In northwestern Colorado the White River Plateau may be seen from great distances as a lofty prominence of light-colored cliffs stretching, curving, retreating, and jutting for nearly a hundred miles. In places the promontories seem almost like rows of castles, so towering and sheer as to appear impregnable. But they are not as inaccessible as that. In the 238,000-acre **Flat Tops Wilderness,** a superlative part of these uplands is reachable if one goes north forty miles from Rifle, Colorado, then east fifty miles from Meeker to Trappers Lake. By that time an elevation of 9,600 feet has been reached, but the Flat Tops Plateau is even higher; it has an average elevation of 11,000 feet. Here the visitor must leave behind his paraphernalia of civilization, his motorized carriers, and most of the comforts of home in order to enter.

Climbing higher on some of the 160 miles of trails within this area, the hiker accustomed to lower altitudes becomes more easily winded. His pace slows, and he welcomes the opportunity to use his binoculars and scout for herds of deer and elk, which summer by the thousands in these mountains. He may spy a coyote trotting across a grassy expanse, a pika in the rocks, or a porcupine among the trees. He could flush a grouse or ptarmigan, or track the flight path of a golden eagle.

After negotiating sedimentary walls and lava cliffs he breaks out on the high plateaus for which the Flat Tops region is named. From the uppermost points, slightly over 12,000 feet, the views are especially striking, and the vastness of western Colorado is revealed in broad panoramas.

217

Within the wilderness are more than thirty lakes as well as a hundred miles of fishing streams, including the famed south fork of the White River. Angling is one of the most popular pursuits. Hunting is also permitted, but hunters are hampered by rough terrain, areas of blown-down trees, and the possibility in autumn of being trapped on the plateau by an early snowstorm. Among the most rewarding experiences are hunting with camera and the simple enjoyment of solitude and scenery. Along the trails may be seen geological formations such as the Chinese Wall and the Devil's Causeway, beds of alpine flowers, large areas of insect-killed Engelmann spruce and forest regrowth, stands of white-barked aspen with their fluttering leaves, parklike meadows, and beaver ponds.

Campgrounds are available in the vicinity of this wilderness, and accommodations may be secured in surrounding towns. Access is from U.S. routes 6, 24, 40, and Interstate 70, and Colorado routes 131 and 132. District ranger offices are at Meeker, Eagle, Rifle, and Yampa.

Information: Supervisor, White River National Forest, Federal Building, Ninth and Grand Avenue, Glenwood Springs, Colorado 81601; and Supervisor, Routt National Forest, Hunt Building, Steamboat Springs, Colorado 80477.

In the Ute Indian language, *rawah* means "wilderness," and the **Rawah Wilderness** of northern Colorado is a small (27,000 acres) but exemplary parcel of wild upland. So high is it, in fact, that some of the trails may not be free of snow until mid-July, and in case of an early September snowfall, the summer can be very short. Nevertheless, this "island of wilderness," at an average elevation of 11,000 feet, provides the setting for cool and pleasant wilderness trips. Sunlight reflects from melting snowbanks and sparkles in the churning waters that cascade over fallen boulders. Pools of water and tranquil lakes mirror the spruce and fir that have withstood winter wind and weight of snow. Wildlife, typical of the Rocky Mountains, includes deer, bears, bighorns, beaver, coyotes, foxes, mink, ptarmigan, and the ubiquitous Steller jays.

This wilderness measures three miles wide and fourteen miles in length, and is located along the crest of the Medicine Bow Mountains. Trails lead to lakes, streams, and summits. One-day excursions by foot or horseback take visitors to the heart of the area. Longer trips of up to a week allow time for more leisurely enjoyment of wild aspects. However, before embarking, a hiker is well advised to check with forest rangers for up-to-date details on trails, fishing, and points of interest. Resort personnel in the vicinity can provide accommodations and arrange pack trips. Campgrounds are available on some approach routes. The area is seventy-five miles west of Fort Collins on Colorado Route 14.

Information: Supervisor, Roosevelt National Forest, 301 South Howes Street, Fort Collins, Colorado 80521.

🌲 The **Mount Zirkel Wilderness,** ten miles northeast of Steamboat Springs, Colorado, lies so high along the Park Range and the Continental Divide that it has fourteen peaks near 12,000 feet. Snow does not melt away substantially until late June, and even then some patches remain all summer. The meltwaters help to supply more than sixty-five lakes in the area, many of which contain brook, rainbow, and cutthroat trout. Typical high-country animals such as pikas, grouse, and ptarmigan are present, and hunting for deer and elk in the autumn is said to be excellent. Trails enter the wilderness from all sides, and traverse the length of it. Groups of more than fifteen people or with more than ten horses should check at ranger district offices before entering the wilderness. Campgrounds are available on adjacent lakes and streams, and accommodations may be obtained in nearby villages. U.S. Route 40 passes twenty miles to the south of the area; several Colorado state routes and forest roads reach points nearer the boundaries.

Information: Supervisor, Routt National Forest, Box 1198, Steamboat Springs, Colorado 80477.

🌲 At one point in the Front Range of the Southern Rockies people can drive up over the mountains and through an alpine wilderness. The Trail Ridge Road, in **Rocky Mountain National Park,** reaches 12,183 feet and for eleven miles remains above tree line. This permits observation from automobiles of a sweeping panorama characteristic of the Southern Rockies: snow-covered mountain peaks in the distance, breathtaking drop-offs into forested valleys, and colorful but fragile tundra vegetation. The novice who wants to sample wilderness can approach it here without much physical effort. He can also observe wide changes in vegetation between the entrance, at 8,150 feet, and the high point of the road.

The park has nature trails, visitor centers, guided walks, campfire programs, and roadside exhibits. If the novice getting introduced to the wilderness would like a short walk in a sylvan setting, he can hike around Bear Lake and observe the golden-mantled ground squirrel close at hand. The way leads near groves of white-barked aspen trees as well as among coniferous trees and over giant boulders.

Another brief venture into the wilderness is the hike from Bear Lake to

Dream Lake, a distance of one mile, but it is a crowded mile in summer. In any case, the hiker gains magnificent views into the heart of the Rockies. Other short "practice hikes" may be indulged in by the novice. He can gradually lengthen his travels, gaining experience, and eventually take long-distance jaunts. About 300 miles of trails lead into the park's backcountry. Mountain climbing, of course, is a more rigorous exercise and each season brings its share of persons who want to climb Longs Peak (14,256 feet elevation at the summit) or other challenging eminences in the park. However, this requires experience and expertise, for tragedy has too often been the lot of those who started up the mountains ill-prepared. A problem for any hiker is the chance of sudden storms, with the possibility of lightning, plunging temperatures, poor visibility, and snow. Rock-climbing ascents and overnight trips of any kind require registration with a park ranger. Campgrounds are available at several points in the park, but no lodging, except on private lands. Accommodations may be secured at numerous places outside the boundary.

As usual in wilderness areas, the best time of year in Rocky Mountain National Park is not necessarily summer. Autumn could be best of all—less snow in the mountains, not as many thundershowers, fewer insects, and far more color, especially when whole slopes of quaking aspen turn vivid gold or orange. Some animals are more active and more often seen, such as elk, bighorns, deer, and coyotes. In case of an early snowfall, the scenery takes on additional spectacle, and the backcountry additional hazards.

Among the features in this wilderness are glaciers, remote lakes, cascades, and sweeping, ice-carved canyons. Before departing, however, hikers would be wise to consult park rangers and examine the available sales maps and literature at park visitor centers. These make more understandable the ecological and geological features with which the wilderness traveler will be associated.

The park, seventy miles northwest of Denver, is accessible via U.S. routes 34 and 36. The Trail Ridge Road connects Route 34 on both sides of the park, leads over the mountains, and into Shadow Mountain National Recreation Area on the western side.

Information: Superintendent, Rocky Mountain National Park, Estes Park, Colorado 80517.

🌲 One of the most familiar scenes in the Rocky Mountains is that southwest of Aspen, Colorado, where the Maroon Bells are reflected in Maroon Lake. These jagged crests and pyramid peaks, with sweeping groves of aspen trees and mats of spruce-fir forest, epitomize the Rockies perhaps as much as any specific section. The skyline rises to 14,265 feet. Sedimentary beds are exposed in dramatic and colorful cliffs. Arctic plants, such as lilies, forget-me-nots, and phlox, grow on the upper tundras. Each ecological "niche" holds a distinctive contingent of plant and animal species: elk in the high country, jays in the woods, and ouzels among the moss on the banks of streams.

Such is the **Maroon Bells–Snowmass Wilderness,** 66,380 acres of relatively unspoiled and picturesque mountain terrain. Of special photogenic interest are the aspen, whose white trunks seem to change shape with each movement of shadow and sunlight. One of the most spectacular short hikes in the Rocky Mountains is that from Maroon Lake, reached by paved road from Aspen, to Crater Lake, inside the wilderness area. Though short, less than four miles round trip, the hike begins at 9,600 feet and rises above 10,000 feet, so that a person unaccustomed to the altitude will gasp for air if he goes very fast. But going fast is folly indeed, especially in mid-July, when the snowbanks are melting, the waterfalls roaring, and the Colorado columbine covering acres of open rocks and forest glades with its blue and white blossoms. Fields of sky-blue flax, together with larkspur and geraniums, enhance the display. The trip is immensely colorful: Overhead the portals of maroon rock invade blue sky—or are wreathed with clouds. Clear stream pools are tinted with emerald shades. Grasses and forbs, a rich green, grow hip-high in places. The finale is Crater Lake, a blue-green, willow-lined body of icy water at the base of the Maroon Bells, whose layered, tilted crags rise to more than 14,000 feet.

Trails lead to high lakes, hot springs, passes with panoramic mountain views, and numbers of cascading streams. Commercial outfitters are available for persons interested in short riding excursions or extended trips. Accommodations are available in Aspen and nearby communities. District ranger offices are located in Aspen and Carbondale. Access roads or trails reach the wilderness from all sides.

Information: Supervisor, White River National Forest, Federal Building, Glenwood Springs, Colorado 81601.

Southwest of the Maroon Bells, the **West Elk Wild Area** embraces parts of three mountain ranges—Beckwith, West Elk, and Anthracite—that rise to 12,920 feet above sea level. Pinnacles, canyons, high, thin walls, and soaring stratified rock layers are the prominent features of this wilderness; coniferous forests and aspen groves fill the sheltered valleys. Open meadows grow thickly with grasses and wild flowers. Picturesque willow-lined lakes contain abundant trout, depending on the numbers and success of anglers. The high country is home to deer and elk in summer, as well as bighorns, bears, and smaller mammals.

Hiking trails reach into all quadrants of this 62,000-acre wilderness. Several one-day trips can be made to fishing lakes and alpine meadows. Other excursions, by foot or horseback, may take up to a week, not counting layovers or side trips. Access is by trail from all directions and prospective wilderness travelers should consider other destinations in Gunnison National Forest while planning their trip. Secondary roads approach the wilderness; the nearest major highways are Colorado Route 135 and U.S. Route 50. Packers and outfitters are available in the vicinity. Improved campgrounds may be found on adjacent forest lands; a full range of food, lodging, and supplies is in Gunnison, twenty-five miles to the south.

Information: Supervisor, Gunnison National Forest, Box 138, Delta, Colorado 81416.

🌲 High on the Cannibal and Calf Creek plateaus southwest of Gunnison, Colorado, the U.S. Bureau of Land Management has set aside 40,400 acres containing a vast expanse of relatively level tundra above 12,000 feet. It is called the **Powderhorn Primitive Area** and embraces, in addition to tundra, a series of life zones ranging down into spruce, fir, pine, and sagebrush. Parts of it are breeding and wintering grounds for elk, but there are also coyotes, deer, bears, beaver, grouse, eagles, and other animals—perhaps even mountain lions. Dedicated late in 1973, the area was freed of mineral prospecting, mining, and lumbering activities. Grazing and recreational pursuits are allowed, although motorized vehicles and equipment are prohibited. Access is via State Route 149. Food and lodging are in nearby communities.

Information: State Director, Bureau of Land Management, 1961 Stout Street, Denver, Colorado 80202.

🌲 Being so high in elevation, the wilderness areas of Colorado remain at least partially inaccessible most of the year simply because of heavy snow blocking access roads or trails or both. It may be possible to enter on skis or snowshoes, but winter travel at high altitude can be hazardous; devotees of this sport must be experienced, sturdy, and equipped with up-to-date information and, where required, permission to enter. **La Garita Wilderness** is an example of high-elevation terrain; within its 49,000 acres are two peaks whose summits reach above 14,000 feet. Trails are free of snow from about June 15 to October 15. It is a busy period because animals such as bighorns, deer, and elk move up into the high country to take advantage of fresh green grass in spring. The hiker encounters other evidence of animal life, such as beaver ponds, and may see mountain lions, coyotes, bears, grouse, and ptarmigan. Trout fishing is a popular pursuit.

No developed campsites are provided within the wilderness, but campgrounds exist on approach routes. Access is via Colorado Route 149 from the south, and by forest roads from other directions. The nearest food and lodging may be obtained at Saguache or Gunnison. As in other wilderness areas, motorized vehicles are prohibited.

Information: Supervisor, Rio Grande National Forest, Monte Vista, Colorado 81144; and Supervisor, Gunnison National Forest, Box 138, Delta, Colorado 81416.

🌲 How much of the **Uncompahgre Primitive Area,** near Ouray, Colorado, is a wilderness seems at this writing to be a matter of question. The area is so replete with mines and access roads that the U.S. Forest Service recommended against wilderness status after hearings held in 1964. Furthermore, there are thousands of acres of private land mixed in with the proposed area, with no assurance that either landholders or miners would always conduct themselves in a manner compatible with wilderness preservation.

After hearings in 1971 and in response to considerable public pressure, the Forest Service modified its proposal. Hemmed in by traditions and laws (the 1964 Wilderness Act permits valid mining rights to be retained), the Service proposed a sort of hybrid unit that would incorporate wilderness, mining, and recreation uses. To be sure, the mountains are magnificent—Uncompahgre Peak rises to 14,309 feet—the mines are historic and interesting, and the roads provide access to the high country. From Ouray, which is cupped in a bowl of massive cliffs, it doesn't look like there could be any access to the alpine country beyond those summits. But there is, and the Forest Service has attempted to find a compromise solution to the conflicting problems. The one certainty is that wilderness values are being eroded.

The Uncompahgre Primitive Area presently has 69,253 acres, and the U.S. Geological Survey calls it one of the most intensively mineralized regions in the United States. It also has timber and forage, so the opportunities for commercial use are substantial. The area has already yielded over $330 million worth of gold, silver, copper and lead with some mines still going strong, and production expected to be good for years to come. Hence the conflicts and pressures.

But the wilderness values are also superlative, and one solution to the land management problems proposes the incorporation of adjacent lands where wild values are still intact. Thousands of elk and deer roam the mountains. Bighorns, bears, and coyotes occupy their niches. The smaller mammals include marten, mink, fox, bobcat, porcupine, and beaver. The little pika looks out from its rocky outposts. Among the birds are grouse, eagles, and ptarmigan. The abundance of lakes and streams makes trout fishing

223

possible—where the waters are not yellowed with mining residue. The principal recreation activities, in addition to fishing, are backpacking, camping, hunting, skiing and snowshoeing. The photographic opportunities are extraordinary, especially in autumn when great waves of glowing gold signify the turning of aspen leaves.

Access is via U.S. Route 550, the celebrated "Million Dollar Highway," between Ouray and Silverton. There are also approaches over lesser roads, as from Telluride. Accommodations are available at Ouray, Silverton and other points around the area. Campgrounds are located on adjacent national forest lands.

Information: Supervisor, Uncompahgre National Forest, Box 138, Delta, Colorado 81416.

🌲 To miners the San Juan Mountains mean only one thing, and for years they have dug from these peaks how many fortunes in gold and silver? Even now the towns of Telluride, Ouray, and Silverton, a district where more than $350 million worth of silver, gold, lead, zinc, and copper were produced, possess an "outpost in the wilderness" character that pioneer miners must have felt. Indeed, considerable wilderness remains in the San Juans, rather surprising because minerals still exist in places, locked in the rocks for possible future extraction. The mountains are covered with mining claims, and even though many have been abandoned, the presence of established wild areas is something of a triumph of mind over metal.

On the western edge of the San Juan Mountains, seven miles southwest of the Telluride mining area, lies the **Wilson Mountains Primitive Area,** its 27,000 acres adjoining the flat-topped mesa country of the Colorado Plateau. Typical of the Southern Rockies, its peaks soar up to more than 14,000 feet. One rock formation, Lizard Head, is a nearly vertical spire that rises 300 feet from its base. Wilson Peak itself rises from the valley floor with the same dramatic effect as the Jungfrau rises above Interlaken in Switzerland. The vegetation ranges from coniferous forests and aspen groves to alpine meadows of grass, sedge, and wild flowers to rocky ledges covered with lichens or nothing at all. In the long winters, during which thirty-three feet of snow may fall, avalanches are not uncommon. In sheltered places the snow or ice may remain all year.

Remnants of mines, dumps, and mining paraphernalia have littered the mountains since the late 1800s. Nearly $2 million worth of precious metals was extracted before the mines and prospects were abandoned. Some of the mines were so high—13,000 feet—that the mining season each summer was very short indeed.

Colorado Route 145 passes near the eastern boundary of the area, but closer approach is only by primitive road or trail—and winter snows block these early in the autumn. Tourist accommodations are available in Telluride.

Information: Supervisor, San Juan National Forest, Oliger Building, Box 341, Durango, Colorado 81301; and Supervisor, Uncompahgre National Forest, Eleventh and Main, Delta, Colorado 81416.

The **Weminuche Primitive Area** combines the former San Juan and Upper Rio Grande primitive areas, located approximately twenty-five miles northeast of Durango, Colorado. The name, pronounced "*wem*-in-ooch," honors the Weminuche subtribe of Ute Indians, and it is quite a honor. Some of the most beautiful wilderness in the Southern Rockies is located within this 346,833 acres. The high green meadows of spring burst forth with vivid color, contrasting with the dense but discontinuous forests of spruce, fir, and ponderosa pine. The woods sweep down to the edges of valleys and give way to open meadows, or they rise to high altitudes and yield to tundra vegetation or barren rock. "The Window" is not a tiny opening through which one looks but a monumental gate of rock through which a giant could stride.

The western part of the wilderness is especially scenic because streams and glaciers have attacked it and carved deep gorges into the ancient rock. This has left sharp dividing ridges and peaks such as the Needle Mountains, and some points reach above 14,000 feet. The eastern part of the wilderness is more volcanic, in reality a deeply dissected plateau whose southern edge drops off in a wall as much as 5,000 feet high. Into this plateau streams have cut nearly impassable canyons. In many places the terrain is too steep to support much vegetation, but elsewhere fir, spruce, pine, and aspen grow.

Cold-water rivulets gush down the gorges from melting snow. Dozens of lakes and nearly 150 miles of streams provide innumerable challenges for fishermen. For sightseers there are Chicago Basin and the remnants of early mining activities, Rio Grande Pyramid, the Knife Edge, Emerald Lake, and hot springs.

Although the area is covered by some 300 miles of trails, a hiker will be lured away from them for various reasons: to approach a herd of elk in a meadow, to camp in an out-of-the-way place, to scale the higher peaks, to search for cutthroat trout, to find the mountain goats that are being established . . .

Access is via U.S. routes 160 and 550, and Colorado Route 149. Campsites with a few primitive facilities are located at Emerald Lake, within the wilderness area. More fully equipped campgrounds are available on surrounding national forest lands. Accommodations may be reserved in surrounding towns, and packers and outfitters may be contacted with regard to extended trips.

Information: Supervisor, San Juan National Forest, Oliger Building, Box 341, Durango, Colorado 81301.

In the midst of the Southern Rockies lies a desert, the kind that early settlers might have called forbidding, cold, and desolate. It lies at an elevation of 8,200 feet in the San Luis Valley, thirty-eight miles northeast of Alamosa, on Colorado Route 150. Ever since they were first described by Lieutenant Zebulon Pike in the winter of 1806–1807, these dunes have been to a large degree unmolested, and in 1932 were set aside as **Great Sand Dunes National Monument,** which now covers 36,740 acres.

Owing to a peculiar combination of natural resources, strong winds pick up sand from loose soils on the floor of the San Luis Valley and carry it toward the imposing 14,000-foot Sangre de Cristo Mountains. Since the mountains have a curvature facing the southwest, these winds are trapped except where they whistle through three low passes. High-flying dust gets over the mountain, but heavier grains of sand fall short. This process has gone on so long that some of the world's tallest dunes, 700 feet high, have formed. At present, the coming and going of sand appears to be fairly stable, for the extent and location of dunes has changed very little in the last fifty years.

It takes about three hours to walk to the top of the dunes and back, but since there are no trails a hiker can pick his own route and wander in this sandy wilderness for many more hours than that. He may explore Medano, Sand, and Mosca creeks, whose waters run for a while then sink into the sand. Early and late in the day are best for summer hiking because of the cooler air and sand; they are also best for photographers because the low angle of sunlight accentuates the contours of the dunes. Vegetation is not entirely lacking on the sands, for grass, legumes, and sunflowers may be found. Surrounding the sands are sagebrush, cactus, and stands of aspen, spruce, fir, and pine. A short nature trail has been laid out near the Monument headquarters and visitor center, and published data are available on the birds, mammals, and other life of the region. A longer hike can be taken up the Mosca Pass trail, outside the Monument. Picnicking and camping areas are available within the Monument, and limited supplies a mile to the south. A full range of tourist accommodations may be found in Alamosa, thirty-eight miles to the southwest.

Information: Superintendent, Great Sand Dunes National Monument, Box 60, Alamosa, Colorado 81101.

PART VI

The Central Lowlands

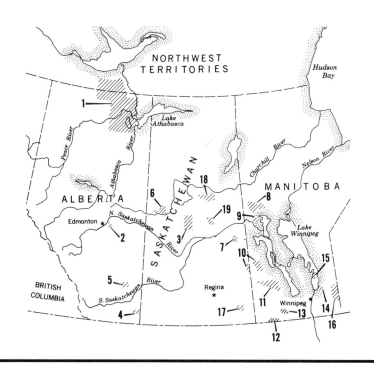

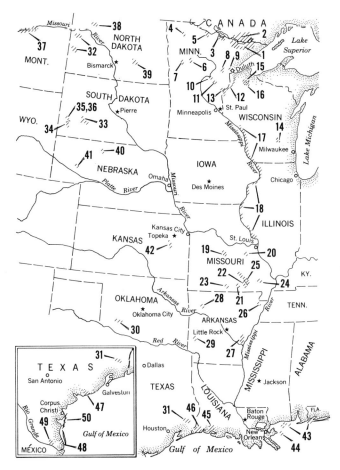

1. CANADA'S PRAIRIE PROVINCES

1. Wood Buffalo National Park, Alberta–Northwest Territories
2. Elk Island National Park, Alberta
3. Prince Albert National Park, Saskatchewan
4. Cypress Hills Provincial Park, Alberta
5. Dinosaur Provincial Park, Alberta
6. Meadow Lake Provincial Park, Saskatchewan
7. Wildcat Hill Wilderness Area, Saskatchewan
8. Grass River Provincial Park, Manitoba
9. Clearwater Provincial Park, Manitoba
10. Duck Mountain Provincial Park, Manitoba
11. Riding Mountain National Park, Manitoba
12. Turtle Mountain Provincial Park, Manitoba
13. Spruce Woods Provincial Park, Manitoba
14. Grand Beach Provincial Park, Manitoba
15. Hecla Provincial Park, Manitoba
16. Whiteshell Provincial Park, Manitoba
17. Moose Mountain Provincial Park, Saskatchewan
18. Lac la Ronge Provincial Park, Saskatchewan
19. Nipawin Provincial Park, Saskatchewan

2. WOODS AND WATERS

1. Boundary Waters Canoe Area, Minnesota
2. Quetico Provincial Park, Ontario
3. Voyageurs National Park, Minnesota
4. Agassiz National Wildlife Refuge, Minnesota
5. Lake Agassiz Peatlands Natural Area, Minnesota
6. Itasca State Park, Minnesota
7. Tamarac National Wildlife Refuge, Minnesota
8. Savanna Portage State Park, Minnesota
9. Jay Cooke State Park, Minnesota
10. Mille Lacs Kathio State Park, Minnesota
11. Mille Lacs Wildlife Management Area, Minnesota
12. St. Croix National Scenic Riverway, Minnesota-Wisconsin
13. St. Croix State Park, Minnesota
14. Horicon National Wildlife Refuge, Wisconsin
15. Rainbow Lake Wilderness, Wisconsin
16. Flynn Lake Wilderness, Wisconsin
17. Upper Mississippi River Wild Life and Fish Refuge, Illinois to Minnesota
18. Mark Twain National Wildlife Refuge, Iowa-Missouri
19. Lake of the Ozarks State Park, Missouri
20. Meramec State Park, Missouri
21. Irish Wilderness, Missouri
22. Current River Scenic Area, Missouri
23. Carman Springs Wildlife Refuge, Missouri
24. Mingo National Wildlife Refuge, Missouri
25. Ozark National Scenic Riverways, Missouri
26. Big Lake National Wildlife Refuge, Arkansas
27. White River National Wildlife Refuge, Arkansas
28. Upper Buffalo Wilderness, Arkansas
29. Caney Creek Back Country, Arkansas
30. Wichita Mountains National Wildlife Refuge, Oklahoma
31. Big Thicket National Biological Reserve, Texas

3. PRAIRIE

32. Theodore Roosevelt National Memorial Park, North Dakota
33. Badlands National Monument, South Dakota
34. Wind Cave National Park, South Dakota
35. Custer State Park, South Dakota
36. Norbeck Wildlife Preserve, South Dakota
37. Charles M. Russell National Wildlife Range, Montana
38. Lostwood National Wildlife Refuge, North Dakota
39. Chase Lake National Wildlife Refuge, North Dakota
40. Valentine National Wildlife Refuge, Nebraska
41. Crescent Lake National Wildlife Refuge, Nebraska
42. Prairie National Park, Kansas

4. GULF COAST

43. Gulf Islands National Seashore, Florida-Mississippi
44. Breton National Wildlife Refuge, Louisiana
45. Lacassine National Wildlife Refuge, Louisiana
46. Sabine National Wildlife Refuge, Louisiana
47. Aransas National Wildlife Refuge, Texas
48. Laguna Atascosa National Wildlife Refuge, Texas
49. Santa Ana National Wildlife Refuge, Texas
50. Padre Island National Seashore, Texas

1. CANADA'S PRAIRIE PROVINCES

North America's largest national park, a subarctic wilderness of 11,072,000 acres, nearly the size of Vermont and New Hampshire combined, has been delineated on the boundary between Alberta and the Northwest Territories, at latitude 60°N. It consists of wet glaciated plains, shallow lakes, marshes, meadows, meandering streams, muskegs, and salt flats, ideally suited to insects and other invertebrates, and readily usable by birds, beaver, moose, and many furbearers. But all is not perpetually wet underfoot, and there are woods of spruce and pine where bears and bison roam; indeed, the latter, the largest remaining herd on the continent, are a hybrid combination of wood and plains bison brought together fifty years ago and saved from extinction. More than 12,000 of these animals wander in this park, and from them it gets its name, **Wood Buffalo National Park.**

Most famous of the park's seasonal residents, however, are the rare and endangered whooping cranes. Not until 1954 did men know where this bird flew to nest each year after leaving its winter home in Aransas National Wildlife Refuge on the Texas coast of the Gulf of Mexico. The journey covers 2,500 miles one way, but obviously the whooping cranes consider remote nesting grounds supplied with insect larvae and crustaceans worth every mile of the flight. Other species of birds are much more abundant. For example, the autumn concentration of migrants on the delta of the Peace and Athabasca rivers, one of the world's largest freshwater deltas, numbers in the hundreds of thousands.

Probably very little of the park will ever be developed for visitor use simply because few visitors use more than 5 or 10 percent of any national park. However, some of the park's environments are accessible by road and, though dangerous, by water. Frozen or not, Wood Buffalo is open all year, although no public facilities are maintained during winter. The land route is north from Edmonton via the Mackenzie Highway and Route 5 to Fort Smith, a distance of 850 miles (half of it gravel). Visitors can fly from Edmonton to Fort Smith but rental cars are not available at Fort Smith. Aircraft cannot land in the park and are subject to height restrictions when flying over certain areas of it. Picnicking and camping facilities are available but limited, both inside and outside the park; however, wilderness camping is

231

allowed under permit. Food, lodging, and supplies may be obtained at Fort Smith and Hay River, outside park boundaries. Hiking, canoeing, swimming, sightseeing, nature study, and fishing are the major activities; fish species include pike, walleye, goldeye, trout, whitefish, and inconnu.

Information: Superintendent, Wood Buffalo National Park, Fort Smith, Northwest Territories.

🌲 Large herds of elk once roamed the Beaver Hills of Alberta, which accounts for the name of **Elk Island National Park.** The park is an island in the sense that it consists of wild forests, lakes, and bogs on a rolling landscape amid flat agricultural plains. Glacial debris was dropped in abundance, and the vegetation has developed only within the last 10,000 years, after melting of the ice. Aspen and poplar are the most common trees at present; beneath them grow such ground cover as sarsaparilla, wintergreen, violet, and bunchberry. The bogs, of course, with their sphagnum moss, cranberry, blueberry, and cloudberry, are fascinating from a botanical point of view, and as a matter of fact there is so little of this natural landscape left in the surrounding region that visiting here is like going back into the past when only Cree Indians roamed the hills and woods. Deer, elk, bison, beaver, and other species still exist as though the world outside had never changed.

Located twenty-three miles east of Edmonton on Route 16, this 48,000-acre park has exhibits, educational programs, trails, campgrounds, and opportunities for hiking and canoeing. Food and lodging are available in Edmonton and other communities nearby.

Information: Superintendent, Elk Island National Park, R. R. 1, Fort Saskatchewan, Alberta.

🌲 Though many of the plains and prairies of North America have been converted to agricultural uses, obviously the farther north they are the less they have succumbed to man's domination. Vast flat or rolling areas of near pristine terrain still exist in the Arctic and subarctic with little or no assurance of being perpetuated as wild, but others have been given full protection by the Canadian government. In the geographical center of Saskatchewan, for example, **Prince Albert National Park** preserves a meeting ground for grassland prairies and boreal coniferous woods. A special feature is the abundance of delicate and subtle relationships among natural life systems. Ordinarily, it is difficult to perceive these arrangements, much less understand them, but the government has provided nature trails, naturalist services, an interpretive center, and other informational facilities in this 957,440-acre park.

Quetico Provincial Park, Ontario.

More than 150 miles of trails lead into the distinctive environments: open prairie; aspen woodlands; forests of spruce, pine, balsam fir, larch, and white birch; lakes; ponds; streams; bogs. Each has a recognizable and distinctive concentration of plants and animals, and a hiker should absorb significant details about these ecosystems before he goes among them. For example, on the prairie, while walking through grasses, bedstraw, meadow rue, yarrow, vetch, and among wild roses, he should remember that this is the place to look for badgers and coyotes. Formerly, he could have found plains bison, but now must be content to see them in fenced paddocks near the southern entrance to the park.

The open aspen woods provide a pleasant environment through which the hiker goes quietly in the hope of seeing elk or bears. He enters coniferous forest and discovers that on higher ground white spruce is more familiar, while black spruce remains in lowlands and jack pines on sandy soil. In this forest, he may be lucky enough to see an endangered mammal once widespread in the American wilderness—the gray wolf. On approaching grassy lakes or winding shallow streams, he should be alert to the opportunity of flushing moose, beaver, and muskrats. Thus the mammals keep to certain habitats, and the birds as well: hawks and herons at marshes, loons on lakes, and pileated woodpeckers among the trees.

233

This park is located thirty-five miles northwest of Prince Albert, Saskatchewan, and is accessible on routes 263 and 264. It is open all year. Winter camping is available and winter sports include cross-country skiing and snowshoeing. In summer campgrounds and facilities for fishing, canoeing, swimming, and the like are available. Permits are required for fires and overnight use at any season in the backcountry. All commercial accommodations may be reserved at Waskesiu Lake.

Information: Superintendent, Prince Albert National Park, Waskesiu Lake, Saskatchewan S0J 2Y0.

🌲 **Cypress Hills Provincial Park,** in the southeastern corner of Alberta, is crisscrossed by roads, and has a townsite and developed campgrounds. Nevertheless, some parts of its 49,620 acres possess a touch of mountain, foothill, and prairie ecosystems inhabited by elk, deer, moose, pronghorns, coyotes, and wild turkeys. In an otherwise agricultural region one finds here a wealth of wild flowers, including orchids; an undergrowth of shrubbery such as wild red raspberry; and woods of white spruce, lodgepole pine, and poplar. Geologic interest attaches to fossil beds containing remnants of rhinoceroses, crocodiles, and saber-toothed cats. Access is via Route 48 from Medicine Hat, twenty miles to the northwest. In winter there is skiing, sledding, skating, and ice-fishing. Accommodations are available in Elkwater.

Information: Superintendent, Cypress Hills Provincial Park, Elkwater, Alberta.

🌲 Persons who wish to see a wild area of badlands can visit **Dinosaur Provincial Park,** twenty-six miles northeast of Brooks, Alberta, along the Red Deer River (not to be confused with Dinosaur National Monument, Utah-Colorado). Access to most of the wild badlands in this 22,072-acre park is limited, as a major portion is restricted and accessible only by means of a guided bus tour. However, in the nonrestricted area a loop road and various walks and self-guided nature trails are available. Wildlife in the park includes coyotes, cottontails, deer, and pronghorns. Displays of dinosaur remains and other paleontological, archeological, and historical objects are also present. It should be noted that digging or collecting of any materials in the park is prohibited by law. Access is from country roads off Canadian Route 1 near Brooks, where food and lodging may be secured.

Information: Park Officer, Dinosaur Provincial Park, Patricia, Alberta.

🌲 Most of Saskatchewan's **Meadow Lake Provincial Park** is being managed under the multiple-use concept (logging, hunting, outdoor recreation, commercial fishing, cottage subdivisions, etc.). But a sizable portion of the 381,440 acres of the park is being set aside as a natural and primitive area with canoe routes, wilderness campsites, and hiking trails. Many park lakes are closed to motorboats, and all islands in lakes are classified primitive. The forest is composed of boreal species such as jack pine, black and white spruce, aspen, white birch, and tamarack. Native species of fish include whitefish, walleye, pike, perch, and lake trout. Brook and rainbow trout have been introduced, as have splake and coho salmon. Though the region has a great many lakes and streams, annual precipitation amounts to only sixteen inches, nearly half of which falls in summer. The park is located on the western Saskatchewan boundary, 210 miles northwest of Saskatoon. Access is via routes 4, 26, 104, 224, and others. Facilities include picnic sites, swimming areas, campgrounds, nature trails, boat-launching ramps, stores, cabins, and accommodations.

Information: Extension Services Branch, Department of Natural Resources, Administration Building, Regina, Saskatchewan S4S 0B1.

🌲 In 1971, under its Parks and Protected Areas Act, Saskatchewan designated 41,500 acres in the eastern part of the province as the **Wildcat Hill Wilderness Area.** Located about 200 miles northeast of Regina, the reserve protects part of the Pasquia Hills, the source of several trout streams. In these hills are canyons, muskegs, and spruce-pine-aspen forests, all home to a fauna that has not been thoroughly studied as yet. Timberwolves are found in the hills, as are caribou, black bears, moose, deer, and other mammals. Passage is rough through thick brush and muskegs, but that has helped keep the area relatively pristine through the years. Sport fishing is permitted; pike and walleye are found in Bankside and Fir Head lakes, and brook trout in the major streams. No motorized vehicles are permitted within the wilderness boundaries. The area can be approached via the Fir River road, northwest of the town of Hudson Bay, or from trails off provincial routes 163 and 109. Food and lodging may be obtained in the town of Hudson Bay.

Information: Extension Services Branch, Department of Natural Resources, Administration Building, Regina, Saskatchewan S4S 0B1.

🌲 **Lac la Ronge Provincial Park,** 147 miles north of Prince Albert, Saskatchewan, lies on the dividing line between rocks of the Precambrian shield to the north and sedimentary rocks to the south. It also embraces a transition of northern coniferous forest with deciduous woods. The park covers 381,440 acres of lake, marsh, stream, and forest domain. Lac la Ronge (the lake itself) is immense, studded with countless islands and endowed with a multitude of hidden bays, some of huge size and complexity but with only a single small entrance. Anglers and boatmen here would do well to have a reliable compass. Good maps are available for purchase. The area is primitive, with only a few outlying camps offering accommodations. Camping facilities are available along the main access road, Provincial Route 2. At the village of La Ronge are food, lodging, and other tourist facilities. Northward are immense tracts of provincial forest lands with fly-in fishing camps. Like all Saskatchewan provincial parks, Lac la Ronge is a multiple-use area where some logging is permitted.

Information: Extension Services Branch, Department of Natural Resources, Administration Building, Regina, Saskatchewan, S4S 0B1.

🌲 Swimming, boating, fishing, and hunting are the main recreation activities in **Nipawin Provincial Park,** a 161,280-acre region of jack-pine forest on the Wapawekka Upland. Cabins and campgrounds are located on Upper Fishing Lake and Lower Fishing Lake; there is also a campground at McDougal Creek. Food, supplies, and a boat-launching ramp are available. One lodge is open all year. Access is via provincial routes 106 and 120, about eighty-five miles northeast of the town of Prince Albert.

Information: Extension Services Branch, Department of Natural Resources, Administration Building, Regina, Saskatchewan S4S 0B1.

🌲 **Moose Mountain Provincial Park** is the location of hundreds of campsites, several resorts, a golf course, fire tower, highways, logging, petroleum exploration, and other accoutrements or activities of civilization. Notwithstanding, it covers 96,086 acres and is classified as 80 percent natural by the Saskatchewan Department of Natural Resources. What may not be true wilderness is at least a touch of the original "knob-and-kettle" country of numerous mounds and lakes left from glacial times. Moose still live here and there are hiking, riding, and bicycle trails among the hills and ponds. The park is made more valuable by the fact that it is surrounded by agricultural and other developed lands, as well as roads on virtually every square mile. It thus possesses some of the last vestiges of what wilderness there was in this part of the Canadian plains. The woods are chiefly poplar and white birch. Fishing is for pike, pickerel, and perch. Camping and accommodations are plentiful, with access via Provincial Route 9 a few miles north of Carlyle.

Information: Extension Services Branch, Department of Natural Resources, Administration Building, Regina, Saskatchewan S4S 0B1.

🌲 Manitoba has more than 100,000 lakes, and since many are wild the setting is ideal for canoeists. There are also sand beaches, rocky ridges, escarpments, dense forests, wildlife, and game fish such as lake and brook trout, northern and walleyed pike, and smallmouth bass. Ice-fishing in winter is popular. More than two million acres have been set aside by the provincial and national governments to preserve some of these riches, and authorities are trying to avoid overuse by human beings. However, hunting and other direct utilization of the renewable resources are permitted in certain places under control.

Grass River Provincial Park, above 54° north latitude, should appeal to lovers of the north woods; it covers 566,000 acres and has eight major lakes.

Canoeists may follow the historic Grass River as well as other parts of the park's lake and stream system. Primitive camping opportunities are available on Simonhouse, Iskwasum, and Reed lakes. Visitors may swim in Simonhouse Lake, depending on the temperature of the water. Access is via Provincial Route 391 along the southern boundary. Lodging is available within the park. The Reed Lake campground is adjacent to a store.

Information: Director of Parks, 409 Norquay Building, Winnipeg, Manitoba.

🌲 A few miles south of Grass River Provincial Park on Route 10 is **Clearwater Provincial Park,** 147,000 acres of pure blue lakes, forests, and streams. Waterfowl and moose abound. Clearwater Lake is known for its sandy beaches and good-sized lake trout. Swimming, fishing, and boating are among the major recreational activities. Camping and accommodations are available within the park.

Information: Director of Parks, 409 Norquay Building, Winnipeg, Manitoba.

🌲 **Duck Mountain Provincial Park** attests to the fact that not all of Manitoba is made up of lowlands, prairies, and lakes. The Duck Mountain Plateau rises some 1,200 feet from the surrounding agricultural lowlands; in the southeastern corner of the park is 2,727-foot Baldy Mountain, the highest point in Manitoba and accessible by road. An "island in the sky," the park contains floral and faunal associations not only of woods and meadows but of lakes. The area is a major wintering ground for elk. There are also moose and

237

bears, with numerous smaller mammals and birds. Recreation activities in this 315,000-acre area include swimming, fishing, camping, picnicking, boating, and, in winter, ice-fishing, snowmobiling, snowshoeing, and cross-country skiing. Cottages are available. Access is via provincial routes 366 and 367; Route 10 passes to the east of the park.

Information: Director of Parks, 409 Norquay Building, Winnipeg, Manitoba.

🌲 **Riding Mountain National Park** encompasses 734,720 acres of rolling plateau and prairie country, part of the Manitoba Escarpment, which abruptly rises 1,500 feet above the lowlands. With a diversity of habitats— streams, lakes, marshes, muskegs, grasslands, hardwood groves, coniferous forest—this area is markedly abundant in vegetative species and forms of birds and mammals. The timberwolf and Canada lynx live here, but far more often seen are coyotes, bears, deer, elk, moose, and beaver. Wild orchids grow in the bogs. Anemones bend on windswept slopes. Prairie areas have a spectacular wild-flower display during most of July and August.

Daily interpretive programs are offered during the summer season. Sport fishing is permitted in a number of lakes and streams. The angling season lasts from May 15 to September 30 except for Clear Lake which is open year round. The park may be visited in all seasons, but a full range of facilities such as restaurants, commercial accommodations, and stores are open only during the period from mid-May to mid-October in Wasagaming Service Center. Campgrounds, from fully serviced to primitive types, are available from May to September. Winter camping is also allowed at some of the primitive campgrounds adjacent to the main roads. There is a network of trails in the park for self-guiding nature study, horseback riding, backcountry packing, cross-country skiing, and snowshoeing. Access is via Provincial Route 10, some sixty miles north of Brandon and 165 miles northwest of Winnipeg.

Information: Superintendent, Riding Mountain National Park, Wasagaming, Manitoba R0J 2H0.

🌲 **Turtle Mountain Provincial Park,** 47,000 acres, consists of rolling, forested hills, valleys, and lakes along the boundary between Canada and North Dakota. Deer, ruffed grouse, and waterfowl are among the wild residents. However, the park management concept is one of a natural environment with extensive public use. Developed campgrounds and day-use facilities are located on Max and Adam lakes, the latter four miles from the

International Peace Garden also within the park. Access is via Provincial Route 10. Accommodations are available in communities outside the park. Information: Director of Parks, 409 Norquay Building, Winnipeg, Manitoba.

🌲 **Spruce Woods Provincial Park,** in the valley of the Assiniboine River, thirty miles east of Brandon, in southwestern Manitoba, covers 58,000 acres of aspen and spruce forest and shifting sand dunes. The park management concept here emphasizes the unique natural attributes of the land. Hiking trails lead through habitats where wildlife and wild-flower concentrations may be observed. West of the park extends the Spruce Woods Provincial Forest. The Trans-Canada Highway passes to the north and Provincial Route 258 to the west. One camp and picnic ground has been developed, and accommodations may be secured in nearby communities. Information: Director of Parks, 409 Norquay Building, Winnipeg, Manitoba.

🌲 **Grand Beach Provincial Park,** fifty-seven miles north of Winnipeg on provincial routes 12 and 59, covers 8,500 acres. Located on the shore of 250-mile-long Lake Winnipeg, it incorporates three miles of sandy beach suitable for swimming. The topography also includes giant boulders, and sand cliffs fifty feet high, once the shoreline of ancient Lake Agassiz. Facilities are provided for boating, camping, and nature study. Wilderness-type camping is available on Elk Island, recently added to the park and accessible only by water. Food, lodging, and supplies may be secured in the park. Information: Director of Parks, 409 Norquay Building, Winnipeg, Manitoba.

🌲 Lake Winnipeg has a number of islands, large and small, and the Hecla Archipelago, ninety miles north of the capital city of Winnipeg, has been set aside as **Hecla Provincial Park.** Covering 213,248 acres of land and water, the park encompasses Hecla, Black, Deer, and numerous smaller islands. It is the settlement site of Icelandic immigrants driven from their homes a century ago when the Iceland volcano of Hecla erupted. Hecla Island is connected to the mainland by a causeway and will in due course have a replica of an Icelandic village; there are now campgrounds, picnic sites, tennis courts, and a golf course. But the other islands are to be kept in a wilder state, and even on Hecla one may observe moose in the spruce-fir woods, sandhill cranes and

239

pelicans in the marshes, and blue heron rookeries at several localities. The park is also a sanctuary for loons, western grebes, mallards, canvasbacks, Canada geese, and other birds on the Central Flyway. Stands of birch and poplar occur, and orchids grow along the trails. Fishermen seek principally northern pike, walleye, and perch. Access to Hecla Island is via provincial routes 8, 234, and 233; the other islands can be reached only by boat.

Information: Director of Parks, 409 Norquay Building, Winnipeg, Manitoba.

🌲 Largest of Manitoba's parks is **Whiteshell Provincial Park,** 675,840 acres of lakes, black spruce woods, wildlife, islands, rivers, beaches, granite hills, a Canada goose sanctuary, and ceremonial grounds where Indians, possibly of Ojibwa origin, laid out boulders in strange patterns. The park's 200 lakes have several connecting rivers and portages that provide excellent canoe routes into the wilderness. Remote lakes and islands are particularly conducive to wilderness camping. A few short hiking trails exist, but the canoe is the best mode of transport here. (Several major trail systems are under construction.) Special maps of certain canoe routes are available for would-be voyageurs. On more than a dozen rivers are waterfalls, rapids, swimming and camping sites, and fishing holes. Anglers seek mostly northern pike, walleye, and smallmouth bass. Self-guiding trails help identify features of interest in the forest. One common sight is the poorly drained spruce swamp hemmed in by rocky ridges and covered with deep, springy sphagnum moss. The hiker also passes groves of aspen, jack pine, fir, and white spruce. The forest floor is virtually a living botanical museum. Lady's slipper still grows in secluded places. Ferns form extensive banks and carpets. Columbine, harebell, blueberry, twinflower, and lily-of-the-valley are some of the other species.

The park is located in southeastern Manitoba, eighty miles east of Winnipeg, and may be reached on the Trans-Canada Highway and provincial routes 44, 211, 306, 307, 312, and 313. Campgrounds and accommodations are abundant. Some of the camps have canoes, skis, motorboats, and other recreational equipment. In more urbane moments, visitors may play golf and tennis or get out on horseback trips. During winter, when the lakes freeze and a blanket of snow settles over the area, visitors indulge in ice-fishing, skiing, snowshoeing, skating, and snowmobiling. Special toboggan routes have been designated.

Information: Director of Parks, 409 Norquay Building, Winnipeg, Manitoba.

2. WOODS AND WATERS

When the voyageurs completed a day's travel they hauled their canoes out on the shore, cooked a meal of buffalo meat and pemmican soup, sang of maidens lost and found, danced a round or two to springtime, and then rolled up in their *sacs de couchage* for a night of sleep in the northern woods. Few were the calls that cleaved the silence: the quivering notes of a loon, perhaps, or the howl of a distant wolf. To the voyageurs, rivers and lakes were arteries of transportation to the West and Northwest, and the only way they could progress was by their own armpower in propelling canoes, by brute strength in carrying canoes and cargo over rocky portages, and by sheer tenacity in plunging ahead against winter storms on sled routes. Today, some of the land over which they roamed is much the same as it was then and the modern visitor can test his own endurance, pull his canoe out on shore, eat, sing, and go to sleep as the loon calls out on the lake.

🌲 The largest preserved segment of voyageur country is encompassed in two contiguous areas: the **Boundary Waters Canoe Area,** which contains 1,029,000 acres of lakes and woodland in Superior National Forest of northern Minnesota, and the **Quetico Provincial Park** of Ontario, which has an area of 1,120,000 acres. To preserve the wilderness values (which are slowly recovering from decades of logging, burning, and other commercial uses) authorities have imposed restrictions with which all travelers must comply. For example, entry is by permit only, size of party is limited to ten per campsite, and duration of stay is limited to fourteen days per campsite. Motor-propelled water craft (or snowmobiles in winter) are confined to specific routes. Nonburnable, disposable food and beverage containers are not permitted. Containers of fuel, insect repellent, medicines, personal toilet articles, and other items not foods or beverages are permitted. All empty containers and other refuse must be burned or packed out. Both the Quetico Provincial Park and the Boundary Waters Canoe Area have similar regulations.

These rules are necessitated by the popularity of the lakes, streams, and woodlands; without restraints the waters would become so filled with modern

241

voyageurs in July and August that the wilderness values could be badly damaged. Already the 1,200 miles of canoe routes in the Boundary Waters Canoe Area attract more than 130,000 persons each year.

Once abiding by the rules, an unforgettable experience may be had in canoeing deep into these watery wildlands. Notes from our journal of a seventy-mile voyage from Ely, Minnesota, north into Canada and back recall a typical north-woods adventure:

Afternoon pleasant; swimming great. Floated out to an island and swam from there for a while. Not too many flowers blooming in July but the blueberries are ripe. Saw and heard many birds—gulls, woodpeckers, chickadees, song sparrows—and had loons for company most of the day. Mosquitoes and horse flies pretty bad at night. . . .

Today we did 6 or 7 portages, some long, some short, some uphill, some down, some level. Came in to camp tired, ate supper and went to bed early. Loons called a little. . . . Camped on the shore of Robinson's Lake, which has many embayments. Each lake is distinctive; each has its own configurations, its own islands. There is some sand along the shores, but mostly rocky. In places, very smooth polished granite comes down in a steep slope. Loons swam in a tight circle, calling and calling, then flew off to another lake. We hear the songs of thrushes, sparrows, warblers and vireos every morning. Saw two moose at sunset. Not many deer here. . . .

Friday night. Camped on a deep embayment in McIntyre Lake. Surrounded by wood pewees. Six loons flew over calling—a rapid, forlorn, throbbing call repeated and rising in crescendo, pitch and rapidity. The smell of the pines and spruce and cedar are not as noticeable as at first; we are beginning to blend in with the wilderness and feel at home.

The best time to go is in late August and September, when the insects and crowds have diminished, the days are clear, the nights sharply cool, the water delightful, and fall color beginning among the trees. Although the forest is mostly a coniferous one of pine, spruce, fir, cedar, and larch, there are mixtures of deciduous species such as birch and aspen. In winter, the scene changes dramatically, and public use is increasing significantly during this period. Visitors go in by ski or snowshoe past several portages, set up camp, and work out from there—exploring, fishing through the ice, observing the winter wildlife.

Although the timberwolf is considered an endangered species in the United States, it maintains a stable population level in the northeastern part of Minnesota. Within the Superior National Forest the timberwolf is protected. The fisher and pine marten, now quite common in this region, were once on the verge of extinction. To the north, woodland caribou maintain viable populations. With more mature forests developing through succession in the Boundary Waters Canoe Area and adjacent areas, the habitat is becoming more favorable for reentry by caribou. Among the other mammals are moose, otters, beaver, black bears, mink, and muskrats—best seen by paddling along the shorelines early or late in the day.

Access from the south is principally through Ely, Minnesota, 100 miles north of Duluth, on State Route 1. Other entry points are near Crane Lake, Grand Marais, and Tofte. North of the border, Canadian Route 11 crosses a portion of Quetico Provincial Park near Atikokan, Ontario. Outfitters on both sides can supply or conduct parties. Maps and permits are essential and available, as are listings of rules and regulations.

For information on the Boundary Waters Canoe Area, write the Supervisor, Superior National Forest, Box 338, Duluth, Minnesota 55801. For Quetico Provincial Park, write the District Manager, Ministry of Natural Resources, Atikokan, Ontario P0T 1C0.

🌲 The third area of major significance in preserving some of the original lake and forest region is **Voyageurs National Park,** authorized by Congress in 1971. It embraces the Kabetogama Peninsula and other lands west of the Boundary Waters Canoe Area, and when land acquisition is complete will consist of approximately 220,000 acres. Included are major waterways and more than fifty lakes, many accessible only by trail. There are also streams, bogs, and forests, varied habitats utilized by beaver, mink, otters, deer, bears, wolves, fishers, moose, and other mammals. In the waters are walleye, northern pike, smallmouth bass, and even the rare lake sturgeon. In the words of the eminent naturalist Sigurd F. Olson, the Quetico-Superior region, including this park, "is the most magnificent and beautiful lake and river country on the continent, possibly in the world, nowhere is there such a combination of smooth glaciated and lichen-covered rocks, red and white pines, bogs, forests in such fantastic and glorious profusion."

The major activities are boating, fishing, canoeing, camping, photography, and nature study. Access is via U.S. Route 53 between International Falls and Virginia, Minnesota. Accommodations may be secured in nearby communities.

Information: Superintendent, Voyageurs National Park, Box 50, International Falls, Minnesota 56649.

🌲 More than 61,000 acres of the bed of old Lake Agassiz, an enormous inland lake during the Ice Age, have been preserved in **Agassiz National Wildlife Refuge,** eleven miles east of Holt, in northwestern Minnesota. The terrain is flat, and freshwater marshes occupy nearly half of it. The rest consists of willow patches, spruce-tamarack bogs, grasslands, and stands of aspen, oak, elm, and ash. Years ago the area was drained, flooded, burned, and otherwise altered by man. The refuge was established in 1937 and since has been flooded and managed primarily for waterfowl production. A little of the original wild Minnesota has been restored, and visitors can see not only the tens of thousands of ducks and other bird life in the proper season, but also moose, muskrat, mink, deer, and beaver. Access is via county state aid Highway 7. No campgrounds or accommodations are available on the refuge, but adjoining Michigan wildlife-management areas have prmitive campgrounds. Food and lodging may be secured in Thief River Falls, twenty-three miles south of the refuge on U.S. Route 59 and State Route 32.

Information: Manager, Agassiz National Wildlife Refuge, Middle River, Minnesota 56737.

🌲 A large bog virtually undisturbed by man for more than 11,000 years is a rarity on earth today, and the state of Minnesota intends to keep the **Lake Agassiz Peatlands Natural Area** undisturbed. It is open only during daytime, and visitors may not camp or picnic. Covering 19,200 acres, the bog and peatlands have developed naturally since the recession of glacial Lake Agassiz. The layers of peat, up to thirty feet deep, possess extraordinary scientific value in determination of the geologic history of the region pursuant to glaciation. Snow covers the land for nearly half of each year and the soil is frozen to depths of as much as twenty inches. The vegetation is distributed in accordance with moisture, nature of the soil, and other factors. The boreal forest consists mostly of spruce, fir, pine, and aspen; there are also cedar bogs, swamps, fens, sphagnum heaths, and other types of peatlands. Wolves, deer, moose, foxes, and smaller mammals, plus birds, amphibians, reptiles, and invertebrate fauna inhabit the delicate ecosystems. The area is located south of local road 31 in Koochiching County in far northern Minnesota.

Information: Director, Division of Parks and Recreation, Centennial Building, St. Paul, Minnesota 55155.

🌲 Minnesota's **Itasca State Park** is famed as the origin of the 2,552-mile-long Mississippi River; the park's name comes from Latin *veritas caput*, "true head," applied by the eminent explorer Henry Schoolcraft. The park covers 32,054 acres, including a portion designated as a wilderness area. Though its grand original forests of white pine were nearly logged off before they could be saved, the woods are recovering and on the trails one may encounter spruce, fir, sugar, and red maples; red, white, and Norway pines; basswood; and other species. Thanks to its glacial heritage, the park is endowed with

Wood Buffalo National Park, Alberta-Northwest Territories. Courtesy Parks Canada.

Trunk of persimmon tree.

Theodore Roosevelt National Memorial Park, North Dakota.

numerous lakes and ponds, with hiking trails weaving among them. Many kinds of small orchids grow in the bogs and some, such as lady's slippers, grow on uplands. Beaver dams and houses, eagles' nests, and springs are a few of the natural features. To understand the scientific and historic aspects of the park, visitors may make use of museums, nature trails, naturalist programs, bird and mammal guides, and history booklets. Indian burial mounds also may be seen. The park has a full range of facilities, including campgrounds, picnic areas, a lodge, inn, cabins, stores, and bathing beaches, as well as boat rental services. Itasca State Park is located 200 miles northwest of Minneapolis, and is accessible on U.S. Route 71 and state routes 31 and 113.

Information: Director, Division of Parks and Recreation, Centennial Building, St. Paul, Minnesota 55155.

🌲 Tamarack is another name for the larch, a coniferous tree whose peculiar characteristic is that it turns color in autumn and loses its needles each winter. It is a common tree of the north woods swamps. In **Tamarac National Wildlife Refuge,** Minnesota, three types of habitats converge: northern coniferous forest, prairie country of the Red River Valley, and northern hardwoods. The 42,000 acres of the refuge contain two dozen lakes that freeze in winter but open in early April to receive a number of species of waterfowl that nest there. However, more than two-thirds of the refuge is forested, and the bird population is principally composed of species adapted to woodlands; in spring there are flights of ring-necked ducks, mallards, wood ducks, blue-winged teals, robins, purple martins, evening grosbeaks, redwings, and yellow-headed blackbirds. Hikers along refuge trails may also see white-tailed deer, beaver, and muskrats. Scenic drives and a nature trail facilitate close study of the refuge. Fishing, picnicking, and boating are permitted in accordance with regulations, but no campgrounds exist. Food and lodging may be secured in nearby communities. Access is via country roads a few miles northeast of Detroit Lakes, Minnesota.

Information: Manager, Tamarac National Wildlife Refuge, R. R., Rochert, Minnesota 56578.

🌲 A six-mile-long section of one of the continent's famous fur trade routes, that between Lake Superior and the Mississippi River, is preserved in **Savanna Portage State Park.** It was highly unpopular with the voyageurs, swampy, closed in by softwood, hardwood, and coniferous forests, and difficult to traverse. Still they managed to carry their canoes and loads of fur over it. The grueling route is marked and kept open for modern travelers who wish to get an idea of what the French and English fur traders had to endure. The park contains 14,605 acres; a hiking trail follows the portage route and there are camp and picnic sites. Accommodations may be secured in nearby communities. The park is surrounded by Savanna State Forest, in sugar maple country. Access is via country roads off State Route 65 north of McGregor.

Information: Director, Division of Parks and Recreation, Centennial Building, St. Paul, Minnesota 55155.

🌲 **Jay Cooke State Park,** 8,920 acres, includes the rugged basalt gorge of the St. Louis River. Rich sediments deposited from melting glaciers cover the rocky terrain and support forests of conifers and deciduous trees. The park is known for its spring displays of white trillium. In addition, it has wild sarsaparilla, bunchberry, wintergreen, and trailing arbutus. The area is also a good place from which to observe the late spring migration of warblers. There are naturalist programs, hiking and ski trails, campgrounds, picnic areas, and an inn. Accommodations may be secured in Duluth, eighteen miles to the northeast, and in other nearby communities. The park is reached on state routes 23 and 39.

Information: Director, Division of Parks and Recreation, Centennial Building, St. Paul, Minnesota 55155.

🌲 On Mille Lacs Lake, 100 miles north of Minneapolis, was once the Woodland Dakota Sioux village of Kathio. About 1745 the Sioux were driven out by Chippewa Indians. Today, 6,785 acres around the site have been set aside as the **Mille Lacs Kathio State Park,** which also contains the Rum River and Lakes Ogechie and Shakopee. Landscapes consist principally of meadows, hills, and second-growth northern forests. Among the recreational activities are hiking, swimming, camping, boating, fishing, skiing, and snowshoeing. A visitor center features displays and programs that interpret the archeological findings in the park. Accommodations may be secured in nearby communities. Access is via U.S. Route 169 between Aitkin and Milaca.

Information: Director, Division of Parks and Recreation, Centennial Building, St. Paul, Minnesota 55155.

🌲 A few miles southeast of Mille Lacs Kathio State Park is the **Mille Lacs Wildlife Management Area,** 37,964 acres of terrain managed primarily for the production and preservation of waterfowl, grouse, deer, bears, foxes, bobcats, raccoons, beaver, otters, mink, and muskrats. About twenty-five miles of trail exist, and hiking, skiing, and snowshoeing are encouraged, but motor-vehicle access and use are strictly regulated. The area is located between Onamia and Mora, Minnesota.

Information: Resident Manager, Mille Lacs Wildlife Management Area, Onamia, Minnesota 56359.

🌲 Rivers set aside under the Wild and Scenic Rivers Act of 1968 are not necessarily wilderness, but since man-made developments are few and far apart, motorboat use is restricted, and the banks kept reasonably natural, a canoeist floating downstream has at least the illusion of traveling the river as the Chippewa Indians and early fur traders did. One hundred miles of the upper St. Croix River, plus its principal tributary, the Namekagon River, for another hundred miles, have been designated the **St. Croix National Scenic Riverway.** Along a considerable part of its distance, the river constitutes the boundary between Minnesota and Wisconsin, and were a canoeist to proceed downstream through more settled and agricultural areas, he would eventually float out onto the Mississippi River about twenty-five miles southeast of Minneapolis and St. Paul. The wild, protected upstream areas are generally without cities, and the area of the Riverway proper is 62,800 acres.

The terrain is principally of glacial origin, but ancient Precambrian bedrock can be seen in rapids areas, and along the riverbanks are outcrops of Cambrian sandstones. The forest that lines the banks is composed of many species of trees, both hardwood and pine. The canoeist passes marshes, fertile bottomlands, and patches of pondweed and wild celery growing in the water. Between November and April the river is frozen; temperatures can go as low as 46 degrees below zero. The summer extreme is 110 degrees. April to June are the cool, moist months when fishermen get out on the river in search of trout, smallmouth bass, muskellunge, and sturgeon. Late summer and early autumn are usually dry and cool.

In the scenic area, the rivers range in width from 40 to 1,200 feet, are mostly shallow and gravelly, and have some 250 islands. Maximum gradient is more than eight feet per mile, but passage is neither especially difficult nor dangerous. The streams are mostly clear and free of harmful pollutants. Deer and upland game birds attract hunters; there are also bears, moose, coyotes, raccoons, and the aquatic furbearers: beaver, muskrats, mink, and others.

Camps, hotels, resorts, cabins, and campgrounds are available in the vicinity. Primitive campsites are being designated along the riverbank. Access to the river is limited, but numerous roads approach the area, including U.S. routes 8, 35, 53, 61, and 63.

Information: Superintendent, St. Croix National Scenic Riverway, Box 579, St. Croix Falls, Wisconsin 54024.

🌲 Adjacent to the St. Croix National Scenic Riverway, the State of Minnesota has established on the north bank of the stream the **St. Croix State Park.** Its 31,557 acres take in forests of jack pine, spruce, and hardwoods, meadows, streams, cedar swamps, steep hillsides, and early Indian village sites. There are more than 120 miles of marked trails, including three self-guiding nature trails, and a small nature center with naturalist programs. Visitors may find primitive and developed campsites, picnic areas, beaches for swimming, plus a lodge and bicycle and canoe concession. A portion of the park has been set aside as a Scientific and Natural Area for research and study. Access to the park, located about eighty-five miles north of St. Paul, is by river, country roads, or State Route 48.

Information: Director, Division of Parks and Recreation, Centennial Building, St. Paul, Minnesota 55155.

🌲 One of the most fertile and productive marshes in the United States lies in southeastern Wisconsin. A product of the glacial age, it has been dammed, ditched, and drained by man in attempts to "improve" its "usefulness," but it has, for the present at least, been restored to something of its original state, and is protected as **Horicon National Wildlife Refuge.** The 20,730 acres are managed for production of waterfowl and as a refuge for migratory species, and so the area is not comparable to wilderness that has remained more or less pristine since the coming of man. Nevertheless, it is big enough to offer at least a hint of what the original marshes must have looked like thousands of years ago. Canada geese pass through by the tens of thousands in spring and fall, and there are more than 220 other species on the refuge bird list. The marsh is surrounded by fields, towns, and good access roads; the major communities are Waupun, Mayville, Horicon, and Beaver Dam, where food and lodging may be secured. Fishing for northern pike and bullheads and hunting for deer are permitted under regulations. At this writing the refuge manager advises us that Horicon is not a wilderness area and although it has been proposed for that status "it is not expected to qualify."

Information: Manager, Horicon National Wildlife Refuge, Route 2, Mayville, Wisconsin 53050.

🌲 A few miles southwest of Apostle Islands National Lakeshore, within Chequamegon National Forest, are the proposed **Rainbow Lake** and **Flynn**

249

Lake wildernesses. These areas, adjacent to each other, cover 12,000 acres. In the waters of the region are trout, pike, and bass. On land, the common mammals are deer, bears, snowshoe hares, and squirrels. At times the air resounds with the call of the loon or coyote. These proposed wildernesses are located near Drummond, Wisconsin, through which U.S. Route 63 passes. Accommodations and public and private campgrounds are available not far away. At present no special recreation restrictions or controls are in effect except for regulations necessary to protect the forest. Bills under study by Congress contain specific restrictions and management procedures which will be instituted once legislation is enacted and approved.

Information: Supervisor, Chequamegon National Forest, Park Falls, Wisconsin 54552.

🌲 It may not be the largest but it has the longest boundaries of any inland U.S. wildlife refuge. The **Upper Mississippi River Wild Life and Fish Refuge** stretches 284 miles between Rock Island, Illinois, and Wabasha, Minnesota, encompassing islands, waters, channels, marshes, woods, and wildlife. Obviously it is a thread of naturalness through lands of intensive human use, and a list of eminent persons who have plied these waters or served on shore reads like a Who's Who of American history: Marquette and Jolliet, Zebulon Pike, Jefferson Davis, Zachary Taylor, Keokuk, Chief Red Bird, William Beaumont, and John Muir, to name a few. Indians with names unknown occupied surrounding lands and built burial mounds in effigies of bears, birds, and lizards. There are old forts and villas, some in a splendid state of preservation, that help to show how men lived when the banks of the Mississippi were truly wilderness.

By beaching a boat on one of those elongated woody islands in the midst of the river, a person can almost forget the tide of civilization that washed these shores. He has a resource of more than 250 species of birds, 50 of mammals, and 113 of fish to remind him of the original inhabitants. Bald eagles still winter here. As a major migration route, the river and its shores serve as a natural pathway for ducks, swans, warblers, and other species on the Mississippi Flyway. The wood duck commonly nests here. Fishing for walleye, sauger, bass, perch, and catfish is a popular pastime, but there is also giant sturgeon in the river. There are fine lookouts such as those at Fire Point, in Effigy Mounds National Monument, and in several state and private parks here and there where camping facilities are provided. Anyone clambering over the cliffs of this river, however, should be aware that rattlesnakes are common.

On this long and protected portion of the "Father of Waters," boating, canoeing, hunting, fishing, camping, picnicking, swimming, and other activities are plentiful, although a few public uses are restricted in favor of wildlife. Access is via many roads including U.S. routes 52 and 61. Accommodations are available in communities at or near the river's edge. Information: Manager, Upper Mississippi River Wild Life and Fish Refuge, Box 226, Winona, Minnesota 55987.

🌲 Farther downriver, between Davenport, Iowa, and St. Louis, Missouri, are islands, sloughs, floodplains, and other links in a chain of waterfowl refuges along the Mississippi Flyway. In the 30,000-acre **Mark Twain National Wildlife Refuge,** which is divided into twelve units along the Mississippi and Illinois rivers, hundreds of thousands of ducks relax on their sometimes grueling journeys. One of the last wintering concentrations of bald eagles south of the 49th parallel is here. To enjoy boating, hiking, fishing, hunting, and other outdoor activities it would be well to obtain a refuge map that shows the location of the various units and tells when they are open for public use. Access is via roads paralleling or crossing the Mississippi River, especially U.S. Route 61 and local roads. Food and lodging are available in nearby communities.

Information: Manager, Mark Twain National Wildlife Refuge, Box 225, Quincy, Illinois 62301.

🌲 A touch of the original Ozarks is maintained in Missouri's **Lake of the Ozarks State Park,** 130 miles in an air line southwest of St. Louis. Although the lake is actually a reservoir backed up by Bagnell Dam on the Osage River, and the park is intruded by an airport with regularly scheduled flights, the area has been under federal or state protection for forty years and at least parts of its 16,550 acres have a relatively wild aspect. This is one of the few places where the Ozark deciduous forest, famed for its fall colors, receives substantial public protection. Within the park are eighty-nine of the lake's 1,375 miles of shoreline; two public beaches have been developed. Facilities for boating and camping have been provided. Fishing is a favorite pastime. Accommodations are available in communities on the approaches to the park. Access is via U.S. Route 54 and state routes 42 and 134.

Information: Superintendent, Lake of the Ozarks State Park, Kaiser, Missouri 65047.

🌲 In east-central Missouri lies the 7,155-acre **Meramec State Park,** covered with forests of walnut, dogwood, oak, and redbud. Formerly the region was inhabited by Mound Builders, then by Shawnee, Delaware, and Osage Indian groups. Daniel Boone once prospected along the Meramec River. The original virgin forest has been gone for years, but wildness can still be found on trails that lead through the recovering woods. Caves have eroded in the underlying dolomitic rock; one, Fisher Cave, contains stalactites and stalagmites, extends about a mile underground, and is open to the public. Camping, picnicking, lodging, swimming, canoeing, boating, fishing, and dining facilities are available within the park. Lodging may also be secured in neighboring communities. Access is via Missouri State Route 185 between Potosi and Sullivan.

Information: Superintendent, Meramec State Park, Sullivan, Missouri 63080.

🌲 Adjacent to the Eleven Point National Scenic River is the proposed **Irish Wilderness** of 17,880 acres, popular with hikers and backpackers. Located some twenty miles northwest of Doniphan, in southern Missouri, it possesses typical Ozark Mountains phenomena: Karst topography, limestone cliffs, caves, sinks, and a deciduous forest in which the scars of early logging have nearly healed. Access is via country roads off U.S. Route 160. Also within Mark Twain National Forest are the **Current River Scenic Area,** and the 6,000-acre **Carman Springs Wildlife Refuge.** Native animals in the region include deer, turkeys, rabbits, collared lizards, roadrunners, and blue herons. Accommodations and campgrounds are available nearby.

Information: Supervisor, National Forests in Missouri, Box 937, Rolla, Missouri 65401.

🌲 The **Mingo National Wildlife Refuge,** in southeastern Missouri, contains a swamp in which Huck Finn might have gotten lost. However, during Mark Twain's day every effort was being made to convert this watery area to farmland, and it was cut, logged, drained, farmed, grazed and burned, with consequent reduction of animal life. Now that it is being managed primarily as natural habitat, the fragile oak forest is recovering and the cypress swamp ecology being rejuvenated. Thirty-eight species of mammals roam the 21,673 acres of the refuge, principally white-tailed deer, rabbits, squirrels, and raccoons. Smaller mammals are preyed upon by copperheads, cottonmouths, rattlesnakes, and other reptiles. But waterfowl are the major reason for existence of this refuge, and as many as 275,000 settle on Mingo during migration. The overwhelming majority are mallards, of which a few, as well as a large flock of Canada geese, spend the winter. The refuge is home to rails, turkeys, herons, and other birds. Visitors may hike, fish, picnic, and at certain times hunt and take a twenty-five-mile self-guided auto tour.

Access is from Missouri State Route 51, 130 miles south of St. Louis. Food and lodging may be obtained in nearby communities.

Information: Manager, Mingo National Wildlife Refuge, Route 1, Box 9A, Puxico, Missouri 63960.

🌲 So many things are appealing about the Ozarks that a trip on the Current and Jacks Fork rivers leaves engraved in the mind uncountable elements of a midwestern montage: deep, clear waters tinted blue-green; canopies of maple and sycamore; dolomite cliffs standing bright in the morning sun; the erratic flight of a kingfisher; a green heron poised over the water, waiting for a fish or crayfish; the music of thrushes or whippoorwills, or simply the still air and insect cadence of a summer evening. To keep such things in their natural state along the watercourse, Congress established the **Ozark National Scenic Riverways,** an action that restricts the human uses of these rivers and their banks to recreational pursuits.

Canoes can be put into the water below Montauk Springs, 175 miles south of St. Louis, and floated down the Current River to Gooseneck, a winding distance of 105 miles. Along the way are springs, caverns, and plentiful opportunities for fishing. At several places on the river and in nearby towns can be found lodging, meals, and stores. Secluded campsites, picnic spots, and trails are available here and there at the water's edge. A portion of the Jacks Fork River, accessible near its upper end not far from Mountain View, Missouri, is likewise available for river running. At Two Rivers, it flows into the Current River, down which the trip may be extended. Altogether, the established riverways protect some 134 linear miles of these Ozark streams. Additional recreational opportunities are available in the adjacent Clark and Mark Twain national forests. The region is especially magnificent in October, when the leaves turn many shades of red and yellow. Access is via numerous local routes, principally off U.S. routes 60 and Interstate 44.

Information: Superintendent, Ozark National Scenic Riverways, Van Buren, Missouri 63965.

🌲 On the boundary between Missouri and Arkansas is a small area of swamps in which grow bald cypress, water elm, water locust, and willow, and periodically flooded hardwoods consisting of oak, pecan, mulberry, maple, birch, and cottonwood. Since the land for miles beyond has been drained and devoted to cotton, this represents a high-value sanctuary for whatever wildlife is left—or migrates through. It is administered by the U.S. Bureau of Sport Fisheries and Wildlife as the **Big Lake National Wildlife Refuge.** Within its 11,000 acres are a few stands of virgin cypress, with trees 150 feet tall, indicative of the woods that once covered the region. Thousands of waterfowl, shorebirds, and other species regularly utilize refuge lands, as do human visitors, who fish, hike, boat, picnic, and observe the natural scene in quiet surroundings. Access is via country roads east of Manila, Arkansas. Food and lodging are available in nearby communities.

Information: Manager, Big Lake National Wildlife Refuge, Box 67, Manila, Arkansas 72442.

 Along the Mississippi River some eighty miles southeast of Little Rock, Arkansas, lies the **White River National Wildlife Refuge,** in lands so low that most of the area is regularly submerged each year under White and Mississippi floodwaters. Within its 113,300 acres are bayous, channels, sloughs, and some 169 lakes (at low water), plus a southern hardwood forest of oak, pecan, sweetgum, cypress, and tupelo—all of which mean food and shelter to wildlife, especially birds. The penetrating call of the chuck-will's-widow carries through the woods on summer nights. The warmth of the climate is attested to by egrets, ibises, and herons. In spring and fall, migration travels bring peak populations of 300,000 ducks, mostly mallards. Human visitors may find food and lodging in De Witt and Helena. The refuge is on Arkansas State Route 1, which leads south of U.S. Route 70 between Memphis and Little Rock. Part of the refuge is pending official classification as wilderness, but most of it is selectively managed for wildlife. Fishing, hunting, and camping are permitted, but inquiry should be made about possibly flooded access routes.

Information: Manager, White River National Wildlife Refuge, Box 308, De Witt, Arkansas 72042.

Water tupelo—bald cypress swamp, Mississippi.

♣ The proposed **Upper Buffalo Wilderness** conserves the sources of the Buffalo River in northwestern Arkansas. Its 10,590 acres are mountainous and rough, with high cliffs, jumbled canyons, deep hollows, and waterfalls. The area is located approximately forty-five miles southeast of Fayetteville. Campgrounds are available on adjacent forest lands, and accommodations may be secured in towns of the region. Access is via country roads and state routes 16 and 21.

Information: Supervisor, Ozark National Forest, Box 1008, Russellville, Arkansas 72801.

♣ In the Ouachita Mountains of western Arkansas lies the **Caney Creek Back Country,** a roadless region of 10,236 acres covered with oak, beech, and pine forests. Hikers pass clear streams and rock outcrops and climb to ridgetops for panoramic mountain views. Wildlife includes deer, turkeys, and bears, and in the streams may be found bass, sunfish, and chub. The area is located fifty-five miles west of Hot Springs. Access is by forest roads and state routes 8, 38, and 84. Campgrounds are located nearby and food and lodging may be secured in local resort areas.

Information: Supervisor, Ouachita National Forest, Box 1270, Hot Springs, Arkansas 71901.

♣ West of the Mississippi River, the scarcity of wilderness, or even mountains, in large portions of the Midwest results in heavy human recreation pressures on ranges that do exist. Nearly two million people a year visit the **Wichita Mountains National Wildlife Refuge** in Oklahoma. But human beings usually seek comforts with their outdoor life, and the 8,900-acre wilderness area within that refuge is so rugged that it remains relatively undisturbed. The mountains are reddish granite, great smooth domes and cliffs with giant boulders scattered about in the natural progress of erosion. Vegetation has covered the steep declivities and tumbled canyons as best it can, from the lichen and cactus that clutch at bits of soil or virtually barren rock, to gullies lined with post and blackjack oak, eastern red cedar, and elm. Finding eastern forest species so far west reminds us that this is a true transition area with overlap of species. One can observe bluejays as well as roadrunners, and eastern as well as western cottontails. Larger mammals —bison, longhorn cattle, elk—have been introduced, and remain mostly in the North Mountain wilderness unit, a strictly natural area preserved for scientific investigation rather than public use.

Yet for all its mountain aspects, this wild land is still a part of the once vast midwestern prairies; little bluestem is the dominant grass, but there are also big bluestem, Indian and grama grasses. Although the effects of the arid West are obvious, and the prairie is not as rich as in more humid parts of the Great Plains, the environment is still distinct. In the Wichita Mountains a wilderness hiker can sample the East, Midwest, and West on a single day's journey. The refuge is reached via U.S. Route 62, and is about eighty miles southwest of Oklahoma City. Food and lodging may be obtained in nearby communities.

Information: Manager, Wichita Mountains National Wildlife Refuge, Box 448, Cache, Oklahoma 73527.

🌲 An outstanding part of the original Midwest that has been virtually eliminated is the proposed **Big Thicket National Biological Reserve** of Texas. Actually this was not so much a "thicket" as it was a huge, magnificent southern forest that spread across gently rolling hills and bottomlands north and west of where Beaumont is today, not far from the Gulf of Mexico and near the Louisiana line. Originally the Big Thicket measured more than a hundred miles in length and sixty miles wide, but after logging, flooding, farming, oil-drilling, and other modifications, nearly all of the original environment was changed. A 1967 study by the National Park Service recommended national monument status for only 2 percent of the original Thicket, and even that was in isolated fragments.

About all such slender remnants can give us today is a suggestion of what this splendid hardwood wilderness originally consisted of: dense forests of beech, magnolia, and chestnut oak; savannas; bogs; spring-fed streams; lakes; sloughs with immense specimens of bald cypress and water tupelo; bayous; patches of pine and palmetto; swamps with alligators; great nesting colonies of herons, egrets, ibises, and roseate spoonbills; curtains of Spanish moss; silverbell and wisteria; twenty-five kinds of ferns; twenty species of orchid; deer, bears, mountain lions, ocelots—the list seems endless. There is little question that the Big Thicket was of national significance, possibly the largest collection of complex and overlapping ecosystems in the country.

It was a crossroads of east, west, north, and south, ecologically speaking, and in that, plus its great size, it approached uniqueness. The list of trees alone is remarkable still and there are well over 2,000 species of plants remaining. In the bogs may be some of the rarest herbaceous plants in Texas. Somewhere in these diminishing woods the last few ivory-billed woodpeckers may be hanging on to life. It was an elegant piece of the real Texas that is still not fully appreciated: Development for homesites continues and efforts to establish a national park have experienced great difficulty.

Yet with dogged Texas tenacity, local citizens, particularly the Big Thicket Association, are still keeping the issue alive. Although some of the choicest remnants are hard to reach, several agencies do provide access into parts of the Big Thicket. The Texas Forestry Association has constructed self-guiding trails into several habitats, and labeled some of the interesting trees, such as sassafras, chinaberry, and trifoliate orange. At the Massey Lake Trail, one can walk through the woods beside a pond into which water drips from the maples in musical cadence after a summer shower. The Alabama Coushatta Indians welcome visitors to their still partly natural reservation sixteen miles west of Woodville. In Sam Houston National Forest are splendid trails, some with explanatory leaflets, through parts of the Big Thicket that have been logged but which are now preserved so that in time their original charm may return. One of these is the Big Thicket Scenic Area, eleven miles north of Cleveland, Texas. In such places can be sampled a little of the "lair of the mysterious," as one author called it.

Many roads lead into and through the Big Thicket region, and travelers should inquire locally for precise directions, or hire a guide. The principal roads of access are U.S. routes 59, 69, 190, and 287. Food and lodging may be secured in Beaumont, Woodville, and other neighboring communities.

Information: East Texas Chamber of Commerce, Box 1592, Longview, Texas 75601; and Supervisor, Sam Houston National Forest, Box 969, Lufkin, Texas 75901.

Santa Ana National Wildlife Refuge, Texas

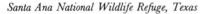

3. PRAIRIE

Two distinct badland regions of the northern plains still exist in their natural state, one in North Dakota and one in South Dakota. As an epithet applied by early explorers, "badlands" summarized the aridity, eroded landscape, heat (110° in summer), cold (more than 40° below zero in winter), and scarce vegetation. These places were simply "hell with the fires out," as one description went. Yet the effect they had on man clearly contradicts the name; Theodore Roosevelt, for example, found far more good than bad, and said that if it hadn't been for what he learned during his years in the badlands of North Dakota he would never have become President of the United States.

🌲 The facts are that quite a covering of vegetation exists and in places the grasses grow waist-high. Not only does the Little Missouri River wind through these soft sandstones and shales, but so do smaller streams and creeks, each with a rippling of water at least during part of the year. At **Theodore Roosevelt National Memorial Park,** composed of three separate units that include the site of Roosevelt's Elkhorn Ranch, the terrain is much as it was when he raced across it on horseback in the 1880s. There are bighorns and deer, long lines of bison, wandering groups of pronghorns, large piping colonies of prairie dogs; plus rabbits, coyotes, magpies, larks, flycatchers, rattlesnakes, and in all, a far richer ecosystem than the word "badlands" implies.

Moreover, the colorful strata—blue, red, yellow, brown—occur in picturesque pinnacles and buttes that are photogenic, especially in morning or in late afternoon following a thundershower. In some places the ubiquitous seams of coal were ignited years ago and have burned underground ever since. There are also forests of petrified wood, long groves of rustling cottonwoods, wide, rolling prairies, deep canyons, and cliffs from which panoramic views may be obtained. Size of the area is 70,436 acres.

A great deal of the park is accessible by road, and exhibits explain the natural as well as historic features. Visitors who want to get an idea of the kind of wilderness that thrilled Theodore Roosevelt should be equipped to hike in the more remote sections of the park, taking care to prepare themselves for the heat and aridity that are a part of the summer environment. Permits are required for backcountry use. Access is via Interstate 94 at Medora, and U.S. Route 85; accommodations are available in Medora and other towns of the region.

Information: Superintendent, Theodore Roosevelt National Memorial Park, Medora, North Dakota 58645.

🌲 The badlands of South Dakota, some fifty miles southeast of Rapid City, near Interstate 90, are more stark and arid than the Little Missouri River badlands of North Dakota, but they still do not constitute "desolate wastes." In fact, the survival and even flourishing of plants and animals in environmental extremes is as fascinating here as it is in southwestern deserts. The grassland–bison–prairie dog community dominates, but a walk through wilder parts of **Badlands National Monument**, 243,508 acres, may bring visitors in contact with deer, pronghorns, bighorns, bison, badgers, and coyotes. Eagles fly over, and swifts and swallows nest in the cliffs. Patches of juniper hug the hollows and stands of cottonwood and wild roses grow in moist places. Unfortunately, however, the original populations of wolves, grizzlies, and mountain lions are gone, with little likelihood that they will be restored. In effect, they are as gone from here as the camels, cats, hyaenodons, and titanotheres that roamed the region millions of years ago. Fossil remains of such prehistoric mammals are abundant in these friable soils.

The Monument, administered by the National Park Service, is provided with exhibits, a self-guiding trail, scenic drive, summer educational programs, campgrounds, picnic area, accommodations, and publications. Early morning, when the air is cool and clear and when long shadows accent the colorful ridges, is one of the best times for seeing and photographing the badlands. Accommodations may be secured in and near the Monument.

Information: Superintendent, Badlands National Monument, Interior, South Dakota 57750.

🌲 Several other protected prairie sites in South Dakota have wild aspects. **Wind Cave National Park** consists of 28,059 acres of relatively unspoiled rolling grassland, even with descendants of some of the original occupants, including bison, black-tailed prairie dogs, pronghorns, deer, elk, coyotes, badgers, raccoons, meadowlarks, and sharp-tailed grouse. The animals are directly or indirectly sustained by the rich vegetation of prairie grasses, both tall and short; and there are deciduous forests characteristic of the East as well as coniferous trees typical of the West. Underneath is the Pahasapa limestone, which has been warped, fractured, and dissolved out into at least twenty-five miles of underground passages. Tours may be taken through Wind Cave from April 1 to October 31; the cave is closed in winter but the park is not. There are camping and picnicking facilities as well as exhibits and hiking trails. Access is via U.S. Route 385 north of Hot Springs, and

State Route 87 south from Custer State Park. Tourist accommodations and facilities are available in nearby towns. Limited food service is available in the park in summer. Visitors should remember that bison can be extremely dangerous and should not be approached on foot.

Information: Superintendent, Wind Cave National Park, Hot Springs, South Dakota 57747.

🌲 In the Black Hills, adjacent to Wind Cave National Park, are the 72,000-acre **Custer State Park** and **Norbeck Wildlife Preserve,** famed for the Needles Highway that passes through both. Mount Rushmore National Memorial is located within the Norbeck Preserve, as is Harney Peak, 7,242 feet, highest point east of the Rocky Mountains. The terrain is rugged and scenic, the Cathedral Spires being sharp-pointed pinnacles of durable granite that have resisted centuries of erosion. It is also pleasantly forested with pine, spruce, birch, and quaking aspen. Rolling, grassy hills are home to more than a thousand American bison, easily observed by visitors, and kept within bounds by an eight-foot-high fence around the entire park. There are also hundreds of deer, elk, and pronghorns. Campgrounds, lodges, resorts, and other facilities are available. The park and preserve are crossed by U.S. Alternate 16 and South Dakota State Route 87.

Information: Superintendent, Custer State Park, Hermosa, South Dakota 57744.

🌲 The **Charles M. Russell National Wildlife Range** is an elongated refuge surrounding the Fort Peck Reservoir, on the Missouri River in northeastern Montana. Its 1 million acres, bordering 180 miles of the river's course, are mostly ponderosa pine "breaks" originally set aside to harbor sharp-tailed grouse and pronghorns. However, wildlife populations of several species are substantial. For example, half a million mourning doves may concentrate here at certain times of the year. Many of the animal species originally here when Lewis and Clark came through in 1805 are being reintroduced—e.g., elk, bighorns, bison, and Canada geese. Indeed, much of the primitive beauty and natural environment described by the early explorers remains, providing habitat for such endangered species as the black-footed ferret, osprey, peregrine falcon, and bald eagle.

Access is via U.S. routes 2 and 191; roads reaching into the wilder areas are apt to be hazardous at times and advance inquiry should be made. Accommodations are available in surrounding communities. Camping, boating, swimming, fishing, and hunting are permitted. Off-road vehicular travel is not allowed.

Information: Manager, Charles M. Russell National Wildlife Range, Box 110, Lewistown, Montana 59457.

🌲 As for true and original prairie, precious little remains. In **Lostwood National Wildlife Refuge,** near the Canadian border fifty miles northwest of Minot, North Dakota, are 26,747 acres of rolling prairie dotted with lakes and sloughs, carpeted with grasses, and sprinkled with aspen, silverberry, and wolfberry. The wetlands are some of the best remaining breeding grounds for North American ducks. Shorebirds are also plentiful, and indeed more than 250 species of birds have landed at one time or another in the refuge. Sharp-tailed grouse are especially abundant. Deer and pronghorns also wander among the many glacial potholes in this northern prairie. The area is managed primarily for protection and production of waterfowl, but it has wild aspects that are attractive in a region devoted to agriculture. Access to refuge headquarters is via State Route 8; visitors should stop there before entering. Food and lodging may be secured in towns twenty miles away.

Information: Manager, Lostwood National Wildlife Refuge, R. R. 1, Lostwood, North Dakota 58754.

🌲 A small touch of primitive lake and prairie habitat remains in the **Chase Lake National Wildlife Refuge,** thirty-five miles northwest of Jamestown, North Dakota, on country roads near Interstate 94. Chase Lake covers half of the 4,385-acre refuge and is surrounded by wide-open, rolling grassland. Temperatures each year range as widely as − 42° to 118°, but the refuge is a wildlife mecca, renowned for having the world's largest colony of white pelicans. In migration, other birds—cranes, geese, ducks, whistling swans—settle briefly here and sharp-tailed grouse are common. Food and lodging may be obtained at points along Interstate 94.

Information: Administration of Chase Lake is carried out by the Manager, Arrowwood National Wildlife Refuge, R. R. 1, Edmunds, North Dakota 58434.

🌲 In **Valentine National Wildlife Refuge** is another type of prairie, the sandhills of north-central Nebraska. The 71,516 acres of the refuge were as badly mauled by human manipulations as other parts of the sandhills, but here man helped the land to recover from draining, overgrazing, and the disastrous introduction of exotic wildlife. It still takes some manipulation to keep carp out of the lakes so that aquatic vegetation will grow for the benefit of wild ducks. Each year thousands of teals, mallards, pintails, redheads, and

261

other waterfowl nest on the refuge, and hundreds of thousands of ducks during migration land to feed and rest on the exceptionally clear waters (more than 10 percent of the refuge is composed of lakes and marshes). This is also a good place to observe the greater prairie chicken, a member of the grouse family, performing its dance-and-strut routine at mating time in early spring.

Many species of birds and mammals occupy the sandhills, and fishing for bass, bluegill, walleye, and northern pike is popular, even through the ice in winter. Picnic areas are available within the refuge, but not campsites; camping must be done outside, and recreation areas are not far away. Accommodations are available in nearby communities. U.S. Route 83 passes through the refuge and good sand trails lead to some of the wetlands.

Information: Manager, Valentine National Wildlife Refuge, Kennedy Star Route, Valentine, Nebraska 69201.

Another 46,000 acres of sandhill country have been set aside as the **Crescent Lake National Wildlife Refuge,** twenty-eight miles north of Oshkosh, Nebraska. Like Valentine, this refuge abounds in lakes and attracts many species of waterfowl. The human visitor who doesn't mind windmills here and there on the horizon should enjoy the grass-covered ridges and valleys, natural marshes, meadows, ponds, and lakes, and lively collections of wildlife in a sandy setting. Venturing off the improved roads, however, offers difficulties, due to the sand. Access is via country roads north from U.S. Route 26. The nearest food and lodging may be obtained in Oshkosh.

Information: Manager, Crescent Lake National Wildlife Refuge, Ellsworth, Nebraska 69340.

Few landscapes in North America have been so fully utilized for agriculture as the tallgrass prairie, and few original scenes so thoroughly modified. In fact, it is now difficult to tell what the original vegetation, which covered more than 250 million acres, consisted of, and ecologists have been hard put to find anything remotely resembling it. A tiny scrap exists in Pipestone National Monument, Minnesota, but a few protected acres hardly constitute wild prairie. The plow has prevailed.

Even so, scientists have identified a patch of some 50,000 acres in the Flint Hills of eastern Kansas as a place where tallgrass grows in a rocky environment that resisted cultivation. Bills were introduced into Congress in 1962 to establish a **Prairie National Park** there but the measures were defeated. The efforts go on, but as of this writing there is still no Prairie National Park, no place to see where the original plainsmen rode across young America.

4. GULF COAST

One of the most badly battered parts of the North American continent is the U.S. coast of the Gulf of Mexico. It has been so crisscrossed with roads and pipelines, and its shores so laved with oil and other residues of civilization that it will take a long time to heal. Even under natural conditions, there is little margin for survival of organisms, if only because of the salt that is violently sprayed over coastal environments during hurricanes and other heavy storms. Yet despite this multiple devastation, nature hangs on, and if some of the coastal sanctuaries are less than wild it is only because the wounds of civilization have yet to be covered.

🌲 Thanks to public concern about the vanishing breeding grounds of birds and turtles, and the loss of outdoor recreation sites, some offshore islands have gained protective status. The **Gulf Islands** of Florida and Mississippi were recently authorized by Congress and have come under the administration of the National Park Service as a national seashore, a new area in the making, as it were. The park includes white sand beaches near Pensacola, Florida, offshore islands, and portions of former military installations in coastal Mississippi and Florida, a total of 20,430 acres. The beaches, historic sites, and reasonably wild Gulf Coast flora and fauna will be preserved for enhancement of recreational opportunities. Swimming, boating, and other facilities are planned, and hiking trails will lead into more remote sections. Camping and picnicking facilities are now available. Access is by boat, or from approach routes U.S. 90 and 98. Tourist accommodations may be obtained at various points along the coast.

Information: Florida Unit Manager, Gulf Islands National Seashore, Box 100, Gulf Breeze, Florida 32561; and Mississippi Unit Manager, Gulf Islands National Seashore, Box T, Ocean Springs, Mississippi 39564.

🌲 **Breton National Wildlife Refuge** consists of Breton Island and the adjacent Chandeleur Islands, southeast of New Orleans in the Gulf of Mexico. The number and size of these barrier isles depends on how much their location, dimensions, and shapes are altered by severe storms; currently

263

the area is about 5,000 acres. Established in 1904 as the second national wildlife refuge, these islands constitute breeding grounds for sea turtles, saltwater fish, and thousands of birds—principally royal and sandwich terns, laughing gulls, and black skimmers. As many as 120,000 nests may be found from May through August. During winter, the islands host about 25,000 redhead ducks and 200,000 lesser scaups. All this takes place on scraps of land averaging less than a mile wide but curving in a gentle arc for twenty miles through the warm subtropical waters. On this low-lying terrain may be found sandy beaches, ponds, inlets, marshes, and patches of black mangrove and black rush. Public use is permitted throughout the year, except at nesting sites, which are posted with "Area Closed" signs. Access is by boat only and though twenty-five miles from the nearest land, the islands are visited frequently in spring, summer, and fall by fishermen who fish from the beaches. Overnight camping and motorized land vehicles are prohibited. Horn and Petit Bois islands, once part of the refuge, were transferred in 1971 to the Gulf Islands National Seashore.

Information: Manager, Delta-Breton National Wildlife Refuges, Venice, Louisiana 70091.

To hundreds of thousands of water birds, summer and winter, **Lacassine National Wildlife Refuge** is a segment of Louisiana marsh in which they can nest today as their ancestors used to do all over the southern coast. Half of the refuge's 31,765 acres are devoted to an artificially managed freshwater pool, but the anhingas, herons, egrets, cormorants, and eagles that nest there seem to consider it wild enough. Roseate spoonbills have begun to nest. December is the time of peak population, with nearly half a million migratory birds that include mallards, pintails, and widgeons. The refuge harbors the largest concentration of white-fronted geese on the Mississippi Flyway and the largest population of fulvous tree ducks on any U.S. refuge.

Access is by boat only, though refuge headquarters may be reached on Louisiana Route 3056, eleven miles southwest of Lake Arthur. Food and lodging may be secured in Lake Arthur, Jennings, and Welsh, less than twenty-two miles away. No camping or picnicking is permitted on the refuge.

Information: Manager, Lacassine National Wildlife Refuge, Box 186, Lake Arthur, Louisiana 70549.

West of Lacassine is a Louisiana coastal strip that, despite Damoclean threats of petroleum exploration, retains a great deal of its former integrity. Ibis, egret, heron, alligator, crab, all share the broad flat marshes of **Sabine**

National Wildlife Refuge, twenty miles southwest of Lake Charles on Louisiana State Route 27. It is surprising to find so sizable a refuge—142,846 acres—in petroleum and agricultural country, and while some of the other marshes around are black with oil, these are not. They abound with familiar marsh grasses (*Spartina*), and for miles the tallest shrubs one can see are *Baccharis* and black willow.

So extensive has been the dredging of channels for ships in this region that the balance between salt- and freshwater has been altered. One consequence is the destruction of cypresses, which now stand as dead white snags in Sabine marshes. Another is the loss of freshwater habitat, which compels authorities to maintain dikes for the capture and retention of rainwater. Nature keeps changing things, too, and the vegetation is anything but constant. There used to be sawgrass, a sharp-edged sedge, for miles around, but a recent hurricane coated most of it with seawater and then departed without much rain to wash off the salt. The resulting salt burn left only patches of sawgrass surviving.

The flat and muddy marshes still possess some of their original richness. Canals are constantly roiling with skittering crabs and schools of fish, and in other parts of this region, there are times when crayfish-catching jubilees attract 100,000 hungry human beings. The major benefits of such a nursery accrue to wading birds, and with so many natural foods, the refuge has been popular; more than 300 species of birds have been observed there. The greatest populations are in December and January. Muskrats, mink, otters, deer, foxes, and other mammals—even red wolves—may be seen on the refuge. The coypu, a South American aquatic rodent more commonly known as the nutria, has invaded the marshlands and mowed down great patches of bullwhip grass (bulrush) and hogcane.

There are places along the road to stop and fish or scan the marshes for birds. The Fish and Wildlife Service has installed a nature trail at one point, along which may be observed alligators and other inhabitants; at the end of the trail a small observation platform has been constructed. To climb higher towers out in the marsh, and to utilize some of the 125 miles of canals and bayous in the refuge, permission must be obtained. Food and lodging may be obtained at Cameron and other local communities.

Information: Manager, Sabine National Wildlife Refuge, Sulphur, Louisiana 70645.

A circular one-way road leads into a portion of the handsomely vegetated **Aransas National Wildlife Refuge,** on the Texas coast, 140 miles southwest of Houston. Dense clusters of blackjack oak, thickly grassed meadows, broad marshes where bent and curling vegetal stalks make geometric designs with their reflections in the water, small ponds, sifting streams—this atmosphere envelops the traveler, perhaps half mesmerizes him, not long after entering. We visited on an afternoon when rain fell in torrents, and the water-laden winds swept across the sandy shores and went deep into thickets of fragrant red bay. Afterward, the low sun shone through a veil of orange, illuminating the land in a soft, warm glow. We missed the whooping cranes, which arrive here in October after a 2,500-mile flight from northern Canada and stay until flying north the following April. But we saw wild turkeys feeding in the meadows, alligators peering from the sloughs, raccoons probing the marshes, javelinas in a hurry through tall grass, and white-tailed deer at nearly every turn.

Aransas contains 54,829 acres. Not all of it is open to the public, and some is even utilized for petroleum production, in accordance with prior rights. This is not intolerable, or even noticeable, and when someday the commercial uses are discontinued, nature will still prevail, as always.

The natural ecosystems are varied. There are tidal pools, marshes, dunes, ponds, meadows, mottes (clumps of oak trees), forests, and tangles of wild grape. For all the hurricanes, some of the oaks reach thirty feet in height, even at the edge of the sea. The refuge was established to protect the vanishing wildlife of the Texas coast—none of which is closer to extinction than the whooping crane. The protection of a large area is vital not only for the grassy seaside flats where the cranes take up residence, but for the broad territory over which they prowl in search of crabs, worms, clams, snails, insects, acorns, and plant tubers.

A good time to visit Aransas is between November and March, when the whooping cranes and other water birds are present, but a visit at any time is rewarding. Hiking trails and picnic sites are available, but overnight camping must be done at nearby state parks or private campgrounds. Access is via routes 35 or 774; food and lodging may be secured in towns along the approach roads.

Information: Manager, Aransas National Wildlife Refuge, Box 68, Austwell, Texas 77950.

🌲 The farther south one goes in Texas, the more the land comes to resemble México and Central America. Great stalks of giant yucca rise above thickets of prickly pear cactus and flowering shrubs. Ocelots, jaguarundis, and armadillos prowl the thorny underbrush. Close to shore, the terrain is occasionally of whitish hardpan, but for the most part the rich subtropical vegetation—grass, mesquite, catclaw, and succulent coastal prairie species— entirely covers the soil. With a warm climate, often hot and humid, the southern tip of Texas amounts to a bird paradise, and the 330 species recorded at **Laguna Atascosa National Wildlife Refuge** and **Santa Ana National Wildlife Refuge** is a record for the U.S. refuge system; it is nearly half of all species found in the contiguous forty-eight states.

Laguna Atascosa is a 45,150-acre coastal area once part of the Rio Grande delta. It is located twenty-seven miles east of Harlingen, on county roads off State Route 106, and has tour roads that permit access to the edges of wild areas. Its terrain is to a large degree open, and often is a wintering ground for three-fourths of the redhead ducks on the continent.

Santa Ana Refuge, on the other hand, is nearly fifty miles inland, on the bank of the Rio Grande, just off U.S. Route 281 near McAllen, Texas. In its thick, moss-draped forests live such tropical birds as chachalacas and green jays, easily observed by visitors. Chachalacas, in fact, haunt the road and mill about like chickens in hopes of a handout. Other easily visible indicators of the tropics are trees, some of which are labeled near refuge headquarters: chapatillo, Barbados cherry, granjeno, tepehuaje, and wild bougainvillea.

Though the Santa Ana Refuge is small (2,000 acres) it is extremely complex biologically, and one of the few vestiges of original Rio Grande Valley subtropical ecosystems. Twelve miles of trails wind through its dense forests, and a six-mile self-guiding road reaches other points of interest. Early morning and late afternoon are the best times to visit, but the air vibrates with calls and notes of birds all day. For photographers, blinds facilitate close-up pictures of wildlife. Visitors may obtain food and lodging in nearby cities and towns.

Information: Santa Ana and Laguna Atascosa refuges are both administered by the Manager, Laguna Atascosa National Wildlife Refuge, Box 2683, Harlingen, Texas 78550.

🌲 Offshore, in the Gulf of Mexico, an elongated sand island extends for more than a hundred miles along the Texas coast. Most of it has been reserved as **Padre Island National Seashore,** and while vehicles are permitted to run the beach, and there are petroleum installations in places, a hiker can still get a wilderness feeling by exploring back away from the shore and among the large expanses of well-vegetated dunes. He may share this domain with a sandhill crane, which often stands like a lonesome sentinel on the top of a dune and surveys the coastal terrain. Or hear a pack of coyotes barking, which seems a little strange as close as this area is to Corpus Christi. Winds blow the sea oats into sprawling designs, and "railroad vine," a wild morning glory, sends out long strings of lavender blooms.

The sea dominates, however, and flocks of shorebirds patrol the strand line.

Pelicans skim the waves farther out, and terns sail high on the winds. This dynamic environment is troubled by the debris of man, for it seems that all the refuse cast overboard from ships in the Gulf of Mexico—and even as far away as the Canary Islands—comes to rest on the shores of Padre Island. Large sheets of plastic, chunks of tar, nylon rope, loading platforms, and even five-ton shrimp-boat refrigerators are among the debris deposited. It is more than the National Park Service can clean away each day; Padre Island is a victim of ocean dumping. Hikers along the beach should wear hard-soled shoes to avoid injury from stepping on nails or glass.

From Corpus Christi a good highway, Route 22, leads across a causeway to Padre Island, thence south ten miles to the entrance of the national seashore. For ten miles south of that point the beach can be negotiated by ordinary passenger cars, but from there on only four-wheel-drive vehicles are permitted. At Malaquite Beach, near the northern end, visitors have access to showers, a snack bar, gift shop, and other facilities. Camping is permitted only on the beach. Campers traveling to remote parts of the shore or hikers going inland should carry food and water. Hiking is arduous, and the heat, humidity, insects, and rattlesnakes make it unadvisable to walk through the grasslands. Travelers should also be prepared for hot sun, glare, and steady wind. A self-guiding trail helps explain natural features. Accommodations are available in Corpus Christi and on Padre Island.

Information: Superintendent, Padre Island National Seashore, Box 8560, Corpus Christi, Texas 78412.

PART VII

The Northeast

1. EASTERN CANADA

2. GREAT LAKES

1. Isle Royale National Park, Michigan
2. Apostle Islands National Lakeshore, Wisconsin
3. Porcupine Mountains Wilderness State Park, Michigan
4. Pictured Rocks National Lakeshore, Michigan
5. Big Island Lake Wilderness, Michigan
6. Seney National Wildlife Refuge, Michigan
7. Tahquamenon Falls State Park, Michigan
8. Betsy Lake Natural Area Preserve, Michigan
9. Sleeping Bear Dunes National Lakeshore, Michigan
10. Rondeau Provincial Park, Ontario
11. Huron Islands National Wildlife Refuge, Michigan
12. Gravel Island National Wildlife Refuge, Wisconsin
13. Hog Island National Wildlife Refuge, Wisconsin
14. Spider Island National Wildlife Refuge, Wisconsin
15. Shoe Island National Wildlife Refuge, Michigan
16. Pismire Island National Wildlife Refuge, Michigan
17. Scarecrow Island National Wildlife Refuge, Michigan
18. West Sister Island National Wildlife Refuge, Ohio
19. St. Lawrence Islands National Park, Ontario
20. Georgian Bay Islands National Park, Ontario
21. Killarney Provincial Park, Ontario
22. Lake Superior Provincial Park, Ontario
23. Pukaskwa National Park, Ontario
24. Neys Provincial Park, Ontario
25. Sibley Provincial Park, Ontario

3. NORTHERN MOUNTAINS

26. Adirondack Forest Preserve, New York
27. Catskill Forest Preserve, New York
28. Harriman State Park, New York
29. Bear Mountain State Park, New York
30. Letchworth State Park, New York
31. Allegany State Park, New York
32. High Point State Park, New Jersey
33. Lye Brook Wilderness, Vermont
34. Bristol Cliffs Wilderness, Vermont
35. Great Gulf Wilderness, New Hampshire
36. Presidential Range Wilderness, New Hampshire
37. Wild River Wilderness, New Hampshire
38. Dry River–Rocky Branch Wilderness, New Hampshire
39. Kilkenny Wilderness, New Hampshire
40. Carr Mountain Wilderness, New Hampshire
41. Caribou–Speckled Mountain Wilderness, Maine
42. Baxter State Park, Maine
43. Allagash Wilderness Waterway, Maine
44. Moosehorn National Wildlife Refuge, Maine
45. Acadia National Park, Maine

4. COASTAL LOWLANDS

46. Cape Cod National Seashore, Massachusetts
47. Monomoy National Wildlife Refuge, Massachusetts
48. Fire Island National Seashore, New York
49. Great Swamp National Wildlife Refuge, New Jersey
50. Brigantine National Wildlife Refuge, New Jersey
51. Cohansey Natural Area, New Jersey
52. Pine Barrens, New Jersey
53. Bombay Hook National Wildlife Refuge, Delaware
54. Great Cypress Swamp, Delaware

1. EASTERN CANADA

A vision of lowering clouds and blustery weather, squalls of rain, and bleak, rocky coasts being lashed by furious seas is enough to chill the ardor of fair-weather tourists. However, Newfoundland is not always like that. In summer the waters warm up to swimming temperatures, the winds abate, the sun bathes newborn patches of orchid and iris, and the white beach sands, undisturbed for miles in **Gros Morne National Park,** gleam as though there had never been any winter. Actually, even in storm and even in winter, the environment here can be highly dramatic, and travelers should hope to have a touch of several kinds of weather.

Gros Morne is like something from the coast of Norway. Great cliffs that rise 2,000 feet from the sea, sheer rocky headlands, deep fjords, islets, and piles of broken boulders characterize this western edge of Newfoundland. The park's 448,000 acres protect the more outstanding parts of the Long Range Mountains, of which the highest point, Gros Morne, reaches 2,644 feet. The rocks are extremely old—on the order of 1.1 billion years—and mostly gneisses and schists, carved into sharp relief during the latest advance of glacial ice. Over this high and precipitous terrain water falls in scenic cascades, some so far it turns into mist before reaching the bottom. The vegetation is limited not only because soils are thin but because of heavy snow, a short summer, and high winds. These winds have stunted the growth of spruce and fir in unprotected places along the coast or pruned the trees down literally to a shrubby carpet called "tuckamoor." On the highest mountaintops, climatic extremes leave little but tundra, with lichens the principal form of life. This is the home of the arctic hare, an endangered species being protected by the park. By contrast, lower sheltered places have bogs, grasslands, and forests of fir, spruce, birch, and maple.

Trails reach these different habitats, and visitors can climb to the summit of Gros Morne. In remote areas they may glimpse caribou, moose, and black bears. Bald eagles and ospreys fly over the headlands, and with good luck a hiker may sight the gyrfalcon and rock and willow ptarmigan. Fishermen along the streams, indulging the competition of mink and otter, take salmon and brook trout. However, some of the most fascinating environments are those at the edge of the sea and under its surface. The 250 species of marine

Maple leaf and star moss, Baxter State Park, Maine.

algae in Bonne Bay alone attest to an extraordinary richness. A cold part of the Labrador Current brings in tons of plankton, which forms the fundamental food for other life. Shellfish, cod, halibut, herring, and mackerel are all abundant, and whales, porpoises, and seals swim past during fall and winter.

The park, accessible via the Trans-Canada Highway and provincial routes 44 and 73, is still new, so camping facilities are limited; in fact, the wilderness aspects are to be sustained permanently, so development will always have limits. Trails are now being constructed so as to permit overnight hikers access to extensive wilderness mountain areas.

Outside the park are private camping and accommodations, including cabins on the Lomond River at the park boundary; cabins, a motel, and a tourist home in Woody Point; cabins in Rocky Harbour; and motels in Cow Head, at Deer Lake, twenty-four miles to the southeast, and at Daniels Harbor, thirty miles north of the park. Most facilities and activities are oriented toward summer use, but cross-country skiing and snowshoeing are possible in winter.

Information: Superintendent, Gros Morne National Park, Box 130, Rocky Harbour, Newfoundland.

🌲 To visitors flying over eastern Newfoundland in January, the land below appears too solidly frozen ever to thaw out. But this is deceptive, for the landscape does unfreeze; indeed, the Labrador Current tempers climatic extremes and produces mild winters along the coast. As a result, forests of maple, spruce, and fir are studded with such plants as orchids and dogwoods. In fact, bogs are numerous, filled with pitcher plants, sphagnum moss, leatherleaf rhodora, and the like. This domain at the edge of the sea, often fjordlike, musical with the songs of thrushes and warblers, replete with moose and bear, has been designated **Terra Nova National Park,** a protected area of 97,920 acres on the eastern shore of the island, forty-eight miles southeast of Gander.

The park protects many features of interest. Geologists will find in this most northerly extension of the 2,000-mile-long Appalachian Mountains ancient sediments dating back 600 million years. They will also find surface disruptions resulting from Ice Age erosion and deposition. Botanists will find boreal forests with such typical northern plants as twinflower and fireweed. Aquatic biologists may observe in the coastal environment kelp, mussels, barnacles, periwinkles, seals, whales, and seabirds.

Terra Nova National Park is traversed by the Trans-Canada Highway. Though open in winter, when snowshoeing is popular, the park has most of its activities in summer. Among these are swimming, canoeing on lakes and streams, hiking, riding, fishing in freshwater for brook trout, Arctic char, and ouananiche (salmon), and fishing offshore for cod, herring, lumpfish, mackerel, and caplin. Food and lodging may be obtained both inside and outside the park.

Information: Superintendent, Terra Nova National Park, Glovertown, Newfoundland.

🌲 The northern portion of Cape Breton Island, Nova Scotia, typifies the classic mountainous coasts of eastern Canada: sheer dark granite, schist and sandstone cliffs rising out of the sea, headlands covered with Scotch lovage, dense forests of balsam fir and spruce, waterfalls, and a high plateau with muskegs and heath barrens. Such is **Cape Breton Highlands National Park,** with spectacular headlands a thousand feet above the sea.

Within the forest live lynx, bears, red foxes, mink, moose, otters, marten, and bobcats. Beaver have become well established. Caribou, once native here, were reintroduced, but are now scarce. The region is well-known for its shorebirds, many of which are long-distance migrants. The park also remains a notable locality for observation of land birds because such groups as warblers and crossbills are often abundant. In park waters live brook and sea trout, and in pools along the Cheticamp River can be found Atlantic salmon.

The park is open all year, though visitor services are limited in winter. Wilderness permits are required for overnight trips into the interior. Trails lead along the coast, around lakes, beside streams, and up into relatively open country inland. Illustrated talks, nature trails, and exhibits explain the natural features. Campgrounds and picnic areas are located along Route 19, the "Cabot Trail," which winds in and out of the park on the west, north, and east sides. Accommodations and food may be secured at Cheticamp, Pleasant Bay, Cape North, and Ingonish. The area is located 280 miles northeast of Halifax and is reached via the Trans-Canada Highway.

Information: Superintendent, Cape Breton Highlands National Park, Ingonish Beach, Nova Scotia.

🌲 To see something of the original inland Nova Scotia, one should visit **Kejimkujik National Park,** named from a Micmac Indian word applied to the largest lake in the park and signifying "place that swells"—though the meaning of this is obscure. The northern deciduous hardwood and coniferous forests have been cut and burned for 200 years, but now with the destruction stopped, and with favorable climatic conditions, some of the original wilderness aspects will be restored. As it is, Kejimkujik presents natural environments for hiking, camping, canoeing, boating, fishing, photography, and nature study. Specific canoe routes have been designated along streams and lakes in this 89,600-acre park. Most of the area is roadless and trailless. Before a canopy of leaves covers the forest each spring, a wild display of violets, trailing arbutus, trillium, orchids, and irises brightens the woodland. Heaths inhabit the bogs, and there are even a few greenbriar and witchhazel shrubs from the south. Deciduous trees include red oak, maple, birch, and beech, and among the conifers are red and black spruce, balsam fir, white pine, and hemlock. Porcupines live in the hemlock stands, squirrels and white-tailed deer in mixed woods, and bears in boggy areas—especially at blueberry time. The water routes harbor beaver, muskrats, raccoons, and otters. Birds also fill the woods, and there is an abundance of frogs, toads, salamanders, snakes, and turtles. The waters are ideal for speckled and brown trout and white perch.

Campgrounds are open year round, with a two-week limit. Food may be obtained near the park entrance; accommodations can be secured in nearby towns such as Annapolis Royal, Liverpool, Bridgewater, and Halifax, the latter 100 miles to the northeast. Canadian Route 8 passes the park entrance. Nature trails and information services are available.

Information: Superintendent, Kejimkujik National Park, Box 36, Maitland Bridge, Annapolis County, Nova Scotia.

🌲 Where unusual natural phenomena are talked about, the Bay of Fundy, between Nova Scotia and New Brunswick, comes in for its share of renown as locale of the world's greatest tides. In the vicinity of **Fundy National Park,** which occupies 51,200 acres with nine miles of frontage on the bay, the tides rise as high as forty-two feet, magnified by the bay's shape and size. To see them sweeping in and out, up the rivers and back, first crashing, flooding, and filling, then withdrawing and exposing whole flats, a visitor could well wonder how animal life adapts to such excessive wetting and drying. The fact is that quite a community of organisms depends upon this tidal estuary, especially birds that explore the exposed flats for food. As long as the expectable happens, and the tides are not excessive—i.e., neither too low nor too high—each organism seems to do very well in its adopted niche. But once every few years comes a tide so high that it sweeps away sharp-tailed sparrows and the nests ordinarily placed back far enough for safety. A high winter tide can bring in blocks of ice containing mud and stones, which are scattered over the bordering marshes. On the return tide, grasses can be broken off and muds torn from the marshes and taken out to distant sand

276

flats. If the tide stays out too long the exposed animals could freeze. How wildlife communities survive in the face of such environmental variables is one of the mysteries of this region.

At most locations along the coast, the tide rises and falls at about one inch per minute. However, certain rivers at the head of the bay exhibit a phenomenon called "tidal bore." In these rivers, the incoming tide takes the form of a solid wall of water from several inches to over a foot high. Tidal bores do not exist in the park, but may be observed in the nearby Petitcodiac River.

Fundy National Park itself has more than tides and beaches. There are shorebound cliffs up to 200 feet high, dense Acadian forests of mixed deciduous trees—aspen, maple, beech, and birch—and conifer groves of balsam fir, pine, and spruce. The topography is a rolling plateau, remnant of an ancient range of mountains whose rocks are 500 million years old. Trails lead to streams, rivers, and lakes where fishing for speckled trout and Atlantic salmon is permitted with a park license; all other forms of plant and animal life are protected. Wildlife includes moose, white-tailed deer, porcupines, beaver, raccoons, and snowshoe hares.

Campgrounds are available, and interpretive programs, including guided hikes, enhance a visitor's understanding of the park. Provincial Route 114 crosses the area, which is located fifty miles south of Moncton, New Brunswick. Accommodations are available in and near the park.

Information: Superintendent, Fundy National Park, Alma, New Brunswick.

🌲 **Kouchibouguac National Park** (the name means "River of the Long Tide") surrounds a bay on the northeastern coast of New Brunswick. The environment is coastal, with a concentration of different land-sea ecosystems: estuaries, lagoons, marshes, tidal flats, sandspits, barrier islands, dunes, and bogs. The forest, principally spruce, pine, and fir mixed with maple and birch, has sphagnum bogs around which grow laurel, Labrador tea, and tamarack. Mammals are not common, but more than two dozen species of fish have been identified in marine and freshwater habitats, and birds are abundant, owing to the park's location on the Atlantic Flyway. Recreational facilities, including campsites, are being developed for human use of this 55,680-acre park. Private camping facilities, food, and lodging may be obtained nearby. Access is via Provincial Route 11, about sixty miles north of Moncton.

Information: Superintendent, Kouchibouguac National Park, Kouchibouguac, New Brunswick.

🌲 There has always seemed to be some indefinable magic in the words Gaspé Peninsula, and certainly persons who have visited this seaward arm of Québec have expressed its charms in different ways; the soft birch woods with stands of spruce; the flocks of birds wheeling over blue waters in bright sunlight; the gentle fog on a rainy morning; the sight of whales coming round the point; angling for speckled trout in the inland streams; or chartering a boat and going to sea in search of cod, mackerel, salmon, or herring. There are a hundred moods, or a thousand, and the Canadian government has preserved a microcosm of the Gaspé world in **Forillon National Park,** located on Gaspé Bay, at the eastern tip of the peninsula.

With so many specific and interchangeable forest associations, a botanist in this 58,880-acre area would be hard put to study them all before the wild geese headed south and winter came. Not only are the forests rich, but the park encompasses dunes, rocky points, salt marshes, and marine vegetation. The wilderness hiker cannot hope to know all of what he sees in this complex series of ecosystems, but there are guided tours that at least provide a good introduction. Moreover, trails lead to hidden beaches, cascading streams, waterfalls, and mountain summits. The coast in places rises in 600-foot sea-sculptured cliffs, which in summer are adorned with nests of cormorants, kittiwakes, guillemots, and gulls. The highest point in the park is 1,800 feet. Elsewhere, visitors come upon small coves, inland lakes, and such fairly numerous and widespread mammals as lynxes, deer, moose, bears, and red foxes.

Provincial Route 6 runs around and through the park; food, lodging, and campgrounds are available along this road, and within the park proper are other campsites. Loop trails lead along streams and to the higher parts of the park; in winter, snowshoe and cross-country ski trails are maintained. Deep-sea fishing trips may be arranged locally, as can pleasure cruises into Gaspé Bay or the Gulf of St. Lawrence.

Information: Superintendent, Forillon National Park, Box 1220, Gaspé, Québec.

🌲 On the south side of the Gaspé Peninsula, the Port-Daniel River flows from the mountains to the sea through a valley filled with spruce and white birch. This is the milieu of **Port-Daniel Provincial Park,** 16,000 acres just north of Provincial Route 6 near the village of Port-Daniel. Speckled trout are taken from lakes in the park and Atlantic salmon from the river. There is no hunting. Campsites and housekeeping cottages are available. Access is via local roads that reach several lakes in the park.

Information: Superintendent, Port-Daniel Provincial Park, New Carlisle, Québec.

🌲 In the Shickshock Mountains of the Gaspé Peninsula, south of the St. Lawrence River, **Gaspesian Provincial Park** protects literally a window of the past. Whereas nearly everything else for miles around was inundated by glaciers during the Ice Age, these uplands remained virtually untouched—in effect refuges for the flora that had evolved to that time. Likewise, the valleys between Ste.-Anne-des-Monts and Rivière-au-Renard appear to have been little disturbed by the ice. As a result, flora preceding glacial times continues to flourish in this park. Mountains of granite and serpentine rise to more than 4,000 feet, and are devoid of trees at that elevation. The rest of the 318,720-acre park is well supplied with forests and wildlife, and is especially popular with anglers in search of speckled trout. Adjacent to the south boundary is **Little Cascapedia River Provincial Park** of approximately 200,000 acres; on the north and west lies **Chic-chocs Provincial Park** of about 300,000 acres.

Access to all three is by Route 299; lodge, chalet, and camping accommodations are available in Gaspesian Park.

Information: Superintendent, Gaspesian Park, Ste.-Anne-des-Monts, Comté de Gaspé-Nord, Québec.

Matane Provincial Park contains 288,000 acres of scenic forest, stream, and mountain country between the St. Lawrence River and the Shickshock Mountains. It is easily accessible, with roads paralleling the park's major lakes and streams, a boon to anglers in search of salmon and gray trout. And there are camping and picnicking sites. But away from these the visitor feels engulfed in wild forests, or finds quiet pools endowed with solitude. These may have to be shared, however, with moose or other mammals inhabiting the dense coniferous woods. Access is via country roads from Route 10 at Matane or Cap-Chat. Food, supplies, and lodging must be obtained in nearby communities. Adjacent to the park on the south is **Dunière Provincial Park** of nearly 200,000 acres, and not far to the south is **Causapscal Provincial Park,** of almost 200,000 acres.

Information: Director, Parc de Matane, 263 Avenue St.-Jerome, Matane, Québec.

Rimouski Provincial Park, thirty miles south of the town of Rimouski, contains 192,000 acres of lakes, streams, and typical mixed forest, with wilderness camping and picnic sites. Some cabins are available within the park but no supplies. Access is by country roads south from Route 232. Fishing and hunting are permitted, a legacy from the early days when parts of the area were owned by hunting and fishing clubs. Other activities include swimming, hiking, and boating.

Information: Director, Rimouski District Office, 1 Ouest, Boulevard St.-Germain, Rimouski, Québec.

♠ The vast Saguenay beaver reserve in eastern Québec was set aside in 1955 to assure the conservation of beaver and permit it to be trapped for the benefit of the Indians of the region. Within it is the **Port-Cartier-Sept-Îles Provincial Park** of 2,080,000 acres. Located north across the St. Lawrence River from the Gaspé Peninsula, it is a remote wilderness still in the process of development for public use. Its subarctic forests consist of black and white spruce, birch, fir, and dwarf shrubs. Wet bogs are common on this flat terrain. There are glacial deposits in the form of flat terraces, and places where granite gneiss outcrops. This is a good park for wilderness travel and camping, at least in certain places; but once out in the vast forest with its ill-defined drainage patterns, the traveler is strictly on his own and had better be well-prepared. Moose and bears inhabit the woods. Speckled trout fishing and picnicking are the major forms of recreation. Housekeeping cottages are available, with other services in the nearby towns of Sept-Îles and Port-Cartier. The area is approached on Provincial Route 138, and entered on a local road north of Port-Cartier, but inquiry should be made about further travel in the wilderness.

Information: Superintendent, Port-Cartier–Sept-Îles Provincial Park, 818 Avenue Laure, Sept-Îles, Québec.

♠ Adjoining Port-Cartier–Sept-Îles Provincial Park on the southwest is **Baie-Comeau–Hauterive Provincial Park,** of well over a million acres. Moving westward across Québec, north of the St. Lawrence River, we come to **Labrieville Provincial Park,** some 200,000 acres in area, reached on a gravel road fifty-one miles northwest of Forestville; and **Chicoutimi Provincial Park,** about 600,000 acres, on Provincial Route 172 east of the city of Chicoutimi.

Since these parks are in various stages of development, up-to-the-minute information should be obtained from the Department of Tourism, Fish, and Game, Hôtel du Gouvernement, Québec, Québec.

♠ **Laurentides Provincial Park** was established for one essential purpose—to protect the thousands of caribou that once roamed in great herds through the woods and over the hills of this part of southeastern Québec. But in time the caribou disappeared, perhaps under pressure of hunting, which was stopped in 1927, or perhaps simply because the animals emigrated to some other locality. They had plenty of room where they were, for the park contains 2,374,400 acres, yet it might just have been that they became too

280

Mistassini Provincial Park, Québec. Courtesy Québec Direction Générale du Tourisme.

Bonne Bay, Gros Morne National Park, Newfoundland. Courtesy Parks Canada.

numerous for the environment to sustain them, and hence slowly departed. The reasons are still unclear. In any case, careful scientific attempts were begun in 1966 to restore the animals, several of which were netted, drugged, straitjacketed and flown in from 400 miles away. But it is a long process, and even to restore a herd of 1,000 will very likely take many years.

Visitors to this park today are more apt to see speckled trout than caribou; at least that is one of the principal lures to anglers. Cottages, campgrounds, secondary roads, trails, and streams are the ingredients that go into a visit here. Route 54 passes through the park, which is located thirty miles north of the city of Québec.

Information: Superintendent, Laurentides Provincial Park, Edifice de la Faune, Box 7200, Orsainville, Québec, G1G 5E5.

🌲 Some fifty miles northwest of the city of Québec, **Portneuf Provincial Park** protects a portion of the Laurentian Mountains. From upper elevations of 2,500 feet rivulets and streams cascade down through heavily wooded valleys. The forests are principally red spruce, but there are also fir, maple, and birch. Moose are common and the waters abound with speckled trout. Bears and wolves also inhabit the park. In summer the major activities are fishing, swimming, and picnicking; in winter, trails are marked for snowmobiles. Housekeeping cottages and campgrounds are available in the park. A railroad bisects this 186,800-acre park. Access is via country roads branching from Provincial Route 367.

Information: Superintendent, Portneuf Provincial Park, Edifice de la Faune, Box 7200, Orsainville, Québec, G1G 5E5.

🌲 On the St.-Maurice River, halfway between the cities of Montréal and Québec, lies **La Mauricie National Park,** a rolling, glaciated hill country of 132,474 acres covered by forests of maple and birch, stands of conifers, scattered aspen groves, more than sixty lakes, and streams so abundant they have not been counted. Canoeists and hikers heading into this park very promptly leave civilization behind and enter a wilderness almost as wild as when the early Attikamegue Indians traveled in it. Working out from remote camping spots, the traveler can explore wild bogs replete with sundews and pitcher plants. Flowers bloom not only in the woods but along the shores of lakes and in the water itself. The likelihood of seeing moose, raccoons, and black bears is rather good; coyotes, timberwolves, foxes, and lynxes are the main predators but are less often encountered. Rich marshy shorelines abound with amphibians and invertebrates. If the traveler wants to fish, he can try for lake trout, northern pike, and smallmouth bass. However, a

Québec fishing permit is required and anglers must register at the park gates upon arrival.

The park is accessible from routes 19 and 55 to Shawinigan, then Route 351 south, toward St.-Gérard des Laurentides. The use of motorboats is prohibited in the park with the exception of Lake Mapizagonke and Lake Edouard, where motors of less than ten horsepower are allowed. Developed campgrounds are available, but private accommodations may be secured only in neighboring communities such as Shawinigan and Grand-Mère. The park is open all year, with June 15 to September 15 the main season. Guided canoe trips by experienced naturalists are scheduled during summer months.

Information: Superintendent, La Mauricie National Park, Box 758, Shawinigan, Québec G9N 6V9.

🌲 **St.-Maurice Provincial Park,** forty miles northwest of Grand-Mère, contains 92,160 acres of lakes, streams, and rolling hills, with forests of jack pine, balsam fir, spruce, and birch. The abundance of lake and speckled trout makes the area especially attractive to fishermen. Campgrounds and limited cabin facilities are available, and secondary roads reach to numerous destinations in the park. Access is via Route 19 from Trois Rivières.

Information: Superintendent, St.-Maurice Provincial Park, 175 6ᵉ Rue, Edifice Hôtel de Ville, Box 36, Shawinigan, Québec.

🌲 Between St.-Alexis-des-Monts and St.-Michel-des-Saints lies **Mastigouche Provincial Park,** named from Montagnais Indian words meaning "small wood" or "small bear." It is located in the Laurentian uplands of rolling hills, lakes, streams, and typical northern forests. The waters contain speckled trout and ouananiche, or landlocked salmon. The park spreads across the hills for 454,400 acres, and is located west of Grand-Mère, adjacent to La Mauricie National Park and St.-Maurice Provincial Park. Access is via country roads on all sides. Housekeeping cottages are available.

Information: Superintendent, Mastigouche Provincial Park, C.P. 297, St.-Alexis-des-Monts, Cté Maskinongé, Québec.

🌲 On the Laurentian Plateau of southern Québec, adjoining Mont-Tremblant Provincial Park on the southeast, is **Joliette Provincial Park,** 176,640 acres of mountains, gorges, rivers, and woods. Fishing for speckled trout and northern pike is a popular recreation; hunting for small animals is also permitted. The larger forms of wildlife include moose, deer, and bears. The park is in the process of being developed for visitor use, and accommodations may be secured in St.-Michel-des-Saints, St.-Donat, and other nearby communities. Access is via side roads off provincial routes 18 and 43. Information: Superintendent, Joliette Provincial Park, 5075 Fullum Street, Montréal, Québec.

🌲 **Mont-Tremblant Provincial Park,** formerly called Trembling Mountain, does not commemorate volcanic or seismic activity, but simply an early Indian legend based on the rumble of mountain brooks. This wild area of 640,000 acres is located in the rolling Laurentian Mountains, and there are enough stairstep ledges, cliffs, and steep valleys to allow for a considerable number of waterfalls and cascades. Lakes encircled by dense north woods give Mont-Tremblant a picturesque quality, and the waters are heavily utilized by anglers. Motorboats are permitted only on certain lakes. The park is reached via Route 11 northwest from Montréal, and several secondary roads provide access to points within the park. Beyond that, large roadless areas are entered only by canoe or on trails or by means of cross-country hiking. Campgrounds are available and boats may be rented but no lodging, supplies, or gasoline may be obtained except in neighboring communities. Campgrounds will be restricted to areas near the entrance, leaving the park itself for nature-oriented activities.

Information: Superintendent, Parc du Mont-Tremblant, Via Lac-Supérieur, Comté de Terrebonne, Québec.

🌲 Forty miles northeast of Ottawa lies **Papineau-Labelle Provincial Park,** 448,000 acres of rolling glaciated hills that rise to 1,600 feet. Among the many lakes and streams stretches a forest of yellow birch with stands of red, white, and gray pine. Wildlife includes deer, moose, hares, and partridges. Hunting for small wildlife is permitted; fishermen may try their luck for gray and speckled trout, pike and walleye. Country roads lead into the park from several sides, principally from provincial routes 11, 309, and 321. Housekeeping cottages are available.

Information: Chief, Outaouais District Office, Park Branch, 653 Boulevard St.-Joseph, Hull, Québec; and Chief, Park Office, Papineau-Labelle Provincial Park, Val des Bois, Québec.

🌲 **La Verendrye Provincial Park,** on Route 58 in southwestern Québec, is a heavily forested fisherman's paradise, its waters abounding in northern pike, lake trout, walleye, sturgeon, whitefish, bass, and other species. Lakes and streams are separated by rocky ridges and dense coniferous forests over a wide area of 3.2 million acres. Within the park live about 3,000 Algonquin Indians. Canoeing is especially attractive, and there are splendid opportunities for extended wilderness journeys. Maps and booklets depicting recommended canoe routes are available from 'provincial authorities. Fishing, sailing, and swimming are also popular. Visitors may secure food, lodging, and campsites within the park. Not far to the south lies **Pontiac Provincial Park,** of approximately 200,000 acres, accessible on forest roads west of Maniwaki.

Information: Director, Park Office, Le Domaine, Parc de la Verendrye, Via Val-d'Or, Québec.

On the western boundary of La Verendrye Provincial Park lies **Kipawa Provincial Park** of approximately 1 million acres. Composed of elongated and irregularly shaped lakes with countless bays, arms, and inlets on their shores and islands, the park is a mecca for anglers. In its pure waters live gray trout, walleye, pickerel, and northern pike. Moose and bears live in the dense woods of pine and birch. Fly-in camps are available at remote locations. Nearby are camps where package tourist plans include float plane round trip, cottage, boats, motors, gasoline, bait, and other supplies; in some cases visitors must bring their own sleeping bags and groceries. Cottages and other accommodations are available in Kipawa, west of the park. Access is via country roads from provincial routes 46 and 62.

Information: Director, Tourism Branch, Department of Tourism, Fish, and Game, Cité Parlementaire, Québec.

Aiguebelle Provincial Park protects 64,000 acres of northern forest and lake country. Its waters contain lake trout weighing up to twenty pounds, plus pike and walleye. Small lakes and streams may be reached on foot; boats can be rented on La Haye, Du Sault, and Patrice lakes. Accommodations are available at Renault, which may be reached on Provincial Route 46 south of Macamic.

Information: Director, Tourism Branch, Department of Tourism, Fish, and Game, Cité Parlementaire, Québec.

Three hundred miles north of Montréal the provincial government of Québec has set aside three reserves of extraordinary size. **Mistassini Provincial Park** contains 3,328,000 acres of relatively level land forested with spruce and balsam fir. Abundant lakes and streams discharge immense quantities of water toward James Bay. "The lakes in this part of the province," advises the Provincial Park Service, "are generally not free of ice before the third week in May, and this is when the best fishing begins. Indeed angling is by all odds the park's leading attraction; lake and speckled trout, pike and walleye throng its waters." Access from the south is by provincial routes 167 and 113; there is also a small airport nearby. Lodges, cabins, and campgrounds are available in the park.

Information: Director, Chicoutimi District Office, Case Postale 66, Roberval, Québec.

🌲 Around the sprawling headwaters of the Broadback and Chibougamau rivers lies the **Assinica Reserve Provincial Park,** which adjoins Mistassini Provincial Park on the southwest. Its 2 million acres of lakes, streams, and woods are an angler's haven, with trophy-size trout the favorite. Also present are pike, walleye, and whitefish. Food and lodging are available within the reserve at fishing camps, accessible only by float-equipped aircraft. The nearest community is Chibougamau, which may be reached by automobile, bus, and daily weekday flights in summer from Montreal, 455 miles to the south.

Information: Director, Chicoutimi District Office, Case Postale 66, Roberval, Québec.

🌲 On the south, Mistassini Provincial Park is joined by **Chibougamau Provincial Park,** 2,176,000 acres, long a hunting ground for Montagnais Indians seeking fur pelts. Like Mistassini, this park has beaver, otters, hares, foxes, wolves, black bears, and moose. It also possesses an abundance of walleye, pike, and trout in its lakes and rivers. Boats may be rented. Accommodations are available, from campgrounds to lodges, and a snack bar offers food. Access is via Provincial Route 167 northwest of Roberval.

Information: Director, Chicoutimi District Office, Case Postale 66, Roberval, Québec.

🌲 Québec has established other provincial parks, some still mostly undeveloped. Wilderness travelers with an appreciation of the "unknown" may want to investigate such areas as the huge **James Bay Provincial Reserve,** north of Matagami, inhabited by Indians of the Cree tribe. Altogether the provincial parks of Québec cover nearly 33 million acres, three times the size of Switzerland and about the same area as the entire Canadian or U.S. national park systems.

Information: Government of Québec, Department of Tourism, Fish, and Game, Hôtel du Gouvernement, Québec, Québec, G1A 1R4.

🌲 Largest of Ontario's reserves is **Polar Bear Provincial Park,** on the southern shore of Hudson Bay. Its 5,952,000 acres are accessible by boat and by land and sea aircraft to Winisk, Site 415, and Sutton River, the latter equipped for float aircraft only. The park is maintained as a true wilderness, Ontario's first. It consists of near-Arctic tundra, taiga, and seacoast that supports populations of polar bears, caribou, snow and blue geese, and other species. Related to this area is **Winisk Wild River Provincial Park.** The Winisk River flows north into Hudson Bay through Polar Bear Provincial Park, and Ontario officials have designated it a wild river, to be managed with few or no recreational facilities. The river and surrounding protected area cover 593,920 acres. Access is by boat or air only. Food and lodging for both areas may be obtained at the Ministry of Transport and Communication airport in Winisk. Persons entering this region should be experienced in wilderness travel and must take all their life-support equipment with them. Food is available at the Hudson Bay Company store in Winisk village.

Information: District Manager, Ministry of Natural Resources, Box 190, Moosonee, Ontario P0L 1Y0.

🌲 Where once the Cree Indians camped in summer is **Nagagamisis Provincial Park,** on the southern shore of eleven-mile-long Nagagamisis Lake. The name means "Lake with Fine Sand Shore," and there are good swimming beaches. In the waters live pike and walleye, while ponds or woods are home to moose, beaver, foxes, bears, and other species. The forest is typical of northern Ontario: conifers of spruce, fir, and pine mixed with aspen and white birch. Part of the park's 11,878 acres has been developed for recreation purposes: camp and picnic sites, trails, and canoe routes. Boat rentals and a store are operated by private outfitters outside park boundaries. Services are available from the first Friday in June to the second Sunday in September. The roads are unplowed in winter. The nearest location of complete tourist facilities is in Hornepayne, twenty-one miles to the south. Access is via Provincial Route 631.

Information: District Manager, Ministry of Natural Resources, Hearst, Ontario.

🌲 The 10,970 acres of **Greenwater Provincial Park,** twenty miles northwest of Cochrane, Ontario, include glacial esker ridges that provide scenic views of more than two dozen surrounding lakes, many of them "kettle"-type lakes. The northern part of the park is accessible only by trail, and hikers will find a number of routes through the undulating forest ridges of poplar, white birch, white spruce, and balsam fir. They may be able to see beaver, moose, and muskrats in the wet places, or red foxes, ruffed grouse, and black bears on drier terrain. In the clear waters live brook and lake trout and other aquatic organisms. Swimming, camping, and picnic areas are available in the park. Food supplies may be obtained in the park from a catering service three days out of the week, or may be obtained at a distance of nine miles from the park. Boats and canoes may be rented. Park services, such as conducted nature hikes, are provided from about the first Friday in June to the second Sunday in September. Accommodations may be secured in Cochrane and advance reservations are advisable. The park is reached by driving nine miles north of Provincial Route 11, near Cochrane.

Information: District Manager, Ministry of Natural Resources, Box 730, Cochrane, Ontario P0L 1C0.

🌲 Anglers seeking a wilderness experience along with good fishing could well consider Ontario's **Missinaibi Lake Provincial Park,** 112,640 acres of north woods domain on the old canoe route between Michipicoten, on Lake Superior, and James Bay. The lake itself, a very intricate, elongated lake with numerous arms and bays, covers 17,000 acres, and fishermen can choose the methods to suit their skills; pike are caught throughout the waters, but lake trout must be sought for in deep holes, whitefish and pickerel at Whitefish Falls and Jenner Bay, and speckled trout at the lake's outlet. Smallmouth bass are also present. In the woods or marshes may be seen moose, bears, wolves, and foxes. Canoeing is encouraged by the creation of new routes or rehabilitation of old, and good maps are available for persons who wish to paddle off on their own into this park and the regions beyond. One route covers 203 miles from Mattice Station, on the Canadian Pacific Railway, to Moose Factory, on James Bay. Descriptive data are available for some of the easier routes, together with details on availability of guides, supplies, and rental equipment.

Access to Missinaibi Lake Provincial Park is via sand and gravel road fifty-five miles north of Chapleau. Park officials do not recommend use of this road prior to May 15 of each year. Park services are available from the first Friday in June to the second Sunday in September. Since the park is just being developed, it has only a few constructed campsites. However, there is an open area for recreational vehicles, plus drinking water, boat docks, and launching ramps. Food supplies, accommodations, and rental boats may be secured in Chapleau.

Information: District Manager, Ministry of Natural Resources, Chapleau, Ontario.

🌲 **Obatanga Provincial Park,** thirty-four miles north of Wawa, Ontario, on Route 17, is a 34,035-acre locale of numerous small marshy lakes that provide good refuge for water birds and good boating, canoeing, and fishing for human visitors. Pickerel and northern pike are the fish most often taken. Camp and picnic sites are available. Food and lodging may be secured at lodges north and east of the park.

Information: District Manager, Ministry of Natural Resources, White River, Ontario P0M 3G0.

🌲 **Esker Lakes Provincial Park** protects a 7,680-acre area of lake and forest country into which trails and canoe routes lead. Sinuous ridges of glacial origin—eskers—are prominent. Fish in the area waters include trout, walleye, smallmouth bass, and northern pike. Motorboats are not permitted on park lakes. The park is not open in winter, although snowmobiles are permitted on roads, trails, and portages. The park is open from the first Friday in June until the second Sunday in September. Camping and related facilities are confined to Panagapka Lake. Supplies are available in the park, but accommodations must be obtained in nearby communities. Access is via provincial routes 11 and 66.

Information: District Manager, Ministry of Natural Resources, Swastika, Ontario.

🌲 In **Mississagi Provincial Park** dozens of lakes, streams, and beaver ponds, tracts of evergreen and hardwood trees, and rugged, rocky terrain typical of the Precambrian Shield provide numerous wilderness recreational opportunities. The park, over 7,000 acres in size, is surrounded by 97,000 acres of park reserve. A variety of canoe routes and walking trails is available and the area is renowned for its lake trout fishing. Being in the transition zone between northern boreal forest and southern hardwoods, the park has a varied plant and animal life. A developed camping area is available. Located sixteen miles north of Elliot Lake, the park is reached from Route 17 via routes 108, 546, and 639. Supplies and lodging are available in Elliot Lake.

Information: Parks Supervisor, Ministry of Natural Resources, Box 190, Blind River, Ontario P0R 1B0.

🌲 **Mattawa Wild River Provincial Park** is over 8,000 acres and was established to preserve twenty-five miles of the Mattawa River, which flows from near Lake Nipissing to its junction with the Ottawa River, in southeastern Ontario. Two to three days are needed to canoe the entire distance, which requires at least seven portages. Side trips may be made into lakes and up tributary streams along the way. Fishermen may take pickerel, smallmouth bass, and northern pike in all waters; brook trout are found in some of the streams and lake trout in the larger bodies of water. In traversing the route, canoeists pass marshes, gorges, waterfalls, rapids, black granite cliffs, wooded banks, and Samuel de Champlain Provincial Park, where there are exhibits on the history of the region. The area is located some 200 miles upstream from the city of Ottawa and is accessible via Route 17, the Trans-Canada Highway, to Route 63, which reaches the west end of the waterway on Trout Lake. Ontario's wild river parks are managed to encourage compatible recreation uses, and are designed chiefly for the canoe-camper. Here the canoeist can follow the routes of early voyageurs and well-known explorers such as Samuel de Champlain and Alexander Mackenzie. Campsites are available throughout the trip. Food, lodging, and supplies are available in North Bay and other communities in the region. Canoes may be rented in North Bay. Activities in addition to canoeing include picnicking, boating, fishing, and swimming.

Information: District Manager, Ministry of Natural Resources, Box 3070, 222 McIntyre, West North Bay, Ontario P1B 8K7.

Algonquin Provincial Park consists of 1,862,400 acres of lakes, streams, and forest straddling the highlands between Ontario's Georgian Bay and the Ottawa River. The western two-thirds of the park are covered mainly by forests of sugar maple, beech, and yellow birch, while coniferous trees—spruce, pine, cedar, hemlock—rim the thousands of lakes and streams. The eastern side of the park is lower and drier, with extensive deposits of sand left by the last glacier, which melted back from the Algonquin area just 11,000 years ago. Today these sites support extensive forests of white, red, and jack pine and while there are fewer lakes, the east side boasts two spectacular rivers for the canoeist. Wildlife includes loons, ravens, beaver, black bears, deer, moose, and wolves. The main sport fish are lake trout and brook trout.

There are two main ways to enjoy Algonquin Park. For car campers, campgrounds and interpretive facilities exist along the thirty-seven miles of Route 60, which cuts through the southern part of the park. The essence of Algonquin, however, is its vast interior network of over a thousand miles of canoe routes. Portages tend to be longer than those in other famous canoeing areas, such as Quetico Provincial Park, but a great variety of routes is available from which to choose.

Algonquin Provincial Park is not a wilderness in the ecological sense that it is pristine and untouched. It has been logged since the mid-1800s and nowadays forest-management policies inside the park resemble those outside. Hunting and trapping are permitted. Thus it may not qualify as true wilderness in the minds of some persons, but it is nevertheless perceived as one by a great many others.

Maps and specific details may be obtained from the park.

Information: Park Superintendent, Ministry of Natural Resources, Box 219, Whitney, Ontario K0J 2M0.

Grundy Lake Provincial Park is a 6,310-acre park of interest to fishermen. In its five lakes, as well as in nearby rivers, there are pike, bass, and pickerel (walleye). The park has typical northern forest trees spread out over ancient granite. Hiking, camping, picnicking, swimming, and boating are the major recreational activities. However, the use of outboard motors is prohibited on all lakes within the boundaries of the park. Supplies are available in the park, but accommodations must be obtained in nearby communities. Access is via Route 69 about fifty miles southeast of Sudbury, Ontario.

Information: Superintendent, Grundy Lake Provincial Park, Ministry of Natural Resources, Parry Sound, Ontario P2A 1S8.

Bon Echo Provincial Park gets its name from the unusual reverberations of sound between cliffs along the narrows of Mazinaw Lake. Bon Echo Cliff, rising 375 feet, borders the lake for more than a mile and still bears centuries-old paintings by the Algonquin Indians. The 15,500-acre park is located on Route 41, six miles north of the village of Cloyne, and has swimming beaches, campsites, an eleven-mile canoe route, a sixty-five-mile hiking route, and self-guiding nature trails. Boat rental facilities, supplies, and accommodations are available outside the park.

Information: Superintendent, Bon Echo Provincial Park, R. R. 1, Cloyne, Ontario.

*Allagash Wilderness Waterway, Maine. Courtesy
U.S. Department of the Interior.*

Martin Lake, near The Appalachian Trail, Maine.

2. GREAT LAKES

Isle Royale, the largest island in Lake Superior, has more than 120 miles of trails, which traverse the uplands of this roadless island as well as the shores of bogs, lakes, and streams. The effect on hikers is one of relaxation and fascination because they are treated to continuous pleasures—a veiled orange sunrise over the lake, navelike groves of birch, tall grass meadows, fragrant spruce, white and scarlet baneberries, summer mists—and know that they are at least fifteen miles from the nearest highway. They can step to the edge of a fjordlike cove and see a moose plunge in for a swim to the other side. Or hike from one end of the island to the other, about forty miles, then return by concessioner's boat, observing such sights as common mergansers skittering across the water. These are among the scenes protected in **Isle Royale National Park,** the 539,341 acres of which preserve the whole island and surrounding islets.

Perhaps the most unusual sight would be that of some of the island's two dozen wolves, which help keep the moose population of 600 to 1,000 beneficially pruned; however, the wolves are shy and retiring and seldom seen by visitors. Sites where early Indians dug out copper may still be recognized, as can the more recent remains of summer homes once built on the island and now retreating into history.

Little of man is left, except for present-day visitors who come by boat from Houghton or Copper Harbor, Michigan, or Grand Portage, Minnesota, or by float plane, and stay only a relatively short time. Food, lodging, and supplies are available in the park, but reservations for accommodations should be made well in advance. The visitor season is mid-May through mid-October. Because of heavy public demand to enter the park, prospective travelers should obtain the latest details on regulations and restrictions before firming up their plans to travel there. Maps and boat schedules are available.

Information: Superintendent, Isle Royale National Park, 87 North Ripley Street, Houghton, Michigan 49931.

🌲 Off the Bayfield Peninsula of northwestern Wisconsin, seventy miles east of Duluth and Superior, lies a cluster of twenty-two islands, twenty of which have been incorporated into the **Apostle Islands National Lakeshore.** The islands vary in size from Gull Island (three acres) to Stockton Island (10,053 acres). Total area of the Lakeshore is 42,000 acres. The islands are heavily wooded with maple, aspen, birch, yew, hazelnut, pine, and spruce. Some have bogs. Along some of the islands and the mainland are found arches, caves, and strikingly eroded cliffs. Most have deer—and deer flies, the latter a nuisance to visitors in July and August unless precautions are taken. All islands are surrounded by water that is nearly always too cold to swim in, but fishermen may find rewards in taking sizable lake trout. The area has only recently been authorized by Congress; lands are now being acquired and some years will pass before all are open to the public and a full range of recreational facilities is available. The islands are, of course, best reached by boat; excursions leave Bayfield daily during the summer. Visitors with their own craft should be aware of Lake Superior's reputation for dealing disaster in time of storm. At the Red Cliff Indian Reservation, on the tip of the peninsula, Chippewa Indians operate campgrounds, charter boats, guide service, a museum and craft center, and other services and facilities. Food and lodging may be obtained in nearby communities. Access is by State Route 13.

Information: Superintendent, Apostle Islands National Lakeshore, 1972 Centennial Drive, R. R., Bayfield, Wisconsin, 54814.

Porcupine Mountains Wilderness State Park, on the Lake Superior shore of Michigan's upper peninsula, is part of a state system being developed under the 1972 Wilderness and Natural Areas Act passed by the Michigan legislature. Under terms of this act, the state is designating wilderness, wild, and natural areas that emphasize ecological values and opportunities for solitude and personal exploration. Porcupine Mountains Park was originally set aside in 1945 to protect virgin pine and hemlock forests, lakes, wild streams, waterfalls, old mines, rugged lake shore, and mountainous terrain. More than eighty miles of trails provide access to most parts of this 58,000-acre area, but backpackers must register at the park office before setting out. Disposable glass or metal containers may not be taken into the interior. Rustic and modern campgrounds are available, as are shelters, cabins, boat-launching ramps, and picnic areas. The park can be reached via Michigan state routes 64 and 107. Tourist facilities and supplies may be secured in nearby communities.

Information: Supervisor, Porcupine Mountains Wilderness State Park, Route 2, Ontonagon, Michigan 49953.

🌲 For forty miles between Munising and Grand Marais, on the northern peninsula of Michigan, the shoreline of Lake Superior has been set aside by the federal government as the **Pictured Rocks National Lakeshore.** Though not yet fully developed, it will eventually contain 73,653 acres, dedicated to the principle that even where the water is too cold for swimming, a wild shoreline is worth preserving. Boating is popular, and scenic cruises leave from Munising in summer. Hikers can cover miles of sandy and pebbly beaches. Or they can explore inland along old trails and roads, discovering hidden lakes and ponds of a much more swimmable temperature than Lake Superior. Indeed, there is a kind of tropical luxury in the vegetation—moss-covered logs, rich bogs, white groves of birch, stands of hardwoods, hemlock, pine, spruce, and fir. In the spring flowering season, and during autumn color, the photographer will find abundant close-up opportunities and will be vexed by limitations, such as the brevity of a visit or the shortness of daylight hours.

Pictured Rocks National Lakeshore contains colorful sandstone cliffs, caves, arches, rock columns, sand dunes, waterfalls, and wildlife. White-tailed deer, black bears, coyotes, and migratory birds may be seen. Great Lakes fish have had their problems, but fishermen here can still expect to take lake trout and whitefish, or the introduced coho salmon. Inland waters contain trout, perch, bass, pike, and sunfish.

Complete facilities for public use will not be available for several years, and some of the land within Lakeshore boundaries is still private property. Nevertheless, several primitive campgrounds are available, with additional sites in nearby state and national forests. Food, lodging, and supplies are available at Munising, Melstrand, and Grand Marais. Access is via state routes 28 on the west and 77 on the east.

Information: Superintendent, Pictured Rocks National Lakeshore, Munising, Michigan 49862.

🌲 The proposed **Big Island Lake Wilderness** of 6,600 acres, lies in Hiawatha National Forest near Munising, Michigan. The entire region between Lake Superior and Lake Michigan is studded with lakes, and the wilderness hiker will find trails and old logging roads as "springboards for exploration." Ponds, lakes, swamps, and mixed conifer and hardwood forests are the principal features on this glacial moraine topography. Here and there stand impressive groves of beech. If the traveler goes quietly, by foot or canoe, his chances of seeing coyotes, raccoons and other mammals—perhaps even a rare wolf or moose—will be enhanced. Fishermen in Hiawatha National

Forest can search for trout, bass, perch, walleye, coho salmon, smelt and steelhead. Access is via country roads south of Munising. Numerous campsites may be found on adjacent forest lands, and in neighboring communities are resorts, food, lodging, supplies, and rental boats or canoes.

Information: Supervisor, Hiawatha National Forest, Escanaba, Michigan 49829.

🌲 **Seney National Wildlife Refuge,** on the northern peninsula of Michigan, includes land that was once logged, burned, drained, and farmed. One would think that only a hollow shell would be left, and it is true that vanished soils and forests take centuries to recover their former integrity. Yet nature eventually heals the scars, and if we haven't an old wild area we have a new one. For the last forty years the refuge has been protected, and in its way offers a showcase of man's capacity to conserve. The western third has had little or no exploitation.

Upper-peninsula coniferous forests, marshes, streams, and ponds constitute the major environments. Wildlife is recovering well, and among the more than 200 species of birds seen here are bald eagles, sandhill cranes, great blue herons, Canada geese, mallards, black ducks, ring-necked ducks, common and hooded mergansers, and teals. The refuge is large enough—95,455 acres—and the management program diligent enough to make the habitat restoration successful so far. Moreover, visitors are encouraged to look in on the operation. A visitor center contains exhibits and audio-visual programs. Two auto tours are available in summer, one guided, one self-guiding. A 1.4-mile nature trail leads to an observation tower. Picnicking is permitted as are, under applicable laws, hunting and fishing. Entry into wilder sections of the area, particularly the western 25,150 acres classified as wilderness, should be discussed with the refuge manager. Access is via Michigan Route 77 south of Seney. Lodging is available in nearby communities.

Information: Manager, Seney National Wildlife Refuge, Seney, Michigan 49883.

🌲 **Tahquamenon Falls State Park,** Michigan, preserves a portion of the river—"the rushing Tahquamenon"—where, according to Longfellow, young Hiawatha built his canoe. The Upper Falls are 200 feet wide and have a sheer drop of forty feet. Canoeists can float downstream to the shore of Lake Superior, passing swamps, hills, and 300-year-old woods of pine, spruce, hemlock, cedar, birch, beech, maple, ash, and basswood. With luck they may glimpse moose in the shallows or eagles in flight above the stream. Hikers can follow portions of the riverbank. Self-guiding nature trails have been developed, as have opportunities for fishing, camping, and picnicking. This 19,188-acre park is accessible along State Route 123 between Newberry and Eckerman. Food and lodging may be obtained in nearby communities. For an extension of the wild experience, visitors may enter the 14,137-acre **Betsy Lake Natural Area Preserve,** which borders Tahquamenon Falls State Park on the north. It contains large lakes, wooded sand dunes, swamps, marshes, ridges, and picturesque pine and spruce woods.

Information: Manager, Tahquamenon Falls State Park, Box 57, Paradise, Michigan 49768.

🌲 Hour after hour, the water changes color: somber and gray, pale green, deep blue, red with the setting sun, then purple, then perhaps a moon-washed silver. When viewed through pines and maples, across the grassed-over dunes, Lake Michigan seems different from the other Great Lakes—or from any lake. Precious little of its natural shore remains intact as a wild environment, but in 1970 Congress authorized the **Sleeping Bear Dunes National Lakeshore,** northwest of Traverse City. Most of the land has yet to be acquired by the federal government, but eventually the area will encompass 60,000 acres, including the Manitou Islands offshore, and thirty miles of Lake Michigan shoreline.

There is, of course, more than dunes and beach. Visitors can canoe on the rivers, hike through forests of hardwoods and pines, watch in the marshy ponds or off windy points for birds, fish for pike and trout, and examine the rich botanical treasures of bogs and swamps. The wildest terrain is found on the outer islands; South Manitou has a remnant of virgin forest containing white cedars more than 500 years old, plus elder, ash, and basswood.

Visitors may climb the dunes, drive on back roads, or take a boat to South Manitou Island. Food and lodging are available in local communities. The latest details should be obtained from the seasonal National Park Service visitor center, 4.4. miles south of Glen Haven, and at headquarters in Frankfort. Main access to the area is via U.S. Route 31 and state routes 22 and 72.

Information: Superintendent, Sleeping Bear Dunes National Lakeshore, 400½ Main Street, Frankfort, Michigan 49635.

🌲 **Rondeau Provincial Park,** 11,500 acres, has been protected since 1894. Located on the northwest shore of Lake Erie, its trees include hickory, sassafras, walnut, and tulip poplar—one of the few such hardwood forests still in its natural state in Canada. Marshes, woods, and lakes are the principal habitats, and summer visitors may think at times that mosquitoes are the principal inhabitants. Less than 10 percent of the park has been developed. Ducks and shorebirds are especially numerous during spring and fall migrations. Roads and trails lead through the park and there are opportunities for boating, swimming, picknicking, camping, fishing, horseback riding, and hiking. Rondeau Bay is located approximately sixty miles east of Detroit, Michigan. It is accessible on Canadian Route 3 south of Morpeth, Ontario.

Information: Superintendent, Rondeau Provincial Park, R. R. 1, Morpeth, Ontario.

🌲 A few islands in the Great Lakes have been given wilderness status, including the **Huron Islands** in Lake Superior, **Gravel, Hog, Spider, Shoe,** and **Pismire islands** in Lake Michigan, **Scarecrow Island** in Lake Huron, and **West Sister Island** in Lake Erie. All are U.S. national wildlife refuges, and since there has been little or no human development, they have remained superlative nesting sites for herons, gulls, and waterfowl. They have no public-use facilities, are accessible only by boat, and are of interest chiefly to naturalists.

Information: Regional Director, Bureau of Sport Fisheries and Wildlife, Twin Cities, Minnesota 55111.

🌲 Considering the attractiveness of islands in the upper St. Lawrence River, it is little wonder that of the thousand between Kingston and Brockville, Ontario, few remain with even a vestige of original wilderness intact. The Canadian government has designated seventeen islands and about eighty rocky islets as **St. Lawrence Islands National Park,** but even on those, only a few spots are pristine. Nevertheless, by boating among them, hiking and camping on them, and fishing for bass, pike, and muskellunge, the modern traveler can at least imagine what the islands must have been like originally. The oak-hickory forests, burned and cut over, recover slowly. Gulls, herons, ducks, and other water birds are common along the shores. Access is via Canadian routes 2 and 401, and U.S. routes 37, 68, and 81. Parking facilities, camping, and a boat ramp are available at Mallorytown Landing, where picnicking and swimming may be enjoyed. Accommodations can be secured along river shores outside the park.

Information: Superintendent, St. Lawrence Islands National Park, Mallorytown, Ontario.

🌲 Though small in land area, 3,480 acres, **Georgian Bay Islands National Park** consists of about fifty islands scattered along forty miles of Georgian Bay, with the exception of Flowerpot Island, located three miles from Tobermory, at the north end of the Bruce Peninsula. In places forested with mixed coniferous-deciduous woods, and in places barren, the islands range in size up to five miles long. The Canadian government provides exhibits, talks, guided walks, and other outdoor programs, but by and large the islands remain wild and undisturbed, an atmosphere enhanced by the expanses of water between them and by the abundance of wild animals: deer, muskrats, beaver, foxes, otters, raccoons, woodchucks, skunks, and others. Beausoleil Island is one of the last refuges of the rarely seen massasauga rattlesnake, a reptile more common to the South and West. Some islands have good hiking; canoeing is facilitated by numerous sheltered coves, and anglers seek pike, walleye, bass, perch, lake trout, and maskinonge.

Camping is permitted in developed sites, open between May and September, and primitive sites, available all year. Food, lodging, and supplies must be obtained on the mainland, with Honey Harbour and Tobermory the nearest sources. Boat transportation to the islands may also be arranged there through private enterprise.

Information: Superintendent, Georgian Bay Islands National Park, Box 28, Honey Harbour, Ontario P0E 1E0.

🌲 Ontario's size—nearly twice that of Texas—permits a system of more than a hundred provincial parks, many of large size and within easy reach of population centers. **Killarney Provincial Park,** for example, contains 84,990 acres, located on Route 637 an hour's drive south from Sudbury and six hours' driving time northwest of Toronto on routes 400, 103, and 69. Situated along the rugged shoreline of Georgian Bay, a part of Lake Huron, it includes white quartzite hills called the Killarney Mountains. Men have inhabited or visited this area since 700 B.C., attracted first by populations of fish and wildlife, then by scientific values of boreal forest communities and by natural beauty. Plans are to keep the park in a primitive or wilderness state, attractive to canoeists, hikers, anglers, photographers, scientists, and the like. Primitive campsites are available in the park; and it has been proposed that snowmobiles and motorboats be prohibited from the park. Canoe routes have been delineated in a booklet obtainable at the park.

Information: District Manager, Ministry of Natural Resources, Sudbury, Ontario P3E 1G1.

🌲 On the eastern shore of Lake Superior, seventy-five miles north of Sault Ste. Marie, lies **Lake Superior Provincial Park,** a "natural environment" area of 336,640 acres set aside by the Ontario government primarily for recreation and education. It has an unusual number of geological features, including volcanic lava flows, dikes, faults, glacial era spillways and terraces, kames, kettles, and eskers. About a third of the coastline within the park consists of gentle topography with sandy beaches; the rest is rugged, steep, and abrupt. Inland, on rolling hills, are clear, cold lakes and hardwood forests dominated by sugar maple and yellow birch. The ground cover consists of a rich mixture of ferns, lilies, clubmosses, sedges, and grasses. Weather is changeable: a few days of clear skies, then variable winds and increasing humidity, followed by a few days of rain. Sometimes fog banks move in from the lake and remain for days.

Park waters contain brook, lake, and rainbow trout, pickerel, whitefish, chub, and herring. Some fifty species of birds nest in the area. Heavy winter snowfall and lack of forage tend to restrict mammalian life, but moose get along well in this environment, sometimes presenting a hazard to motorists on Route 17, the Trans-Canada Highway, which runs through the park. Deer, bears, wolves, foxes, and other species also inhabit the region. Although controlled, considerable logging is still permitted within certain portions of the park. Trapping and a one-month hunting season on moose are also allowed.

Public-use activities include camping, hiking, picnicking, study on nature trails, and swimming, but little access has been developed beyond the main road. Canoeists may enjoy wilderness travel and remote camping, but the numerous streams and lakes are not as conveniently connected into travel routes as in Quetico and Algonquin parks. Nevertheless, some trails have become well established, with portages cut through; the Sand River route, for example, is a four-day, thirty-five-mile itinerary along the eastern side and across the center of the park. Other routes, not quite as long, reach lakes Gamitagama, Mijinemungshing, Anjigami, and Rabbit Blanket. All supplies must be carried by travelers to this park; food and lodging are available only in communities outside.

Information: District Manager, Ministry of Natural Resources, Box 1160, Wawa, Ontario P0S 1K0.

🌲 **Pukaskwa National Park,** Ontario, is relatively new, so developments are presently limited. Approached on the Trans-Canada Highway, Canadian Route 17, through Marathon, it lies on the northeast shore of Lake Superior. Trails will eventually lead over mountains, past large lakes, and through dense woods of spruce, pine, poplar, and birch. Animal life includes caribou, moose, deer, wolves, black bears, lynx, and smaller species. Within the park's 464,000 acres are wild streams with rapids and waterfalls; along fifty miles of Lake Superior shoreline, between the White and Pukaskwa rivers, are bays, beaches, rocky headlands, and islets, an environment for wilderness canoeing. Canadian authorities intend to keep Pukaskwa a wilderness park with limited access; as yet no roads lead into it. The nearest accommodations are along Route 17.

Information: Superintendent, Pukaskwa National Park, Marathon, Ontario.

🌲 **Neys Provincial Park** is an 8,150-acre "natural environment park," a category of reserves which contain outstanding aesthetic, natural and/or historical features designed for recreation and education. Such parks may include facilities for camping and picnicking, hiking and nature interpretation. (Other kinds of parks in the Ontario system include primitive, wild river, natural reserve, and recreation.) Neys Provincial Park is located sixteen miles west of Marathon on Route 17. Although endowed with a long and wide sandy beach, the waters of Lake Superior are usually too cold for swimming here. Trails lead into the woods, where caribou, moose, foxes, and other animals live. Trout fishing in the lake and along streams leading into it is a popular recreation pursuit. Camp and picnic sites and a self-guiding nature trail are available. Food and lodging may be obtained in Marathon.

Information: District Manager, Ministry of Natural Resources, Box 280, Terrace Bay, Ontario P0T 2W0.

🌲 Separating Thunder Bay and Black Bay, in western Ontario, is **Sibley Provincial Park,** a 59,500-acre "natural environment park" that includes the Sleeping Giant. This rock eminence rises in rugged cliffs above Lake Superior, and hikers who climb the trail up on it have panoramic views of the lake, bays, and numerous bodies of water on Thunder Bay Peninsula itself. The dense forest and occasional open places are populated by abundant wildlife, including bears, deer, and moose, the latter being often observed at Joeboy Lake. For anglers, the park's lakes and streams possess pike and northern bass. For students of nature there are exhibits, films, walks, talks, and self-guiding nature trails. The park also has a road system. Swimming and picnicking are permitted, and there are more than 200 tent and trailer sites. Accommodations may be secured in nearby communities. Located twenty-four miles east of Port Arthur, the park may be reached via Provincial Route 587 (south of routes 11 and 17).

Information: Superintendent, Sibley Provincial Park, Ministry of Natural Resources, 14 North Algoma Street, Port Arthur, Ontario.

3. NORTHERN MOUNTAINS

The largest wilderness in the eastern United States may not seem very wild at all when the traveler enters it. As he heads for the nearest mountain he encounters a barrage of No Trespassing signs along the roads, and on trying to reach the shore of the first lake encountered, he may find barriers instead of beaches. It is possible that he will find so many ski runs, resorts, railroads, reservoirs, villages, and logging trucks that he will flee before finding the solitude he originally sought. Yet the solitude is there, millions of acres of it: wild lakes, canoe routes, remote trails, and even virgin forests. This paradox is New York's **Adirondack Forest Preserve,** which is not to be compared with national or state parks—except possibly those of Great Britain, where private property is part of the scene, like it or not.

Actually, the wild part is the paradox, considering how thoroughly men burned and ripped out the forest, killed off the fauna, and settled in the scenic spots. Photographs of that era show awesome destruction that even now has not healed over, and will not for another century or more. By 1885 New Yorkers had had enough, and thereupon established the Preserve, a somewhat optimistic exercise at the time because so much terrain had been swept into private hands.

The die was too much cast to change man's rapacious habits overnight. Eventually pressures on the Preserve grew so great that its protection had to be placed under the state constitution. And even that did not stop the onslaught: there have been more than a dozen constitutional amendments authorizing stream regulations, timber cutting, highway construction, and land exchanges. Nevertheless, like ups and downs in the investment market, the trend has been unquestionably up, toward conservation of a priceless asset and support for the letter of the law: ". . . the Forest Preserve . . . shall be forever kept as wild forest lands. They shall not be leased, sold or exchanged, or be taken by any corporation, public or private, nor shall the timber thereon be sold, removed, or destroyed."

The destruction of yesteryear shows symptoms of being arrested, and today a park with a shotgun pattern of private property in it is better than no park at all. Indeed, it is admirable that more than 2 million acres of reasonably wild land still exist in what was long the most populous state in the nation.

And if the present-day visitor sticks to his determination, he can find not only real wilderness and hundreds of miles of trails, but experiences he might never have thought possible. The Preserve contains fifteen wilderness areas totaling a million acres, plus primitive areas, canoe areas, wild forests, and other designations. Scores of woodland trails lead to streams, marshes, ponds, and summits, and the New York State Department of Environmental Conservation issues trail leaflets for routes in each major region, for example: Blue Mountain Lake, Schroon Lake, Moose River, and Lake George. The Northville–Lake Placid Trail alone traverses approximately 133 miles and takes about nineteen days to hike. It connects the southern Adirondack foothills and the High Peaks region. Along it, the hiker-angler can try his luck for trout, pickerel, bass, and pike. Stands of spruce and hardwood have grown so well in the last protected half century that the wounds of early days are partly covered. In places, the only accommodations are trailside lean-tos. Elsewhere, attractive campsites may be found.

Many shorter trails, of course, provide opportunity for briefly sampling the wild Adirondack environment. One of them goes from the Adirondack Museum to the summit of Blue Mountain, a distance of two miles and a climb of 2,000 feet. A three mile trail to the top of Black Mountain provides wide views of the Lake George region. On Lake George itself, nearly fifty of the 200 islands are available for camping. At special localities in the Adirondacks, canoe routes have been established and are delineated in maps of the Department of Environmental Conservation. Blue Mountain Lake, to cite one, is at the remote headwaters of the Raquette River, start of a nearly unbroken eighty-mile string of lakes and waterways. Some 170 miles of watercourses are being designated as wild, scenic, and recreational rivers.

Nor is there any longer an "off season," since recreationists long ago discovered the advantages of wilderness hiking in autumn, winter, and spring. The Department of Environmental Conservation has designated ski and snowshoe trails of varying difficulty and issued a brief guide to them.

To hikers with a passion for mountaineering, the Adirondacks constitute a paradise of forty-six mountains over 4,000 feet in elevation. Highest of all, and highest in New York State, is Mount Marcy, 5,344 feet. Indians had to ascend through dense virgin forests and scrubby alpine growths of balsam fir to gain the summit. Today, four well-marked trails converge on the mountaintop, and a booklet, "Trails to Marcy," published by the Department of Environmental Conservation, describes them in detail.

Ascending the trail on a sunny September day, a hiker finds himself in a veritable cathedral whose colorful "windows," fragments of yellow, orange, green, and brown, are composed of overlapping birch and maple leaves. Tall

303

tree trunks appear as Gothic columns in the shadows, and the forest floor is a soft mosaic of needles, leaves, and gray rocks covered with lichens. Downed trees sprout with layers of shelf fungus and constitute the homes of spiders and insects. Watching all this and attempting to avoid the exposed roots of birches and maples along the trail calls for tricky footwork.

There is the awesome silence of a cathedral as well, but most of the time it is broken by numerous noises: the strumming of leaves that imparts to the vales a hollow, whispery rattle; the hammering of woodpeckers; the scratching of chipmunks among the leaves; and shrill warnings of squirrels. Across brooks, past lean-tos, beneath steep, rocky walls and cave shelters near waterfalls, beside deep ravines, the trails lead over saddles and up to increasingly prominent ridges from which views of the MacIntyre Range and valleys beyond can be obtained. Because the mountain is so popular, it is a good idea to avoid weekends and holidays; at other times there is more likelihood of lean-tos being unoccupied and trails less crowded.

A new master plan has been approved for Adirondack preserved areas, and new efforts are being made to strengthen regional planning. State authorities intend to acquire scenic easements to halt the "erosion of open space," and to accelerate the purchase of private lands. They will also keep an eye on places where overuse could reduce the values for which the wilder lands were set aside. Then perhaps the newcomer will find more readily and easily the forest solitude and wild lakes for which the Adirondacks are renowned.

Many access points exist. Interstate 90, the New York State Thruway, lies south of the boundary; Interstate 87 is to the east. New York routes 28 and 30 crisscross the Preserve. Accommodations are available at resorts and villages in and around the area, and details about these can be obtained from the New York State Department of Commerce or local chambers of commerce.

Information: Director, Division of Lands and Forests, Department of Environmental Conservation, 50 Wolf Road, Albany, New York 12201.

🌲 Fifty miles to the south of the Adirondacks is the **Catskill Forest Preserve**, 246,940 acres of lakes, streams, rounded ridges, steep mountain slopes, and dense forests. The highest point is Slide Mountain, 4,204 feet elevation. A fine system of trails reaches into remote sections, passing scenic waterfalls and climbing to panoramic overlooks. This is the locale of New York's famed Rip Van Winkle legend. The Preserve is located about twenty miles west of Kingston and is accessible on state routes 23-A, 28, 42, and others. There are camp and picnic sites, beaches, boat ramps, and fishing spots. Food and lodging may be obtained in the park.

Information: Director, Division of Lands and Forests, Department of Environmental Conservation, 50 Wolf Road, Albany, New York 12201.

🌲 One may think of wilderness in the vicinity of New York City as anomalous, but over a period of three quarters of a century the Palisades Interstate Park Commission has built up a chain of reserves that protect diabase cliffs along the Hudson River, rolling woodlands, granite ridges, marshes, lakes, and scenic mountains in the states of New York and New Jersey, virtually within sight of Manhattan. Largest of these reserves are the adjacent **Harriman State Park** and **Bear Mountain State Park,** the combined area of which exceeds 51,000 acres. Despite the ills of noise and air pollution, the latter frequently reducing visibility from high points overlooking the Hudson River Valley, and despite roads that cross both parks, there is an opportunity to take off on trails and climb up into lonely oak woods. During spring the songs of birds and the fresh smell of new growth fill the air; in September a hiker hears the pop of acorns as they fall to the rocky ledges. Trails are abundant; The Appalachian Trail winds across the park area. One of America's leading nature-education complexes (museums, nature trails, and other installations) may be visited at Bear Mountain. Outdoor recreation facilities include swimming, boating, picnicking, camping, fishing, and in winter, skiing and ice skating. Cabins and cafeterias are available. Access is via the Palisades Interstate Parkway, Seven Lakes Parkway, and other routes.

Information: General Manager, Palisades Interstate Park Commission, Bear Mountain, New York 10911.

🌲 **Letchworth State Park,** thirty-five miles upstream (southwest) on the Genesee River from Rochester, New York, preserves seventeen miles of deep, winding, forested canyons where light-colored shales and sandstones outcrop in steep cliffs as much as 600 feet high. The river plunges over three picturesque waterfalls, the highest 107 feet. Within the boundaries of the 14,340-acre park are hiking trails plus food, lodging, camping, tennis, fishing, picnicking, and swimming facilities, but a suggestion of the original wilderness remains. The forest, typical mixed deciduous hardwoods and conifers, provides colorful foliage displays in autumn. Access is via state routes 36, 194, 245, 246, 408, and 436.

Information: General Manager, Genesee State Park Commission, Castile, New York 14427.

🌲 New York's **Allegany State Park,** on the Pennsylvania boundary between the Allegany River Reservoir and the Seneca Indian Reservation, contains hundreds of cabins and camping sites as well as roads, restaurants, stores, and tennis courts. At certain times of year, hunting for turkeys, grouse,

Canada geese, Brigantine National
Wildlife Refuge, New Jersey.

deer, squirrels, raccoons, and rabbits is permitted. Nevertheless, the area is large enough—65,000 acres—to possess some wilderness characteristics. Although it was formerly logged and farmed, the traces of man's works are being obliterated by nature, and some of the old logging roads now provide pathways through the woods of birch, beech, maple, and hemlock. Located in the northern part of the Allegheny Plateau, the park is rough, with ridges, valleys, and large glacial boulders, but not as rugged as the Adirondacks. The rocks are chiefly shales, sandstones, and conglomerates, some highly fossiliferous. Among recreational activities are skiing, skating, tobogganing, sledding, and snowmobiling in winter, and camping, picnicking, swimming, hiking, nature study, and trout fishing in summer. Access is via U.S. Route 219, State Route 17, and local roads.

Information: Superintendent, Allegany State Park, R. D. 1, Salamanca, New York 14779.

🌲 On the New York border, forty miles due south of the Catskill Forest Preserve, is a mountain park in neighboring New Jersey that possesses beaver colonies, a white cedar swamp, tumbling streams, and forests of hemlock, pine, and spruce. This is **High Point State Park,** whose ridges rise to the

306

*Laughing gulls,
Brigantine National
Wildlife Refuge, New Jersey.*

Birch bark, Maine.

highest point in New Jersey, 1,803 feet. Situated along Kittatinny Ridge, with its scenic views, the park's 12,396 acres constitute a refuge for wildlife and a place of interest for hikers; The Appalachian Trail passes through the eastern edge of the park. Facilities include a lodge, cabins, campgrounds, picnic areas, refreshment stands, and nature-study areas. Swimming, fishing, and hiking are among the leading activities. Access is via New Jersey Route 23 near Colesville, in the extreme northwest corner of the state. Adjoining the park on the south is the 14,843-acre **Stokes State Forest,** which includes scenic Tillman Ravine, a natural gorge maintained in its wild state.

Information: Manager, High Point State Park, R. R. 4, Box 287, Sussex, New Jersey 07461.

In southern Vermont, about fifteen miles north of Bennington, the proposed **Lye Brook Wilderness** of 14,334 acres contains highland meadows, valleys, streams, ponds, and mixed deciduous-coniferous woods. It has been protected as a "backwoods area" for several years and may be entered on several forest trails. The Appalachian Trail passes through the eastern portion of the area. Access is via local roads off U.S. Route 7, to the west. Campgrounds are available in other sections of Green Mountain National

307

Forest to the north and south. Food and lodging may be secured in nearby towns.

Information: Supervisor, Green Mountain National Forest, 151 West Street, Rutland, Vermont 05701.

🌲 The proposed **Bristol Cliffs Wilderness,** about ten miles northeast of Middlebury, Vermont, lies in the northern part of Green Mountain National Forest. Though small—6,500 acres—it provides an introduction to the gentle woods and remote wild parts of the Green Mountains. From higher elevations a traveler obtains panoramic views of New York's Adirondack Mountains, across Lake Champlain to the west. Access is from Vermont State Route 17, on the north, State Route 116 from the west, and from country roads. Accommodations may be secured in nearby towns.

Information: Supervisor, Green Mountain National Forest, 151 West Street, Rutland, Vermont 05701.

🌲 The highest mountains in New England, the Presidential Range of eastern New Hampshire, capped by Mount Washington at 6,288 feet, are both rugged and rounded, enclosed within the White Mountain National Forest. For decades travelers have gone to the summit of Mount Washington by cog railway or motor road or hiked up the trails, first through dense, luxuriant coniferous forest and then across open rocky slopes devoid of all but alpine vegetation. The potential hazards of such a hike are some of the most severe in the East because the weather can quickly change from delightful to disastrous, the temperatures plunge, and winds exceed 200 miles an hour. Yet the views are worthwhile, and on a good day distant panoramas of New England peaks and forests can be seen in every direction. Had it not been for early human foresight in restricting commercial development of these slopes, we would not now have the **Great Gulf Wilderness,** which encloses a deep glacial basin on the eastern side of the Presidential Range.

Forested below, treeless above, this area contains 5,552 acres bounded on the south by the Mount Washington Auto Road and on the west by The Appalachian Trail. At lower elevations a system of trails leads through forests of spruce, fir, and northern hardwoods. White-tailed deer feed on the steep slopes. Lynx and bobcats prowl in the shadows. Grouse and partridge blend with the carpet of decaying leaves. Some of the greatest values are related to quiet and solitude that outsiders may not have expected in a region so long occupied by man. Access is via the Mount Washington Auto Road, which branches westward from State Route 16, south of Gorham, New Hampshire. Accommodations are available in nearby communities.

Information: Supervisor, White Mountain National Forest, Laconia, New Hampshire 03246.

🌲 Not all of the wild places of eastern North America have wilderness designation, yet it is possible to hike for hundreds of miles without encountering outposts of megalopolis. The means for this are long trails, those narrow and sometimes rugged "manways" that lead on and on through the woods and along the ridges. Foremost is **The Appalachian Trail,** a 2,000-mile route of connected pathways conceived more than half a century ago and initially completed in 1937. The Trail was not intended to be easy—it climbs into high rocky reaches, goes over rough terrain, plunges precipitously down steep slopes, and frequently goes through wet and soggy marshes. Yet being so much on ridgetops, many segments of the Trail are reasonably dry, and anyway, the hardships—if such they be—are a part of the wilderness experience.

Lean-tos, lodges, and campsites are about the only facilities, apart from places where the Trail must pass through developed areas, and on the side trails there are usually not even primitive shelters. Under the National Trails System Act of 1968 this route falls within the jurisdiction of the U.S. Department of the Interior, but it is also maintained and traditionally kept in condition by local hiking clubs along its fourteen-state route from Georgia to Maine. These in turn have banded into the Appalachian Trail Conference, which publishes trail guides that are virtually indispensable for full enjoyment of the Trail and understanding of the primitive America through which it passes.

In New England the Trail goes through gentle Connecticut lowlands, north over the Berkshires of western Massachusetts, through remote parts of the Green Mountains, Vermont, then northeast into New Hampshire's White Mountains, over Mount Washington and the Presidential Range, then on a 279-mile mountain-hopping trajectory through the wild coniferous woods of Maine. The northern terminus is atop Katahdin, highest point in Baxter State Park—and in Maine. Many roads give access to the Trail, and food and lodging may frequently be secured along these roads not far from the Trail. For a brief description of the southern half of the route, see page 326.

Information: Appalachian Trail Conference, Box 236, Harpers Ferry, West Virginia 25425.

🌲 Part of the great massif of New Hampshire's Presidential Range— Mount Adams, Mount Jefferson, Mount Madison, Mount Washington—is included within the proposed **Presidential Range Wilderness.** The area of

12,000 acres lies adjacent to several scenic areas and to the Great Gulf Wilderness. The terrain is almost an Arctic one at the top (Mount Washington reaches an elevation of 6,288 feet) and environmental conditions can be severe at any time of year. Indeed, local people claim that on these mountains is some of the world's worst weather. When the sky is clear, or at least partly cloudy, travelers on the summits can get splendid views of the New England landscape. These views are certainly unobstructed by trees; the terrain is rocky, steep, sometimes slick, and sometimes obliterated if a sudden fog rolls over a ridge. An auto road and cog railway provide access to the top of Mount Washington. The Appalachian Trail lies along the summit ridge. Accommodations may be secured in nearby communities.

Information: Supervisor, White Mountain National Forest, Laconia, New Hampshire 03246.

🌲 The proposed **Wild River Wilderness** of 20,000 acres, southeast of Gorham, New Hampshire, possesses an unusual diversity of flora and fauna that makes it scientifically attractive. On the marshes and grasslands live moose and beaver. In remote woods of birch, spruce, and fir are bears and bobcats, plus other predators such as coyotes. Up the Wild River and in alpine zones the scene changes again. Altogether, its proponents class the area as a high-quality wilderness. Some forty miles of narrow, primitive paths reach into this wild habitat, and The Appalachian Trail passes along the western boundary. Access is from trails and forest roads off State Route 113. U.S. Route 2 passes to the north. Campgrounds and accommodations are available in surrounding areas.

Information: Supervisor, White Mountain National Forest, Laconia, New Hampshire 03246.

🌲 Wilderness lovers often are enthusiastic about New Hampshire's Presidential Range because of the opportunities for solitude where the uplands have remained in a reasonably pristine state. Such is the case with the proposed **Dry River–Rocky Branch Wilderness,** at the southern edge of the Presidentials and just east of Crawford Notch State Park. Its 23,100 acres possess a rugged topography that has remained intact as a wild area. In the view of the Sierra Club, it possesses large trailless areas where solitude is paramount and a wilderness experience in the purest sense can be found. Elevations range from 3,600 to 5,385 feet; a harsh climate prevails, and in the rocky alpine zones, only small, tenacious forms of life survive. With the spruce grouse, snowshoe hares, and Canada jays, a hiker would think himself closer to the Arctic than he is. The wildlife alone provides a lively experience, but there are also deep ravines, sheer walls, tumbling, clear brooks, and roaring cascades. The Dry River—not dry at all—contains rare virgin forest. Hunting, fishing, and rock climbing are the major activities; more than sixty-five miles of trails and seven shelters are maintained by the U.S. Forest Service and the Appalachian Mountain Club. Access is by trail and forest road off U.S. Route 302 and New Hampshire State Route 16. Campgrounds and accommodations may be found on and near surrounding forest lands.

Information: Supervisor, White Mountain National Forest, Laconia, New Hampshire 03246.

🌲 In the northernmost part of White Mountain National Forest, the proposed **Kilkenny Wilderness** contains Mount Cabot, Mount Waumbek, and headwaters of the Upper Ammonoosuc River. From rugged ridges with spruce trees down into valleys of fir, hemlock, maple, and birch, the 24,000 acres provide habitat for coyotes, beaver, moose, and other mammals. There are few trails. Present recreational uses include hiking, climbing, and hunting. Campgrounds and accommodations are available in surrounding areas. Access is via country roads off U.S. Route 2 and State Route 110. The area is located in the Pilot and Pliny ranges between Berlin and Lancaster, New Hampshire.

Information: Supervisor, White Mountain National Forest, Laconia, New Hampshire 03246.

🌲 The proposed **Carr Mountain Wilderness,** in central New Hampshire, reaches an elevation of 3,470 feet and covers 10,000 acres. Though not endowed with spectacular mountain scenery, the area has spruce-covered ridges, hardwood forests, and marshy lowlands attractive to wildlife. Deer, moose, beaver, and bobcats are the principal mammals. Waterfowl occupy ponds, and the streams are stocked with trout. Fishing, hunting, and hiking are the principal uses; there are presently about eleven miles of trails, some of them old abandoned logging roads. Access is via trails and forest roads off State Route 25. Food and lodging may be secured in surrounding towns, and campgrounds are available not far away.

Information: Supervisor, White Mountain National Forest, Laconia, New Hampshire 03246.

🌲 Some of the granite of Maine's mountains is so coarse-grained that the included feldspar crystals give the hills a speckled aspect, especially in the proposed **Caribou–Speckled Mountain Wilderness,** east of Evans Notch and about twelve miles southwest of the town of Bethel, Maine. This 12,000-acre area contains both Caribou and Speckled mountains, where fire has almost denuded the low, rounded summits, and severe weather prevents a rapid recovery. In fact, vegetation on the upper levels consists mostly of heaths, mosses, lichens, and stunted conifers. For the hiker, such treeless ridges afford fine views of the Presidential and Mahoosuc ranges. Some of the twenty miles of trail lead along pure mountain streams and through rich vegetation of oak, beech, birch, spruce, hemlock, and white pine. The woods in spring resound with the notes of songbirds. Deer are abundant; other mammals include moose, bears, and coyotes. Still, the "speckles" give an unusual appearance to this wild area: In addition to feldspar, one may see crystals of amethyst, beryl, tourmaline, quartz, and other minerals.

Access is via trails and country roads off State Route 113. U.S. Route 2 passes to the north. Campgrounds are available on forest lands and lodging may be secured in nearby communities.

Information: Supervisor, White Mountain National Forest, Laconia, New Hampshire 03246.

Baxter State Park is a wild region of lakes and ponds, dense woods, steep mountain cliffs, cascades, and waterfalls. Hiking beside its brooks we get a feeling of gratitude toward former Governor Baxter and the Maine legislature, which determinedly set aside 201,018 acres to be kept "forever wild." Although some hunting as well as predator and insect control were authorized, the park is still maintained primarily as a wilderness, with public recreation secondary. There are some campgrounds, campsites, lodges, bunkhouses, and other accommodations, but these, like the roads, are simple and unobtrusive.

Indeed, Katahdin is one of the wildest mountains in the eastern United States. Its ice-scoured peaks, scattered boulders, classic glacial features, woods, and streams make it "a cross-section of interior Maine," as Governor Baxter himself put it. Birch, beech, and maple predominate among the deciduous trees, while the conifers are dominated by spruce and balsam fir. A moose goes crashing away through the woods. Deer, bears, wildcats, mink, weasels, and smaller mammals reside permanently, and the birds include Canada jays and spruce grouse.

Campgrounds in Baxter State Park are open from May 15 to October 15. Canoeing, hiking, camping, fishing, and mountain climbing are among the favorite wilderness pursuits here. Katahdin is a much-written-about mountain; a detailed description may be found in the *Guide to the Appalachian Trail in Maine*, available locally or from the Appalachian Trail Conference. Baxter is an elite park without any illusion that "parks are for people." It is a wild segment of the original Maine, and people are allowed to use it only if they do not abuse it. Here Maine remains what Thoreau called it: a damp and intricate wilderness. Access is by country roads from Greenville, Millinocket, and Patten.

Information: Supervisor, Baxter State Park, 116 Aroostook Avenue, Millinocket, Maine 04462.

🌲 Northward through the woods of Maine flows the Allagash River. From Telos Landing, near Baxter State Park, where canoes can be launched, to the St. John River, where the Allagash ends, is a hundred miles of more or less wild rivers, lakes, rapids, and waterfalls. The government of Maine has designated it the **Allagash Wilderness Waterway**. Both paddles and poles are required to negotiate this stream. The canoeist makes his way across placid lakes, but then finds white water at Chase Rips. Around Allagash Falls, which are forty feet high, he portages for a third of a mile. At several points come opportunities for side trips, especially up Allagash Stream to Allagash Lake. Here and there may be seen old historic places reminiscent of early logging, such as the site of the Eagle Lake and Umbazooksus Railroad. Short hikes can be taken to old fire towers, and fishermen can try their luck occasionally for brook trout, togue, and lake whitefish.

The forested aspect of the waterway is preserved by means of restrictions on timber harvesting within one mile of the waterway and prohibition of nonwilderness activities within 400 to 800 feet. The wilderness area covers 200,000 acres, of which more than 30,000 are water. Although not marked by signs, except at campsites, it is patrolled by waterway rangers and other state officials. Good maps are highly desirable for a canoe trip here. Warm clothes should be worn on account of the generally cool climate.

Campsites are scattered along the route, and camping is limited to those areas. Only canoes are allowed; square-stern types are permitted and may be fitted with one outboard motor not to exceed ten horsepower. In certain places motors are prohibited entirely. Road access to points on the river is by forest roads from Greenville, Millinocket, Patten, Ashland, and Allagash Village; some of the roads are private and advance permission must be secured before using them. Accommodations are available in communities on approach routes.

Information: Director, Maine Bureau of Parks and Recreation, Augusta, Maine 04330.

🌲 Among the shadowed woods of fir, pine, and spruce in northern Maine lives a scattered population of deciduous trees, such as maple, beech, and

313

birch. This luxuriant forest is interrupted only by occasional bogs and marshes or streams that enter cold blue lakes. Among the trees live deer, black bears, moose, and dozens of other species of mammals. Two hundred kinds of birds have been observed in the region, including woodcocks. In early spring at dawn or dusk the male woodcock climbs high into the air from a clearing, whistles as it flies in an undulating pattern, then plunges down in a mating ritual. Such are the scenes at **Moosehorn National Wildlife Refuge,** on U.S. Route 1 near Calais, Maine. The refuge is divided into two units, one on the St. Croix River, where tide fluctuations exceed twenty-eight feet, and the other on Cobscook Bay. The combined area of both units is 22,665 acres, with open spaces in which to hike, photograph, study from exhibits and self-guiding tours, ski, snowshoe, and fish. Accommodations are nearby.

Information: Manager, Moosehorn National Wildlife Refuge, Box 285, Calais, Maine 04619.

🌲 The coast of Maine is composed of more than crashing waves and rocky cliffs, though that dramatic picture is memorable indeed. The spruce and shrubbery, flowers, tidal pools, and free flights of birds in their evolutionary habitats all suggest more delicate aspects. Visitors may spend a morning with a naturalist at tidal pools, and for three hours have not a dull moment observing sea anemones, sponges, red and green algae, sea lettuce, periwinkles, starfish, urchins, barnacles, chitons, whelks, mussels, and limpets. Terns and eagles fly overhead; an osprey dives for fish offshore; guillemots sweep from the cliffs to skim the waves and splash into the sea. Old carriage roads ascend into forests of spruce and birch to the summit of Cadillac Mountain, at 1,530 feet, the highest point on the Atlantic coast. There it is possible not only to get a wide blue view of granite islands in a tranquil sea, but also to hear the notes of warblers and find the nest of a junco hidden beneath a dwarf fir tree. On Isle au Haut lie some of the wilder portions of the coast; a hiker passes black spruce trees with purple cones suspended in colorful clusters, and photographs knee-high flowery clumps of dwarf laurel, akin to the famous mountain laurel of farther south. All this is preserved in **Acadia National Park,** 34,000 acres of wild seacoast where parts of the original land and seascapes are retained. The park is located forty-five miles southeast of Bangor, accessible on several roads, including state routes 3, 102, and 198. Food and lodging may be secured in Bar Harbor and other nearby communities, although reservations for summer lodging should be made well in advance. Trails, museums, roadside exhibits, guided walks, and other opportunities exist for public enjoyment. There are campgrounds in and around the park.

Information: Superintendent, Acadia National Park, Bar Harbor, Maine 04609.

4. COASTAL LOWLANDS

The eastern edge of the United States is endowed with hundreds of miles of offshore sandy islands, deposited by currents and sifted by constant winds. Some are little more than elongated sandspits, in places so narrow that waves wash over them or even cut them apart. They are vulnerable to violent weather, repeatedly altered in shape, and shifted in location. Yet their attributes of sparkling sand, rolling waves, brisk sea breezes, and wide-open naturalness make them highly attractive and valuable for recreation purposes. Little wonder that some of the best are preserved as parks, refuges, and wilderness areas.

Cape Cod National Seashore embraces the entire forty-six-mile east coast of Cape Cod, and some of the interior of the Cape as well. Not only were beach sands piled high into dunes, but glacial gravels have been laid down in giant sweeps, often punctuated by sunken basins, or "kettle ponds," where enormous chunks of ice once remained for a time before melting and allowing the mantle to settle. In these sunken ponds and lakes grow forests of Atlantic white cedar that eventually yield to red maple. Out where there is less protection from the elements grow forests of pitch pine, sometimes seared and killed by salt spray hurled inland during high winds and heavy surf. On the bay side are moors of heath, salt marshes, and tidal creeks all biologically productive with such diverse life as savanna sparrows, razor clams, marshfire glasswort, and fiddler crabs.

All lands within the authorized boundary of the Seashore have not been acquired, but certain beaches, dunes, forests, ponds, trails, museums, picnic sites, lighthouses, and historic sites are open to the public. Privately operated campgrounds and accommodations are available in the surrounding area. Access is via U.S. Route 6, ninety miles southeast of Boston.

Information: Superintendent, Cape Cod National Seashore, South Wellfleet, Massachusetts 02663.

From a distance Monomoy Island, which makes up **Monomoy National Wildlife Refuge,** appears to be low, barren, and lifeless. But as one

315

approaches it, across a narrow inlet south of Cape Cod, he watches herring gulls and terns flying in leisurely but erratic circles above the dunes. Over beds of eelgrass and sea scallops in the shallow bay behind Monomoy visitors approach the beach, leap into the water, and pull ashore. For as far as they can see—the island is eight miles long—there appears to be nothing but sand and beach grass. But crossing the dunes and proceeding inland they enter protected vales deep enough to tap the water table, where freshwater floats above saline. This moisture supports wild plum, shadbush, bayberry, blackberry, chokecherry, high-bush blueberry, pines, ferns, and an abundance of poison ivy. Parts of the island have marshes, swamps, and even short streams.

The seaward beach belongs to gulls and terns, eider ducks, sanderlings, plovers, and red-throated loons. Actually, Monomoy is a major stopover for birds migrating along the Atlantic Flyway, and some 250 species have been sighted through the years. Summer brings as many as forty rare Hudsonian godwits. Terns nest by the thousands, laying their eggs in warm sand. The size of the island—3,300 acres—is sufficient to shelter large bird populations, and to protected interior thickets come land migrants such as sparrows and warblers.

A few buildings on the island will eventually be removed, leaving only the lighthouse, built in 1828, to suggest man's early occupation. Now a day-use wilderness area, Monomoy has no facilities for public use or recreation, and camping is not permitted. Access is by boat only, and can be hazardous. The nearest accommodations are on Cape Cod, which is reached via U.S. Route 6, ninety miles southeast of Boston. Boats and lodging are available in Chatham.

Information: Manager, Monomoy National Wildlife Refuge, 191 Sudbury Road, Concord, Massachusetts 01742.

🌲 Off the south shore of Long Island lies another barrier beach, once the site of beach cabins that were badly damaged in a severe spring storm. Instead of renewing the attempts of men to settle in so severe an environment, but rather to preserve the barrier and prevent commercial development of it, the State of New York and the federal government cooperated in the establishment of **Fire Island National Seashore,** twenty-six miles of sand, surf, beach grass, wild roses, marsh, and sunken thickets of serviceberry, black gum, and holly. Waterfowl abound in spring, summer, and fall. The authorized boundary of the Seashore encompasses only twenty-six miles of the thirty-two-mile-long island, and the boundaries are within several communities that have been exempted from condemnation of land. A few beach cabins and expensive summer homes remain.

The island is accessible by road and ferry. Food and lodging may be secured on Long Island. Camping is permitted in the Seashore at Watch Hill, but reservations are required.

Information: Superintendent, Fire Island National Seashore, 65 Oak Street, Patchogue, Long Island, New York 11772.

🌲 Twenty-five miles west of New York City is **Great Swamp National Wildlife Refuge,** near Morristown, New Jersey, covering 5,051 acres. More than half of it is a swamp that remains surprisingly untouched in a vast metropolitan region. Moreover, life is abundant: 19 species of fish, 39 of reptiles and amphibians, 30 of mammals, and 205 of birds. A mile-long system of boardwalks allows human beings to penetrate the swamp discreetly, peer from observation blinds out over pond-marsh-meadow environments, and make their way through thick beech woods and sweetgum groves where copses of blueberry grow ten feet high.

If the noise of aircraft overhead is not too loud, one can hear the songs of meadowlark, redwing, towhee, warbler, titmouse, thrush, and pewee, punctuated by the croaking of green frogs. Black soggy soil forms a souplike bed of nutrients for oak and maple seedlings. Here and there grow patches of ferns, sphagnum moss, and skunk cabbage, the latter with foot-long leaves. A walk along this elevated pathway has its rejuvenating effect, and more such swamps would be thoroughly welcome in the eastern megalopolis. A community, according to Thoreau, is to be saved not so much by the righteous men within it but by the woods and swamps around it.

The refuge, open during daylight hours, is reached via country roads off U.S. Route 22 or Interstate 287 south of Morristown. There are nature trails, an outdoor education center, and opportunities for scientific study and photography. Neither camping nor picknicking is permitted. Picnic sites may be found in the nearby Morristown National Historical Park and other areas. The nearest campgrounds are at Mahlon Dickerson and Lewis Morris county parks. Accommodations may be obtained in nearby towns and cities.

Information: Manager, Great Swamp National Wildlife Refuge, Pleasant Plains Road, R. D. 1, Box 148, Basking Ridge, New Jersey 07920.

🌲 It is difficult to grasp that a natural area teeming with life thrives within sight of Atlantic City, New Jersey, but eleven miles across Reed's Bay lies **Brigantine National Wildlife Refuge.** Its woods, waters, and marshes teem with hundreds of thousands of birds, chiefly Canada geese, black brants, laughing gulls, terns, herons, egrets, ibises, and grebes. Only because the refuge is large enough—20,000 acres—to support the food needed by these birds can they remain. The osprey, for example, needs a relatively undisturbed domain in which to nest, and a source of fish nearby.

In the shallows live white perch, flounder, fluke, and blue crabs, plus innumerable smaller animal forms, and beds of algae and eelgrass—which are attractive to brants. Thus Brigantine is an extraordinary feeding ground and "nursery" directly on the Atlantic Flyway. Northbound waterfowl migration reaches a peak in late March and early April, and on bright warm days in May one can see migrating warblers and other transient species. Ducks hatch in June and July, and return migration begins in August. The most spectacular concentrations occur in November, when more than 150,000 birds assemble on the Refuge. In winter the chances of seeing bald eagles are good, and of course there are other year-round residents.

Though the refuge is mostly salt marsh suitable for birds, it also contains forested uplands of pine and mixed hardwoods, and is home to thirty-eight species of mammals. A portion of the protected area may be toured by automobile, and visitors may take a circle route on dikes that retain freshwater ponds. Geese have the right-of-way—and frequently cross the road. Alert observers may require several hours to negotiate that loop road, and not just because it is fascinating to watch one family of geese after another. From observation towers they can see snowy egrets darting into the water after fish; least terns hovering, diving, hovering; and glossy ibises sifting among the grass in shallow water. Along the road may be heard a constant chorus of laughing gulls, and at several points dozens of them share small marl banks with handsomely patterned ruddy turnstones.

Unfortunately, a pall of smoke at times rolls in from Atlantic City. But, hopefully, the adverse effects of civilization will diminish and visitors may continue to enjoy the trails, observation points, photographic blinds, and other aids without disturbing this coastal ecosystem. Access is via U.S. Route 9 off the Garden State Parkway near Oceanville. Accommodations are available in nearby communities.

Information: Manager, Brigantine National Wildlife Refuge, Great Creek Road, Box 72, Oceanville, New Jersey 08231.

🌲 Apart from federal sites, the State of New Jersey has assessed its own natural lands and adopted a program of preserving what remains. Some of this involves restoration of the natural scene and acquisition of new lands to enhance wild areas. The closest thing to original wilderness in the state is the **Cohansey Natural Area,** a 12,400-acre tract of salt marsh in Cumberland County, Delaware Bay region. It has been little used and not much polluted, and is a good example of coastal plain vegetation surrounded by salt marshes. However, it is not yet fully owned by the state. Many other areas, however, have been designated as state parks, forests, and natural areas.

Information: Director, Division of Parks and Forestry, Department of Environmental Protection, Box 1420, Trenton, New Jersey 08625.

🌲 Certain wild areas near urban centers have special attributes, such as the **Pine Barrens** of New Jersey, thirty miles southeast of Philadelphia. On these rolling sandhills, which cover a major part of New Jersey, pine forests have spread around bogs, sumps, seeps, lakes, and grassy meadows. Old roads and trails abound, leading hikers into remote places. In an atmosphere scented with pine, one discovers rivers and lakes tinted with tannin, and valleys cushioned with banks of fern. At night katydids scratch out a rhythm that is matched by choruses of crickets. And if the natural scene ignites in the hiker a new curiosity about ecology or geology, he can satisfy much of it at the Batsto Nature Center, a few miles east of Hammonton, on New Jersey Route 542. Although parts of the Pine Barrens have been utilized for homes, roads, cranberry bogs, blueberry farms, and military installations, several large units have been kept reasonably free of encroachment and are supplied with campgrounds and other facilities.

Information: Superintendent, Wharton State Forest, Batsto, R. D. 1, Hammonton, New Jersey 08037.

🌲 On Delaware Bay, ten miles northeast of Dover, lies the 15,110-acre **Bombay Hook National Wildlife Refuge,** most of it a brackish tidal marsh of value to migrating and wintering waterfowl. But there are also winding rivers, wooded swamps, deciduous forests, thickets, and freshwater ponds, all of which, in a largely urbanized region, attract many species of mammals, birds, and reptiles. Deer feed in the meadows, and human visitors out early in the morning might glimpse a fox, otter, or raccoon. Half a dozen species of turtles and half a dozen kinds of snakes are frequently seen in the marshy habitats. The Refuge has observation towers and nature trails, but no campgrounds. Food and lodging may be obtained in nearby communities. Access is via State Route 9 east of Smyrna, Delaware, but much of the Refuge can be visited only by boat. The best bird observations are between October 1 and November 30.

Information: Manager, Bombay Hook National Wildlife Refuge, R.F.D. 1, Box 147, Smyrna, Delaware 19977.

🌲 If it weren't for the efforts of private citizens and groups of citizens, some wild areas might never be salvaged. This is especially true, at the national level, of such organizations as the Nature Conservancy. A good example at the state level is the preservation of the **Great Cypress Swamp** of Delaware (not to be confused with the Great Swamp National Wildlife Refuge of New Jersey, the Great Dismal Swamp of Virginia, or the Great Cypress Fresh Water Reserve of Florida). It is located on the headwaters of the Pocomoke River near Selbyville, Delaware. This tract was ditched, drained, cut, burned, and put to agricultural use, mostly in the 1930s when few persons cared about the ecology of a region if it could be made economically productive. As a result, the once-vast cedar and cypress swamps that covered the Delmarva Peninsula were nearly destroyed. Peat was burned out and a new forest of maple and sweetgum grew up.

In 1961, however, a nonprofit organization called Delaware Wild Lands, Inc., which initiated conservation efforts throughout the state, went to work acquiring lands and planting cypress and cedar seedlings, pine and smaller flora in an effort to restore the natural scene. Of the original 50,000 acres only about 12,000 remain relatively wild, and of this only about 6,500 acres can be called true swamp. Delaware Wild Lands owns 4,500 acres of the true swamp. Today canoeists can paddle among groves of bald cypress with their characteristic exposed "knees." Someday, perhaps, most of the original heartland of the swamp can be obtained and given major public protection. Then it may approach the wild aspects it had when the pioneer naturalist Thomas Nuttall, came in the early nineteenth century and called it "one of the most frightening labyrinths you can imagine."

Information: President, Delaware Wild Lands, Inc., 1011 Washington Street, Wilmington, Delaware 19801.

PART VIII

The Southeast

Appalachian Trail

OHIO

ILLINOIS | INDIANA

MD.
Washington, D.C.
DELAWARE

River

Ohio

Louisville

MISSOURI

WEST
VIRGINIA

Richmond

Chesapeake Bay

KENTUCKY

Nashville

Knoxville

VIRGINIA

Cape Hatteras

ARKANSAS

TENNESSEE

NORTH
CAROLINA

Raleigh

Columbia

SOUTH

CAROLINA

MISSISSIPPI

ALABAMA

Macon

Atlanta

Jackson

Montgomery

Charleston

GEORGIA

Savannah

Atlantic Ocean

Mobile

New
Orleans

Jacksonville

Ocala

Gulf of Mexico

St. Petersburg

FLORIDA

Miami

Key West

Florida Keys

1. SOUTHERN MOUNTAINS

1. Great Smoky Mountains National Park, North Carolina–Tennessee
2. Blue Ridge Parkway, Virginia–North Carolina
3. Mount Mitchell State Park, North Carolina
4. Shenandoah National Park, Virginia
5. Shining Rock Wilderness, North Carolina
6. Linville Gorge Wilderness, North Carolina
7. Cumberland Gap National Historical Park, Kentucky
8. Cranberry Wilderness, West Virginia
9. Dolly Sods Wilderness, West Virginia
10. Otter Creek Wilderness, West Virginia
11. Spruce Knob–Seneca Rocks National Recreation Area, West Virgina
12. Laurel Fork Wilderness, Virginia–West Virginia
13. James River Face Wilderness, Virginia
14. Ramseys Draft Wilderness, Virginia
15. Mammoth Cave National Park, Kentucky
16. Beaver Creek area, Kentucky
17. Big South Fork of the Cumberland River, Kentucky-Tennessee
18. Cohutta Wilderness, Georgia-Tennessee
19. Joyce Kilmer Wilderness, North Carolina–Tennessee
20. Cheoah Bald Wilderness, North Carolina
21. Snowbird Creek Wilderness, North Carolina
22. Ellicott's Rock Wilderness, South Carolina–North Carolina–Georgia

2. WOODS AND SWAMPS

23. Okefenokee National Wildlife Refuge, Georgia
24. Suwannee National River, Florida
25. Great Dismal Swamp, Virginia–North Carolina
26. Congaree Swamp, South Carolina
27. Prince William Forest Park, Virginia
28. Carolina Sandhills National Wildlife Refuge, South Carolina

29. Savannah National Wildlife Refuge, South Carolina–Georgia
30. Piedmont National Wildlife Refuge, Georgia
31. Sipsey Wilderness, Alabama
32. Bradwell Bay Wilderness, Florida
33. Lake Woodruff National Wildlife Refuge, Florida
34. Myakka River State Park, Florida
35. Big Cypress Fresh Water Reserve, Florida
36. Corkscrew Swamp Sanctuary, Florida

3. ATLANTIC SHORE

37. Cape Hatteras National Seashore, North Carolina
38. Pea Island National Wildlife Refuge, North Carolina
39. Assateague Island National Seashore, Maryland-Virginia
40. Chincoteague National Wildlife Refuge, Virginia
41. Cape Lookout National Seashore, North Carolina
42. Cape Fear, North Carolina
43. Cape Romain National Wildlife Refuge, South Carolina
44. Wolf Island National Wildlife Refuge, Georgia
45. Cumberland Island National Seashore, Georgia

4. SUBTROPICS AND SEA

46. St. Marks National Wildlife Refuge, Florida
47. Cedar Keys Wilderness, Florida
48. Everglades National Park, Florida
49. Florida Keys Wilderness, Florida
50. John Pennekamp Coral Reef State Park, Florida
51. Biscayne National Monument, Florida
52. Passage Key National Wildlife Refuge, Florida
53. Island Bay National Wildlife Refuge, Florida
54. Pelican Island National Wildlife Refuge, Florida

323

1. SOUTHERN MOUNTAINS

The crystal clarity of the streams is only one of the extraordinary values of southern mountains. On high gray cliffs in **Great Smoky Mountains National Park** the sun's rays stream through petals of brilliant pink dwarf rhododendron. A visitor hears the pervasive drumming of grouse. At Gregory Bald, a summit on the boundary between Tennessee and North Carolina, one can photograph at least six color variants of flame azalea, and botanists insist that there are at least a dozen more. On the way to Ramsey Cascades, the forest is like a cathedral, and during the last two weeks of October the intricate woods turn into a fantasy of yellow and red.

It is fruitless to try to encompass all of these mountain impressions in two or three visits; a lifetime would be inadequate. Two special periods are spring (especially May and June), when some of the flowers are at their best, and October, when autumn color is richest. In summer, the heat and humidity make hiking a decidedly damp experience, and even then it would be desirable to concentrate on just one section. For example, Mount Le Conte is worth not only trail hikes from six different directions, but a stay at the lodge on top, the only accommodations within Great Smoky Mountains National Park. (Reservations should be made well in advance.) Or from Cades Cove, trails lead off in at least half a dozen directions—to waterfalls, ridges, "balds," wild gardens, and secluded valleys.

Likewise, weeks could be spent in the Clingmans Dome, Oconaluftee, Cataloochee, Cosby, and Fontana areas. The seventy miles of The Appalachian Trail through the park could be hiked in a few hours, but hikers whose attention is diverted by trillium, frogs, firs, bears, bees, berry patches, trout, turkeys, woodchucks, and photo viewpoints will scarcely get started before nightfall of the first day.

The park, with 514,669 acres, has a full range of educational and other facilities for outdoor enjoyment, and is located forty miles southeast of Knoxville, Tennessee, on U.S. Route 441. Campgrounds are available in and near the park. There is a hotel at Elkmont, inside the park; food and lodging may be secured in Cherokee, Gatlinburg, and other nearby towns.

Information: Superintendent, Great Smoky Mountains National Park, Gatlinburg, Tennessee 37738.

Quantico Creek, Prince William Forest Park, Virginia.

🌲 North from the Great Smoky Mountains, through heavily settled and cultivated terrain, a surprisingly large percentage of the Appalachian Mountains is protected in one way or another, and there are two principal routes through the southern highlands, one by road, the Blue Ridge Parkway, and the other by The Appalachian Trail. At present, the **Blue Ridge Parkway** extends 469 miles through Virginia and North Carolina, linking Great Smoky Mountains and Shenandoah national parks. The Parkway is designed for leisurely travel on a ride-a-while, stop-a-while basis. Though the right-of-way is generally less than a mile in width, it passes through some remote areas where hikes can be taken, and in places expands to units thousands of acres in size; several established wilderness areas lie adjacent to the right-of-way. The Parkway is replete with nature trails, exhibits, and historic restorations. One attractive site along it is Craggy Gardens, a ridgetop concentration of Catawba rhododendrons near Asheville, North Carolina, that burst into bloom in June. Another special locality devoted to interpretation of wildlands ecology is the Peaks of Otter, north of Roanoke, Virginia. The Parkway is unusually spectacular in autumn, especially when the bright-yellow leaves of tulip trees and the rich red of maples are at their peak of color. Food, supplies, and lodging are available at various points along the Parkway. There are many access routes; on the west, in the valley below the Blue Ridge, Interstate 81 parallels the Parkway for much of its length.

Information: Superintendent, Blue Ridge Parkway, Box 7606, Asheville, North Carolina 28807.

🌲 **The Appalachian Trail,** its southern terminus on Springer Mountain in Georgia, leads through much wilder and far less accessible terrain than that reached by the Blue Ridge Parkway, and is much longer—2,000 miles from Georgia to Maine. The southern thousand miles of it goes over the Nantahala and Cheoah Mountains, the Great Smokies, along the Blue Ridge, and across the Potomac River at Harpers Ferry. It passes in view of Mount Mitchell, North Carolina, highest point in the eastern United States, 6,684 feet, now protected in **Mount Mitchell State Park,** accessible by auto on a side road off the Blue Ridge Parkway. In places the Trail passes along "jump-off" ledges where cliffs fall away for a thousand feet. It passes remote mountain farms, valleys, old homesteads, and long miles of coniferous and deciduous forest refreshingly far from the hustle of human activity. It is accessible and hikable in every season: when layers of leaves lie deep on the path in autumn, or when a blanket of snow and ice covers the ridges. However, the trail is exceedingly popular and during vacation periods shelters along the way are

(top) Mountain laurel, Great Smoky
Mountains National Park,
North Carolina-Tennessee.
(above) Skunk cabbage shoots in January,
Prince William Forest Park, Virginia.
(right) Grasshopper on sawgrass,
Everglades National Park, Florida.

filled to overflowing. The seventy miles of the Trail within Great Smoky Mountains National Park have come under such heavy demand that the National Park Service took steps in the summer of 1972 to control use of trail shelters. Permits are issued for use of the twelve-person shelters, and when capacity is reached, hikers are encouraged to take alternate routes that also provide shelters. Side trails lead to points of interest as well as to sources of food, lodging, and supplies. Hikers should equip themselves with the various trail guidebooks published by the Appalachian Trail Conference because, for one thing, they should know where drinking water is located along the way. For a brief description of the northern section of the Trail see page 309.

Information: Director, Southeast Regional Office, National Park Service, 3401 Whipple Avenue, Atlanta, Georgia 30344; and Appalachian Trail Conference, Harpers Ferry, West Virginia 25425.

In **Shenandoah National Park,** between Waynesboro and Front Royal, Virginia, 80 miles of ridgetop and valley terrain is recovering from heavy logging, blight, and other changes wrought by man. Views from the summits, traversed by the celebrated Skyline Drive, include panoramas of rolling piedmont to the east and the Shenandoah River Valley to the west. High-country forests have attractive aspects at all seasons. Persons hardy enough to reach the summits in winter may find snow and rime by day and perhaps rare red and green auroras at night. Spring fogs and mists nourish masses of azalea and mountain laurel in May and June; during autumn, chlorophyll fades from the leaves and unmasks brilliant yellows, oranges, reds, and purples. It may be a little less easy to see black bears in Shenandoah than in the Great Smokies, but they are there, largely in the wilder and more rugged southern section of the park. An unusual number of species of salamanders exists in the Appalachians, especially in moist places. Thus deciduous forests, though once cut and logged, are actually complex ecosystems, and the wilderness is clearly restoring itself.

The Appalachian Trail traverses the length of the Park, and side trails lead east and west, down thickly wooded slopes, into hemlock groves, past waterfalls, beside prominent rocky crags, and through secluded vales. Within the park are lodging, camping, and picnic sites, self-guiding trails, exhibits, and museums. Access is from the north or south end, or via U.S. routes 33 and 211, which cross the park.

Information: Superintendent, Shenandoah National Park, Luray, Virginia 22835.

🌲 In North Carolina, just off the Blue Ridge Parkway, are the **Shining Rock Wilderness,** twenty miles southwest of Asheville, and **Linville Gorge Wilderness,** forty-five miles northeast of Asheville, both administered by the U.S. Forest Service. Shining Rock, from the mountain of the same name, which refers to outcrops of white quartz, covers 13,000 acres of jumbled scenic mountains in the southern highlands, a few miles east of the Great Smoky Mountains. Its ridges and slopes, endowed with the music of waterfalls, are covered with dense deciduous forests and occasionally flowering trees and shrubs. Although access is by the Parkway or U.S. Route 276, no roads go within; the heart of the wild country may be reached only by trail. Entry permits are required for both areas.

Linville Falls is reached via the Blue Ridge Parkway, and a short walk leads visitors to an overlook from which to view the thirty-foot-high cascade. But travel farther down the gorge, into the rugged 7,600-acre wilderness, must be by trail or through the trailless woods. Roads do approach the east and west rims and from viewpoints visitors may see into the gorge. Several trails descend into the depths, past chimneys, spires, and cliffs. Because of its difficulty of access, Linville Gorge has been little exploited, and hikers go through virgin forests of oak, pine, maple, sourwood, silverbell, and other species of trees. Beneath these are thickets of heath and laurel, plus such animals as deer, bears, grouse, copperheads, and timber rattlesnakes. A picnic ground is nearby; campgrounds may be found along the Parkway and in neighboring national forests. Accommodations are available in nearby communities.

Information: Supervisor, National Forests of North Carolina, Box 2750, Asheville, North Carolina 28802.

🌲 In our Industrial Age it is a little hard to realize that the old Wilderness Road, hacked out of primeval forest by Daniel Boone and thirty axmen in 1775, still has some wilderness left. Agriculture and logging have modified much of the Allegheny Plateau country in Kentucky and Virginia, and strip mining has left ugly artificial terraces where once were forest and wildlife. But in the vicinity of Cumberland Gap, an area of 20,169 acres of the Allegheny Plateau still remains roadless, administered by the National Park Service as part of **Cumberland Gap National Historical Park.** This stretch of land, covering nearly fifteen miles along Brush and Cumberland mountains, is not very wide, and the noises of civilization are usually not very far away. But the fact remains that this terrain still possesses something of the primitive character it had when settlers and soldiers tramped through the Gap to get to the Kentucky settlements. Deciduous hardwood forest covers the knifelike summit ridge, dips into the valleys, and hides the streams, caves, and limestone sinks; it yields only to cliffs that rise up out of the woods as promontories from which a hiker can see across neighboring valleys. On a clear day he may even observe the Great Smoky Mountains, seventy miles due south. Pines mix among oak and hickory, and the rugged slopes are thicketed with mountain laurel and rhododendron. Dogwood and redbud flower conspicuously in spring. And in the shadows move grouse, deer, bobcats, raccoons, opossums, squirrels, and other life forms.

A trail runs the length of the park, crossing the 6,375 acres of the designated wilderness. There are camping and picnic sites (open May 1 to October 31) and a museum nearby. The site is accessible via U.S. routes 58 from the east and 25-E from the north and south. Accommodations may be secured in nearby towns.

Information: Superintendent, Cumberland Gap National Historical Park, Box 340, Middlesboro, Kentucky 40965.

In Monongahela National Forest, West Virginia, may be found several sites of unusual interest. One of the still reasonably wild areas is the proposed 36,300-acre **Cranberry Wilderness,** a once-logged, once-roaded basin that is healing rapidly so that primeval aspects of the forest are returning—except, alas, for the great specimens of chestnut oak that once grew here. A part of the Allegheny Plateau, the area rises to a summit of 4,600 feet on Black Mountain. The forest is typical mixed northern hardwoods, with spruce at higher levels. Trout fishing is popular along the streams and hunters enter the mountains in search of deer, turkeys, and smaller wildlife. Black bears are fairly abundant. Water is available on most trails except, of course, along high ridges; hikers should carry and use water-purification tablets if they drink or cook along the headwaters. The presence of midges and other insects calls for repellents in summer. Forty miles of trail exist, and hiking in trailless areas is rewarding if the hiker can make his way through thickets of rhododendron.

At the southeast edge of the wilderness is Cranberry Glades Botanical Area, an extensive bog that harbors plants and animals characteristic of the far north. The flora includes sundews, pitcher plants, bog rosemary, orchids, buckbean, Canada violets, and Canada mayflowers. A boardwalk leads through woods of spruce, hemlock, and alder before reaching the bogs. The Cranberry Mountain Visitor Center, nearby, has displays and educational programs to help explain natural features and processes. The proposed wilderness area may be reached off state routes 150 on the east and 39 on the south, as well as Forest Service Road 86 to the north. Campgrounds and motels are available in the vicinity.

Information: Supervisor, Monongahela National Forest, Box 1231, Elkins, West Virginia 26241.

🌲 The Allegheny Plateau has for centuries been dissected by streams that originate in the ridges and flow down through sandstone, conglomerate, and other forms of sedimentary rock. Where Red Creek and its tributaries have incised deep canyons into the plateau west of Petersburg, West Virginia, lies the Dolly Sods Scenic Area of about 10,200 acres. Endowed with sphagnum bogs, spruce and hardwood stands, blueberry patches, rhododendron thickets, and waterfalls, the proposed **Dolly Sods Wilderness,** named for open meadows or "sods" once used by the Dolly family, constitutes a varied and scenic eastern wilderness. Prior to extensive logging before the turn of the century the high-country plains were covered with virgin stands of red spruce and hemlock, with northern hardwoods in the coves. Uncontrolled logging and fires changed the character of the landscape, but under protection by the U.S. Forest Service for more than forty years, Dolly Sods is slowly recovering. Deer and snowshoe hares are abundant, but bears appear to be declining in population. The high ridges provide good watching points for observing hawk migration in the autumn. Closed to all vehicles, the heart of the area provides solitude for persons who prefer to travel on foot. Trails reach many parts of the area. Campgrounds and accommodations may be found in the vicinity. Access is via mountain roads in the northeastern part of Monongahela National Forest.

Information: Supervisor, Monongahela National Forest, Box 1231, Elkins, West Virginia 26241.

🌲 The proposed **Otter Creek Wilderness,** a high, bowl-shaped basin in Monongahela National Forest, is approximately 18,000 acres in size, and although cut over sixty years ago it has been partly healed by nature and is on the way to becoming an outstanding wilderness. Otter Creek is an attractive mountain stream containing native brook trout, and the region constitutes one of the few black bear–breeding areas in West Virginia. Hikers find forty miles of trails, some leading along Otter Creek up to its origin, others along mountain ridges. Coal Run has attractive waterfalls. Caving, camping, trout fishing, swimming, and nature study are among the human recreational activities here. Bogs contain collections of plants typical of more northern ecosystems. A few stands of virgin hemlock remain in remote places.

331

Some parts of the deciduous forest are relatively open; in other places, off the trails, explorers would have to skirt dense thickets of rhododendron and greenbrier. As with other natural areas in this region, the West Virginia Highlands Conservancy has stimulated interest in use and protection of the valley and has fought commercial intrusions. Considering how much of West Virginia has already been given over to industry, it seems time to reclaim substantial parts of the state for simple enjoyment of the natural scene. Access to the Otter Creek area is via State Route 72. Developed campgrounds are located just outside the area, principally off U.S. Route 33 to the south. Motels and lodges may be found in Parsons, Elkins, and other nearby communities.

Information: Supervisor, Monongahela National Forest, Box 1231, Elkins, West Virginia 26241.

🌲 The United States and West Virginia governments, recognizing the extraordinary scenic and recreational values of the Allegheny Plateau, have taken steps to keep the best parts of it unmarred by industrial development. Within Monongahela National Forest, 100,000 acres have been set aside as the **Spruce Knob–Seneca Rocks National Recreation Area**, where ridges and rocky peaks burst out of forests that are replete with rushing streams, including the headwaters of the Potomac River. Recreational activities include hiking, swimming, canoeing, boating, and fishing. Nearby are other places of natural science interest, such as Gaudineer Scenic Area with its virgin spruce forest, and Canaan Valley and Blackwater Falls state parks. Access is over several roads, including U.S. routes 33 and 220 and state routes 4, 28, and 32. Campgrounds and accommodations are available throughout the region.

Information: Supervisor, Monongahela National Forest, Box 1231, Elkins, West Virginia 26241.

🌲 In the headwaters region of the Potomac River, in Virginia and West Virginia, lies the proposed **Laurel Fork Wilderness** of up to 11,656 acres. Old logging roads and railroad grades now provide footpaths to a forested mountain terrain that has grown over since the logging era. The name comes from the stream draining the area, and probably refers to rhododendron, which local residents call laurel. Beavers, deer, turkeys, and other animals are common. Elevation ranges from 2,600 feet to 4,100 feet. This area is in the remote eastern edge of the Allegheny Mountains, about ten miles south of the Spruce Knob–Seneca Rocks Recreation Area. Approach roads include state routes 19, 28, and 642, and forest road 55. Campgrounds and accommodations are available in the surrounding region.

Information: Supervisor, George Washington National Forest, Harrisonburg, Virginia 22801; and Supervisor, Monongahela National Forest, Box 1231, Elkins, West Virginia 26241.

🌲 The proposed **James River Face Wilderness** actually does face the James River. It is a steep face; the mountain profile descends 2,300 feet in three miles to the James River Water Gap, where the usually placid river flows gently but strongly eastward, cutting across upturned northeast-trending sedimentary rocks of the Blue Ridge. The face is so steep it has not been logged. Among the trees are Carolina hemlocks at their northern limit. Deep canyons, remote hollows, high ridges, and dense deciduous woods characterize the 8,800-acre wild land. The south bank of the James River is particularly interesting with large rocks, fast water, and deep holes. The Appalachian Trail passes through here and the Blue Ridge Parkway lies adjacent. In addition, a network of footpaths in this area includes the Gunter Ridge Trail, Belfast Trail, Piney Ridge Trail, and Balcony Falls Trail. Campgrounds are available along the Parkway or on adjacent forest lands. Accommodations may be obtained in nearby communities, including Roanoke, thirty-five miles to the southwest. Access is via forest roads and state routes 159 and 781.

Information: Supervisor, Jefferson National Forest, Box 4009, Roanoke, Virginia 24015.

🌲 To see what Virginia was originally like, a good place to begin is along Ramseys Draft, a clear trout stream between Shenandoah Mountain and Bald Ridge, twenty miles northwest of Staunton. The proposed **Ramseys Draft Wilderness** possesses rare uncut, never-logged forests with giant specimens of hemlock, sugar maple, and oak. The terrain is typically Appalachian: steep, northeast-trending ridges and little flatland. Animal life consists of deer, bears, raccoons, turkeys, and other species. Trails and an abandoned road are open to hikers and horseback riders. The 6,700-acre area is located about twenty miles southeast of the proposed Laurel Fork Wilderness, and is accessible via U.S. Route 250. Food and lodging may be secured in nearby communities, though lodging facilities are likely to be filled to capacity in times of heavy travel. Staunton is the nearest large city where lodging is likely to be assured.

Information: Supervisor, George Washington National Forest, Harrisonburg, Virginia 22801.

🌲 **Mammoth Cave National Park,** Kentucky, has a surface area of 51,000 acres, bisected by the winding Green River. Although years must pass before the cut-over forest recovers something of its original nature, the park has wild values both above and below ground. It is in the midst of classical Karst topography, a limestone terrain dissolved into sinkholes, valleys, channels, and caverns. Mammoth Cave proper has more than 150 miles of known interconnecting passages, and there are numerous other subterranean chambers—known and unknown. Access to underground features is strictly controlled not only on account of the extreme fragility of gypsum and limestone formations, but because of the special equipment and skills required to negotiate difficult passages. On the surface are trails, including self-guiding nature trails, that lead through the deciduous forest past sinks, caves, and emerging underground rivers to points overlooking the Green River Valley. A park concessioner offers riverboat excursions. Lodging and food are available in and near the park, which is located ninety miles south of Louisville off Interstate 65.

Information: Superintendent, Mammoth Cave National Park, Mammoth Cave, Kentucky 42259.

🌲 At this writing, the **Beaver Creek** area in McCreary County, Kentucky, is one of a number of eastern U.S.A. units proposed for inclusion in the national wilderness preservation system. This locality of approximately 5,000 acres is entirely within the Beaver Creek drainage. It lies below a nearly continuous cliff line that ranges from 20 to 200 feet with many small waterfalls, numerous rock houses, arches, a few small caves, clear, free-flowing streams, stands of young pine and hardwoods, and a variety of wildlife. Forest Service management and administrative planning have been aimed toward some kind of protective classification, and the site has remained relatively undisturbed since acquisition in the middle and late 1930s. Access is by foot travel only, and only one short section of developed trail exists at present. This is along the lower portion of Beaver Creek. However, for the physically able, a hike into the trailless area is well worth the effort. Approach is via local roads east of Winchester, Kentucky. The Mountain Parkway passes through Daniel Boone National Forest. Campgrounds are available in the forest, and accommodations may be obtained in nearby communities.

Information: Daniel Boone National Forest, 27 Carol Road, Winchester, Kentucky 40391.

🌲 The **Big South Fork of the Cumberland River,** in Kentucky and Tennessee, is presently being studied for possible recreation, park, and wilderness values. About 120,000 acres are under consideration for a national park, which suggests that the resources are worthy of national attention. An interagency federal report calls the massive bluffs and deeply entrenched valleys of the Big South Fork one of the most spectacular river areas in the eastern United States. Though the valley is nowhere deeper than 700 feet, it nevertheless presents an awe-inspiring view of cliffs rising out of deciduous forests, deep, narrow passages along the river, waterfalls, "chimney rocks," caves, side canyons, palisades, and more than a hundred natural bridges and arches. In the moist ravines grows luxuriant vegetation. Pine and oak dominate the drier locations, while the mixed hardwood forest consists of hemlock, beech, mountain magnolia, poplar, maple, and associated species. Presently the principal river recreation is floating the streams in canoes, kayaks, rubber boats, and johnboats—a swift-running or at times placid experience with uninterrupted passage through scenic wilderness country. Spring and early summer are the best times for floating. The area has been determined to meet all the criteria for inclusion in the national wild and scenic rivers system. A part of it is currently within the boundaries of Daniel Boone National Forest, accessible via U.S. Route 27. Campgrounds and accommodations are available nearby.

Information: Supervisor, Daniel Boone National Forest, 27 Carol Road, Winchester, Kentucky 40391.

🌲 Sometimes it seems that the lands least wanted in the past are the most wanted now, places that were previously so remote or rugged that men stayed away. For such reasons the proposed **Cohutta Wilderness,** now surrounded by 5 million people within 150 miles, has been spared even the logger's saw—at least in several places. The Cohutta Mountains of northern Georgia, 115 miles north of Atlanta, contain virgin stands of native trees—some individuals of immense, or even record, dimensions. Elsewhere old logging paths constitute a kind of primitive trail system. The evidences of early cutting have been nearly obliterated by nature and, hopefully, the land will now be considered too steep and the soil too shallow for commercial exploitation. Cohutta country, which lies in the southern part of the Blue Ridge, consists of deep rocky gorges with plunging streams and roaring waterfalls overhung by hemlock and poplar. However, the U.S. Forest Service warns that the many beautiful and enticing waterfalls in Chattahoochee National Forest are also dangerous. Many people have attempted to climb these waterfalls and fallen, some to their death, from the wet and slippery rocks. The best advice is to keep a proper distance. In places the streams contain naturally reproducing populations of trout; the Jacks and Conasauga rivers, whose watersheds lie within the Wilderness, are said to be among the few high-quality trout streams remaining in Georgia.

Wildlife includes black bears, deer, turkeys, ruffed grouse, foxes, raccoons, and bobcats. Unfortunately, wild boars have been introduced. Access is via State Route 2 and forest roads. Shelters and campgrounds are available in other parts of Chattahoochee National Forest. Food and lodging may be secured in nearby towns. Campsites and nature trails are available in Fort Mountain State Park, about ten miles to the south. The southern terminus of The Appalachian Trail is on Springer Mountain, thirty-five miles to the southeast.

Information: Supervisor, Chattahoochee National Forest, Box 1437, Gainesville, Georgia 30501.

🌲 The Joyce Kilmer Memorial Forest, just south of Great Smoky Mountains National Park, has existed for many years as a tribute to the author of the poem "Trees." Now the proposed **Joyce Kilmer Wilderness** takes in an expanded territory that includes the upper parts of Santeetlah, Slickrock, Yellowhammer, and other creeks in the Nantahala National Forest of western North Carolina. Because of its remote location, in rugged, mile-high mountain country on the Tennessee border, and owing to the difficulty of penetrating some of the dense thickets and steep forested slopes, the area possesses much virgin forest. In other portions, the forest has regrown over logged areas and the old lumber roads have now become trails. Among the notable trees are yellow poplar, hemlock, oak, sycamore, basswood, and beech, including some huge trees of 80-inch diameter and over 150 feet in height. As for fishing opportunities, the waters of Slickrock Creek are known as one of the finest native brown trout fisheries in the eastern United States. Access to this 32,500-acre wild area is via U.S. Route 129 and forest roads. Campgrounds are available just outside the boundary and accommodations may be secured in the surrounding region.

Information: Supervisor, Nantahala National Forest, Box 2750, Asheville, North Carolina 28802.

🌲 The proposed **Cheoah Bald Wilderness** is well known to Appalachian Trail hikers. Traveling through Nantahala National Forest in western North

Carolina, they climb up over this wide-open summit and get good views of the misty southern highlands, then proceed northward, down to Fontana Dam and beyond to Great Smoky Mountains National Park. The wilderness area of 19,000 acres covers all sides of the mountain as well as its 5,062-foot summit. On one side is the scenic Nantahala Gorge. There are cliffs, cascades, deep virgin forests on steep slopes, spires of blue slate, and hiking trails that penetrate the remote and quiet coves. Approach roads include U.S. routes 19 and 129 and State Route 28. Accommodations may be secured at resorts and villages in the region.

Information: Supervisor, Nantahala National Forest, Box 2750, Asheville, North Carolina 28802.

🌲 The proposed **Snowbird Creek Wilderness** of western North Carolina is a 15,000-acre area of rugged ridges, deep forests, waterfalls, and rushing streams. Trails lead up Snowbird and Sassafras creeks, and the hiker is required to ford the streams at intervals. This can be a difficult task at high water; the region receives up to eighty inches of rainfall a year. Snowbird Creek is noted for its trout fishing, but the interior of this area is difficult to penetrate, so travelers should be well equipped and experienced in wilderness travel. Approach is via U.S. Route 129 and forest roads. Food and lodging are available in the surrounding region.

Information: Supervisor, Nantahala National Forest, Box 2750, Asheville, North Carolina 28802.

🌲 Where Georgia, South Carolina, and North Carolina meet lies the proposed **Ellicott's Rock Wilderness,** a hundred miles northwest of Atlanta. Within its 3,600 acres are the Chattooga River, Fork and Glade mountains, and hardwood forests that have been so well protected for so many years that unusually large oaks and poplars exist. The topography of high ridges and deep valleys affords rugged and interesting hiking opportunities. Access is via state routes 28 and 107. A number of campgrounds may be found just outside the area, and accommodations are available in nearby communities.

Information: Supervisor, Sumter National Forest, 1801 Assembly Street, Columbia, South Carolina 29201; Supervisor, National Forests in North Carolina, Box 2750, Asheville, North Carolina 28802; and Supervisor, Chattahoochee National Forest, Box 1437, Gainesville, Georgia 30501.

Canoe waterway and bald cypress forest,
Okefenokee National Wildlife Refuge, Georgia.

Grand Prairie, Okefenokee National Wildlife Refuge, Georgia.

2. WOODS AND SWAMPS

At the origin of the Suwannee River is the famed Okefenokee Swamp, preserved as the **Okefenokee National Wildlife Refuge.** The river constitutes the southwestern outlet of the swamp, a vast basin of tannin-tinted waters that seem stable and stagnant at first glance but are actually rich, fresh, and flowing. As any canoeist who has made his way up the channels to Big Water Lake will vow, the swamp has a decided current.

In fact, deep within Okefenokee, where the cypresses are strung with Spanish moss, the spatterdock beds are dotted with yellow blossoms, and shrubby banks of white-flowered Gordonia seem to float above the surface, a visitor gets the impression of anything but stability. He steps out on land and thinks he is on terra firma, only to find that his steps start small trees and shrubs bobbing up and down: He has anchored to a broad floating island. The swamp is in reality a giant peat bog filling a huge saucer-shaped sandy basin.

To catalog the beauty and natural phenomena of Okefenokee would take a long time. Its major environments are cypress forests, where buttresses and trunks line canoe routes like walls and their knees protrude from the mirrorlike waters; "prairies" that are actually watery expanses covered with lily pads that measure up to twelve inches across; and true islands on which grow southern forests of pine, oak, maple, and magnolia.

Okefenokee National Wildlife Refuge is located in southeasternmost Georgia, off U.S. routes 1 and 441 south of Waycross, and forty miles northwest of Jacksonville, Florida. Inside the swamp, one feels a thousand miles from civilization. Thanks to restrictions imposed by the U.S. Department of the Interior, ·Okefenokee is not likely to be overrun by the modern specter of too many tourists. Entry permits are required for overnight canoe camping and on each of the seven designated canoe trails in this 377,528-acre wilderness no more than one party will be permitted each day. The minimum size of each party will be one canoe and two persons and the maximum ten canoes and/or twenty persons. Parties may camp only one night at each site; there are either wooden platforms or dry islands on which to rest. Open fires are prohibited (except on island campsites) and all trash must be carried out.

With enforcement of such "quality control," Okefenokee should continue to provide a wilderness experience for visitors, though not necessarily a comfortable experience. On summer evenings the mosquitoes can be fierce. Deerflies are sometimes a menace. Care must be taken to avoid alligators and poisonous snakes, and hence swimming is not allowed. The heat and humidity are often high and oppressive. Heavy rains drench the swamp in summer, and lightning frequently bangs around like a flashing sword. Peat "blowups" in the watery passageways may require the traveler to get out and pull his canoe through. There is also the possibility of getting lost if the canoeist strays from the main routes.

This points up the suitability of the habitat more for wild animals than for man. With so many parts of the swamp inaccessible to human beings, no one knows how many alligators there are, but refuge officials estimate about 6,000. This makes life harrowing for raccoons, a favorite food of alligators, but the populations seem to be in balance. Bears eat just about anything they can find, from palmetto buds and acorns to honeybees. Prothonotary warblers nest in swamp trees, and red-cockaded woodpeckers in pines. There are eleven species of herons, egrets, and bitterns living on the swamp prairies, but perhaps the most famous residents there are Florida sandhill cranes. Armadillos, barred owls, wood ducks, soft-shelled turtles, frogs, fish, crayfish, droves of damselflies—there seems to be no end to the list of Okefenokee inhabitants. To get an introduction to the swamp, visitors can take short boat excursions or canoe trips on their own. Museums, self-guiding trails, and observation towers are available, plus a mile-long boardwalk into the wetlands on the east side. Accommodations are available outside the boundaries of the Refuge. Access is by U.S. routes 1, 23, and 441, and state routes 2, 94, and 177.

Information: Manager, Okefenokee National Wildlife Refuge, Box 117, Waycross, Georgia 31501.

🌲 A field investigation report was made by the U.S. Department of the Interior in 1964 on the proposed **Suwannee National River.** Originating in Okefenokee Swamp, Georgia, the Suwannee flows 250 miles south through Florida to the Gulf of Mexico. Though Stephen Foster never saw it, he made it famous in his popular song, "Old Folks at Home." The Interior Department report concluded that with its crystal-clear springs, sculptured limestone banks, and wealth of flora and fauna, the river and its environs emerged as a resource of unique character with a combination of outstanding features. It was considered one of the foremost opportunities in the Southeast for preservation of a free-flowing stream of its type. In the balmy climate (average annual temperature is 70°) the stream flows through dense woods of willow, cypress, ash, oak, gum, and magnolia. On higher, drier sites grow pines with an understory of palmetto. Human construction has not yet ruined the river, and a band of trees lines the river for most of its route, which at least gives the illusion of wilderness travel. Deer, turkeys, bears, and wildcats still thrive in the region, as do numerous smaller mammals and birds. Fish in the river include largemouth bass, Suwannee bass, crappie, bluegill, and other species. Swimming is a popular pastime at springs along the route. Canoeing and boating opportunities are exceptional.

At this writing, establishment of the Suwannee as a national river is still under study. Meanwhile, the river is widely enjoyed as a recreation resource, especially from such points as Suwannee River State Park, Florida, on U.S. Route 90, some seventy-five miles west of Jacksonville. Food, lodging, campgrounds, and other facilities are available along the river. Hopefully, the recreation experience will continue to possess at least a touch of the wild country that William Bartram wrote about so engrossingly in his excursions during the colonial era.

Information: Director, Florida Department of Natural Resources, Tallahassee, Florida 32304.

Wild swamps and river bottoms in the southeastern United States cover millions of acres; there are vast tracts along the Santee River in South Carolina, the Altamaha and Ocmulgee rivers in Georgia, the Tensas River in Louisiana, and various streams in Florida. Grand Bay Swamp in Georgia covers about 20,000 acres, Corkscrew Swamp in Florida more than 10,000 acres, and Reelfoot Lake in Tennessee some 20,000 acres. One of the largest true wilderness swamps remaining is the **Great Dismal Swamp,** which covers about 500,000 acres on the boundary between southeastern Virginia and northeastern North Carolina. Ever since George Washington, men have been digging canals in attempts to drain this swamp and make it "useful," but even though some ecological changes were wrought, it still remains an enormous system of natural lakes, woods, and wetlands. Giant cypresses grow out of the deep-water areas. In places half water, half land, the gums, magnolia, and pawpaw prevail. On more or less dry islands grow poplars, oaks, and hollys.

Yet all this only introduces the complexity of the Great Dismal Swamp. A host of other trees grow in it, of course, and many kinds of wild flowers. The place is so colorful and fragrant at times with such plants as yellow jessamine, camellia, azalea, and pepperbush that one wonders why it was ever called "dismal." Perhaps the name came from the dark waters, deep shadows, and poisonous snakes that abound. Colonel William Byrd, who surveyed the Virginia–North Carolina boundary through the swamp in 1728 called it a body of "dirt and nastiness" and said that "foul damps ascend without ceasing, corrupt the air, and render it unfit for respiration."

But the woods are filled with songs of warblers and frogs in spring. Butterflies feed on the nectar of heaths. Bears dig out honey from holes in the oaks. River otters hunt crayfish in swamp channels. The big short-tailed shrew is considered unique to this area. And the little grass frog, no bigger than a dime, inhabits the bog environment. Even in winter the swamp is a lively place. Biologists estimate that a million robins use Great Dismal Swamp as a winter roost. More remarkable yet is the roost in an evergreen shrub and boggy area where 30 million blackbirds, cowbirds, grackles, and starlings gather.

Perhaps the most extraordinary paradox is that this swamp still exists, lying as it does virtually on the outskirts of the metropolitan Norfolk area. It is accessible simply because U.S. Route 17 and other roads approach it or cut across it. Fortunately, through what is one of the most remarkable corporate gifts of recent times, the Union Camp Corporation donated nearly 50,000 acres in the heart of the swamp, including Lake Drummond, to the United States through The Nature Conservancy. This land is now managed by the U.S. Department of the Interior as a national wildlife refuge. On October 9, 1972, Congress authorized a study to determine the feasibility and desirability of preserving the entire swamp. This study was targeted for completion in October, 1974. Therefore, except for limited public access, all camping, accommodations, and other facilities are virtually nil until plans can be formulated and a determination made of the priorities between wildlife and man in this highly fragile environment. Suffice it for now that so valuable a part of the American heritage, which George Washington called a "glorious paradise" for wildlife, has been saved.

Information: Regional Director, Bureau of Sport Fisheries and Wildlife, U.S. Department of the Interior, John W. McCormack Post Office and Courthouse, Boston, Massachusetts 02109.

🌲 Not all of these near-pristine swamps of the southeastern states are yet assured of protection. A few miles south of Gadsden, South Carolina, lies the **Congaree Swamp,** a surprisingly uncut section of virgin lowlands along the Congaree River. The strip is narrow, and as of this writing still private land, but has happily not been decimated. It is a rare example of an original southern hardwood swamp. Rich soil, often inundated by the winding Congaree River, supports trees of unusual dimensions: a bald cypress 160 feet tall; a sweetgum 117 feet; a willow oak 155 feet; even a holly eight feet in circumference and 95 feet tall. The "knees" beneath the cypress trees in places rise more than six feet out of the mud. There are nineteen species of sedge, thirteen grasses (including giant cane); seven kinds of oak; five hickories; and such uncommon trees as swamp cyrilla and flatwoods plum. The swamp is of ecological interest because several relatively undisturbed ecosystems are found in close association: forests, lakes, bogs, sloughs, creeks, and rivers.

State and county roads provide access to the swamp area, but since the lands are private, entry requires permission from the property owners. Once out in a johnboat, drifting down Cedar Creek beneath the silent shadows of giant trees, a visitor is apt to feel a sense of isolation not too common in Carolina's woods. A proposal to establish a Congaree Swamp National Monument has been pending for years; the National Park Service considered the site a biological community of rare quality and considerable scientific value, complementing the well-preserved upland forests in Great Smoky Mountains National Park.

🌲 South of Washington, D.C., is a notable parcel of 11,000 acres called **Prince William Forest Park,** on Quantico Creek near the Quantico Marine Base in Virginia. More than thirty-five miles of trails provide circuits through meadows, pine and oak woods, and along streams. During wet seasons the forests are full of colorful mushrooms. In spring the parade of wild flowers—bluet, fawn lily, lady's slipper—is led off by skunk cabbage, which may open its blossoms as early as January. The brilliantly colored foliage of autumn, and the dry, clear days in October, provide an exceptional environment for hikes. Pyrite mines, beaver dams, lakes, and secluded rocky glens are a few of the attractions. Facilities are limited to a picnic area, campground, and group camps. The park, administered by the National Park Service, is located just west of Interstate 95 near Triangle, Virginia. Accommodations are available in nearby towns.

Information: Manager, Prince William Forest Park, Box 208, Triangle, Virginia 22172.

🌲 Sixty miles northeast of Columbia, South Carolina, is a section of rolling sandhills where agricultural attempts were abandoned years ago and some 46,000 acres set aside as the **Carolina Sandhills National Wildlife Refuge.**

343

The resilience of nature has been remarkably demonstrated because the wild aspects of the land are rapidly rebounding. Deer and beaver, says the U.S. Department of the Interior, have staged tremendous comebacks. Obviously the ecosystem is healing, for there are also bobcats, foxes, opossums, large flocks of ducks and geese, and the once-vanished wild turkey. The forest itself is regrowing to more than pine and scrub oak. A self-guided auto tour, several miles of trails, a wildlife observation tower, and a photo blind provide visitors with opportunities to study sandhill ecosystems at close range. Facilities are also available for picnicking and fishing. Access is via state routes 33 and 145. Accommodations may be secured in nearby communities.

Information: Manager, Carolina Sandhills National Wildlife Refuge, McBee, South Carolina 29101.

🌲 More than 13,000 acres along the lower Savannah River, half in Georgia, half in South Carolina, constitute the **Savannah National Wildlife Refuge,** and notwithstanding highways across it, dikes, impoundments, and the remains of an intensive nineteenth-century rice industry, the existing marshes, swamps, and woods are regaining some wild aspects. They certainly attract birds—including migrants from both the Atlantic and Mississippi flyways. Ducks, coots, and gallinules are common in winter. Ibises collect in large numbers during the summer to feed on fish. Anhingas, herons, egrets, alligators, white-tailed deer—the refuge is a microcosm of southeastern habitats. Hiking, wildlife observations, and limited fishing and hunting are permitted. The fish most often caught are bluegill, crappie, bass, and flounder; also to be found along the river are rockfish, catfish, and redbreast. In the northern part of the refuge grow hardwood forests and some nearly virgin stands of slash pine. Access is from U.S. Route 17, tne miles north of Savannah, Georgia. Food and lodging may be secured in nearby communities.

Information: Manager, Savannah National Wildlife Refuge, Route 1, Hardeeville, South Carolina 29927.

🌲 Some of the hill country on the east side of the Ocmulgee River, about fifteen miles north of Macon, Georgia, has been preserved as the **Piedmont National Wildlife Refuge.** Its 33,000 acres contain oak-pine forest, which with wildlife communities of deer, turkeys, quail, and red-cockaded wood-peckers, are recovering from the timber-cutting and farming practices of the past. It is a quiet land, except for the call of the turkey gobbler, the songs of warblers in spring, or the chants of chuck-will's-widows at evening. There is also the music of tumbling streams. In mid-April the flower display begins with crimson maple blooms and bursts of white dogwood, and later the orange blooms of yellow poplar open in the treetops. Trails reach the more remote sections of the refuge. Access is via state routes 11, 18, 83, and 87. Accommodations may be obtained in Macon and other nearby communities. Visitors should check with the refuge manager for current information and regulations.

Information: Manager, Piedmont National Wildlife Refuge, Round Oak, Georgia 31080.

🌲 Along the Sipsey Fork of the Black Warrior River, in northwestern Alabama, lies the proposed **Sipsey Wilderness** of up to 12,000 acres. It is characterized by narrow ridges, deep valleys, connected canyons, numerous waterfalls, and a diversity of plant life. This area of Alabama lies in a transition zone between the piney woods country of the Coastal Plain and the hardwoods of the Appalachian Mountains, hence pines and hardwoods mix here, depending on the slope, exposure, moisture, depth of soil, and other environmental factors. Part of the area has been protected for more than half a century as the Bee Branch Scenic Area. There are sheer sandstone cliffs covered with ferns and mountain laurel. Campgrounds and accommodations may be secured in the national forests or in neighboring towns. Access is via state, county, and forest roads northeast of Haleyville, Alabama.

Information: Supervisor, National Forests in Alabama, Box 40, Montgomery, Alabama 36101.

🌲 The proposed **Bradwell Bay Wilderness,** in the Florida Panhandle, twenty-five miles southwest of Tallahassee, is not a seashore site but a "bay" known to southeasterners as a forest community in a swampy habitat. Since the area of about 22,000 acres is roadless, the swamp is difficult to get to. Perhaps that is the reason a small patch of virgin slash pine, some individuals in which are over a hundred feet tall, remains on an island within the swamp. Also present are cypress, black gum, and other species in a rich subtropical ecosystem. The animal life includes alligators, deer, bears, and turkeys. The site can be approached via U.S. Route 319 and State Route 375. (St. Marks National Wildlife Refuge lies about ten miles to the southeast, on the coast of the Gulf of Mexico.) Accommodations are available in nearby communities.

Information: Supervisor, National Forests in Florida, Box 1050, Tallahassee, Florida 32301.

🌲 In **Lake Woodruff National Wildlife Refuge,** twenty miles west of Daytona Beach, Florida, are marshes, meadows, hardwood swamps, pine woods, scrub lands, and lakes along the St. Johns River. These ecosystems form attractive stopover points for migratory birds accustomed to each: ducks on the water; warblers in trees and shrubs; ground doves in open places; phoebes on dikes in marshes. Some species of birds are resident year round, including anhingas, herons, egrets, wood ducks, vultures, hawks, ospreys, pine warblers, yellowthroats, redwings, grackles, and cardinals. Although managed for the benefit of waterfowl, and rare and endangered species of wildlife, there are still wild aspects in this 18,400-acre refuge. Mammals, for example, inhabit the refuge, and visitors may see deer, bobcats, and raccoons, among others. The subtropics are represented by alligators, armadillos, and associated life forms. Access is via State Route 40. There are no campgrounds or accommodations on the refuge, but food and lodging may be secured at nearby DeLeon Springs or at DeLand, seven miles away.

Information: Manager, Lake Woodruff National Wildlife Refuge, Box 488, DeLeon Springs, Florida 32028.

🌲 In **Myakka River State Park,** seventeen miles east of Sarasota, a touch of original Florida remains in 28,875 acres of protected lakes, streams, and subtropical woods. The park was named after the Myacca Indians, who discovered the valley centuries ago and utilized its rich soils, wildlife populations, and forest resources. More than 200 species of birds are known from the area. Swimming is not permitted, but boats may be rented for use on the river and Myakka Lake, and anglers may fish for bass, bream, perch, and catfish. A three-mile trail leads through hammocks of live oak and cabbage palm to a primitive campground; all supplies, including water for cooking and drinking, must be packed in and all refuse packed out. Other campgrounds, closer to roads, are available within the park, as are cottages, food, and supplies. A scenic drive passes through the park, and guided tours are provided. Access is via State Route 72.

Information: Manager, Myakka River State Park, Route 1, Box 72, Sarasota, Florida 33577.

🌲 Much of the region in the vicinity of Corkscrew Swamp is still devoid of urbanization and heavy industry, a fortunate circumstance though there is ample farmland. Even so, the ecological balance of southern Florida's natural environments is so dependent on fresh water, largely from Lake Okeechobee, that attempts are being made to establish a freshwater reserve. Drainage, settlement, and other man-made alterations could wipe out many of the original biosystems, including those in Everglades National Park, a situation some Floridians think is already far advanced. This **Big Cypress Fresh Water Reserve,** when established, would include thousands of acres north of the Tamiami Trail, and would conserve water for neighboring human communities, too. It would also, surprisingly, help the shrimp-fishing industry off Sanibel Island and in the Dry Tortugas; the life cycles of numerous organisms in Florida Bay are dependent on estuarine nursery zones that are linked to seasonal flows of fresh water and assorted debris from inland. Access is via local roads.

🌲 Of all the great "strands," or islandlike groves of cypress forest that once grew in southern Florida, only a few have remained unlogged. The largest is preserved in the 11,000-acre **Corkscrew Swamp Sanctuary,** owned and operated by the National Audubon Society. Even lumbermen themselves contributed to saving this swamp, joining thousands of donors who raised hundreds of thousands of dollars to purchase the tract. Named for a small creek that meanders in a corkscrew pattern, the swamp is a complete ecosystem dominated by cypress trees as much as 130 feet tall, 25 feet in circumference, and 700 years old. There are also abundant epiphytes, or air plants, that grow on the limbs and trunks of trees, ferns of enormous size, maple, myrtle, orchids, hanging strands of Spanish moss, vines of strangler fig, wild hibiscus with vivid red flowers up to eight inches across, marshes covered with willows, and lakes of lettuce. These latter do not contain the table variety, but a green, leafy, free-floating plant called water lettuce (*Pistia stratiotes*), which was frequently seen by William Bartram on his wide-ranging travels through the southeastern states in the 1770s. Since then water lettuce has been largely crowded out by water hyacinth (*Eichhornia crassipes*), introduced from the tropics nearly a century ago.

Even in June, when drought has nearly drained Florida's ponds and lakes, the water lettuce survives and there is still an aspect of luxuriance in Corkscrew Swamp. Going into the area is like entering a broad green tunnel. The sun seems far away and irrelevant, though of course it nourishes the living organisms. Odors of brackish water and decaying life assail the senses as one goes deeper, walking on a loop trail and boardwalk more than a mile long. White-eyed vireos sing in the trees, and storks and ibises fly overhead, barely seen through the canopy of interlaced leaves. Carolina wrens zip in and out of the understory and trill melodious songs that travel for long distances through the woods. The forest rattles with "drumbeats" as pileated woodpeckers drill in dying trunks.

Beneath the birds and the shrubbery lies a stratum of reptiles and other ground- or water-dwelling organisms, of which the most conspicuous are alligators. A side trail leads to a central marsh surrounded by forest; in it, alligators can be seen among the leaves of water lettuce.

In summary, Corkscrew Swamp contains a part of the original American heritage: the largest remaining stand of virgin bald cypress and some of the oldest trees in eastern North America. The Sanctuary, sixteen miles west of Immokalee, is reached off Florida Route 846. There are picnic sites near the area but no camping. A full range of food and lodging may be secured in Naples, thirty miles to the southwest on U.S. Route 41.

Information: Director, Corkscrew Swamp Sanctuary, Box 1875, R. D. 2, Sanctuary Road, Naples, Florida 33940.

Little blue heron on water lettuce,
Corkscrew Swamp Sanctuary, Florida.
Photograph by Michael Sutton.

Key deer, National Key Deer Refuge, Florida.

3. ATLANTIC SHORE

Part of the Outer Banks of North Carolina were incorporated more than forty years ago into the first national seashore in the United States. Named after its most prominent headland, **Cape Hatteras National Seashore** protects a seventy-one-mile-long stretch of sand and varies in width from a few yards to three miles. Although a road runs the length of the islands of Bodie, Hatteras, and Ocracoke, and villages exist at intervals, the shifting shores and steadily changing dunes extend virtually undisturbed—as close to a wild beach as can be found these days in such a settled region. But sand and sea oats are by no means the only environment. Hatteras Island has woods of holly, pine, and oak, and freshwater and saline marshes abound. There are even ponds and lakes, all of which have been attractive to migrating waterfowl for unknown millenniums. Usually by late October thousands of Canada geese and snow geese begin arriving for the winter. The thickets are full of warblers in spring.

May at Cape Hatteras can be bitterly cold, but there is just enough of the tropics to attract egrets and herons. Mosquitoes are abundant at times, as are blowing sands, and of course, occasional hurricanes that pound the islands with high winds and raging waves. But the sandbanks are flexible and resilient; they change at the commands of wind and wave. Although determined attempts have been made to hold back the waves—by sandbagging, sand-pumping, and dune stabilization with brush and grass—the sea has consistently won. It has taken two Cape Hatteras lighthouses and lapped at the base of the present one. Clearly, these islands are dynamic, and while the seaside erodes, the bayside expands in widening marshes. As the experience of Monomoy and Fire Island has suggested, such islands are not the place for permanent human habitations.

Cape wildlife seems always restless. Laughing gulls chatter without seeming to stop. Sanderlings skitter along the wet beach, hunting for sand fleas and other small crustaceans. Visitors may swim, beachcomb, fish, hunt waterfowl, camp, picnic, and observe wildlife. Visitor center exhibits and naturalist programs explain the many seashore phenomena. Accommodations are plentiful. Access is via U.S. Route 158, south from Nags Head.

Information: Superintendent, Cape Hatteras National Seashore, Box 457, Manteo, North Carolina 27954.

🌲 Some wildlife refuges, managed for the production of wild animals, are not classified as wilderness because of the presence of dikes, artificial ponds, and various necessary environmental manipulations. Nevertheless, they are open to the public for wildlife-oriented recreation (hiking, bird watching, nature study, and the like) and thus represent at least an approach to wilderness where there may be no true wilderness for hundreds of miles. **Pea Island National Wildlife Refuge,** located within the boundaries of Cape Hatteras National Seashore, contains 5,915 acres of sand dunes, ocean beaches, brushland, marshes, and ponds, and 25,700 acres in Pamlico Sound. It is an important wintering ground for snow geese, Canada geese, whistling swans, and several species of ducks. Located on the northernmost 13.5 miles of Hatteras Island, the refuge may be reached on North Carolina Route 12 from Nags Head. Visitors may walk along the dike of the North Pond to observe wildlife. Camping facilities and other accommodations may be obtained in or near the surrounding national seashore.

Information: Manager, Pea Island National Wildlife Refuge, Box 606, Manteo, North Carolina 27954.

🌲 Off the Maryland and Virginia coast, **Assateague Island National Seashore** will consist, when land acquisition is completed, of 39,630 acres and thirty-seven miles of sandy shore, ocean, bay, dunes, myrtle thickets, marsh, and pine woodlands. The area is known not only for its native wildlife but for its wild ponies, legendary survivors of the wreck of a Spanish galleon, and sika deer, natives of Japan. A natural avenue for migrating birds, its location on the Atlantic Flyway makes the island a mecca for thousands of ducks, geese, warblers, willets, and other species. Associated with the Seashore are Assateague State Park, Maryland, and Chincoteague National Wildlife Refuge, Virginia. Much of the island is still in a primitive state, with access only at each end. Swimming, camping, picnicking, fishing, photography, and nature study are among the most popular activities. Accommodations are available in communities on the mainland, but of course are crowded on holidays and weekends. Access is via Maryland State Route 611 and Virginia State Route 175.

Information: Superintendent, Assateague National Seashore, Route 2, Box 294, Berlin, Maryland 21811.

🌲 **Chincoteague National Wildlife Refuge,** located on Assateague Island from the Maryland boundary south into Virginia, contains 9,447 acres, and is probably best known for its population of wild ponies. There is a great deal more than ponies, however, and visitors should allow at least two days to cover the varied habitats. First there are the beach and backwater, separated by grass-covered dunes, stretching for miles in a relatively wild environment. Then the woods begin, deep forests of pine, holly, oak, myrtle, sumac, sassafras, cherry, and maple, with occasional marshes. And finally, freshwater ponds that harbor ospreys, ducks, geese, ibises, and other water birds.

The best time to be in these woods, or at the ponds or on the beach, is early morning, preferably from sunrise on, because the air and water are usually calmest then and the songs of orioles, warblers, and indigo buntings can be heard. Old roads through the woods make good hiking trails; driving on levees is permitted at certain hours of the day. Campgrounds, food, and lodging are available on Chincoteague Island, two miles to the west. Access to both Chincoteague and Assateague islands is via State Route 175.

Information: Manager, Chincoteague National Wildlife Refuge, Box 62, Chincoteague, Virginia 23336.

South of Cape Hatteras the protected Outer Banks continue without interruption for forty miles to the south in **Cape Lookout National Seashore.** Actually the Seashore was authorized in 1966, but the land has not been acquired by the U.S. government, and as of this writing there are no federal facilities. When acquisition is completed, the size of the Seashore will be 24,500 acres. The land is presently unoccupied, a narrow, broken strip of sand, sea oats, and marsh grass that curves forty miles from Ocracoke Island to the tip of Cape Lookout. It is known collectively as the Core Banks, very likely after the Coree Indians who once lived in the region. The islands were once a center of intensive mullet fishing. The Seashore will also include Shackleford Banks, another sand segment that extends at a right angle from Cape Lookout eight miles in a northwesterly direction to Beaufort Inlet. Access is by boat or air. Accommodations may be secured in Beaufort and other mainland communities.

Information: Superintendent, Cape Lookout National Seashore, Box 690, Beaufort, North Carolina 28516.

In 1965 the U.S. Department of the Interior conducted a study of the **Cape Fear** area, south of Wilmington, North Carolina. The sandspits, beaches, salt marshes, and live-oak forests were found to be wild and primitive and judged to be of national significance. A 13,000-acre Cape Fear National Monument was proposed, but the land at that time was privately owned by one person, and the proposed monument was never established. At this writing the project is dormant.

351

🌲 The seas have washed away parts of Atlantic islands no telling how many times, but the resilient land and life come back. New channels, new islands, new marshes are formed. If live oaks, magnolias, pines, and palmettos are destroyed in one place, they spring up in another. An example is **Cape Romain National Wildlife Refuge,** which, including adjacent waters, protects 60,000 acres along fifteen miles of the Atlantic shore. Located twenty miles northeast of Charleston, South Carolina, it is typical alligator country, and loggerhead turtles nest on the sandy beaches. But the Cape belongs mostly to birds. Some come and go with the seasons, but more than a hundred species nest here, and it is not unusual to see bald eagles every day. Sandy areas are occupied by turnstones, dowitchers, knots, and plovers. On treeless islands, terns and brown pelicans nest. Willets and dunlins prefer mud flats. Rails keep to marshes, coots and gallinules to ponds, and warblers to woods. A continuous movement of birds takes place, and in summer the avian population changes to egrets, herons, ibises, and other summering species. Visitors may fish, photograph, swim, and study the natural scene, but certain restrictions apply, especially when birds and turtles are nesting. Access is off U.S. Route 17, but boats are required to reach the offshore isles. Accommodations may be obtained in communities on the mainland.

Information: Manager, Cape Romain National Wildlife Refuge, Route 1, Box 191, Awendaw, South Carolina 29429.

🌲 **Wolf Island National Wildlife Refuge,** on the Atlantic coast at the mouth of the Altamaha River, is located ten miles offshore from Darien, Georgia. Wolf Island itself is little more than 500 acres in area, but refuge authorities administer a total of 4,218 acres, which includes lands leased from The Nature Conservancy. The wild land and seascape, with vegetation consisting mainly of sea oats, sandburrs, myrtle, and marsh plants, is much more attractive to gulls, plovers, knots, pelicans, oyster catchers, skimmers, and other birds than to men. Indeed, there are no human-use facilities or developments in the area, which is mostly tidal marsh, and visitors approach by boat principally to observe the bird life. Sandy beaches exist, but they are important nesting areas, especially for loggerhead turtles, and human beings who want to swim should proceed to other areas along the Georgia coast. At certain times of the year, public entry is restricted or prohibited. "The island's value to birds, turtles, marine fishes and other wildlife," says the U.S. Department of the Interior, "can best be maintained by preserving the area in a natural condition. Intensive management and public use would destroy the very things that now make the refuge important." The nearest food and lodging are in communities on the mainland.

Information: Wolf Island National Wildlife Refuge is administered by the Manager, Savannah National Wildlife Refuge, Route 1, Hardeeville, South Carolina 29927.

🌲 Off the coast of Georgia lie the Golden Isles—Wassaw, Ossabaw, St. Catherines, Sapelo, St. Simons, Jekyll, and Cumberland—a string of attractive islands where a little of the original Georgia remains. Southernmost and wildest is Cumberland Island, inaccessible except by boat or air, and endowed with ocean beaches and dunes, salt marshes, freshwater lakes, ponds, and swamps, palmetto thickets, and forests of sabal palm, magnolia, cedar, pine, and moss-hung live oak. After years of effort it was finally authorized by Congress in 1972 as **Cumberland Island National Seashore.** The island covers about 40,000 acres, measures seventeen miles from end to end and is located on the Georgia-Florida boundary at the mouth of the St. Marys River. Deer are common, but most of the other mammals are small. Extensive marshes provide feeding grounds for fish and waterfowl as well as breeding sites for the clapper rail, long-billed marsh wren, sharp-tailed and seaside sparrows, marsh rabbit, and other species. The beaches are ideal for swimming. Offshore, fishermen may take pompano, snapper, flounder, Spanish mackerel, and channel bass. At present, Cumberland Island is closed to public use while land acquisition and development proceed.

Information: Superintendent, Cumberland Island National Seashore, Box 960, Kingsland, Georgia 31548.

Young alligator on water lettuce, Corkscrew Swamp Sanctuary, Florida. Photograph by Michael Sutton.

4. SUBTROPICS AND SEA

For a long time they were unwanted lands, hot, humid, remote, almost impenetrable, alive with cottonmouths and alligators. Unwanted, that is, except by the animals that occupied them, a delicately balanced subtropical wildlife evolved into unique ecosystems. Such were the Everglades, the Florida gulf islands, the keys, the cypress swamps. Naturalists early recognized their long-range value and were aghast to think how impoverished the American heritage would be without them. After protracted battles, these naturalists, sometimes led by local citizens with an almost evangelic zeal, convinced the U.S. Congress that reserves should be established before it was too late. Thus, a string of wildlife reservations was inaugurated at a time when little was known about ecology. Then, as settlement swept southward (or outward from such cities as Miami) the wild places became pockets of original Florida almost in a sea of alien construction. Their value grew, though the threat of being dismantled in favor of industrial progress remained even after two major projects—a jetport in the Everglades and a cross-Florida barge canal—were canceled in midconstruction.

🌲 On the Gulf of Mexico, twenty miles south of Tallahassee, lies the **St. Marks National Wildlife Refuge,** of which 17,746 acres of salt marsh, woods, and swamps have been set aside as wilderness. Over the approximately half a century that the refuge has existed some phenomenal concentrations of wildlife have become routine: 1,200 Canada geese, 120,000 ducks, and 30,000 coots. Many of these are visible from roads that lead along portions of the wilderness boundary. Also seen are ospreys, white-tailed deer, otters, raccoons, opossums, alligators, and even an occasional black bear. With luck, the visitor may see rarer species such as bald eagles and sandhill cranes. Boating and fishing are also possible among the islands in Apalachee Bay and along coastal waterways. Hikers may take advantage of trails through pine, oak, magnolia, palmetto, holly, and bald cypress forests, or investigate such environments as the tidal creek, bayou pool, marsh, and bay. Access is via U.S. Route 98. Accommodations may be secured in nearby communities.

Information: Manager, St. Marks National Wildlife Refuge, Box 68, St. Marks, Florida 32355.

🌲 The **Cedar Keys Wilderness** is composed of a group of islands with white sand shores, mangrove swamps, and hammock forests of cabbage palm, laurel oak, and red bay trees. Four islands—Seahorse, North, Snake, and Deadmans keys—are included in the wilderness, and although none is very far from the mainland, they are difficult to get to by boat because of shallow mud flats around them. But birds get to them by the thousands, which is a major reason for the sanctuary. The isles are small—378 acres total for the four—but their importance to migratory and colonial birds is immense: As many as 50,000 egrets, cormorants, herons, and other species are raised on the keys each year, and bald eagles and ospreys also nest. The islands also support the most northerly nesting colony of endangered brown pelicans on the Florida coast; each year about 400 young are raised here. The surrounding salt marshes, mangrove flats, and bay waters provide an abundance of food, including oysters, crabs, shrimp, and fish, and the mild climate has made rookery conditions ideal for no one knows how many thousands of years. But the birds are sensitive to intruders and while they are nesting human access to the islands is prohibited. From mid-July through October, however, the public is permitted on the islands, where photography, nature study, shell collecting, picnicking, and beachcombing are the major activities. Hunting, camping, and building fires are prohibited.

The refuge is accessible from the terminus of Florida State Route 24, sixty miles southwest of Gainesville. Accommodations are available in communities on the mainland.

Information: Manager, Chassahowitzka National Wildlife Refuge, Route 1, Box 153, Homosassa, Florida 32646.

🌲 Far down the western coast of Florida are the Ten Thousand Islands, an intricate labyrinth of mangrove-bordered waterways, and the beginning of the largest subtropical wilderness in the United States, **Everglades National Park.** Sometimes a visitor's first impression is lack of belief that such formless flats and grassy emptiness could have been made into a national park. But closer inspection reveals that the Everglades are far from empty, though it takes a while to understand them. In the first place, they are not one habitat but at least half a dozen. The "everglades" proper is a series of broad limestone flats with jagged-edged sawgrass that stretch for miles and through which sheets of water slowly flow from Lake Okeechobee to the Gulf of Mexico. Spotted across the 'glades are slight elevations (in reality, islands) that support dense tropical hardwood forests and are called hammocks. East of the 'glades, on higher—but not much higher—ground, lie open woods of slash pine with saw palmetto and other shrubs. Like the 'glades, these pine lands evolved over millenniums during which wildfires were common, and thus thrive in their original state when man lets the natural fires burn.

In a few places are cypress swamps, and now and then a hammock of mahogany trees with scattered clumps of paurotis palms. But long before the sea is in sight the waters become brackish, and this supports the growth of scattered mangroves. Near the coast both mangrove and buttonwood become very dense. Then, by contrast, there is a desert on the southern shore, a coastal prairie where yuccas thrive on sand dunes. Finally, out in the shallow bay exists a rich aquatic nursery that sustains much of the wildlife of the Everglades.

To canoeists among the mangroves, this wildlife is at every hand, first oysters clinging to the mangrove roots, then mullet and tarpon leaping out of the water, then rare American crocodiles—much less often observed than alligators inland—rare manatees, bald eagles, and finally a wide terrestrial ecosystem in which deer and raccoons are among the most conspicuous mammalian residents. The farther he travels on these wilderness waterways, the more the visitor begins to see that mammals are not nearly as dominant as in, say, Alaska; Everglades is literally for the birds. At the edge of Florida Bay he watches roseate spoonbills sift the muds for fish, shellfish, crustaceans, and insects, or reddish egrets and great white herons poke about for fish. Overhead fly man-o'-war birds, flocks of white ibis, or great numbers of wood ibis spiraling in the haze. In successful nesting years, rookeries are formed and thousands of birds nest on islands in the mangrove-bordered lakes and in Florida Bay. However, nesting seasons are delicate times and park authorities restrict approach to lakes and keys containing rookeries.

Everglades National Park can, of course, be visited by methods of transportation other than canoes or boats. A highway leads through the heart of it and along this route are self-guided walking trails through each of the principal habitats: pinelands, hammocks, sloughs, 'glades, and mangrove swamps. Visitors may go on public tours into the Shark River area at the northern perimeter of the park. Hiking across the 'glades themselves is simply impractical; besides the hindrance of water, there are potholes of dangerous jagged limestone; moreover, the vicious sharp-toothed blades of sawgrass can lacerate clothing and flesh. From December to April, visitors may accompany rangers and naturalists on regularly scheduled "boat-a-cades" and "canoe adventures," bicycle junkets, "slough slogs," discovery hikes, and other programs that interpret the natural history of the 'glades, hammock, and bay environments.

The park is located thirty-five miles southwest of Miami, on Florida State Route 27. The Tamiami Trail, U.S. Route 41, skirts the northern boundary.

Campgrounds, food, and accommodations are available in and near the park.
Information: Superintendent, Everglades National Park, Box 279, Homestead, Florida 33030.

🌲 The United States mainland may terminate at Cape Sable, in Everglades National Park, but wildlife habitats continue out into the water, to beds of Thalassia grass that wave with the currents in shallow bays—and along the Florida Keys. This 130-mile-long chain of limestone isles reaching out to Key West is to a large degree tamed and settled, a favorite locale for persons who want to escape from winter and enjoy a normally benign environment. However, a sizable number of islands still possess abundant animal life because they have been protected as national wildlife refuges, parts of which are now designated as the **Florida Keys Wilderness.** These came about because of battles around the turn of the century to save plume birds (egrets, herons, spoonbills) from being shot for their use in the millinery trade, and efforts later to save disappearing deer. Crowded by civilization, the key deer, a small-sized race of the white-tailed deer, diminished to fifty individuals that occupied only a few of the Florida Keys, where life with hurricanes has perils of its own without man's interference. This deer, which stands about two and a half feet high, became the object of nationwide attempts to set aside certain parts of the keys, an effort that succeeded in 1957 with the establishment of the National Key Deer Refuge. Since then the deer have multiplied to more than 500.

Landscapes, fish, and much of the wildlife of these keys are distinctly West Indian, even though not even Key West lies within the tropics. Mangroves surround or cover the islands; inland grow palmetto, coppery-barked gumbo-limbo, broad-leaved sea grape, poisonwood, and some 300 other species. Access to some of the refuge islands is by road, and on Big Pine Key a visitor can observe typical deer habitat of pine and palmetto. Scores of islands within the wilderness, however, may be reached only by boat, and if the season is right, a visitor's body soon becomes black with mosquitoes. He may also encounter snakes. Offshore, where nearly 600 species of fish inhabit shallow bays or coral reefs, is an utterly different world, well-known for its color.

Information: Manager, National Key Deer Refuge, Box 385, Big Pine Key, Florida 33040.

🌲 Many wilderness areas in North America have aquatic aspects, but one almost entirely under water is **John Pennekamp Coral Reef State Park** in Florida. Some 48,000 acres of protected ocean waters include a living coral reef, not unlike those in other parts of North America (see especially Cahuita National Park, Costa Rica, and Bocas del Toro National Park, Panamá). The park is twenty-one miles long and extends six miles out into the Atlantic Ocean off Key Largo, fifty-five miles south of Miami. Forty species of coral inhabit the reef—including staghorn, elkhorn, brain, hat, leaf, flower, rose, tube, star, starlet, cactus, and finger—and in this complex world live literally hundreds of species of tropical fish, many exceedingly colorful and unusually patterned. Obviously, swimming is the major method of enjoying this park and submerging in its natural environment, but glass-bottom boats, canoes, and pontoon, motor-, sail- and rowboats are available for rental. Visitors may also launch their own water craft. Tours in glass-bottom boats are conducted daily if surface winds are not too severe and bottom sediments not too roiled. Fishing is also permitted, and anglers will find trout or bonefish in the flats or large saltwater species in the Gulf Stream. No license is required for saltwater fishing in Florida. At a public and administrative site on Key Largo are facilities for parking, picnicking, camping, and purchasing food and supplies. Accommodations may be secured at many points along U.S. Route 1, which passes by the park entrance.

Information: Manager, John Pennekamp Coral Reef State Park, Box 487, Key Largo, Florida 33037.

About fifteen miles due south of Miami, Florida, as the porpoise swims, an underwater wilderness of 96,000 acres has been set aside as **Biscayne National Monument.** Together with the John Pennekamp Coral Reef State Park, which lies just to the south, this area helps to assure protection of a large portion of coral reefs and associated aquatic environments off the upper Florida Keys. Biscayne consists of no mainland shore but it does have about twenty-five islands, among them Elliott, Sands, and Old Rhodes keys, seven miles offshore. Eastward of the keys, some four to five miles farther into the Atlantic, the area is bordered by Pacific, Ajax, Long, and Triumph reefs.

For the most part the water is shallow—less than ten feet between the keys and the mainland and increasing to thirty-five feet out toward the reefs. Nourished by the sun, laved by gently moving, warm-water currents, the saltwater ecosystems are remarkably rich. Beds of sea "grasses" shelter multitudes of small fish, as do the complex coral reefs. Sponges, sea feathers, sea whips, neon gobies, angelfish, and wrasses are only a few of the species visible to snorklers.

The shallows and shores are made up mostly of jagged Key Largo limestone, a fossilized coral reef. Access to the Monument is by boat only; public transportation will eventually be instituted. Facilities on Elliott Key include a primitive campground, picnic area, rest rooms, and saltwater showers. There is no potable water. Hiking during winter months is a popular pastime here. Pleasure boating and fishing are major activities on the water. However, the National Park Service strongly warns swimmers to observe safety rules and not swim alone. Public educational and recreational facilities are planned, but the land space is so small and fragile that developments will never be more than minimal. Boats and equipment may be rented on nearby mainland areas. Accommodations are available in communities south of Miami and along U.S. Route 1. Public and private campgrounds may be found near Homestead; the Monument office is temporarily located in Homestead Bayfront Park.

Information: Superintendent, Biscayne National Monument, Box 1369, Homestead, Florida 33030.

🌲 A number of places remain wild in Florida, some small but nevertheless established as national wilderness areas: **Passage Key,** a nearly barren island in Tampa Bay; **Island Bay National Wildlife Refuge,** part of a maze of mangrove islands in Charlotte Harbor; and a group of islands along the east coast that includes the famed **Pelican Island,** first national wildlife refuge established in the U.S.A. The Wilderness Act specifies that wilderness designation of a refuge must be compatible with refuge purposes. These areas are small and fragile, hence restrictions on public use will be imposed when needed to protect wildlife or the wilderness character of the islands. There are no accommodations or facilities.

Information: Regional Director, Bureau of Sport Fisheries and Wildlife, 17 Executive Park Drive, Northeast, Atlanta, Georgia 30329.

Iztaccíhuatl-Popocatépetl National Park, México.

PART IX

México

1. Iztaccíhuatl-Popocatépetl National Park, Morelos-México-Puebla
2. Zoquiapan y Anexos National Park, México
3. El Tepozteco National Park, Morelos
4. Lagunas de Zempoala National Park, Morelos
5. Nevado de Toluca National Park, México
6. Bosencheve National Park, México-Michoacán
7. Los Mármoles National Park, Hidalgo
8. La Malinche National Park, Tlaxcala-Puebla
9. Cofre de Perote National Park, Veracruz
10. Pico de Orizaba National Park, Puebla-Veracruz
11. Cañón del Río Blanco National Park, Veracruz
12. Lagunas de Montebello National Park, Chiapas
13. Lagunas de Chacahua National Park, Oaxaca
14. Pico de Tancítaro National Park, Michoacán
15. Volcán de Colima National Park, Colima-Jalisco
16. El Gogorrón National Park, San Luis Potosí
17. Cumbres de Monterrey National Park, Nuevo León
18. Cumbres de Majalca National Park, Chihuahua
19. Río Bravo International Park, Coahuila
20. Constitución de 1857 National Park, Baja California
21. Sierra de San Pedro Martir National Park, Baja California
22. Barranca del Cobre, Chihuahua
23. Puerto de los Angeles, Durango
24. Barranca de los Negros, Durango
25. Los Azufres, Michoacan

In México the history of wildland preservation dates back to 1898, when the first forest reserve—which later became a national park—was established. Today the country is in a state of rapid forward movement in this field. A great deal of wilderness remains, even though not publicly preserved, because parts of México are more or less inaccessible or nearly uninhabitable. The country's volcanic backbone has numerous summits still reasonably wild, of which only the most outstanding have been declared national parks. There are uninhabited seashores, stretches of coral reefs that few snorklers know, coastal mangrove swamps with lost waterways, and wild rivers that tumble from pool to pool. The tropical forest is in places so dense that men could penetrate it only with great difficulty and even the newly developed island of Cozumel, nearly ringed by a highway, has marshes and dense forests that only mammals, birds, and insects lay claim to. Indeed, Mexican pilots have a repertory of tales about downed colleagues being eaten alive by ants or jaguars or. . . .

In México, as most anywhere else, park and wilderness concepts are gathering momentum. Increasing numbers of Mexicans are tiring of air pollution, poisoned waters, aircraft noise, and fuming traffic jams. The administration, management, and development of national parks is the responsibility of the Subsecretariat of Forests and Wildlife in the Secretariat of Agriculture. The government recently established a national commission to undertake the necessary construction of facilities in natural areas.

Fortunately, much land is *ejido,* i.e., publicly owned, and so México has the potential for extending its park and wilderness system far beyond existing reserves, principally through expropriation and compensation. One example is the geologically significant Pinacate region south of the Arizona boundary, a vast arid land with high temperatures, high mountains, and giant volcanic craters, which is at this writing being considered by Mexican authorities for establishment as a national park and recreation area. If that happens, the combined Pinacate, Organ Pipe Cactus, and Cabeza Prieta reserves could constitute the largest protected wild desert in the western hemisphere.

Other areas under consideration for park status include the Great Central Desert of Baja California; the Seven Craters in Santiago Valley; Cañón de Urique or **Barranca del Cobre,** one of the world's deepest canyons; **Puerto de los Angeles** and **Barranca de los Negros,** on Mexican Route 40 halfway between Durango and Mazatlán; **Los Azufres;** and various seashore areas on the Caribbean coast.

363

As of 1974, there were no fewer than twenty-one national parks larger than 5,000 acres. Most are little known and some are little used; their lack of facilities or access has made them less attractive to tourists than the more celebrated recreation sites or pre-Columbian ruins. Some have not had their boundaries completely delineated. Most have never been developed for tourism. As a result, the visitor must usually check with Mexican forest authorities for information or get detailed directions from local officials in the town nearest his destination. The official Mexican government road map shows all parks clearly, but it would still be advisable for travelers to gather as many details as possible before starting out. The principal office in México City where information may be obtained is Departamento de Parques Nacionales, Secretaría de Agricultura, Aquiles Serdán 28, 8° Piso, México 1, D.F. Information may also be obtained from the Comisión Nacional de Obras en Parques Naturales, Secretaría de Obras Públicas, Dr. Barragán No. 779, Colonia Bertis Narbeta, México 12, D.F.

In the pages that follow, we give brief general data, personal observations, or the observations of Mexican authorities, and the access and nearest towns. Though this text has been checked by Mexican authorities in the departments of Agriculture and Public Works, it must be remembered that since México is in rapid transition, not all of this data may be up-to-date, and new areas may have been established too late for inclusion in this book. Few of the parks as yet have superintendents and staffs fully equipped to handle correspondence or inquiries, and in some cases little or no information is available anyway; hence a park mailing address is not given. Yet, these summaries should lead visitors to within easy asking distance, and from there they are likely to find town authorities proud of the national *patrimonio* and willing to help visitors enjoy these heritage showpieces. Language is not likely to be a serious barrier because even at worst, sign language and the name of a specific area should be sufficient. Although there are no maps of parks, at this writing, local maps with sufficient information are available.

Perhaps the most carefree, and sometimes most economical, way to visit the national parks—in México as nearly anywhere else—is with an experienced guide, preferably a licensed one. He can compress into a few days or a week the important and secret places that might take newcomers months to find.

🌲 Perhaps as much a "trademark" of México as any other natural feature are the imposing peaks of Popocatépetl and Iztaccíhuatl, located not far beyond the outskirts of México City. These perpetually snow-clad volcanic peaks, with their shawls of thick grass and scattered pine or fir, are preserved in **Iztaccíhuatl-Popocatépetl National Park** (more affectionately known as

Izta-Popo), which covers an area of 64,197 acres. Iztaccíhuatl, in the Aztec language, means "White Woman"; Popocatépetl means "Smoking Mountain," and although the peak is presently dormant, having erupted last in 1868, it occasionally issues enough clouds of smoke to show that it is not entirely asleep. The summit contains a large crater with sulfur deposits. Both peaks may be scaled, and trails lead into the upper regions; in fact, large numbers of people sometimes make pilgrimages up on the mountains. Iztaccíhuatl reaches 17,342 feet, and Popocatépetl 17,887 feet, which suggests that hikers and climbers must be in good physical condition and able to suffer the diminished oxygen supply at such altitudes. México City itself lies at an elevation of 7,240 feet, and thus even visitors arriving by automobile attain a substantial elevation.

The park is easily accessible by a paved road that branches off México Route 115 a mile south of Amecameca and forty-five miles southeast of México City. The road leads through delightful forest until it reaches Paso de Cortés, a saddle between the two peaks. There, a traveler finds open savanna of tall dense grass with only occasional trees on up to the limit of vegetation. Owing to the elevation and climate, these peaks, like so many tropical mountains, are often concealed by clouds. The temperature can also be quite cold, and appropriate warm clothing should be worn. A new hostel exists within the park, but it is designed principally for youth groups. Plans are to construct tourist accommodations in the lowlands just outside park boundaries. Meanwhile, horses and guides may be secured in nearby Amecameca and a full range of tourist facilities is available in México City. The Mexican government intends to enlarge the park trail system and construct a small museum and other educational facilities. For the most part, however, the park will be kept in a wild state as part of the original Mexican heritage.

🌲 Adjacent to Iztaccíhuatl-Popocatépetl National Park on the east is **Zoquiapan y Anexos National Park,** containing 45,000 acres. It is accessible off the main route between México City and Puebla and is about an hour's drive from either city. The village of Río Frío is closest to the park. The landscape is one of typical high-elevation volcanic ridges and meadows partly covered with cold-climate pine and fir forests. Picnic areas, trails, and roads exist in the park. A full range of tourist facilities may be found in Puebla.

🌲 In the state of Morelos, twenty miles southeast of México City, lies **El Tepozteco National Park,** a region of gray-brown, arid cliffs. The park's 60,000 acres are mountainous, and were obviously favored by pre-Columbian

(Left) Santa Elena Canyon, proposed Sierra del Carmen National Park, México; (right) Big Bend National Park, Texas.

Rio Grande, with village of Boquillas, México, and Sierra del Carmen National Park in background. Courtesy U.S. National Park Service.

inhabitants, as evidenced by the ruins of Tepozteco, which include a distinctive pyramidal temple. The rocks of the mountain range are volcanic, principally basalt, and are in places covered with pines and oaks. Picnic sites are available. Access is off Mexican Route 95, or off the México City–Cuernavaca freeway, following Route 115-D to the village of Tepoztlán. Dirt roads and trails lead to points within the park. Food and lodging may be secured in Cuernavaca, about twelve miles to the southwest.

366

🌲 **Lagunas de Zempoala National Park,** twenty-five miles south of México City on the road to Cuernavaca, contains 11,673 acres of volcanic terrain, lakes, and coniferous forests in the Ajusco Range. In addition to pines, alders, oaks, willows, and related species there are numerous heaths and other wild flowers. The elevation reaches 11,375 feet on the summit of Cerro de los Alumbres. Access is off México Route 95 to Tres Cumbres, Huitzilac, and the lakes of the park. Opportunities are available for fishing and camping. Accommodations and meals may be secured in México City, Cuernavaca, or other nearby communities.

🌲 **Nevado de Toluca National Park** is named for a volcano covered with snow a good part of the year that reaches an elevation of 15,020 feet. The summit crater possesses two remarkably blue lakes. A scenic road leads to the summit, affording spectacular views of the surrounding countryside. Lower slopes of the mountain are covered with forests of pine, fir, and oak. The park, which covers 127,500 acres, is located about eighty miles southwest of México City. It is reached on regional roads south and west of Toluca, where Mexican national routes 15 and 55 cross. There is a paved road to Temascaltepec. Food and lodging may be obtained in Toluca.

🌲 Seventy-five miles west of México City, on the road to Morelia and Guadalajara, is **Bosencheve National Park,** 37,500 acres of mountainous terrain endowed with forests of pine and fir. The Laguna del Carmen is a lake where birds congregate during migration. Some of the species to be seen are Mexican ducks and clapper and yellow rails. Access is via Mexican Route 15 and local roads. The nearest community is the spa city of Zitácuaro, in which food and lodging may be obtained.

🌲 **Los Mármoles National Park** (the name means "marbles") covers 47,875 acres in the state of Hidalgo, about 150 miles north of México City. A side road leads southeast from Jacala, on Mexican Route 85, to San Nicolas, within the park. Another approaches the southwest corner of the park at Minas Viejas. The area includes several natural springs and a large canyon called San Vicente. The forest consists of several species each of oak and pine plus fir, madrone, walnut, and tepozán. Food and lodging may be secured at Tamazunchale, northeast of the park.

🌲 A few miles northeast of the city of Puebla lies **La Malinche National Park,** on the boundary between the states of Tlaxcala and Puebla. This huge circular mountain—Malinche Volcano measures more than twenty miles in diameter—reaches an elevation of 14,636 feet. The park covers approximately 114,277 acres, and includes forests of pine and fir. Private property still exists in certain parts of the park, so it is advisable to inquire locally or hire a guide for extended trips. Picnic tables are available. Access is via country roads from Puebla and Tlaxcala. Puebla is on National Route 150 about eighty miles southeast of México City. Accommodations may be secured in Puebla and Tlaxcala.

🌲 **Cofre de Perote National Park,** a few miles west of Jalapa, in the state of Veracruz, contains 29,000 acres centered around the 14,048-foot peak, Cofre de Perote. The name means "Jewel Box of Perote." The Aztec name, Nauhcampatépetl, means "Square Mountain." Millions of years ago the mountain was the center of extensive volcanic activity; some of its lava flows reached the Gulf of Mexico, nearly fifty miles to the east. Climbing through its woods of cypress, alder, oak, fir, and pine toward the summit, hikers get panoramic views of mountain ranges, volcanoes, plains, and when skies are clear, the sea. Access is via country roads off Mexican Route 140, which passes around the east, north, and west of the park. Food and lodging may be obtained in Jalapa and Perote, to the east.

🌲 México's highest mountain, Orizaba, elevation 18,700 feet (third-highest mountain in North America after Mt. McKinley and Mt. Logan), is protected in **Pico de Orizaba National Park,** approximately twenty miles north of the city of Orizaba. The peak is also known by the name Citlaltépetl. The summit of the volcano is perpetually snow-covered, but forests of pine and fir grow at lower elevations. The peak, inactive since 1687, is a major Mexican landmark, though its summit is frequently obscured by clouds. The park contains 49,375 acres and is approached on country roads north of Mexican Route 150. Ciudad Serdán is nearest the points of major interest. There are no tourist facilities.

🌲 **Cañón del Río Blanco National Park** covers 139,225 acres south of the city of Orizaba. Because of choice ecological habitats at various altitudes, sources of water, rich volcanic soils, and a relatively stable climate, the canyon and mountain slopes are a veritable garden of plants that differ markedly from one elevation to another. Below the high-altitude pines and firs is a belt of oaks; below that grows a band of mixed subtropical species such as ash, walnut, poplar, cacao, guava, acacia, and avocado; in the moist canyons live giant ferns, platanillo, limoncillo, horsetails, and other species. The park is without development, but is accessible on local roads southeast from the city of Orizaba, where a full range of tourist facilities may be found.

🌲 In far southern México, in the state of Chiapas near the Guatemalan border, lies **Lagunas de Montebello National Park.** Situated at nearly 5,000 feet above sea level, the temperature in this region of fifty-nine attractive lakes is usually refreshing and springlike. Rains are heavy from May to October but Mexicans prize the area and consider these lakes some of their country's most beautiful. Coloration in the waters varies from emerald and jade to black and white. One lake measures fifteen miles long by one mile wide. The vegetation includes an abundance of ferns and orchids as well as pines, oaks, vanilla, cacao, and hule (rubber tree). The 15,000-acre park is approached on Mexican Route 190, and reached via country roads southeast of Comitán. Food and lodging may be secured in the nearby communities of Comitán and San Cristóbal. Picnic facilities, overlooks, trails, roads, and sightseeing boats are available.

🌲 Along the southern coast of México, on the shores of the Pacific Ocean, are numerous lagoons and bays with native vegetation consisting of mangroves and other tropical species. The place is usually alive with such birds as pelicans, herons, ducks, and chachalacas. The curving sandy beaches and their environs were described half a century ago as a "grand spectacle"; since then, settlers have moved into many coastal environments of México and Central America, and put undisturbed ecosystems to agricultural use. In **Lagunas de Chacahua National Park,** some 200 miles southeast of Acapulco, the Mexican government has attempted to conserve the natural scene, which includes such plants as ebony, ceiba, mesquite, royal palm, mahogany, cedar, and tamarind. The fauna is also rich: deer, boars, hares, foxes, and an abundance of colorful tropical birds such as parrots. The park covers 25,000 acres and is accessible by dirt road off Mexican Route 200 or, of course, by sea and air. Facilities are in the process of being developed.

🌲 **Pico de Tancítaro National Park** was established by decree in 1940, but its 73,290 acres have not yet been precisely delineated or acquired by the

369

Mexican government. Consequently, the area is mostly private property, with only limited public access and no tourist facilities. The park was set aside to protect an extinct volcanic area (maximum elevation 12,664 feet) where pine forests alternate with lava flows. A short distance north lies the famed volcano of Parícutin, the 1,700-foot-high cinder cone left from an eruption in 1943 that destroyed villages and cornfields and drove 4,000 people from their homes. Pico de Tancítaro and its associated volcanoes are located about 300 miles due west of México City. Access is via country roads northwest from the city of Uruapan to the village of Tancítaro. Food and lodging are available in Uruapan.

🌲 **Volcán de Colima National Park** protects a volcano that reaches 12,631 feet elevation and is covered with snow. It emits sulfurous fumes and occasional plumes of smoke. Its sides are cut by deep canyons and the going is so rough, considering sheer cliffs at the top, that Europeans compare it with the Matterhorn. Located on the boundary between the states of Colima and Jalisco, about eighty miles south of Guadalajara, the park covers roughly 55,500 acres, partially clothed in forests of pine, fir, and oak. The park has not been developed. Tonila is the closest village. Access is via local roads off Mexican routes 54 and 110. One route leads from Colima to Tonila to Plan de los Fresnos. Food and lodging are available in the city of Colima.

🌲 About thirty miles south of San Luis Potosí lies **El Gogorrón National Park,** where the protected zone of 62,500 acres contains volcanic phenomena, including hot springs. People of the region swim in these waters because of reputed therapeutic values. The climate is semiarid, the vegetation consisting chiefly of mesquite, cactus, nopal, and pirú. Access is via Mexican Route 57 south of San Luis Potosí. From Villa de Reyes a country road leads to Baños del Carmen, within the park. There are no other developments. Food and lodging may be obtained in San Luis Potosí.

🌲 Situated in the state of Nuevo León is México's largest national park, **Cumbres de Monterrey National Park,** with an area of 616,250 acres. However, a new study of the boundaries may reveal a lesser size because the park is located adjacent to the city of Monterrey, which has expanded to a population of more than a million persons and utilized park land in the process. The mountains form part of the Sierra Madre Oriental, and include scenic ridges, geological formations of immense proportions, arroyos, and waterfalls. Roads, trails, and picnic facilities are available. A full range of tourist facilities may be found in Monterrey.

🌲 **Cumbres de Majalca National Park,** of 11,932 acres, is situated in Chihuahua State, 200 miles south of El Paso, Texas. Its woods of ponderosa pine and oak contrast with surrounding desert lowlands. Erosion has carved the landscape into unusual forms. The park is reached via country road west of Mexican Route 45. Accommodations are available in the park and in the city of Chihuahua, thirty-five miles to the south.

🌲 For many years the Sierra del Carmen, an imposing 10,000-foot range of mountains on the south side of the Río Bravo (or Rio Grande, as U.S. citizens refer to the river along the boundary), has been discussed as a possible national park. The idea of two adjacent border parks is appealing: Sierra del Carmen on the Coahuila side and Big Bend National Park on the Texas side. A more recent suggestion has been to combine the two areas in a proposed **Río Bravo International Park.**

There is little doubt that the mountains south of the border have extraordinary wild and scenic values. In the 300,000-acre section being reviewed by Mexican experts the lower slopes and canyons are sparsely covered with creosote bush, mesquite, sotol, ocotillo, and lechuguilla. In higher regions, grasses become more prominent, and juniper and Mexican cherry are found. At 10,000 feet grow forests of pine, fir, oak, maple, and mountain mahogany. Such are the vegetative contrasts of the Sierra del Carmen, and travel here is much like hiking in the Chisos Mountains of Big Bend National Park. However, for the moment at least, the property on the Mexican side is private and local inquiry should be made as to the status of the park and permissible entry routes.

Owing to altitudinal changes, the fauna of the Sierra del Carmen is also diverse. Birds include white-winged doves, verdins, meadowlarks, and kinglets—familiar species of deserts and desert mountains. Black bears, coyotes, wolves, mountain lions, and white-tailed deer are some of the mammals. As in most deserts, the ecosystems here have their share of lizards and rattlesnakes.

Access to this region is northwest from the Mexican town of Múzquiz. Visitors to Big Bend National Park can obtain panoramic views of the Sierra del Carmen by visiting Boquillas Canyon; at sunset the cliffs rising behind the Mexican village of Boquillas, across the river, present a memorable display of form and color.

🌲 The wilderness values of Baja California are well known: distant desert vistas, deep arroyos, sand dunes, granite mountain ranges, and a remarkable vegetation. **Constitución de 1857 National Park** is located in the Sierra de

Desert bighorn ram.
Photograph by Leonard Lee Rue,
National Audubon Society.

Chachalacas.
Photograph by Jeanne White,
National Audubon Society.

White-winged doves.
Photograph by Allan D. Cruickshank,
National Audubon Society.

Clapper rail. Photograph
by Allan D. Cruickshank,
National Audubon Soci-
ety.

Juárez, roughly fifty miles south of the California border, and covers 12,375 acres. It is endowed with pine forests and there are lakes—the largest being Laguna de Juárez. Potable water and picnic facilities are available.

 **Sierra de San Pedro Mártir National Park** lies about 125 miles south of the California border, and includes 157,500 acres of dramatic granite massifs and folded slate ridges. In the low desert valleys, where life shrivels under summer temperatures approaching 130°, the vegetation is principally cactus, ocotillo, and creosote bush. Climbing up into the mountains one passes through slightly more moist regions of poplar, willow, oak and piñon pine. Where there were roadrunners below, now there are mockingbirds and buntings. Excess hunting has reduced the numbers of larger mammalian inhabitants, but it is still possible to see deer, mountain lions, and bighorns in hard-for-man-to-reach locations.

Higher elevations, having more moisture, are endowed with meadows, pools, springs, and creeks. Manzanita, a shrub belonging to the heath family, clings to craggy ridges, and there are pines, aspen, fir, and incense cedar, not unlike the Sierra Nevada of upper California. East of the park, the highest point in the San Pedro Mártir Range is Picacho del Diablo, 10,126 feet, highest point on the peninsula, and often snow-covered in winter. There are excellent views of the Gulf of California.

Two main roads lead south into Baja California. Mexican Route 1 leads more or less along the west coast. Route 5 goes along the eastern side of the peninsula. The park lies between them, but approximately forty miles from each. Country roads lead toward the park from San Felipe on the east. A road goes through San Matías Pass, north of the park. Local inquiry should be made about road conditions and access points nearer the park. Food and lodging are available in Ensenada, about eighty-five miles in an air line northwest of the park. Developments within the park are just beginning.

La Malinche National Park. Courtesy Pan American Union.

PART X

Central America

The countries covered here are those with the most advanced systems of national parks and wild areas. Costa Rica has been moving faster in this field than most nations of the world, and from a crash program begun in 1969 has emerged with four areas established and others under study. Guatemala recently issued a 344-page report on new proposed national parks, only a few of which are established and developed for public use. Panamá is in the midst of planning its system of national parks, and the places listed are foci of long-term protection and development processes begun in the 1960s.

Hence many areas described in this chapter have not yet received full protection or do not have tourist facilities. But the traveler who can adapt to these tropical environments should enjoy some extraordinary wilderness adventures.

Cloud forest above Río
Grande de Tapantí, Costa Rica.

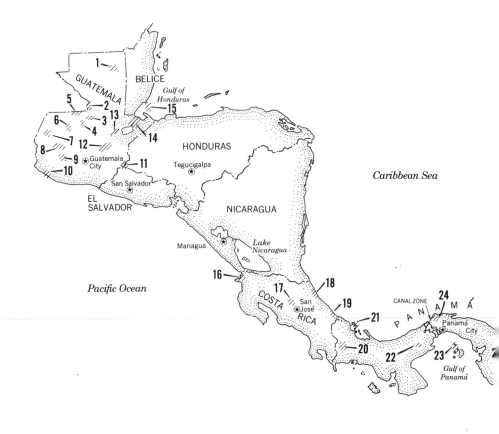

1. GUATEMALA

1. Tikal National Park
2. La Pasión National Park
3. Chisec National Park
4. Lachuá National Park
5. Ixcán National Park
6. Bisis National Park
7. Los Cuchumatanes National Park
8. María Tecún National Park
9. Lake Atitlán National Park
10. Huamuchal National Park
11. Trifinio National Park
12. Sierra de las Minas National Park
13. Sierra de Santa Cruz National Park
14. Río Dulce National Park
15. Los Cayos National Marine Park

2. COSTA RICA

16. Santa Rosa National Park
17. Volcán Poás National Park
18. Tortuguero National Park
19. Cahuita National Park

3. PANAMÁ

20. Volcán Barú National Park
21. Bocas del Toro National Park
22. Altos de Campana National Park
23. Islas de las Perlas National Park
24. Portobelo National Park
25. Fronterizo National Park

1. GUATEMALA

Like much of Central America, Guatemala has vast roadless areas. Large parts of them are earmarked for parks, reserves, recreation areas, or natural monuments; some are being studied for specific designation; others have been withdrawn from settlement or use until their values can be fully determined. In addition there are eighteen major volcanoes whose summits have been more or less unsuited to agriculture and are therefore wild to some degree. The following areas are mostly remote, few reached by roads and few provided with visitor services. Travel should be arranged through the Guatemalan government and local tourist agencies wherever possible. For best results, guides who know the country should be engaged for travel into the interior of remote regions. As a start, prospective travelers should get in touch with the Instituto Guatemalteco de Turismo (INGUAT), the Guatemalan tourism agency, in Guatemala City and elsewhere, about travel and transportation. For detailed information on national parks, at least what data are available, they should write: Director, Departamento de Parques Nacionales, División Forestal, Dirección de Recursos Naturales Renovables, Ministerio de Agricultura, Guatemala City, Guatemala.

🌲 Most remote lowlands in Guatemala are so rainy and hot that modern man has built few settlements there. But early men did and in the Petén, northernmost of Guatemalan provinces, lie hundreds of decaying Mayan ruins. The largest-known archeological complex is preserved in **Tikal National Park,** 200 air miles northeast of Guatemala City. Tikal is the most thoroughly excavated of the Mayan sites in this low tropical forest. Originally constructed sometime before A.D. 550, the buildings were reconstructed, altered, and expanded by the Mayas over a period of nearly 400 years. No one is certain why the Mayas left, but during their period of occupation they enjoyed a bounty of water that was unusual, even in this wet climate. For the region is underlain by porous limestone into which rainfall is usually absorbed and carried away; only during the wet season do broad shallow basins fill with water, but this was evidently enough to sustain the Mayan population.

377

The park's 144,000 acres, and a proposed extension that would more than double the area, are probably wilder now than they were when the Mayas lived here. Surrounding the ruins is a complex tropical forest exhibiting remarkable ecological phenomena. The same basins that provided the Mayas with water keep wild animal populations supplied today. Howler and spider monkeys are conspicuous. Visitors frequently see anteaters, agoutis, coatimundis, and foxes. Less often encountered are ocelots, jaguars, kinkajous, pacas, brocket and white-tailed deer, tayras, raccoons, and opossums. There are more than 300 species of birds, most resident but several dozen regular migrants to and from the north. For example, some twenty-five species of wood warblers spend the winter at Tikal. The rest of the animal kingdom is likewise complex, such as twenty species of lizards, thirty-eight species of nonpoisonous snakes, eight species of poisonous snakes, and who knows how many kinds of ants.

This animal life occupies innumerable ecological niches in the tropical forest. Some ants live in the trunks of cecropia trees, some in thorns of legume trees. The different forest types are dominated by ramon, palm, mahogany, yaxnix, and chicozapote. The plant kingdom is rounded out by ferns, orchids, bromeliads, and others.

Food and lodging are available in the park. Access is by regularly scheduled flights to a nearby airstrip; in addition, the road from Guatemala City to Tikal, via Morales and Poptún, has recently been completed and tourist cars and recreational vehicles arrive regularly at the park. An alternate route to Tikal, via Cobán, is under construction at this writing.

La Pasión National Park, 341,250 acres, lies in the Petén region on the México-Guatemala frontier. Low, hot, and humid, it is rich and productive biologically, but just how much so is yet to be determined. The aquatic life is believed to be of considerable scientific importance. Navigation of the rivers is a spectacular adventure owing to the clarity of the waters and the wild natural scene. The fauna is significant for its tapirs and crocodiles. Access is via road from Flores to Sayaxché, thence by river into the interior.

Chisec National Park, 28,250 acres at the northern edge of the department of Alta Verapaz, is a low-elevation terrain mostly of karst topography—dissolved limestone areas that contain some of the richest cavern ecosystems in the tropics. Rainfall is abundant, some 152 inches per year, with the heaviest rains falling in June, July, and October. Two expeditions by French speleologists, in collaboration with the University of

San Carlos of Guatemala and the Guatemala Association of Natural History, revealed the existence of no fewer than eighty caves, some containing ceremonial burials and paintings of the Mayan Indians—which raises the fascinating subject of Mayan subterranean archeology. Other features include pink stalactites (some, alas, already pillaged) and a natural well or sink 600 feet deep. Jul-Ik, the most extensive known cavern, measures 4,125 feet in length. Some caverns have subterranean rivers, cascades, and pools and at least one has a natural bridge entirely underground. The flora and fauna are typical of the hot, humid tropical forest, except that here there is an interesting, though little-known, subterranean fauna.

Lachuá National Park, 201,875 acres in the northwestern part of Alta Verapaz Department, is located in a region of karst topography where massive limestone formations have been perforated by the solvent action of subterranean waters and the chemicals they contain. Thus, the landscape abounds in caves. The climate is hot and humid, and the vegetation reflects this, being composed principally of palms and broad-leaved tropical trees. More than 300 species of birds inhabit the region. The abundant fauna is characteristic of lowland Guatemala. This park constitutes a particularly good habitat for tapirs. The principal scenic attraction of the region is Lake Lachuá, and in it is a unique aquatic life system. To preserve this watery environment in its natural state the Guatemalans have warned against introduction of exotic fish species. Access to this remote area is by foot, horse, or mule.

Ixcán National Park, 100,000 acres, in the departments of Huehueten-ango and El Quiché on the border with México, is a hot, wet environment that receives as much as twenty-six inches of rainfall a month. The nearly pristine ecosystem is typically humid tropical, resembling that in La Pasión National Park, to the northeast. The area is remote, approached only by trail, and thus its rich fauna, flora, and archeological resources are little known.

Bisis National Park, 133,000 acres, lies in the northern part of El Quiché Department, in hills with an elevational range of between 3,000 and 8,000 feet above sea level. The forests consist of pines, live oaks, deciduous hardwoods, and shrubs, with abundant ferns, orchids, and bromeliads. More than 270 species of birds have been identified, including the rare, colorful quetzal. The area is still relatively pristine, and from these uplands one may look out over the vast wild forest of the Petén region; to the west, the massif of the Cuchumatanes is visible. Access is via Route 7-W and from roads to Cotzal and Chajul.

🌲 **Los Cuchumatanes National Park,** 211,000 acres, in Huehuetenango and El Quiché departments, is a mountainous area ranging in elevation from 9,000 to nearly 12,000 feet. The climate is cold, often freezing, and there are coniferous forests of pine, fir, and juniper. Bromeliads are abundant. The dense woods and related ecosystems provide haven to 125 resident species of birds, including the rare and beautiful quetzal. Among the mammals are squirrels, rabbits, coyotes, deer, and mountain lions. Glacial features, such as moraines, may be observed. Scenic views from the high points are spectacular. Access is via Route 9-N, which crosses the park between Chiantla and San Juan Ixcoy. A short distance to the south are the ruins of Zaculeu.

🌲 **María Tecún National Park,** 78,375 acres, lies in the central Sierra Madre near Lake Atitlán, Totonicapán, Chichicastenango, and Quezaltenango. It consists of uplands that reach an elevation of over 8,000 feet. The flora is punctuated with pines, some of giant proportions, and contains an extraordinary variety of bryophytes. From the high ramparts of the mountains may be obtained views of the Pacific Ocean, surrounding volcanoes, and Lake Atitlán. Access is by local roads.

🌲 **Lake Atitlán National Park** was established in 1955, but has not been managed as a park. In their current inventory of natural areas, Guatemalan government specialists recommend that it be classified as a recreation area instead. This is understandable because of the extent of population around the lake, but the area is worth mentioning here because of its outstanding qualities, easy access, and some degree of naturalness. Indeed, there are persons who would classify Lake Atitlán itself, forty miles in an air line west of Guatemala City, as one of the most beautiful lakes in the world. Located at 5,200 feet elevation in a land of "forever spring," it is ringed by volcanic cones that rise even higher: San Pedro, 9,921 feet; Tolimán, 10,270 feet; and Atitlán, 11,565 feet. The waters are deep blue, or green, or purple, or gold—depending on the hour at which they are viewed, the clarity and color of the sky, and other factors. The lake measures ten miles wide, twenty miles long, and is 1,500 feet deep. It is surrounded by colorful villages and scattered

Strangler fig, Santa Rosa National Park, Costa Rica.

Ojoche trees, Santa Rosa National Park, Costa Rica.

Dry forest, Santa Rosa National Park, Costa Rica.

habitations of Mayan Indians. But despite the deforested slopes and upland agriculture, a hiker can get some idea of what the volcanic wilderness must have been like centuries ago. The lake supports a population of giant pied-billed grebes. These birds, of which only 200 remain, exist on Lake Atitlán and nowhere else. They dive, but cannot fly, their wings having failed to develop sufficiently. Though crowded by human civilization, they face more serious dangers from below; during youth they are vulnerable to attacking pike, bass, or muskellunge. Guatemalan naturalists and conservationists have kept the birds under observation and paid particular attention to nesting areas.

Two access routes, both paved but winding, lead into this scenic crater lake. One branches off the Pan-American Highway due north of Lake Atitlán and proceeds eleven miles to small villages at the shore where excellent meals and lodging may be secured. The other comes in from the east through Patzun. Because the volcanic soil is soft and mobile, travelers should be alert to the possibility of landslides blocking the road or loose rocks on the right-of-way. The interesting Indian village of Chichicastenango is about twenty miles north of Lake Atitlán.

🌲 **Huamuchal National Park,** 57,000 acres on the Pacific Coast near the Mexican boundary, is a region of mangroves, lagoons, and meadows. It is bounded in part by the Tilapa and Ocosito rivers, is located in the department of Retalhuleu, and borders the department of Quezaltenango. The climate is either wet (May to October) or dry (November to April), but heavy rains can fall at any time. Most of the original forest was cut to make room for cultivation of cotton. Nevertheless, the area is one of Guatemala's few remaining possibilities for a Pacific Coast refuge for wildlife—marine turtles, crocodiles, unique fish species, snakes, mammals, and 155 resident species of birds. The area is especially noted for its bird-watching opportunities. There are also attractive beaches in a tropical setting. The area is approached on routes 8 or 9-S, and thence by country roads or by boat along the coast.

🌲 **Trifinio National Park** has been suggested as an international area of 150,000 acres where Guatemala, Honduras, and El Salvador join. Each country, under this proposal, would set aside its own third of the acreage as a national park. Located in the mountains of southeastern Guatemala, in the department of Chiquimula, the elevation reaches nearly 8,000 feet above sea level. The terrain is principally volcanic. Rain rarely falls from November to

April and the vegetation takes on a dry, lower-montane aspect, with such trees as oak, ash, pine, sweetgum, acacia, and wax myrtle. Birds and mammals are not as abundant as in lowland regions and some have been extirpated here. There are numerous ancient ruins in the region; thirty miles in an air line to the northeast, in Honduras, are the Mayan ruins of Copán, once a center of science. The proposed park area may be approached from Guatemala via Route 18 to Esquipulas, or Route 20 to the west; and from El Salvador via Route 12 north of Santa Ana and Metapán.

Sierra de las Minas National Park, 213,035 acres, includes several river basins in central Guatemala. In the upper parts of the mountain range are extensive zones of pine. Orchids, horsetails, and giant ferns abound. The wild ecosystems are home to an abundance of birds, including toucans and trogons, but the most important, on account of its rarity, form, and color, is the quetzal, national bird of Guatemala. The other fauna include serpents (five species of which are venomous), monkeys, tapirs, deer, raccoons, and opossums. High points in the mountains afford panoramic views of the Río Motagua basin to the south and Lake Izabal to the northeast. There are also picturesque streams and waterfalls. Access is off Route 5 (the road to Cobán) on a side road eleven kilometers to Chilascó; or on the other end of the mountains access is via Route CA9 and thence the road to the marble mines of Santa Rosalía.

Sierra de Santa Cruz National Park, 156,000 acres, resembles Río Dulce National Park in flora, fauna, and climate. It is located at the end of the Santa Cruz Mountains just north of Lake Izabal. A large part of the park is still relatively pristine; the region itself is one of the few in Guatemala where mountains are still sparsely inhabited. Magnificent views are to be had of Lake Izabal and the Sierra de las Minas to the south, and the Caribbean Sea to the east. There are numerous canyons, cascades, and caverns. Access is literally by lake and stream; the park is approached on Route 7-E toward Estor, and Route 13 toward El Petén.

Río Dulce National Park, 60,500 acres in the low country of the department of Izabal, on the eastern coast of Guatemala, was established by presidential decree in 1955. Though hot and humid, the region has become renowned for its natural beauty, luxuriant vegetation, and wild animals. Much of it is a freshwater environment, the major body being Lake Izabal.

This lake and its tributaries are known for the clarity of their waters. The canyon of the Río Dulce, through which Lake Izabal discharges its water to the sea, is called by the Guatemalans "one of the most beautiful and impressive places in tropical America." In addition, there are attractive beaches near Livingston where the river empties into the Caribbean.

The rain pours, the sun heats the atmosphere, and a high humidity prevails, but this, of course, nourishes the ferns, orchids, mahogany and cedar trees, and other plants. Though the region still has a dense wet tropical forest—it was originally rich in deciduous trees—most of the commercially valuable timber has been extracted. Palms are abundant, and pines occur in scattered stands. Of special interest are the abundant floating and submerged plants, plus the rich variety of fishes—more than a hundred species. There are crocodiles and, on the Caribbean coast, sea turtles. For naturalists, this is literally a tropical paradise. More than 300 species of birds are resident, plus scores of serpents, at least thirteen species of which are venomous. Monkeys, tapirs, deer, raccoons, mountain lions, and jaguars are only a few of the mammalian species. The rare manatee inhabits aquatic areas. Access is via Route 13, the road to El Petén. Motorists going to Tikal National Park cross the Río Dulce on a ferry. At the eastern end of the park, Livingston is fifteen miles by launch from Puerto Barrios; this latter is a port city 200 miles northeast of Guatemala City and is reached by Route CA9, a paved highway through scenic mountains and valleys.

Los Cayos National Marine Park takes in a proposed 770,063 acres of land and sea north of Puerto Barrios, in the shallow waters of the Caribbean. Included are barrier coral reefs paralleling the coast and dozens of *cayos*, or islets, including the Cayos Zapotillo. Mangrove and fig are a few of the native plants, but man has planted coconut, almond, citrus, casuarina, and other species here. Terrestrial animals are scarce, but they do include the boa constrictor. Land life here has to endure occasional hurricanes. The birds are nearly all marine and/or migratory.

2. COSTA RICA

Motorists traveling south on the Pan-American Highway pass from Nicaragua, which has no national parks, into Costa Rica, one of the most progressive park- and conservation-oriented nations in the western hemisphere. Indeed, less than thirty miles south of the border a traveler may turn west into **Santa Rosa National Park,** the first of its kind in Costa Rica, and a treasure of natural life systems. What a visitor will see depends largely on what time of year he arrives—during the six-month dry season, from December to May, when a warm wind blows and the forest has almost an arid aspect, or during the six-month wet season, when lakes form on the meadows, the heat becomes oppressive, the grass and the woods turn green, and the ground soaks up life-giving moisture. Annual rainfall amounts to nearly eighty inches. Thus controlled by drought extremes, the forest is open and somewhat arid in contrast with other parts of Costa Rica. Some of the trees are actually deciduous, losing their leaves in the dry season.

All this variation is first glimpsed during the four-mile drive from the entrance to the *casona,* a 200-year-old ranch house that was the site of a short but fierce battle for the country's independence in 1856. The house is being stabilized and reinforced structurally and contains exhibits on historic and natural features.

From the house a self-guiding nature trail leads into a richly vegetated swale where bright-blue motmot birds fly among the trees and troops of white-faced monkeys peer down through the leaves and chatter at intruders. To dwellers north of the tropics, few of the trees are familiar, except possibly acacias, mimosas, and oaks. The rest of the woods consist of a remarkable number of tree species.

The animal life is likewise varied. Even in the driest season, a great deal of activity goes on, and the hiker would do well to move quietly and observe carefully. On the forest floor may be seen long columns of ants carrying fresh-cut leaves—an enormous load for them; their industry and the nature of the route they construct seems more miraculous the longer we watch. The more common mammals are deer, peccaries, tapirs, spider and howler monkeys, anteaters, and ocelots.

From the historic house the road winds through open forests, dense woods, and grassy glades for about three miles, then descends through thickening forests with views of the deep-blue Pacific to the west. It levels off in a forest of giant buttressed ojoche trees whose crowns form a shading canopy. Some of the trunks are locked in the grip of strangler figs. The going is easy, for little vegetation blocks the way on the forest floor. There are even a few pools of water in the gravelly beds of streams, and a short dip on a hot day can be very refreshing. In these environments may be glimpsed blue-winged teals, macaws, tinamous, guans, and spot-bellied bobwhites. White-faced monkeys inhabit the upper strata of tree limbs. A human visitor may be startled by the sound of a body hurtling through space and slapping the ground with a thump. This is merely a harmless, four-foot-long iguana leaping down a tree trunk and fleeing. Iguanas are fascinating to watch because of their antics and their striking shapes, designs, and colors.

The route enters a brackish tidal zone where salt-tolerant trees and shrubs alternate with flats of dry and cracking mud. In the shallow estuaries a roseate spoonbill may be glimpsed, and possibly a crocodile. The road ends here, and the last few hundred yards to the sea are over sandy terrain with plants characteristic of deserts. After this the visitor observes one of the finest aspects of Santa Rosa National Park, a wild, gently curving beach, Playa Naranjo, enclosed by distant brown headlands and walled in by woods to landward. The sand has a brownish cast, and so does the water, but it is time for a swim—if one can get used to the sight of shark fins moving offshore. The sharks are likely to be rather small, and the water is shallow for some distance out.

These are the environments of Santa Rosa, and from the single road any part of the 24,750-acre park may be explored. Care should be taken to leave things as they are, because the Costa Ricans have quite a feeling for the protection of their resources, and they went to extraordinary lengths to relocate squatters from this particular park. One might find a clutch of ridley, green, or leatherback turtle eggs in the sand at the beach, but they are best left alone; park wardens have the beach under special surveillance when eggs are incubating.

The park has a small campground. The nearest food and lodging are at Liberia, twenty-three miles to the south. Liberia is also the closest point of air access to this part of Guanacaste Province; the park itself fronts on Route 1, and is about a day's drive from San José, the capital of Costa Rica.

Information: Director, Servicio de Parques Nacionales, Ministerio de Agricultura y Ganadería, San José, Costa Rica.

Among Costa Rica's volcanoes the largest and most dramatic recent eruptions have been at Irazú, above Cartago. But Poás Volcano, twenty miles

*Crater eruption, Volcán Poás
National Park, Costa Rica.*

northwest of San José, has been selected for extensive park protection and development, and with good reason. Whereas Irazú is generally quiet between eruptions, Poás is nearly always erupting, even if only in low key. It contains a hot gray lake that explodes from time to time in a series of geyser bursts that fill the air with clouds of steam and streams of mud. It is all rather eerily silent, at least from the observation point on the rim above. The wide crater is barren and colorless except for a few deposits of yellow sulfur. But away from the crater, and the effects of heat, a dense vegetation exists. Such are the contrasts of **Volcán Poás National Park.**

Along a short self-guiding nature trail from the observation point, through dense oak cloud forest strung with colorful bromeliads, visitors descend into an auxiliary crater containing a green freshwater lake. Up here at over 8,000 feet the air can be cool, and at times frosty. Fog flows over the mountain frequently, cooling and wetting the woods, and hikers who wish to explore off-trail in this 10,000-acre park should have protection against the elements. They should also discuss their route with Costa Rican rangers because part of the park is a strict nature reserve into which public access is limited or prohibited. The vegetation consists of abundant oaks, orchids, ferns, and mosses, the common pink-flowered *Monochaetum,* the ubiquitous *Clusia* tree, and magnolia. Closer to the crater the forest becomes dwarf and finally nonexistent. But most of the mountain, like the country itself, is a veritable wild garden. Indeed, Costa Rican biologists boast that their nation has a thousand species of orchids. On Poás these woods are the last refuge of rare, colorful, long-tailed green birds called quetzals. Squirrels are common, but tapirs, deer, jaguars, and peccaries are more rare owing to the mountain's isolation by surrounding agricultural lands.

387

The park has a visitor center with information on the natural history of the mountain. Picnicking and camping are permitted. Food and lodging may be secured in towns at the southern base of the mountain, or in San José. Access is via Heredia, Route 9, and local roads to the northwest of San José.

Information: Director, Servicio de Parques Nacionales, Ministerio de Agricultura y Ganadería, San José, Costa Rica.

🌲 The mountains of this West Virginia–size country are some of the most rugged and densely vegetated in the Central American cordillera. Typical is the Tapantí area, where oaks and other hardwoods cling to nearly vertical slopes, and waterfalls plunge into remote canyons seldom if ever visited by man. In such mountainous wild areas the Costa Rican government has new park proposals under study.

Down on the Caribbean shores of Costa Rica the weather is much more hot and humid, with tropical forests forming high green walls along the waterways. Such is the case at **Tortuguero National Park,** accessible by air or boat, fifty-six miles north of Puerto Limón. Going into the interior along the rivers and elongated lagoons is about the only way to penetrate this green wilderness, which reverberates with the booming grunts of howler monkeys. Stopping and getting out of one's canoe to walk through the palm swamps is possible but has little point because of the density of trees and difficulty of passage. There are also some heavily vegetated hills, but any substantial penetration into this 45,000-acre wilderness should be with a local guide who knows the region. And even though the forest people of Latin American countries have miraculous ways of getting out of trouble, it would still be a good idea to take survival gear.

With 200 inches of rain a year, and no dry season, this is one of the wettest parts of Central America. Most visitors will be content to see the beach, overhung by coconut palms; it is famed as a major nesting ground for rare and endangered green turtles. In fact, protection of these beaches was the principal reason for establishing the park; green turtle eggs had been increasingly dug·up for human consumption, and the number of turtles returning to lay their eggs each year had fallen dangerously low. Hawksbill and leatherback turtles also visit here. Deeper within the woods live toucans, macaws, parrots, tapirs, anteaters, jaguars, mountain lions, ocelots, and kinkajous. Rare manatees and lungfish inhabit the lagoons.

The Costa Rican government is currently devoting its efforts to park and wildlife protection at Tortuguero rather than to tourism development. The theft of turtle eggs and slaughter of the turtles for their "calipee," a fatty substance locally prized as a food delicacy, is being reduced through land and sea patrols by park rangers. Therefore, there is no camping, food, or lodging in or near the park, and visitors who wish to remain overnight must arrange for their own supplies. Access is via air on weekly flights, or by sea on boats that operate infrequently, from Puerto Limón. Boats may also be chartered in Puerto Limón. Charter trips by air may be arranged in San José, the nation's capital.

Information: Director, Servicio de Parques Nacionales, Ministerio de Agricultura y Ganadería, San José, Costa Rica.

One of the most difficult ways to get to **Cahuita National Park,** in eastern Costa Rica, is to get up at three A.M., take the train out of Puerto Limón, rattle through cacao groves for an hour or so, cross a river on canoe, leap or get hurled aboard a bus, and journey the last five miles over an old rail bed that has gone to pieces and is full of holes. This brings the visitor to the seaside village of Cahuita, where limited food and lodging may be secured. The easiest way to arrive at the same destination is by boat and boatman hired in Puerto Limón, twenty-five miles by sea to the north. In either case, the trip is worth the effort.

Cahuita is a point of land jutting two miles into the Caribbean. In the center is a strip of tropical hardwood forest that resounds with the echoing chorus of howler monkeys—wave upon wave of sound that makes this one of the most memorable wilderness areas in Central America. Fringing the hardwoods are coconut trees that separate the central forest from the sandy shore. Hiking along the interface between land and sea is not always easy: One has to crawl over piles of coconut fronds or negotiate the mouths of small brief streams that originate not very far through the woods. But going slow has its rewards, and hikers may see squirrels drilling holes in coconuts, flocks of green parrots flying overhead, and bright-orange crabs scurrying underfoot.

Offshore is a living coral reef four miles long, a world of sea urchins, tropical fish, massive corals—and the remains of a Spanish vessel that struck the reef at the beginning of the eighteenth century and settled in sixty feet of water. A few objects such as cannons, brick ballast, and an anchor are visible to snorkelers in shallow water, but the rest of the vessel is too deep to be seen from the surface. It is being protected by the government until the park is developed, a museum built, and parts of the vessel placed on display.

Though the park is relatively small, 4,250 acres, a visit can consume several days of hiking, swimming, and nature observations. Facilities are limited; Puerto Limón is the closest site of a full range of hotels, restaurants, and supplies.

Information: Director, Servicio de Parques Nacionales, Ministerio de Agricultura y Ganadería, San José, Costa Rica.

3. PANAMÁ

One expects in Panamá a superhumid environment so wet that no raincoat can provide a defense against the sustained and heavy downpours. And this is exactly the case in certain localities nearly every day of the year. But there are also frosty places such as the proposed **Volcán Barú National Park,** just east of the Costa Rican frontier, some 299 miles west of Panamá City. The volcano rises out of lowlands devoted to the cultivation of coffee, vegetables, banana, and citrus, and reaches an altitude of 11,395 feet, highest point in Panamá. Influenced by the Pacific Ocean, thirty miles to the south, and the Caribbean, thirty miles to the northeast, the climate on this mountain is exceedingly complex. At 6,000 feet the average annual temperature is 60°, a refreshing contrast to the muggy heat of the coasts, and frosts are frequent at higher elevations. Pleasant as this may seem, the mountain is also frequently obscured by clouds, which form nearly every day by 10:00 A.M. Then the mist blows in and rain falls, the precipitation in some places being as much as 109 inches per year. Sometimes there are fierce, high-velocity winds. Usually, however, the mountain is delightful, although it is advisable for photographers to be out at the earliest hours of the morning if they want to see most of it. The situation is better during the drier season from January to April.

Although much of Volcán Barú has been cut and burned for subsistence agriculture, and erosion has subsequently taken its toll, the vegetation returns quickly once the area is conserved from cutting. A few nearly inaccessible pockets have remained uncut, and the virgin forest, replete with ferns, orchids, bromeliads, and carpets of sphagnum moss, survives there. As a consequence of human use, however, the mammals are sparse: tapirs, peccaries, anteaters, deer, jaguars, mountain lions, and sloths. Birds are more plentiful, and much more diverse. Among the spectacular species are quetzals, hummingbirds, and flame-throated warblers. Ornithologists believe that forty species of birds occur here and nowhere else. Other birds are rare and a few are thought to have been exterminated from the mountain.

Primitive trails lead up and around the volcano, but the higher in elevation one goes, the more he leaves springs and tumbling streams behind. Hence, climbers should carry their own water up the final 4,000 feet. Size of the park is 35,375 acres. Thousands of people visit the mountain and hundreds ascend its summit each year. Access to the lower slopes is via country roads from David, a city of 58,997 persons in the province of Chiriquí. However, local inquiry should be made to determine road conditions and routes currently recommended. A paved road leads twenty-five miles north to the resort town of Boquete, on the eastern slope of the mountain. Food and lodging are available in both David and Boquete.

Information: Director, Recursos Naturales Renovables, Ministerio de Desarrollo Agropecuario, Box 5390, Panamá City, Republic of Panamá.

🌲 One of the most attractive regions of Panamá is that in and around the proposed **Bocas del Toro National Park,** on the Atlantic Coast 200 miles west of Panamá City. Many islands and tranquil peninsular embayments exist in this locality, but only a few lie within the park. The principal characteristics are coral reefs, clear water, wide beaches of golden sand, and forests of mangroves and other tropical trees. The various ecosystems teem with wildlife, especially shallow waters surrounding the numerous isles. Birds and turtles nest on the islands. The nearby town of Bocas del Toro has an airport and limited tourist facilities, as well as a beach from which to launch swimming and snorkeling expeditions. Precipitation is about 101 inches a year and the average temperature is 77 degrees F.

Information: Director, Recursos Naturales Renovables, Ministerio de Desarrollo Agropecuario, Box 5390, Panamá City, Republic of Panamá.

🌲 **Altos de Campana National Park** consists of 6,610 acres of humid tropical environments as well as submontane forests less than forty miles southwest of Panamá City. Nearby are the popular beaches of San Carlos and Coronado. Volcán Barú lies far to the west, and is more elevated, but the Trinidad, Tusa, Vallolí, and Peña Blanca ranges rise to a maximum of 3,198 feet, and from the summits one gets good views of the Pacific Ocean to the south. The peaks have largely been denuded of trees, but patches of upland forest remain here and there, especially in ravines. With time, good management, and reforestation the wild woods should grow back. Access is presently difficult, but the improvement of an existing road and perhaps the completion of a loop spur road off the Pan-American Highway should provide access to the boundary before long. There are no facilities; the traveler is on his own. Food, lodging, and supplies may be obtained in Panamá City and other communities of the region.

Information: Director, Recursos Naturales Renovables, Ministerio de Desarrollo Agropecuario, Box 5390, Panamá City, Republic of Panamá.

Volcán Barú National Park, Panamá.
Courtesy Panamá Ministry of Agricultural Development.

🌲 In the Bay of Panamá, fifty miles out in the Pacific Ocean from Panamá City, lies a series of tropical isles being made into a national park. Pacheca, Pachequilla, Chapera, Pájaro, Bolaños, Gibraleon, Bayoneta, Vivienda, Casaya, Casayeta, Lampon, and Chitre islands make up the **Islas de las Perlas National Park,** known for marine and terrestrial life still in a fairly wild state. Large numbers of birds nest on the islands, and there are quiet, protected coves as well as good beaches. No tourist facilities have yet been developed in the park, but nearby is Isla Contadora, with food, lodging and tours. Isla Contadora is twenty minutes by air from Panamá City.

Information: Director, Recursos Naturales Renovables, Ministerio de Desarrollo Agropecuario, Box 5390, Panamá City, Republic of Panamá.

🌲 **Portobelo National Park** lies on the Atlantic coast of Panamá less than an hour's drive northeast of Colón. The harbor is in reality an important historic site, and the ruined sixteenth-century fortifications, customs house, chapel, and other structures are some of the finest ever constructed in the Caribbean. Morgan the pirate captured Portobelo in 1669 and Sir Francis Drake died offshore in 1596. In addition to protecting the historic values, the Panamanian government has wisely set aside 27,170 acres to include wild coastal forests, recreational terrain, and wilderness—the latter making up most of the park. The intent is to preserve the area as a primitive zone, but the coast and beaches will receive heavier use. A paved road leads to the park, where boats and guides can be engaged. But the visitor to Portobelo had better be prepared for water—and lots of it—from the sky. Short but intense showers can literally inundate a person and his equipment (which suggests that cameras, binoculars, and other delicate equipment be thoroughly wrapped in plastic). The annual precipitation is about 109 inches and the average temperature is 69 degrees. The growth rate of plants on this wet northern side of Panamá is phenomenal, and the richness of the vegetation may well be imagined. The largest trees reach a height of 130 feet, but most of the forest is made up of lesser individuals of a large number of species. At the shoreline grow different species of mangrove in an ecosystem considerably different from that on the hills and in the ravines back in the interior.

Persons unfamiliar with the marine, coastal, or tropical forest environments here should secure competent guides before undertaking extensive travels. As a park near to Panamá's populated centers, Portobelo is a refreshing touch of wet tropical wilderness that is easily accessible. Accommodations are available in Colón, Maria Chiquita, or Panamá City, the latter one and a half hours' drive to the south. Access is via a good road branching off to the north of the main Panamá City–Colón highway about ten miles east of Colón. The park extends from Portobelo Bay to San Cristóbal Bay, a distance of about eleven miles, and reaches inland approximately seven miles.

Information: Director, Recursos Naturales Renovables, Ministerio de Desarrollo Agropecuario, Box 5390, Panamá City, Republic of Panamá.

Fronterizo National Park is the most remote and as yet inaccessible of Panamá's national parks. Eventually the Pan-American Highway will be completed near it, but in the meanwhile it remains an isolated, mountainous region of immense biological interest. It is still virgin forest, and contains an undetermined number of complex ecological associations, largely because the altitude varies from 650 to 5,000 feet. Included are montane cloud forests and wet tropical lowland forests. The park is located in extreme southeastern Panamá, 150 miles southeast of Panamá City. Colombia, across the border, is also planning to establish a frontier park. Curiously, one of the motivations is to create a buffer zone against the northward advance of *aftosa*, or foot-and-mouth disease, which may be fatal to cloven-footed animals, both domestic and wild. However, this is not the only reason for establishing the national park; Panamanian officials perceive it as an economic plus for local and international tourism and as a prime site for public education and scientific research. They also see it as a fountain of wildlife naturally replenishing adjacent biotic communities upon which local Panamanians depend for food.

In any case, the terrain appears to be of international significance and has adequate ecological integrity to justify a park of substantial size. The

Panamanian park is expected to have 717,379 acres, and will be Panamá's largest. Anyone wishing to attempt a trip into the area should discuss the matter fully with Panamanian park officials, following their advice and meeting their requirements.

Information: Director, Recursos Naturales Renovables, Ministerio de Desarrollo Agropecuario, Box 5390, Panamá City, Republic of Panamá.

Lake Atitlán, Guatemala.

INDEX

405